W9-AXF-370

QUEEN ELIZABETH II

NICHOLAS DAVIES

QUEEN ELIZABETH II
A Woman Who Is Not Amused

A BIRCH LANE PRESS BOOK
PUBLISHED BY CAROL PUBLISHING GROUP

A Birch Lane Press Book
Published by Carol Publishing Group
Birch Lane Press is a registered trademark of Carol Communications, Inc.
Editorial Offices: 600 Madison Avenue, New York, N.Y. 10022
Sales and Distribution Offices: 120 Enterprise Avenue, Secaucus, N.J. 07094
In Canada: Canadian Manda Group, P.O. Box 920, Station U, Toronto, Ontario M8Z 5P9
Queries regarding rights and permissions should be addressed to Carol Publishing Group,
600 Madison Avenue, New York, N.Y. 10022

Carol Publishing Group books are available at special discounts for bulk purchases, sales
promotion, fund raising, or educational purposes. Special editions can be created to
specifications. For details, contact: Special Sales Department, Carol Publishing Group,
120 Enterprise Avenue, Secaucus, N.J. 07094

Manufactured in the United States of America
10 9 8 7 6 5 4 3 2 1

Library of Congress Cataloging-in-Publication Data

Davies, Nicholas.
    Queen Elizabeth II : a woman who is not amused / by Nicholas
Davies.
        p.   cm.
    "A Birch Lane Press book."
    Includes index.
    ISBN 1-55972-217-7
    1. Elizabeth II, Queen of Great Britain, 1926-   . 2. Queens—
Great Britain—Biography.   I. Title.
DA590.D37   1994
941.085'092—dc20
    [B]   93-46668
                                                              CIP

CONTENTS

AUTHOR'S ACKNOWLEDGMENTS

This is not an official or authorized biography, and there are those at Buckingham Palace who would have preferred such a book to have been written by a historian. There have been many biographies of Queen Elizabeth II, a number written with the blessing and encouragement of members of the Royal Family and members of the Royal Household.

This biography has been written with the assistance of former senior members of a number of royal households who believed that the time had come for an open and honest account of Queen Elizabeth and, in particular, her relationships with her husband Philip, her four children, and other members of the Royal Family.

As a professional journalist, the only claim I would make is that I have endeavored to report accurately in a field where it is extremely difficult to do so. I have pursued rigorous journalistic practices in gathering and checking material.

Many men and women who helped me in researching this book talked to me on the understanding of absolute confidence and complete anonymity. Most did not wish to endanger their relationship with the Royal Family or members of royal households. So their names do not appear at all.

I have frequently been asked, "Did you interview the Queen for your book?" The answer is no. The Queen never gives interviews.

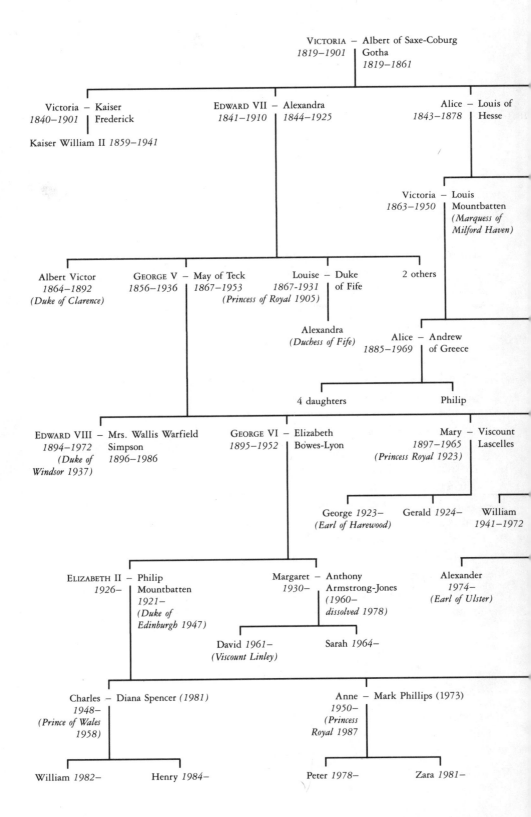

VICTORIA — Albert of Saxe-Coburg
1819–1901 | Gotha
1819–1861

Victoria — Kaiser
1840–1901 | Frederick

Kaiser William II 1859–1941

EDWARD VII — Alexandra
1841–1910 | 1844–1925

Alice — Louis of
1843–1878 | Hesse

Victoria — Louis
1863–1950 | Mountbatten
(Marquess of
Milford Haven)

Albert Victor
1864–1892
(Duke of Clarence)

GEORGE V — May of Teck
1856–1936 | 1867–1953

Louise — Duke
1867–1931 | of Fife
(Princess of Royal 1905)

2 others

Alexandra
(Duchess of Fife)

Alice — Andrew
1885–1969 | of Greece

4 daughters

Philip

EDWARD VIII — Mrs. Wallis Warfield
1894–1972 | Simpson
(Duke of | 1896–1986
Windsor 1937)

GEORGE VI — Elizabeth
1895–1952 | Bowes-Lyon

Mary — Viscount
1897–1965 | Lascelles
(Princess Royal 1923)

George 1923–
(Earl of Harewood)

Gerald 1924–

William
1941–1972

ELIZABETH II — Philip
1926– | Mountbatten
1921–
(Duke of
Edinburgh 1947)

Margaret — Anthony
1930– | Armstrong-Jones
(1960–
dissolved 1978)

Alexander
1974–
(Earl of Ulster)

David 1961–
(Viscount Linley)

Sarah 1964–

Charles — Diana Spencer (1981)
1948–
(Prince of Wales
1958)

Anne — Mark Phillips (1973)
1950–
(Princess
Royal 1987

William 1982–

Henry 1984–

Peter 1978–

Zara 1981–

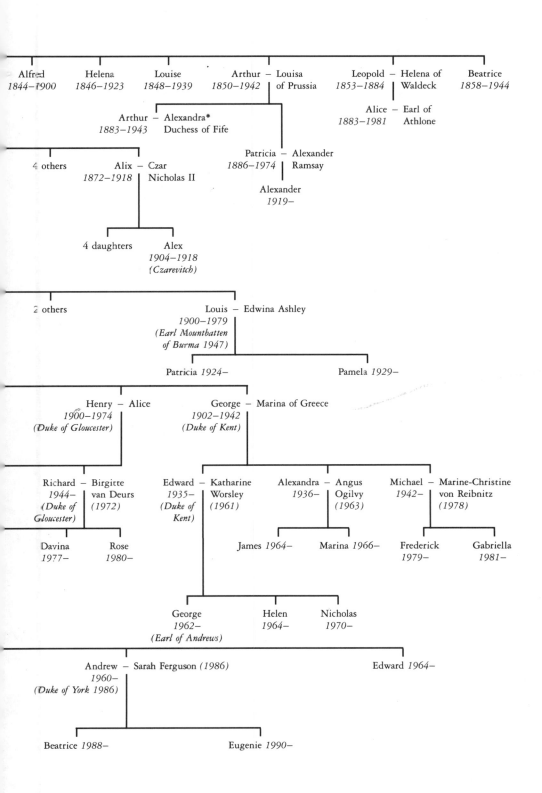

I

THE WINDSORS
AT BAY

ONE

A FAMILY IN DISARRAY

Elizabeth walked out of Crathie Parish Church with her husband, Prince Philip, a few steps behind. A small knot of well-wishers, mostly women, watched as she walked down the path. Dressed in a dark coat and hat and carrying a black handbag, Elizabeth smiled at the group and bowed her head slightly in recognition. Her chauffeur opened the car door and, as she sat down, pulled a tartan rug over her knees. As the car drove off, she turned, smiled again, and waved to the group of women, but none waved back.

With Philip seated beside her, Elizabeth settled back for the few minutes' drive to Balmoral, her Scottish castle. The smile had gone. Now her face was set, serious and glum, as she looked out of the car window, staring at the dark clouds and the trees of autumn shedding their leaves.

Elizabeth had always loved Balmoral, a place full of happy memories—of her childhood in the 1930s, of her early married life. Only a year or so before, her happy, excited grandchildren had played and screamed and rushed around, the old castle full of noise, alive with the bustle of activity. Now as she walked into its cold, slightly disorderly hall, and a maid took her hat and coat, all was peace and quiet.

Elizabeth shivered slightly in the autumn chill and walked through to the drawing room to read the Sunday papers in front of a log fire. Philip followed. They didn't speak, each instinctively knowing, from years of the same regimented life, the order of the day.

Elizabeth's venerated Royal Family, which for so many decades portrayed the image of a united, happy family, had been shown to be as fragile as any other. Even the cherished family reunions at holiday times no longer took place, for her children no longer wanted to attend.

September 1993 saw Elizabeth holidaying alone with Philip in her beloved Scotland, Charles enjoying a beach holiday in sunny Spain with his sons, Wills and Harry, Diana in London trying to enjoy her new life as a single mother, Andrew away on naval duty, and his wife Sarah, virtually expelled from the Royal Family, in London with their children, Bea and Eugenie. Elizabeth's only daughter, Anne, spent the holiday at home in Gloucestershire with her new husband, Commander Tim Laurence. Only Prince Edward, their youngest child, stayed at Balmoral that autumn, but not for long.

Elizabeth loves her grandchildren. One of her great joys is having them around when she is not at Buckingham Palace. She had always looked forward to her annual ten-week holiday at Balmoral surrounded by her family, and especially the grandchildren. Now she hardly ever sees them.

The Sunday papers were, mercifully for once, concentrating their firepower on matters other than the Royal Family, examining instead the civil war in Bosnia, the deteriorating situation in Somalia, President Bill Clinton's health reforms, and President Boris Yeltsin's fight for political survival.

All sections of the press had given the Royal Family a rough time for months, some for years. Yet it seemed only yesterday that Elizabeth could do no wrong and her family was admired and respected by the nation. She had basked in the sensational worldwide triumph of the marriage of Charles and Diana in 1981, the marriage of Andrew and Sarah in 1985, and the excitement surrounding the arrival of royal babies throughout the 1980s.

Suddenly, everything went wrong. The marital disasters of her children and the stubborn behavior of their young wives had transformed the situation almost overnight. For no reason at all, the monarchy itself had been dragged into the equation, and the House of Windsor was facing a deepening crisis. Elizabeth, too, became the focus of attention, and people were asking questions which reached the very nerve center of the British monarchy.

Through the centuries a distinction had always been made between the reigning monarch and all the lesser royals, including the heir to the throne. So long as the monarch behaved like a monarch, all the others could go hang until one or the other would, in turn, become monarch.

During the 1960s, however, it became fashionable to confuse the monarch with the Royal Family. The confusion arose out of a desire to modernize the House of Windsor, to let a little light in on the family, to humanize and popularize them and bring them closer to the people. The light shone upon the younger royals, on "action-man" Charles, on "war-hero" Andrew, on "charity-worker" Anne. The royal advisers enjoyed the limelight shining on Elizabeth's children, for it brought credit to the entire family and the sovereign herself.

As the marriages of the young royals fell apart, however, the media scented blood. They shone their spotlights on the supporting cast of royals, dispatching the star of the show, the Queen who had spent forty years on the throne, to the shadows.

Diana, Princess of Wales, became the star attraction the media wanted to know about. They wanted to know every minute detail of her life. The failure of her marriage added to her attraction for those hungry for a closer insight into the family. And not just in Britain. Within a matter of a few years she had become a world megastar, for everyone remembered watching the TV spectacular when Shy Di walked down the aisle on her wedding day. Tears were shed that day in homes around the world.

Everyone wanted this particular marriage to succeed. A beautiful, young, unknown children's nanny, who seemed vulnerable and innocent, had captured the heart of the heir to the English throne; it was the stuff of fairy tales, every girl's childhood dream. People around the globe felt involved, and the world followed the ups and downs of her marriage. When it fell apart, everyone felt touched by the sadness. Only months before, another royal marriage had collapsed when Prince Andrew and Sarah, his wife of seven years, felt unable to stay together.

Scandals emerged. The lovely Diana, unhappy and alone in her palace, had taken lovers; Fergie's scandalous sexual behavior, complete with incriminating photographs, became common knowledge. Yet no one, except Diana, seemed to mind that Prince Charles had taken a mistress with whom he spent most of his life. And none blamed Prince Andrew when his marriage failed, partly though his own arrogance and weakness.

Royal commentators shook their heads knowingly, and all agreed, "Of course the Queen does an excellent job. But what a tragedy that all her good work should have been set at naught by the appalling indiscretions of the Princess of Wales and the Duchess of York."

Such disproportionate attention had been allotted to the Royal Family, and particularly to the wives of the royal Princes, that everyone supposed that, as the younger royals had fallen into disrepute, so too must the sovereign herself. Some suggested the institution of monarchy had been put in jeopardy. Suddenly, Elizabeth found herself under attack, her entire family under scrutiny, and the nation openly discussing the merits of monarchy as the millennium approached.

Monarchists wanted the world to believe that the reputation and actions of Elizabeth, her courage and strength of character, her blameless life, and her exemplary conduct, shine strongly because they contrast so favorably with those undesirable royals surrounding her.

But there is another school of thought: Some believe the blame for the tarnished image of the British Royal Family lies with Elizabeth herself. Upon reflection, it seems Elizabeth never had time to care sufficiently for her growing family or examine their needs or their failings. From a young age she had acquired a strong sense of her own importance and would never lose it. She had been taught from childhood to believe her role as Queen to be far more important than bringing up a family in a loving environment. Her father had instilled in her a strong sense of duty—to the British people, to the monarchy, and to the House of Windsor. Forever, it would be her guiding, inflexible principle.

Today, all around her, Elizabeth sees the results of the decision she made in dedicating herself to the monarchy, to the good name of the House of Windsor, and to the nation, rather than attending to her family.

At the end of 1993, Elizabeth realized full well her family's sorry state: Charles separated, Andrew separated, Anne divorced and remarried, and her youngest son, Edward, now thirty, preferring to remain a bachelor.

Elizabeth retired to the isolation of Balmoral for her autumn holiday in 1993 to take stock and decide how to deal with the greatest crisis facing her in her forty years on the throne. She had to devise a course of action that would restore faith in the monarchy, redeem the reputation of the House of Windsor, and, if possible, win back the hearts of the British people, who polls showed had been losing their affection for the Crown.

By far the most important person to Elizabeth is her son and heir, Prince Charles, for he will be responsible for shouldering the burden of monarchy and maintaining the status quo of the British constitution in the next century. Both Elizabeth and Charles know that his own conduct will be decisive in determining whether the monarchy survives and prospers into the next generation.

Elizabeth hopes that Diana's determination to force a separation from Charles may prove, in the long term, beneficial to the monarchy. Diana had become the focus of all attention, the only person of glamour within the Royal Family, the only royal the media wanted to see, photograph, film, and write about. Twelve years after her betrothal to Charles, magazine covers around the world still portray Princess Diana in as many guises as they can.

The most dramatic piece of royal theater since the separation was staged by Diana in December 1993, when she announced her retreat from public life to escape the public glare.

She could have made the official announcement discreetly, in private, from Kensington Palace. But instead, Diana chose to move center stage in a blaze of publicity and give a high-profile statement, in a faltering voice, before a charity audience in London's Hilton Hotel. The room was packed with journalists, photographers, and television crews, who had been told beforehand that Diana would be making "a dramatic statement."

Dressed in a dark, bottle-green suit and looking tense, Diana said, "When I started my public life twelve years ago, I understood that the media might be interested in what I did. I realized then that their attention would inevitably focus on both our private and public lives.

"But I was not aware of how overwhelming that attention would become; nor the extent to which it would affect both my public duties and my personal life, in a manner which has been hard to bear.

"At the end of this year, when I have completed my diary of official engagements, I will be reducing the extent of the public life I have led so far. Over the next few months I will be seeking a more suitable way of combining a meaningful public role with, hopefully, a more private life."

As she sat down, Diana looked close to tears.

In effect, Diana announced to the world she wanted to retreat from the limelight into a more private life, for the time being. She wished to spend more time with her two sons, although they spend most of their life away at boarding school. The day after her speech, all 118 charities and organizations of which she is patron received an official personal letter from the Princess of Wales explaining that she would not be able to fulfill functions for them "for the foreseeable future."

In truth, Diana had become lonely in public. Whether appearing at a charity function or touring overseas, Diana had felt vulnerable and alone. The cover-girl publicity she once craved had palled. She felt unable to form close relationships with anyone for fear of media intrusion.

The Palace courtiers were appalled at Diana's determination to make a public statement about her future because they feared the effect might further damage the Crown. They counseled her, suggesting the statement be made from Kensington Palace. Diana would hear none of it. As she had in the past, she would challenge the Palace hierarchy head-on.

Charles was nonplussed by his wife's decision. A year before, they had reached an agreement to work in parallel, rarely meeting in public, and she had happily accepted the arrangement. Now she wanted the arrangement changed.

Elizabeth, Prince Philip, and Charles all asked her what she intended to do with the masses of spare time she would now have for herself. To all, Diana replied, "I don't know, I haven't decided. But you must let me get away. I can't face it anymore."

Elizabeth, in particular, was apprehensive about Diana's decision to leave the public arena. She fears Diana's plea for privacy is part of an unfolding drama of which Diana herself has no idea where it will end. With no charity work and no royal engagements, Diana will have very little to occupy her waking hours and will become more lonely and restless.

Now that Diana has sought to sideline herself, Elizabeth believes an opportunity has occurred for the monarchy to be taken more seriously, and for Charles to reconstruct his own relationship with the British people, which had suffered considerably during the drama of their marital breakup.

However, it did not matter to Elizabeth that Charles had found life impossible with Diana and sought happiness and contentment with another woman, or that he and Camilla were living, to all intents and purposes, as man and wife. All that concerned Elizabeth were the fortunes of the monarchy and the prestige of the House of Windsor.

Elizabeth encouraged Charles to start a new life from the ashes of his marriage. Charles, too, wanted to refocus his life so that the public and the media would see him as doing a useful job for the nation, rather than as a cold, uncaring prince who had caused his beautiful young wife such misery and emotional distress. At the time the breakup became public knowledge, in 1992, Charles felt trapped in the quagmire of his failed marriage, the butt of tabloid trivia and speculation. He said then, "It's been an utterly bloody year."

Now, reinvigorated by the formal, public separation from Diana, Charles channeled his broad range of commitments into a more coherent structure with the help of his private secretary, Commander Richard Aylard, an unstuffy former naval officer. He also took on new, more experienced staff. He employed a deputy secretary, Stephen Lamport, on detachment from the Foreign Office, and two hand-picked assistant secretaries, Matthew Butler, on loan from the City, and Belinda Harvey, to brief him on health and heritage issues. He also brought in two press officers, Allan Percival and Sandy Henny, both professionals with government backgrounds. Charles hoped his new team would be streetwise. He installed new computers and had his offices at St. James's Palace, two hundred yards from Buckingham Palace, freshly painted.

He also employed an unofficial social secretary, Tiggy Legge-Bourke, who had another important role, to work as part-time helper and confidant to William, eleven, and Harry, nine. When Charles traveled with his sons, Tiggy went along as well.

Charles began by bringing his main charity organizations under the single banner of the Prince's Trusts. These have evolved into a formidable network with a combined annual income of $50 million, 470 paid staff, and nearly 9,000 voluntary workers. All have their own separate goals and yet all have the same theme: creating the sort of Britain of which Charles wants to be King.

Directors of his charities now feel the bracing chill of the Prince's personal attention. Charles writes, almost weekly, to the directors with ideas, requests, updates, and details of new projects. Tom Shebbeare, director of the Prince's Trusts, said, "There is never a shortage of things to respond to nowadays. And the Prince is always on the phone."

Ever since leaving the Royal Navy in 1976, when he was twenty-eight, Charles has sought a public role for himself other than attending royal functions week in, week out. The 1980s were the nadir for him. Many times during that decade Charles, a most serious man, found himself taking strong positions on various subjects, such as the environment, architecture, urban renewal, and education, only to discover his views were hardly remembered a few months later. He also discovered that government ministers found his intrusions unwelcome.

In November 1983 Charles found a new role, representing Britain's business interests overseas, as a sort of "cultural and commercial emissary." He has the backing of Prime Minister John Major, who believes the Prince would be a valuable roving ambassador. Many British exporters encouraged Charles's bid to become such an emissary, believing he can help them capture overseas markets.

As Charles planned his new high-profile role, which both he and his mother believed would restore his integrity as heir to the throne, a fresh, and highly damaging, attack burst into the open. Several Church of England bishops claimed Charles would be an unsuitable King because of his private morals, that is, because he committed adultery with Camilla Parker Bowles. They argued that breaking his marriage vows put a question mark over the sincerity of the vows he would make before God at his coronation.

Not since the abdication of King Edward VIII had the Royal Family faced such a challenge. Elizabeth was furious that the Church of which she is head should have chosen such an inappropriate moment to launch their attack on Prince Charles.

The latest opinion poll, taken in December 1993, showed Charles's popularity at an all-time low. It revealed 31 percent of the nation wanted Prince William, then eleven, rather than Charles, to succeed Elizabeth when she dies. All blamed the crisis of confidence over Charles's marriage breakdown.

Charles reacted to the bishops' attack with disbelief, then quick anger that the clergy should attempt to equate marriage and coronation vows. In private, he castigated the clergymen for daring to suggest his unsuitability on moral grounds, describing the church-men's "moral argument" against him as "a bloody cheek; mischievous, fallacious, and aggressive." He told his staff that his marriage vows were a public witness before God of a private commitment to his wife; a pledge of sexual fidelity could never be considered the same as a pledge to serve a nation.

Charles had a point. A king is a symbol of nationhood and history rather than a spokesman for a moral position. A king's authority stems from popular allegiance to an institution rather than trust in an individual.

Elizabeth spoke to her advisers and senior churchmen at Lambeth Palace, the Church of England's London headquarters. All agreed that the misfortunes of the Prince's private life had been a regrettable chapter in the history of the monarchy but were an unjust, unreliable, and unconstitutional test of his fitness to rule. Elizabeth expressed the hope that the vast majority of churchmen understood that and would make sure the country knew that too.

The attack hurt Elizabeth because she believed it to be another attempt to draw attention to the most regrettable and unhappy episode of her reign, the disastrous marriage of Charles and Diana. She also believed it was an attempt to support Diana in the public battle she appeared to be waging against Charles.

Charles had become far more relaxed following the break with Diana. With his passion for hunting, shooting, fishing, and garden-ing, he throughly enjoyed his life as an English gentleman farmer. When at Highgrove, his country home in Gloucestershire, he had as his constant companion Camilla Parker Bowles. They loved to walk and ride together in all weather and enjoyed each other's company at home, listening to opera and classical music and reading rather highbrow books.

Charles had never been happier and more contented in his life. He had come to rely on Camilla completely, for her advice, friendship, and companionship, and he needed her emotionally and physically. For her part, Camilla, too, had found love and happiness with Charles. But both were married to other people, although Charles was now officially separated.

Both Charles and Camilla certainly loved each other. They seemed so comfortable and happy together. As Charles would often tell her, "Our relationship was made in heaven. We were made for each other." And they would often tell each other how much they were in love.

Camilla's husband, Brigadier Andrew Parker Bowles, a close friend of Charles for many years, accepted the situation. He knew Camilla to be Charles's mistress and that she had been since the middle 1980s. Camilla would act as hostess when Charles gave lunch or dinner parties. Close friends accepted them as a couple and treated them as such. Elizabeth knew all this and accepted the situation, although Camilla had never been invited to stay at Balmoral, Windsor, or any other of Elizabeth's homes as Charles's companion.

The majority of the British people, however, disapproved of Charles's new adulterous lifestyle and showed it in every poll. They believed he should have stayed with Diana, and if that were impossible, he should certainly have not become involved with an old flame whose husband was a close friend. The public wanted Charles to set a good example. Throughout 1993 criticism of Charles continued to grow rather than abate, and questions were continually asked about his fitness to be the next King.

Charles would tell Camilla that the criticisms would pass in time and the British people would forget and forgive his transgressions. Camilla wasn't so sure. She proposed that she and Charles separate so that he could reestablish his relationship with the nation and be seen as a responsible, hardworking, worthy heir to the throne. At first, Charles would not hear of such drastic action, telling her it was "unnecessary." But Camilla persisted.

Once before, Camilla had proved she was the strength in their relationship. Following the assassination of Earl Mountbatten in 1979, Charles had wanted her to divorce her husband Andrew and settle down with him. Camilla knew that would be a disaster for Charles personally and for the Royal Family as well. She urged him to forget her and find someone else. Finally, he did so, and within months had met the shy young Diana.

Throughout the autumn of 1993 Camilla continued to press Charles, telling him he was risking his good name, his reputation, and his future by staying with her. For weeks at a time Charles would refuse to listen to her arguments whenever she brought up the subject.

Finally, Camilla persuaded Charles to consider separating for just twelve months. As the sniping at their relationship continued, Charles concluded that perhaps Camilla's plan made sense. He knew his mother would most certainly approve of the separation, putting the Royal Family, the Crown, and more important, the House of Windsor, before his own wishes.

While Charles toured Australia in early 1994, news of his separation from Camilla became public. But Charles's close friends would not speculate on how long the separation would last. They knew Charles would find it difficult, perhaps impossible, to stay away from the woman he loved.

Diana had been fearful that the Buckingham Palace organization responsible for the monarchy's reputation would attempt to isolate her for demanding a separation. Some courtiers were consumed with the need for revenge, determined to sideline Diana for her arrogant disregard of royal convention.

Elizabeth, however, forbade such action. She hoped that Diana would remain close to the family and return to a more public life. She knew Diana to be far and away the British people's favorite royal and therefore someone to be cherished rather than ostracized.

But Elizabeth cannot forget, and has not forgiven Diana for permitting her friends to wash the royal dirty linen in public by revealing details of her married life with Charles. For that transgression strikes at the very heart of Elizabeth's entire life's work.

Diana told the Queen she wanted her prime function in life to be caring for the two Princes. "I want William and Harry to grow up in the real world outside the 'Big House,'" she told her mother-in-law. "I want them not only to experience the everyday life that ordinary people in Britain live, but I want them also to understand the impact of that life on those people. And I am talking about all sorts of people here. Britain must not be a foreign country to my boys."

Implicit in that comment was not only a veiled criticism of the upbringing of Charles and Elizabeth's other children, but also a conviction that when William is crowned King he and the monarchy will be very different from all that has gone before.

For that reason Diana takes the boys everywhere she can—to the cinema, to shows, fun parks, theme parks, Disney World, factories, hospitals, army barracks, museums, and art galleries. It is the reason she insists that whenever she takes them for a treat, such as a burger at McDonald's, they stand in line like everyone else.

Diana told Elizabeth that she has no intention of marrying again; she is prepared instead to sacrifice her personal life for her children. And that is the reason she does not want to divorce Prince Charles. That, however, is not the whole truth.

Diana wants to retain the title of Her Royal Highness The Princess of Wales, with all its attendant privileges, and she did want to be the next Queen of England. That became increasingly unlikely as Diana retreated from public life. A year after the official separation in November 1992, Diana now believes her hopes that one day she would be crowned Queen were naive, as she and Charles remain barely on speaking terms.

Palace advisers expect Charles and Diana to divorce in due course, quietly and without fuss, probably when their younger son Harry, now nine, is thirteen. Both parents believe the final break will be easier for Harry to take when he becomes a teenager.

Whatever happens between her and Charles, Diana remains determined to spend her life guiding and advising young William, ensuring that eventually she will be the power behind the throne when her son becomes King. It is the ambition of a most determined young woman, but whether it is misguided, unrealistic, grandiose, or even touched by megalomania, Diana believes it will all come about one day. In this objective she is challenging not only Elizabeth and Prince Charles, but the monarch's most senior advisers, who are still smarting from their failure to control the "wayward," headstrong Diana.

To friends of this author, Diana has railed about Elizabeth's senior advisers on many occasions. She would tell them, "No one in that place is streetwise in any way at all. Nor do they want to be. They don't believe that they should relate to the world, the real world of today. They believe in their stupidity that the world must relate to them and abide by their values."

And when someone asks her "What is that way?" she tells them in no uncertain terms.

"The old way, the arrogant way, is all they are interested in," she would say. "They want everything to continue as it did in Victorian times, and they want me and my children to behave as if this was still

Victorian England, not the beginning of the twenty-first century.

"From the moment I stepped foot in the palace they tried to tell me how to behave, what to do, in precise detail. When I tried to discuss a point, let alone argue, they would tell me to keep quiet and to listen. They would tell me there was no discussion, for there was no alternative to their way, the way that was set in stone a hundred years ago.

"They would criticize everything. Sometimes I felt back at school. I would be ticked off for appearing at a summer party without tights; I would be admonished for appearing too casual, for not smiling enough, for not chatting to guests. It became impossible."

Diana has talked with Elizabeth about her determination to remain as close as possible to her sons, despite their being away at boarding school for most of the year. She also told Elizabeth of her desire to educate them in her own way, with her values, and that she would not permit any interference from Buckingham Palace.

Diana has spoken to a number of her friends of her plans for Wills and Harry, saying, "I want my boys to really grasp the hopes, the joys, the problems, the fears, the ambitions, and the disappointments of the real world and feel them in their hearts. People in the 'Big House' simply don't show those feelings.

"Charles has never showed his feelings in his life because he was trained never to reveal them, to anyone. He was conditioned by the courtiers from a baby. He is cold because that is how he was conditioned to behave, a product of his own isolated upbringing. Now, and forever, he is the prisoner of his own environment."

A hundred times Diana explained all this to Charles when she fought to retain his love and his affection in the dark days of their marriage. But Charles found it impossible to respond to Diana's emotional demands and her desperate pleas, and, in the end, he turned to Camilla, the person he considers his only true friend in the world. Camilla had saved his sanity once before, and he knew she would respond to his appeals for help now as he struggled with the trauma of his unhappy marriage. As Diana has stated angrily many times since, Camilla was only too happy to do so.

Diana's plan to become kingmaker will be no easy task. Elizabeth has no intention of allowing William, the heir to the throne, to be educated and brought up by the young woman who turned her back on the Royal Family. Nor has Prince Charles. And, most important, neither have the men in gray suits who work in Buckingham Palace and see their life's work as the preservation of the throne and all its traditions.

As heirs apparent, both Elizabeth and Charles were educated in their teens to understand the complexities of the Constitution, the duties of the sovereign, and the historical perspective of the monarchy; so, too, will young William's grooming begin when he becomes a teenager. Carefully chosen tutors, constitutional lawyers, and senior courtiers will be responsible for his education. This will mean William's spending more time at Buckingham Palace under the watchful eye of Elizabeth, not with his mother at home at Kensington Palace. More and more, young William will come under the discipline of the Palace courtiers, who will lose no opportunity to educate him as they see fit.

Even before she decided to withdraw from public life, Diana realized she had been slowly pushed to one side and the spotlight deliberately trained on Charles and the two young Princes. Diana had thought her future secure when Prime Minister John Major declared so in his historic House of Commons statement announcing their separation in 1992. She had reckoned without the senior Palace courtiers who were determined Diana would be sidetracked, her ambitions thwarted, and that one day the Princess of Wales would find herself on the outer margins of royal life.

Six months after the marriage split, Diana found herself removed from the most important royal ambassador roles and given more minor jobs. Harold Brookes Baker, editor of *Burke's Peerage,* commented, "Diana no longer represents the Queen in various parts of the world, and there is no doubt that she has been moved sideways. Her duties are now largely those devised by herself and her charities.

"She woke up one day and found out she was not one of the most important people in the world but just an instinctive pinup who could do good works for needy people."

In the twelve months since the couple separated, Diana's list of official royal duties plummeted by more than 25 percent, from 389 to just 288. Nearly all the dual occasions when she appeared with the Prince of Wales have ceased. She took the decision to attend fewer glittering galas and film premieres, preferring to use her talents at the sharp end of royal business, visiting hospitals and hospices, and throwing herself into charity projects.

To demonstrate her independence Diana ordered new headed stationery, a crown encompassing a capital *D,* showing the world she had become her own person, setting her own agenda, making her own decisions, and in charge of her own destiny. Removing herself from the sphere of Palace influence and striking out on her own had required courage and audacity. But her every step would be watched by Elizabeth's advisers.

As her official work became more discreet, so did Diana's love life. After the glare of publicity surrounding her relationships with the banker Philip Dunne, and the Guards Officers Major David Waterhouse and Major James Hewitt, Diana took great care to shield her love life from the paparazzi.

One reason for Diana's secrecy about the man who had become her close confidant and adviser was that he had a wife and two children at home.

The man Diana turned to for advice, and who helped her through the trauma of the separation, was Michael Corry-Reid, forty-two, a handsome former Guards officer and polo player who owned and managed mailbox shops in London. Diana and Michael Corry-Reid became friends after meeting at Ludgrove Preparatory School, in Berkshire, where their sons attend as boarders.

I had played polo with Corry-Reid for a number of seasons. Following Diana's separation, Corry-Reid talked of his relationship with her: "We are very good friends. She is an absolutely lovely lady. We talk on the phone and I occasionally pop around to Kensington Palace for a drink and a chat. Sometimes we talk for hours; she can be most amusing and has a great sense of humor."

Rumors circulated throughout royal circles that Diana and Corry-Reid were having an affair. He told me, "People are bound to gossip. They always do, particularly since Diana and Charles have separated. I do what I can to help out. Understandably, Diana is sometimes lonely and I help, in my small way, to keep a smile on her face. We laugh a lot and have fun, but much of the conversation is about the boys and their schooling."

Over a drink, Michael added, "If I helped Diana come to terms with her mountains of doubt over her separation from Charles and her decision to bring up her boys as a single mother, then I am most happy. She knows where she can find me at any time. She only has to pick up the telephone."

Corry-Reid has a great zest for life and loves living in the fast lane. He also has a sense of humor and enjoys the good life, parties, dinners, gambling, and late nights. His activities have been somewhat curtailed, however, because he had invested in one of the unfortunate Lloyd's of London insurance syndicates which lost tens of millions of dollars.

An ebullient character, Corry-Reid is a happy-go-lucky, confident man, always with a smile and a cheery word for everyone, the type of man to help Diana through her moments of doubt and her crises of confidence.

And Diana had many crises following her separation. At times she felt vulnerable, helpless, and powerless. She found it difficult to concentrate and kept wondering if she had made the right decision in demanding a separation. She also feared being ostracized by the Royal Family.

Occasionally, she cracked. Sometimes she would break into tears when photographed unexpectedly in the street. At other times the Princess's famous cover-girl looks were contorted by stress. A year after her separation, in October 1993, she broke down in tears for no evident reason when attending the musical *Grease* in the center of London.

Less than a year after the separation Diana would sometimes find herself at home for a week or more with no royal engagements, no charity functions, spending her days swimming, at the gymnasium, or playing tennis, her sons away at boarding school. Much of the time she would be at home alone with nothing to do, bored, world-weary, and afraid of the future. At night she would entertain friends at Kensington Palace over a snack meal and a glass of wine or attend a private dinner party. Often Diana would be a lone woman among couples, which made her feel worse.

Michael Corry-Reid explained how she would talk for hours. He recalled, "Sometimes we would talk until five o'clock in the morning, about every subject under the sun. She desperately needed company, needed someone in whom she could confide, someone whom she could trust. Sometimes she seemed scared of what the future might hold.

But she knew she had her sons to care for and bring up and they always give her strength. She thinks about them all the time."

For Elizabeth there were yet other marriage crises in her family demanding her attention. Andrew and Fergie's love life caught major headlines, too. After their formal separation, Prince Andrew returned happily to the Royal Navy to continue his career. And when the anger and humiliation of Fergie's leaving him had finally subsided, Andrew found a new and happier relationship with her. During the summer of 1993, they discovered they enjoyed being together again, with and without Beatrice, then five, and Eugenie, three. They even found they could laugh together.

They took meals together, went for walks, and swore to each other that they would never let anything come between them and their two daughters. Andrew acknowledged to friends he found the irrepressible Fergie fun to see. Some of their friends believe it possible the two might try to reconcile their differences and give the marriage another chance. This would depend on Fergie and whether she feels capable of coping with the pressures she found impossible to live with.

Despite rumors of rifts and arguments, Sarah, Duchess of York, remained with her American lover, the businessman Johnny Bryan, who took control of her life after her marriage broke up. Fergie came to respect Bryan not simply as a lover, although that is of great importance to her, but also as her adviser and the man she wanted to run her life. Never before had Fergie been in such a relationship where she happily played second fiddle.

Elizabeth's youngest son, Prince Edward, thirty, like his elder brother Charles, is searching for a role in life. In December 1993, he launched his own independent television and film company, Ardent Productions. Edward provided capital for the venture and won backing from the world's wealthiest man, the Sultan of Brunei.

It is most unusual for any member of the House of Windsor to be associated directly with the hard-nosed business world, but Edward's new business cards proclaim "Edward Windsor, Joint Managing Director."

Prince Edward chose the name Ardent to suggest the key values of the company: ambition, motivation, and strength. He had always shown interest in the arts world, and his first job, with the composer Andrew Lloyd Webber, was making tea. He never lived it down. Edward first thought of running his own television company in 1991 and invited experienced hands from the BBC and Britain's independent television stations to join him.

For some years, many rumors had suggested that Elizabeth's youngest son was gay. As he fast approached his thirtieth birthday, such rumors of his sexuality increased since Edward was hardly ever seen in the company of young women, let alone dating them. When asked if he had any girlfriend, he replied, "I enjoy my life."

Throughout the autumn of 1993, however, Edward had been secretly dating a Diana look-alike, twenty-eight-year-old Sophie Rhys-Jones. Tall, blond, shy, and strikingly good-looking, she is an account manager for a public relations consultancy and lives in a rented apartment in West London, a mile from the apartment where Diana lived before her engagement to Prince Charles.

Sophie first met Edward while working on a royal charity project in August 1993. He introduced her to his parents at Buckingham Palace, and Elizabeth invited Sophie to tea and dinner. Throughout the early months of 1994 Sophie became a regular visitor to the palace where Edward has his own suite of rooms.

When Edward's relationship with Sophie became known in December 1993, they were immediately the target of every royal watcher and paparrazi. A scrum of Fleet Street journalists and photographers camped at her apartment and her workplace.

Ironically, Sophie's existence and royal connection filtered into the public's knowledge only a matter of days after Diana had announced her intention of retiring from public life. A gleeful Fleet Street believed they had discovered a new royal girlfriend to take Diana's place. Edward had other ideas.

In a bid to protect Sophie from the royal watchers and photographers who had made life such hell for Diana and Sarah Ferguson, Edward took the unprecedented step of faxing a short letter to every Fleet Street editor.

In part, it read: "I am taking this unusual step of writing to you directly in the hope of stopping your reporters and photographers from destroying that part of my life that I am entitled to regard as private and, more importantly, Sophie's life. . . . I am very conscious that other members of my immediate family have been subjected to similar attention and it has not been at all beneficial to their relationships, therefore please will you call an end to your harassment of both Sophie and me and allow us to try to carry on our lives as normal. It is you who have the power to grant us this. Please will you consider our case seriously."

Both Elizabeth and Philip greeted the news of Edward's girlfriend with some relief, as they had believed their youngest son was destined to remain a bachelor.

Elizabeth's only daughter, Princess Anne, continues to spend prodigious numbers of weeks involved with charity work, and in particular on overseas trips with Save the Children, of which she is patron. In between, Anne spends the greater part of the year at her home, Gatcombe Park, in Gloucestershire, caring for her son Peter, fifteen, and daughter Zara, twelve, and settling down to married life with her new husband, Commander Tim Laurence, whom she married in 1992.

The man who dominated Elizabeth's life, Prince Philip, remains at her side, more so than he has been for much of their married life. Now seventy-two, Philip has become a crusty individual who understands that he must still fulfill his duty, walking the regulation two steps behind his wife whenever they appear in public.

It may have taken Elizabeth many years to come to terms with her irascible, arrogant husband, who brought her much sadness and heartbreak. He still carries out numerous royal engagements each year and still voices his opinions whether they are asked for or not and on any subject of his choosing.

But save for Elizabeth, who no longer tolerates his moods, Philip has become a lonely man, for he has an uneasy relationship with his children. His actions, his harsh words, his discipline have alienated his three sons and his daughter. None of them want to spend time with their father. And due to his behavior toward them, the children no longer see much of their mother, although Elizabeth maintains she would like to see more of her children and grandchildren.

Fit and healthy, Elizabeth, at sixty-seven, believes she has many years of active life ahead of her. She has no intention of handing over the crown to Charles, especially since his separation. She looks forward to remaining Queen until well into the next century, though the stress of the last two years has taken its toll; her hair has grown whiter, the lines around her eyes are more pronounced, and some of the spring has gone from her step. Yet hardly anyone knew of the sacrifices she had made.

II

THE EMERGENT
YEARS

TWO

LILIBET

Elizabeth Windsor was born third in line to the English throne. The reigning monarch, King George V, was her grandfather. George's eldest son, Edward (whom the family called David), was Prince of Wales, heir apparent, and her uncle. George's second son, the Duke of York, was her father; he stood second in line to the throne but would move further down the order of success if Edward married and had a son.

Elizabeth's arrival into the world on a cold, rainy April night in 1926 was awkward and complicated, for hers was a breech birth. Her mother, the Duchess of York, had been in labor for more than twenty-four hours because the doctors persisted in trying to bring about a normal birth. But in the early hours of the morning they performed a cesarean section and Princess Elizabeth was born.

Besides the doctors and nurses, a secretary from the Home Office also attended the delivery to certify the baby's lineage. This quaint English royal custom grew out of the so-called warming-pan plot in 1688, when it was alleged that a substitute baby had been placed in the bed of James II's wife. Though the allegation was false, a senior government official has attended every royal birth since that date to make sure the baby was really of royal birth. Baby Elizabeth was particularly special to her parents because her mother had previously suffered a miscarriage, and there was a fear that she might not be able to bear children. That day Elizabeth's father, the Duke of York, known as Bertie, who became King George VI, wrote to his parents: "You don't know what a tremendous joy it is to Elizabeth and me to have our little girl. We always wanted a child to make our happiness complete, and now that it has at last happened, it seems so wonderful and strange...."

Queen Victoria introduced many of the traditions and ideals of today's Royal Family. It was a German princess, however, Mary of Teck, King George V's wife, who actually transformed the British monarchy from the dull, dowdy image of Victoria to the values of duty, morality, and family life so beloved of the emerging middle class. Mary of Teck also made sure the nation understood that, as monarch, King George embodied extrahuman qualities of king-priest, father of his people, and the sacred and anointed heir of the British nation and the far-flung British Empire.

Queen Victoria recognized that Mary of Teck was remarkable for her intelligence, her ambition, and, above all, her passion for the monarchy. Victoria badgered her eldest grandson, the weak, dissolute, idle Duke of Clarence, second in line to the throne, to marry Mary. They became engaged, but shortly afterward Clarence died of a mysterious illness. Victoria was so intent on Mary of Teck's joining the family that she urged and pushed her second oldest grandson, George, the next in line, to court and marry her. Not wishing to disappoint or displease his grandmother, George did so a year later.

Following Victoria's death in 1901, her son became King Edward VII, and George and Mary, the Prince and Princess of Wales. It wasn't only Queen Victoria who was enamored of Princess Mary, so was Edward VII. He ordered that Mary, his daughter-in-law, be sent all the official red boxes containing the government papers so that she would thoroughly understand the workings of government when she became Queen. It was an extraordinary, even revolutionary idea to involve his daughter-in-law, a German, so closely in the secret affairs of the monarchy and the government, particularly in an era when women were considered second-class citizens.

Some historians go so far as to attribute the survival of the British monarchy to Queen Mary, a most resolute woman. She was determined that the monarchy in Britain should not only survive but thrive, unlike the monarchies of the rest of Europe, which in the early part of this century were either swept away or changed to modern Scandinavian-style affairs. On his deathbed in 1910 Edward VII feared his son George would be the last King of England, but Mary had other ideas.

Queen Mary, Elizabeth's grandmother, ruled the Royal Family, and in particular her husband George V, with firmness and determination. King George would have much preferred to stay at Sandringham, his country home in Norfolk 120 miles north of London, living the life of a country squire rather than carry out the duties of monarchy. Seventy years later, his great-grandson Charles similarly prefers the life of a country gentleman.

Queen Mary seemed to have an uncanny understanding of the British people, and she embodied the formidable ideals of middle-class British womanhood of that era: thrift, service, self-control, and unshakable devotion to the home. Queen Mary persuaded the mass of the people that the Royal Family was "just like us," an ordinary middle-class family, but, at the same time, made her husband the King appear a paragon with whom the people could identify.

Her view of the monarch contrasted sharply with that of her husband's father, Edward VII, who led a life of self-indulgence surrounded by party-goers, gamblers, womanizers, and drunks. He also had a string of lovers, paramours, and even loose women. Mary changed all that. She and her husband George would dine frugally together in Buckingham Palace each night, usually alone, and would be in bed promptly by 11:15 P.M. with the lights out. They hardly ever entertained privately. Yet, despite this frugal lifestyle, she did insist that every evening they dress formally for dinner even when dining alone; she would appear resplendent in a majestic full-length ball gown with a tiara and the King would be dressed in white tie and tails and wearing the Order of the Garter!

Queen Mary took it upon herself to maintain the prestige and influence of the monarchy by example and service to the nation. To illustrate the Crown's new attitude to the nation's morals she began at the palace itself. As if to cast out the adulterers and womanizers who had surrounded the previous King, Edward VII, Queen Mary decreed that all divorcées, whether the wronged party or not, should never be permitted to appear at court; on no occasion would they be introduced to the King or herself, nor would they be permitted to join royal shooting or hunting parties, and must never be granted entrance to the

Royal Enclosure at Ascot. Queen Mary's values and principles would be religiously followed by her daughter-in-law Queen Elizabeth and her granddaughter Elizabeth.

Poor, henpecked George V, never very bright, also had to toe the new royal line of duty and dedication. Fortunately, he had spent most of his adult life in the Royal Navy—hence his nickname the "Sailor King"—and fully understood the meaning of the word *duty*. Mary advised, cajoled, and persuaded her husband to follow her advice, and he did so, despite the fact he could be the most irritable of men.

She was also determined to show the power and the glory of Britain, which in those early days of her reign was the wealthiest and most powerful nation in the world: the Royal Navy had command of the seas across the world, the British army was apparently invincible, and the British Empire at its peak. Mary wanted the whole world to pay homage. One of her more extraordinary ideas turned into the most magnificent show of kingship ever organized by the British Crown outside the country, when a demonstration of obsequious obedience to the British Crown took place in India in 1911, immediately after the coronation. King George with Queen Mary stood on a dais, dressed in their full, heavy, coronation robes and crowns as well as bearing their imperial regalia. The Indian princes, in full view of their massed armies of immaculate Indian troops, paid homage to them while bejeweled elephants knelt before the Emperor.

Back home, Mary insisted the monarchy should also be seen as splendid, wealthy, and powerful. When the King and Queen went to Balmoral for their August holiday, seventeen locomotives were placed along the royal route just in case the royal engine broke down. At royal picnics, liveried footmen would serve the food and wine, and Buckingham Palace was then staffed by one hundred upper and four hundred lower servants; the palace provided a four-course meal with wine and liqueurs each day to the upper servants.

World War I secured the survival of the monarchy in Britain while finishing off those of Germany, Austria, and Russia. Much of the credit for the survival of the English royals must be given to Queen Mary; it was her finest hour.

Mary insisted that the Royal Family share the burdens of the Great War with their subjects. She declared that the court would abandon alcohol "for the duration of hostilities," and when this became known the people understood and appreciated that the Royal Family was not living in luxury while the common folk did without. To show her dedication Queen Mary spent the war touring hospitals, tending wounded soldiers herself, even helping out in the wards. And she was indefatigable. Mary persuaded other female members of the Royal Family to follow her example. One finally complained to her: "I'm exhausted and I hate hospitals." Queen Mary snapped back: "You are a member of the British Royal Family. We are never tired and we all love hospitals."

Queen Mary made sure her sons were at the war front, sharing the appalling conditions like every other mother's son. Her eldest son, the dashing Prince of Wales, was in the trenches; her second son, Prince Albert, commanded a gun turret at the naval Battle of Jutland; and King George himself made frequent visits to his troops in the trenches. During one visit he was thrown from his horse and badly injured. All these patriotic acts won respect for the Royal Family and drew the monarchy and the people closer.

And yet, despite such signal success in rebuilding and remodeling the monarchy, Queen Mary left behind a disaster—the effects of which have continued to plague the Royal Family to the present day: her relations with her own children—her five sons and her daughter— proved an unmitigated failure.

Because of his relationship with his parents, Edward, Prince of Wales, rejected everything they stood for, including, finally, the throne of England, bringing about the biggest crisis the House of Windsor had ever faced. Edward's abdication in 1936 has haunted the Royal Family ever since. Even today Elizabeth judges the success or failure of the monarchy by that yardstick. As the failures and disasters of three of her children's marriages cast deepening shadows over the Crown, Elizabeth has clung to the single fact that the crisis confronting the House of Windsor in the 1990s is nothing compared to those dark days of the abdication. At that time, some believed the abdication heralded the end of the monarchy in Britain.

It is extraordinary that so many senior members of the House of Windsor should have proved to be such deplorable parents, incapable of bringing up their own children even after they themselves had experienced hardships at the hands of their own mothers and fathers.

Queen Mary's understanding of the British people did not extend to her offspring, whom she treated as though she was their hard-hearted teacher rather than their mother. And King George V, brought up in the harsh discipline of the Royal Navy, believed that to spare the rod was to spoil the child. He treated the slightest childish misdemeanor as rebellion to be dealt with sternly and severely.

In such circumstances it is usual for the mother to come to the defense of her offspring, but not Queen Mary. She took the side of her husband because he was the King, and the King could do no wrong. Unfortunately for her children, Queen Mary was no natural mother, and some contemporaries remarked that she didn't have a maternal instinct in her body despite the fact she bore six children. Shortly after being born, each and every child was immediately handed over to the royal nanny because Mary wanted as little to do with them as possible.

All became casualties in one way or another. Bertie, the Duke of York, later George VI, was a stammering, nervous wreck of a young man; George, Duke of Kent, was addicted to cocaine and a practicing homosexual; Henry, Duke of Gloucester, turned into a drunkard and an alcoholic; and the eldest, David, Prince of Wales and heir to the throne, rejected everything his parents had held most dear, including the monarchy.

Bertie was a miserable, sickly child. Queen Mary, who often saw him only once or twice a week, did not notice that his nanny, neurotic and unfit for her job, failed to feed him properly. He spent his early years screaming for food. Shy, retiring, and nervous, Bertie suffered from an appalling stammer, which was put down to constant bullying by his father. Queen Mary considered his legs too bandy, so she ordered that braces be put on both of them, for two years, to straighten them. They caused Bertie enormous discomfort and pain. Because of his poor diet and lack of food, Bertie also suffered from indigestion, which made him nauseous; only after many years did doctors diagnose a duodenal ulcer. Despite this upbringing Bertie displayed remarkable courage. He served in both the Royal Navy and the Royal Air Force, and despite being knock-kneed he won the RAF Tennis Doubles at Wimbledon in 1920.

Queen Mary and King George's youngest son, Prince John, developed epilepsy when he was about seven, due, according to some biographers, to the treatment meted out to him by his strict parents. As a result he was locked away in a small house on the Sandringham estate in Norfolk and cared for by a single nurse. One night at dinner Queen Mary simply announced to the family: "John is unwell and has gone away to be cared for. It is very unlikely that we will ever see him again."

He was, in fact, never seen again by his brothers or sister, or by his parents. He died in 1919 unloved, unnoticed, and unmourned. He was only fourteen.

Queen Mary and King George were surprised and happy when Lady Elizabeth Bowes-Lyon, the youngest daughter of the 14th Earl of Strathmore, eventually agreed to marry their son Bertie after twice refusing his offer of marriage. Lady Elizabeth was one of the prettiest debutantes of the decade and a great attraction to all the young aristocrats. She wasn't at all sure she wanted to become enmeshed in the Royal Family. Lady Elizabeth was sweet and sensible and had formidable charm; she also had a will of her own, and no one could successfully challenge it. In retrospect, the strength and the sweetness were exactly what Bertie needed to counteract his own rather weak, ineffectual character. It did not matter to the family that Lady Elizabeth was not of royal blood and technically a commoner.

At that time, 1923, no one in England dreamed that Bertie would ever be King; his parents were simply keen to find a good, sensible, strong-willed wife for their second eldest son.

Despite, or perhaps because of, Mary's domineering relationships with her own children, she sought a close involvement with her first granddaughter, the baby Lilibet. From the beginning, Queen Mary took the little Princess under her wing as though she had a premonition that one day she would be Queen. When entertaining guests at teatime, a ritual Queen Mary always observed, she would send a car for baby Elizabeth, who would be brought to Buckingham Palace and shown off to the guests as they sat and ate their cucumber sandwiches and rich cakes. Absorbed by her granddaughter, Mary described her in letters as "a white fluff of thistledown," a baby with "the sweetest air of complete serenity."

Fifteen months after Lilibet was born, Queen Mary persuaded her husband that the Yorks should undertake an official royal visit to Australia and New Zealand, a trip by sea that would take them away from Lilibet for four months. While her parents were overseas, baby

Elizabeth was brought to live at Buckingham Palace, and Queen Mary saw her at least three times every day, something she had never done with her own children. Elizabeth could do no wrong, and her grandparents spoiled her shamelessly.

At twelve months of age Lilibet would sit on a rug throwing packs of cards around the room. At eighteen months, she would grab balls of wool and unravel them as she ran around the room and down the corridors. Later she had a reputation for finding boxes of matches, spilling them everywhere, and then, on occasion, lighting them. She would rip the arms and legs off her dolls and teddy bears and throw them round the room. One set of toys she cherished above all, however—her painted lead soldiers, which she would put on parade and pretend to inspect, like a future Queen.

Mary and King George were always arranging photographs of the little Elizabeth. One was particularly striking, of grandmother and grandchild sitting correctly, neither looking at the camera: Queen Mary, wearing a long, flowing dress with a multiple rope of pearls, and Lilibet, sitting on a table, looking almost doll-like, with a small row of coral beads, look aloof, regal. It was Queen Mary's favorite photograph.

Gruff, crotchety King George would not permit his own children even to talk to him unless he addressed them first. In contrast Elizabeth would sit on his knee, pull his beard, and call him all sorts of names, such as "big ears," and he thought her wonderful.

When the twelve-month-old Princess made her first appearance on the famous Buckingham Palace balcony, Queen Mary, not her parents, proudly held her for the crowds to cheer. And in a letter to Queen Mary, Elizabeth's mother wrote: "It almost frightens me that the people should love Elizabeth so much. I suppose that it is a good thing, and I hope she will be worthy of it, poor little darling."

The nickname Lilibet took because, as a child, Elizabeth could not pronounce her own name, and some members of the family have called her that throughout her life. Queen Mary would persuade Bertie and her mother to visit Buckingham Palace and Windsor Castle as frequently as possible so she could watch, and supervise, the child's progress. As a royal child Lilibet, at ages four and five, would return the salute of the guardsmen on duty by madly waving both her arms at them, causing great laughter. She seemed natural and carefree in comparison to the stiff and formal King George and Queen Mary.

For most of her young life Elizabeth lived at 145 Piccadilly, opposite Green Park, only a few hundred yards from Buckingham Palace. Her nanny was Mrs. Clara Knight, forever called Allah—a childish form of Clara, and nothing to do with Islam. Allah was the royal nanny par excellence, and she was rewarded for her work and devotion to the family with the honorary title of "Mrs.," though she never married. In those days the title "Mrs." signified status and earned respect. She was never photographed out of uniform and usually would be seen in her navy-blue belted coat and navy felt hat pushing a royal pram in one of the royal parks.

In August 1930, a few months after Lilibet turned four, her sister, Princess Margaret Rose, arrived, a child who would test Elizabeth's patience as well as her parents', over the ensuing years.

Bertie, the Duke of York, with memories of his awful childhood still in his mind, was determined that his children should enjoy a lyrical youth and look upon their childhood years as a golden age. His wife Elizabeth had fortunately enjoyed a wonderful childhood and wanted her daughters to have the same happy experience. And so it was to be.

Queen Mary had spoiled her eldest son, David, the heir to the throne, because he was the Prince of Wales. But as his life became more dissolute Queen Mary grew closer to the Yorks, especially after Lilibet was born. As a result, she changed her allegiance and began spoiling the Yorks. She decided that Bertie and Elizabeth had become the quintessential Royal Family, living evidence that the monarchy embodied all the radiant domestic virtues, despite the antics of the heir to the throne. For David was proving irresponsible and a gadabout, having love affairs with older and usually married women, gambling, partying, and clubbing with his young racy friends and living the sort of life condemned as sinful by his mother.

In 1930, Mary decided on the publication of a full-length biography of Elizabeth, then three: *The Story of Princess Elizabeth* appeared with the "sanction of her parents" and written by Anne Ring, formerly attached to HRH The Duchess of York's Household. It was a bestseller.

This slim volume offered such paragraphs as: "From the moment of her birth not only has our little Princess been wrapped about with the tender love of parents and devoted grand-parents, of cousins and uncles and friends, but she has been the admiring object of affection from thousands in the country and beyond the seas who have never seen her."

A description of bedtime read: "When Princess Elizabeth's nurse, descending to the Morning Room or the Drawing Room, says in quiet tones, 'I think it is bedtime now, Elizabeth,' there are no poutings or protests, just a few joyous skips and impromptu dance steps, a few last minute laughs at Mummy's delicious bedtime jokes, and then Princess Elizabeth's hand slips into her Nurse's hand, and the two go off gaily together across the deep chestnut pile of the Hall carpet to the accommodating lift, which in two seconds has whisked them off to the familiar dear domain, which is theirs to hold and to share."

Other books appeared, with the full approval of the Royal Family, emphasizing the "joyous, delightful, radiant" family of the Duke and Duchess of York. Film footage and newsreel pictures of the Yorks in the 1930s depicted Bertie, slim and serious, and neatly dressed; his adoring wife, Elizabeth, smiling sweetly; and two little Princesses, perfectly behaved and immaculately dressed in party frocks, playing sweetly together. In the 1930s Princess Elizabeth—described as "the most celebrated and best-loved child in the world"—had apparently become Britain's answer to America's child star, Shirley Temple.

One morning the Lord Chamberlain met Lilibet in a palace corridor and said cheerily, "Good morning, little lady." Lilibet retorted, "I'm not a little lady, I'm Princess Elizabeth." Later that morning Queen Mary knocked on the Lord Chamberlain's door and with Lilibet in tow announced: "This is Princess Elizabeth, who hopes one day to be a lady."

On another occasion, her mother had taken her young daughter along when entertaining a society lady at tea, and Lilibet soon became bored. She rang for a footman and told him, "Kindly ring for a taxi. Our guest is leaving." Elizabeth was immediately sent to her room without her tea.

Hundreds of toys arrived at the house, gifts from total strangers enraptured by the little Princess, but she was permitted only a few dolls and teddy bears. Instead of toys, her nanny gave her a dustpan and brush when she was just three, and she loved to help the maids clean her nursery. Tidiness and cleanliness were traits Elizabeth never lost, and she believed the old adage that cleanliness is next to godliness. At four when she was given her first pony as a Christmas present, she was also given the necessary brushes and grooming kit. Though young, Lilibet was taught that a pony had to be cared for, and she would groom her little horse before every ride. She kept the brushes and kit lined up outside her nursery door.

The 1930s relationship between Palace and media appears extraordinary today. Privileged royal watchers from selected newspapers were invited to Buckingham Palace and Windsor Castle to see the two Princesses at play or at their school lessons; others came to watch the Yorks' Christmas pantomime at Windsor, starring, of course, Elizabeth and Margaret. Ladies-in-waiting and other servants were encouraged to earn pin money by writing about the Princesses' lives in the popular papers and women's magazines.

Today press officers are employed to minimize and spin information about the royals. When Princess Elizabeth was growing up, the Palace could rely on the press and movie news to present the most favorable view of the Royal Family.

Generally, Lilibet lived a solitary and lonely childhood, though she always had Nanny Allah and, of course, her irritating younger sister to play with; nevertheless, she appears to have been a happy child. She had been given a cairn terrier puppy for her third birthday, and she adored it. Always strongly attracted to animals, mainly dogs and ponies, Lilibet would become closely attached to them, spending hours grooming and playing with them. They took the place of other childhood friends, who were few and far between during the years she grew up. While still a child she also began her lifelong love affair with the corgi (Welsh for "dwarf dog"), beginning with her mother's two corgis, Carol and Crackers.

Remarkably few restrictions were put on the girls. That was most unusual at a time when most of the aristocracy still believed that children should be seen and not heard. They could roam through the entire house and were encouraged to jump into their parents' bed in the early mornings. They were even permitted nighttime pillow fights before settling down and listening to Nanny Allah or their mother read a bedtime story.

Margaret MacDonald, "Bobo" to the Princesses, came to work for the Yorks as a nursery maid shortly after Margaret arrived. From caring for four-year-old Lilibet, Bobo was to spend her entire life with Elizabeth. Bobo remained a close personal friend until she died in September 1993 at the age of eighty-nine, one of the most important influences on Elizabeth's life. Bobo lived in a small suite of rooms at Buckingham Palace and still chatted to Elizabeth once or twice a day until the end. For their first ten years together they shared a bedroom, until it was decided that Lilibet, then fourteen, was old enough to sleep alone. Later, Bobo was to become Elizabeth II's official personal maid and dresser, but the relationship was much closer than that. Lilibet confided in Bobo totally, and the loyal Scotswoman knew every secret of the future Queen. The grown-up Elizabeth was to say of her: "I talk over everything with Bobo; she is so sensible and down to earth, and I would trust her with my life."

In 1932, with Elizabeth just six, the Yorks spent most of the time in a new home, Royal Lodge in Windsor Great Park. For four years the family reveled in the countrylike atmosphere of Windsor Park. There Lilibet was given a small garden plot to grow her own vegetables and flowers, and it was in the nearby park that she learned to ride her pony.

As she emerged from the cocoon of her early childhood, Lilibet became a stickler for detail, tidiness, and punctuality. She seemed too self-disciplined, too correct, too orderly for a girl just seven years of age. She would put away her toys neatly, fold her own clothes immaculately, pack up her books according to size, and even arrange her sweets by colors and sizes. She learned to dress herself when just four, doing up all her buttons, but she showed no flair for clothes, happily wearing whatever her nanny put out.

At the age of seven another newcomer entered Elizabeth's life. Miss Marion Crawford, the famous Crawfie, employed by the Yorks as the girls' governess, was also to have a profound influence. She would be responsible for their entire education. From the very beginning their father, the Duke, had little ambition for his children's learning. The only instruction he gave Crawfie, twenty-three, was "For goodness' sake teach the girls to write a decent hand. That's all I ask you." And she did. Both Elizabeth and Margaret have good, strong handwriting.

There was never any suggestion that Elizabeth or Margaret should attend an ordinary school, not even a select private one. Neither the

Duke nor the Duchess, and especially Queen Mary, believed their "royal" children should go to an ordinary school with other pupils. The Duchess had attended a London day school for a while and hated every moment, and she had no intention of inflicting such penance on her own children; a governess was considered far preferable. So Elizabeth's entire education was a quiet, solitary, and lonely undertaking, controlled and organized by the sensible Crawfie.

In 1950 Crawfie published a book detailing the lives of Elizabeth and Margaret in the 1930s. Entitled *The Little Princesses*, it became a Book-of-the-Month Club selection in the United States. One paragraph showed their isolation: "Other children always had an enormous fascination, like mystic beings from a distant world, and the little girls used to smile shyly at those they liked the look of. They would so have loved to speak to them and make friends, but this was never encouraged. I have often thought it a pity. The Dutch and Belgian Royal children walked about the streets in their countries as a matter of course."

In her book, Crawfie also revealed the pugilistic side of Elizabeth's nature, describing the ten-year-old Lilibet as having a "nifty left hook" which, when roused, she used on her sister, Margaret. Crawfie described Margaret as a good "close fighter" and known "to bite on occasions." She added, "But Elizabeth was the one with the temper."

Lilibet and Margaret seldom escaped the confines of their home. They were once taken, as a special treat, for a ride on a subway train, but unfortunately someone recognized the Princesses, who were in the hands of Crawfie and a detective. A royal car had to be called to help rescue them from the crowds that gathered to gaze at them. Occasionally, the girls rode incognito on the top of London buses, but after a few months these trips also were stopped for fear the girls might be recognized.

The girls were taken to one pantomime a year around Christmas and were permitted to attend the annual horse show at London's Olympia. Most of the time they had to rely on their own devices, organizing their own games at home. Often these would involve running around the house with one of the girls pretending to be the horse while the other held the reins.

During the 1930s the Royal Family reached a pinnacle of popularity, which surprised King George V. In May 1935 a celebration was held to mark his twenty-five years on the throne, and the people cheered wherever he went. Coming at the end of the Great Depression, with millions still unemployed and abject poverty everywhere, the Silver Jubilee celebrations provided a wonderful tonic. There were bonfires and parties in the streets and the parks. Indeed, it was recorded that park attendants had to call for extra carts to haul away the thousands of used condoms!

Only twelve months later the monarchy and the nation were enveloped in the trauma of Edward's abdication. In 1936 Lilibet was just ten and hardly aware of the unfolding drama which was to have such an effect on the rest of her life. Lilibet did once meet the American divorcée Wallis Simpson, when King Edward, who had succeeded to the throne on the death of King George, came to visit the Yorks. She even shook hands with the Duke's paramour, whom Queen Mary called "that scarlet woman." What struck Elizabeth at the time was Mrs. Simpson's American accent, which, of course, was strange to her ears.

For her part the twice-married divorcée, Mrs. Simpson, did remember Elizabeth and Margaret. She commented later: "Those girls are unbelievable, wonderfully blonde, brightly scrubbed, and beautifully mannered."

For some time before King George V died, Queen Mary had been anxious about Edward's succeeding to the throne. Both the ailing George and Queen Mary were appalled by the behavior of Edward and Mrs. Simpson. Edward escorted her everywhere in London; Wallis, usually overdressed and bejeweled, would turn up on the arm of the heir apparent at parties, balls, and even the Royal Opera House. Her appearances were treated as sensational and, to many in the 1930s high society, as scandalous, because society knew she was a married woman, still living with her second husband.

Following the sudden death of George V in 1936, Queen Mary feared for the monarchy itself. She simply did not trust her eldest son to do the right thing. Queen Mary told Edward of her fears and suggested that he should put aside his interest in Mrs. Simpson "for the sake of the nation." Mary pointed out in no uncertain terms that as King he was no longer responsible simply for himself but for the entire nation, and therefore he must end his self-indulgence. Mary further bluntly told her son that Britain could not support a twice-divorced woman as Queen.

The family took great care not to discuss Mrs. Simpson or the threat to the monarchy in front of the children. Elizabeth, however, a naturally bright child, sensed something was afoot. She asked her nanny, her governess, and her mother: "What's wrong with Uncle David? Is Uncle David in trouble?"

Elizabeth's natural curiosity wasn't answered directly. In that respect she was in the same position as the vast majority of the British people, who had no idea whatsoever that there was the slightest possibility Edward would abdicate. No British newspapers printed a word of the unfolding drama until the abdication actually occurred.

In October 1936 Mrs. Simpson brought successful divorce proceedings against her husband, Ernest. He would be the second husband she had divorced. In six months, after the decree nisi had been made absolute, she would be free to marry a third time. The satirical magazine *Punch* put the issue into perspective, showing Prime Minister Stanley Baldwin urging King Edward to give up Mrs. Simpson, saying: "All the peoples of your Empire, Sir, sympathize with you most deeply; but they all know—as you yourself must—that the Throne is greater than the man."

Indeed, the Prime Minister did plead with King Edward on many occasions to drop Mrs. Simpson, explaining that the Cabinet, the government, dominion governments, the Church, and public opinion would not accept a once-divorced, much less a twice-divorced woman as Queen. But Edward would not listen; if he could not marry the woman he loved, then he would abdicate the throne.

On Thursday afternoon, December 10, 1936, Elizabeth, aged ten, heard crowds outside her home in Piccadilly calling her father's name and cheering. She went downstairs and asked a footman what all the commotion was about. The servant told her that her father was now King and that meant that one day she would be Queen. She raced back upstairs and told her sister Margaret, then six, the exciting news.

"Does that mean that you will have to be the next Queen?" asked Margaret.

"Yes, someday," replied Lilibet.

"Poor you," said Margaret.

It seems Elizabeth took in her stride the realization that one day she would be Queen. Despite all the comings and goings at the house that day she was more interested in going for a swim.

Downstairs, however, poor Bertie was not at all happy with the turn of events because he had never believed his elder brother would actually abdicate. The news put him in a state of shock for several days, and he had to retire to bed. His wife, now Queen Elizabeth, had just begun to recover from a bad bout of flu. Her response was characteristic: "We must take what is coming to us, and make the best of it." She had never wanted to be too closely enmeshed in the affairs of the Royal Family. Now she was Queen, and the thought filled her with trepidation.

In truth, Edward had been forced to abdicate by the will of Parliament after Tory Prime Minister Stanley Baldwin told him bluntly that Mrs. Simpson would be totally unacceptable to the Parliaments of Britain and the Commonwealth as royal consort. Baldwin asked the King openly during one of their discussions: "Do you really think the people would accept a Queen Wally?" Edward looked at Baldwin for a while without comment. He then nodded his head, saying: "You're right."

The abdication caused the most extraordinary soul-searching in England, but it also had its effect in the United States, for many Americans saw in Mrs. Wallace Simpson a true woman of the people. A few took the refusal of the British government to sanction Edward VIII's love for the woman he wanted to marry as an insult to the United States. After all, it was argued, the wife of the Duke of York, who was to succeed his brother on the throne, was also a commoner. They asked: "What was the difference between a king marrying a commoner from America and a king marrying a commoner from Scotland?" The correct reply of course was that Mrs. Simpson had been divorced, twice, and Elizabeth had never been. And, further, Queen Mary, by far the strongest royal character at the time, was passionately against divorce.

In the 1930s, abdication was viewed as a failure of constitutional monarchy, the very essence of Britain's system of government, which it trumpeted throughout the world as the best of all democratic systems. The establishment, the government, and the church viewed the abdication as a severe embarrassment.

There were also those in the United States, particularly among the young, who believed that King Edward VIII should have refused to abdicate, should have insisted on marrying Mrs. Simpson, should have challenged the government, should have appealed to the British people over the heads of Parliament and married "the woman I love." Winston Churchill also urged such action.

Shortly after Edward's abdication, when it was evident Elizabeth would eventually become Queen, her grandmother took command of her education. Queen Mary was amazed to find that the two Princesses appeared to be learning nothing more than the three Rs— reading, 'riting, and 'rithmetic. At that time Elizabeth, then eleven years old, and Margaret, six, spent only one and a half hours doing schoolwork, from nine-thirty to eleven o'clock every morning, followed by an hour's play and lunch. Then another hour's rest was followed by singing, music, drawing, and dancing. When weather permitted, the girls were taken outside for an hour's walk, as part of their education!

The total education of Britain's future Queen consisted of just seven and a half hours of academic work a week. Mary decreed her granddaughter should study history, so she would learn about Britain's past glories; geography, with emphasis on the scope and extent of her beloved British Empire; poetry, to perfect memory; and Bible reading for her understanding of religious history. She also arranged for the vice-provost of Eton, Britain's foremost public school, Sir Henry Marten, to instruct Lilibet in English constitutional history.

Surprisingly, Queen Mary did not order the further intellectual stimulation or extra academic work that were clearly needed for the development of the two Princesses. Mary and Elizabeth's parents were apparently concerned that their daughters might become bluestockings (studious young women). As a result, Princess Elizabeth succeeded to the throne virtually uneducated in all but the most rudimentary and basic disciplines.

With the full approval of Queen Mary, those courtiers in command at Buckingham Palace decided that revealing the new King in the fullest possible royal splendor would be the best way to overcome the crisis that the abdication had caused the monarchy and to obscure the fact that George was not the rightful heir to the throne. And so the frail George was subjected to the most rigorous and magnificent Coronation Britain had ever witnessed.

The Coronation had a profound effect on eleven-year-old Lilibet. The divine service, the sacred image of the sovereign, and the actual crowning were all explained to her. She already understood that one day she too would be crowned Queen and would take on the responsibilities of the Crown. Queen Mary decided the two Princesses would take part in the Coronation, and they watched the whole three-hour service. Elizabeth took everything most seriously, never smiling throughout. Margaret, too young to understand what was happening, spent a lot of time looking about her. Elizabeth gasped as the hundreds of assembled peers, in their glorious robes, shouted loudly "God Save the King" at the moment the crown was placed on her father's head by the Archbishop of Canterbury. That sense of a monarch's sacred and divine right to rule stayed with Elizabeth well into her adult life and caused ructions in her marriage.

George's coronation in May 1937 was a triumphant success, but he needed the moral support of Queen Mary at the actual ceremony, breaking a centuries-old tradition that no Dowager Queen was present at a crowning. On newsreels and film the world witnessed the amazing spectacle of the Coronation, which left no one in doubt that, with all its dignity, splendor, and sacred rites, the English throne was as strong as ever.

King George and his consort Queen Elizabeth were now determined to produce a male heir, but it was not to be. And Lilibet told her nanny she prayed to God to send her a little brother who could one day be King. The family would never again mention Uncle David or the abdication to Elizabeth until she became Queen at the age of twenty-six.

Uncle David's banishment upset Elizabeth. She had found him a likable man, always laughing and joking with her. The Duke and Duchess of Windsor, the titles awarded them after the abdication, were banished forever, forbidden from returning to Britain, exiled to live wherever they wished outside Britain. They were given an annual stipend, though the amount was never revealed, allowing them to live in comfort, but not splendor, till the day they died. The Royal Family's treatment of the Duke of Windsor has been seen by generations as cruel and needless, but the House of Windsor is severe. Uncle David had put his own personal happiness before duty, and he had to bear the consequences for the rest of his life. All was explained to Elizabeth at a later date, but she had learned a most salutary lesson.

George VI feared his severe stammer would make him incapable of carrying out his role as monarch when he realized he would be expected to continue the tradition, begun by his father, George V, of broadcasting to the nation and the empire at Christmastime. His wife, Queen Elizabeth, hired the Australian speech therapist Lionel Logue, and after months of therapy his stammer improved enough so that on Christmas Day 1937 he managed to deliver his speech. But the nation, which had been informed in advance of his speech impediment, shared the King's ordeal as he struggled with many of the words. His obvious courage and discomfort added to his popularity, for the people warmed to a monarch who had personal problems just as they did.

Meanwhile, the selling of Lilibet to the nation, ordered by Queen Mary to popularize the monarchy, continued inexorably. Now, her name was given to bone china, to hospitals, and even to chocolates; her wax effigy, sitting on a pony, now stood in Madame Tussaud's and her portrait in the Royal Academy, and her picture appeared on the cover of *Time* magazine.

Convinced no male heir would appear and that Lilibet would one day be crowned monarch, Queen Mary again intervened, checking on her granddaughter's education. She again found her education wanting but instead of encouraging a proper formal education, she decided to educate the two Princesses herself. She personally conducted cultural tours of London, taking the girls to the Tower of London, the Royal Mint, the Bank of England, and farther afield to Kew Gardens, Hampton Court, and Greenwich Palace. Queen Mary would march ahead of the children, talking with whoever was in charge, while the girls would hurry on behind, exhausted at the end of two-hour visits. Margaret swore she would never allow her children to see more than three pictures at a time while visiting art galleries, so they would plead for "just one more'" rather than longing to go home.

Elizabeth's education remained in the hands of Miss Crawford, the prim spinster and former primary school teacher from Scotland. Although she had never taught anyone over the age of eleven, Crawfie remained Elizabeth's only teacher until she was eighteen. Then Elizabeth's education ceased altogether. She spent much of her time taking long walks in the park and dancing lessons in Buckingham Palace, reading from books, and resting for long periods. Elizabeth never spent more than two hours a day—ten hours a week—actually studying. It was as if she were living in the nineteenth rather than the twentieth century.

The royal sisters did bring some much needed life to Buckingham Palace, which had never known the boisterous noise of two young girls running, laughing, and enjoying the long corridors and huge rooms of the palace. Servants and courtiers welcomed their arrival and their irreverence for the place, which many considered more a mausoleum than a palace.

The King and Queen loved to spend as much time as possible with their daughters. Weekends were mostly spent at Windsor Royal Lodge, where they all enjoyed do-it-yourself entertainment like charades, card games, parlor games, sing-alongs, and walks together in Windsor Great Park, all simple pleasures. But none of these activities was designed to help expand the mind of either of the young girls.

Elizabeth's family life came to a shattering end as war engulfed Europe and Buckingham Palace was bombed and set ablaze by Luftwaffe raids over London. On September 3, 1939, the day when Britain declared war on Germany, Lilibet and Margaret were at a Girl Guides camp in Scotland. Both were members of the Brownies and the Girl Guides but never took part in any activities or attended any parties where boys were present.

Throughout the war the sisters spent most of their time at Windsor Castle, thirty miles west of London. Although it had been suggested that they be sent to the safety of Scotland or Canada, particularly as Elizabeth was now heir to the throne, the King and Queen refused. They had no intention of leaving the nation to face Nazi Germany alone, and they wanted to keep their family together as much as possible. The girls lived in the Brunswick Tower, a strongly built part of Windsor Castle, while their parents spent the weekdays in the heart of London at Buckingham Palace.

World War II came to the Royal Family as much as anyone else in Britain. More than three hundred high-explosive bombs, as well as incendiaries and buzz bombs, fell around Windsor Castle before the war ended. Most nights during the first three years the family heard the wail of air-raid sirens and the drone of enemy bombers overhead.

When the sirens sounded, the girls were awakened by Bobo and

Allah, who shared their bedrooms throughout the war, and dressed in "siren suits"—warm one-piece suits with hoods (called siren suits because children donned them whenever the sirens sounded). Quickly they made their way down darkened stairs to the basement, where the rest of the staff also took refuge. They carried with them little suitcases containing their favorite dolls, a book, and the diaries their mother gave them at Christmas each year. They slept in a two-tier bunk which had recently been installed, and the girls would sometimes spend the entire night in the tiny basement waiting for the all-clear to sound. Life in Windsor Castle wasn't much fun. In each corridor only one naked lightbulb illuminated the darkness. All the paintings, the silver, the antique furniture, the wall hangings, and the rugs had been carefully stored beneath the castle.

Throughout the war, King George and his wife had no intention of leaving Britain, for they believed that would be tantamount to deserting their people. They hoped, by their example, to instill the same grit and determination in the nation as Prime Minister Winston Churchill did in his wartime speeches. Elizabeth often listened to those stirring radio broadcasts with her parents.

In 1940 Churchill made one of his most memorable speeches: "We shall defend our island, whatever the cost may be, we shall fight on the beaches, we shall fight on the landing grounds, we shall fight in the fields and in the streets, we shall fight in the hills; we shall never surrender."

Following that speech King George and his wife let it be known they had decided to take up arms in case the day came when they needed to defend themselves. Each week they practiced with rifles, tommy guns, and revolvers in specially erected ranges in Buckingham Palace and Windsor Castle. On occasion, Elizabeth and Margaret were allowed to watch their parents and handle the revolvers, but they never learned to shoot. That was to come later.

On the orders of Churchill a secret hideout was built and fully equipped as a bomb shelter at Madresfield, Worcestershire, 120 miles northwest of London, which would become the royal headquarters if ever German forces landed in Britain. At Windsor Castle, baggage for an immediate departure was kept packed throughout the war. The Crown Jewels, wrapped in newspaper and tied with string, were hidden in vaults below ground along with other valuables, ready, at any time, to be brought to a ship at Liverpool. Along with the Princesses, the valuables would sail for Canada.

The day following her sixteenth birthday, Elizabeth enrolled in the wartime youth service scheme, a national organization set up to permit young people over sixteen to "do their bit" to help the war effort. From the outbreak of WWII, Elizabeth had pleaded with her parents to be permitted to help out, in any way possible. Now she was given the chance to prove to the nation, who read of the item in the papers or saw the newsreel film at the local cinema, that the teenage Princess was contributing to the war effort. As a result Elizabeth became accepted as "one of us." And when Buckingham Palace suffered direct hits during a bombing raid in 1941, King George and his wife let it be known they had no intention of quitting London. That decision won them much praise and admiration, since the people saw that their lives were as much at risk as every other London resident.

The war brought advancement of Elizabeth's education with the arrival in London of Mme. Antoinette de Bellaigue, a vivacious Belgian who fled Belgium with her family just ten days before the German invasion. She was hired to teach the Princesses French, and she remained their tutor from 1942 to 1946. She also suggested the Princesses learn German, and they did (but only to schoolgirl level).

Only once during the war did Elizabeth face any real danger. In 1944, she was on a Girl Guide hike in Windsor Park when a flying bomb, sometimes called a "doodle bug" or "buzz bomb," was heard zooming overhead. An army officer in command of the hike ordered the girls to run flat out into a slit trench, and the bomb exploded nearby with a shattering roar. From that moment on an armored car followed the Princesses whenever they went on walks.

All over England, sixteen- and seventeen-year-old girls were encouraged to contribute to the war effort. Elizabeth became increasingly frustrated and annoyed that she was not allowed to carry out more adult duties to help because of possible danger to the heir to the throne. She wanted to become a nurse and tend the wounded and help in hospitals, but her parents would not permit it. After much argument she was eventually allowed to join the Sea Rangers, a group activity for teenage girls interested in seafaring, but this didn't satisfy Elizabeth's craving to carry out more responsible and useful duties.

Finally, in 1945, Lilibet became a soldier, of sorts, in the army transport service. Thrilled to be allowed to dress in khaki, Elizabeth told Bobo: "Now I'm like a real soldier." She was Number 230873, Second Subaltern Elizabeth Alexandra Mary Windsor of the Auxiliary Transport Service (ATS) No. 1. Mechanical Transport Training Centre. Her army records show she was eighteen, 5'3" tall, with blue eyes and brown hair.

For those last few months of war Elizabeth performed the same duties as any other young woman in military transport. She drove a three-ton truck, changed spark plugs, adjusted brakes, greased axles, and changed tires. At last she felt part of the war effort and reveled in her newfound adventure. But even during those months she led a privileged, closeted existence and was never subjected to the rough life of the transport training center. Whereas the other ATS girls lived in barracks, she traveled by chauffeur-driven car between Windsor Castle and the training center each day. She was back home by 4 P.M. and ate in the ATS officers mess.

Victory in Europe was celebrated on May 8, 1945, a day Elizabeth never forgot. She had never tasted such freedom as she did that night. After much pleading on their part, King George permitted his daughters to leave the palace and join in the merrymaking. Chaperoned only by their beloved Crawfie and escorted by a few junior army officers, the Princesses mixed with the crowd, unrecognized by the tens of thousands who joined in the tumultuous celebrations. They ran through the streets of London, danced in Piccadilly Circus, and mingled with the thousands who walked from Trafalgar Square to the palace, where they joined in the wild cheering, singing, and chanting. Crawfie recalled that Elizabeth and Margaret shouted as loudly as everyone else that night: "We want the King, we want the Queen."

Elizabeth had been thirteen at the outbreak of war and nineteen when Japan finally surrendered. At nineteen she was still living a quiet, mainly cloistered life, cut off from the real world as she had been throughout her childhood and teenage years, hardly ever meeting boys her own age and mixing with few girls. At the age of fourteen she still attended all-girl birthday parties. And for her sixteenth birthday Princess Elizabeth, though now a young woman, was given a child's tea party with Jell-O, ice cream, and paper hats.

Boys from Eton would sometimes be invited to rather stiff, formal lunches at Windsor Castle. Elizabeth acted as hostess, sitting in the middle of the table and opposite Margaret, who was already known as an enfant terrible.

Her only real experience of the opposite sex occurred during occasional parties at Buckingham Palace or Windsor when Elizabeth played host to visiting airmen from other nations, among them Americans, New Zealanders, Australians, and Canadians. The parties took place in the afternoon, lasted thirty minutes, and the only beverage served was tea! Other parties Crawfie mentions include occasional madrigal classes, treasure hunts, and games of sardines, but these were only with other girls. Not surprisingly, at the end of the war, on VE-Day, King George wrote of his daughters in his diary: "Poor darlings, they have never had any fun yet."

With the war over, Elizabeth hoped she would spend much more time with her adored Philip. They had first met just before the outbreak of war, in 1939, when she was thirteen. She had been with her parents at the Royal Naval College, Dartmouth, and Philip, then eighteen, was chosen to escort her and Margaret around the school. Immediately attracted by his athletic good looks, blond hair, sporty appearance, and big smile, Elizabeth had never forgotten the young man whom she called "My Viking Prince."

Elizabeth knew Philip to be the son of a member of the Greek royal family which some years earlier had been exiled to Paris. She understood he had been educated in Britain and was destined for a career in the Royal Navy.

For the six years of World War II, she had continually thought of the exciting young naval officer she had seen only a few more times since their first encounter. She had written him letters—not love letters, but friendly ones, giving him news of life in London and of her family.

One of their wartime meetings was at Christmas, in 1943, when Philip, on leave in England, was invited to attend the Royal Family's annual pantomime at Windsor Castle. Elizabeth, sixteen, played the title role in *Aladdin*, and Margaret, Roxana. Elizabeth tried to persuade Philip, then twenty-two, to join in the theatricals, but to her disappointment, he refused. Other royals in the cast included her cousins the Duke of Kent and Princess Alexandra. Elizabeth became visibly animated as Philip clapped and cheered from his front-row seat. Elizabeth leapt from a laundry basket dressed as the young Chinese boy Aladdin, tap-danced, sang solos and duets, and cracked jokes, some quite risqué. Philip laughed aloud in appreciation.

As the war drew to a close, Elizabeth—excited and anxious, like many other young women waiting back home for their men to return from war—desperately hoped that the man she had thought about for so long would return to her. She repeatedly asked Bobo, her one confidante: "Do you think Philip will come back to me? Will he have forgotten me?"

Elizabeth already knew she wanted to marry Philip, but King George had no idea that his beloved child was thinking seriously about marriage. He had other ideas. In his eyes, Lilibet was far too young to contemplate even a serious relationship with anyone, much less think of marriage, and he wanted her to enjoy her young life for a few more years.

In early 1944 King George II of Greece wrote to Elizabeth's father urging him "to take most seriously" the possibility of marriage between his cousin Philip and Elizabeth. King George didn't even mention the letter to Lilibet. When speaking to Elizabeth King George often referred to their family as "the four of us," meaning himself, his wife, Elizabeth, and Margaret. He never included anyone else and never spoke of a future which included any husbands. He apparently yearned to preserve his family in a cocoon, away from the real world, and keep his beloved daughters to himself.

George was annoyed when King George of Greece again raised the question when visiting Buckingham Palace in 1945, announcing to the English George: "It seems Lilibet is in love with Philip, and I know that he adores her."

George VI scowled and replied: "Philip had better not think any more about it at present. They are both too young."

Elizabeth, now twenty, was a good-looking young woman of modest height—five feet, three inches tall—who carried herself well. She had a good figure and shapely legs, her muscles toned by riding. Her hair, light brown and curly, was just above shoulder length. She had a lovely complexion and a ready smile. Queen Mary's lady-in-waiting Lady Airlie commented at the time: "The carriage of her head is unequalled and she has about her that indescribable something which Queen Victoria had, regality."

After the Greek George's second proposal, George VI took a closer look at Lilibet and suggested that she concentrate on her riding lessons and other field sports. He taught her to fish, to stalk deer, and to shoot deer as well as birds. But that wasn't the only reason he wanted to turn her thoughts away from marriage and the opposite sex.

Throughout the war, King George felt he was neglecting his favorite daughter during her teenage years. He felt guilty for his neglect and wanted her to enjoy life now that the restrictions of war had been lifted. He also hoped Lilibet would become the son he had always wanted. He was devoted to her in every sense: wanting her to have the very best in life, to remain single until her middle twenties, to be his close companion, and to spend a good deal of time together. It was a forlorn hope. Lilibet had grown up and she had already made her choice.

Elizabeth had always been an endearing, loving, and obedient daughter. After the war, when George found time to go to Scotland with her, they would spend hours together walking, fishing, riding, and shooting. What she really yearned for, however, was the bright lights of London, now springing to life after the dark days of war. And being in London would bring her closer to Philip, the man she wanted to see as much as possible. But she was dutiful and patient and kept her real thoughts from her father, waiting for the day she would be able to declare her love.

King George realized the time had come for his daughter to start to understand affairs of state. He decreed that she should attend official functions, like launching ships and opening exhibitions, as well as formal lunches and dinners, which were often rather stuffy, boring affairs. After attending a number of these events, Elizabeth realized how inadequate her general education had been and how little she knew of the outside world, of general knowledge, of politics; she felt embarrassed when people she considered important talked of matters she knew little about. She told Bobo: "Sometimes I don't understand what people are talking about at table. And I'm absolutely terrified of sitting next to strangers in case they talk about things I have never heard of."

Elizabeth appeared equally terrified at the debutante dances which, after a wartime hiatus, resumed after the end of the war. King George and his wife encouraged their reappearance so that Elizabeth, now twenty, and Margaret, sixteen, could meet young people, have some fun, and perhaps meet suitable young men whom they might one day marry. But Elizabeth had little or no interest in these dances. She was shy, and found it difficult to handle small talk. Though considered pretty and attractive, she would tend to hold back and stay in the background, making it difficult for young men to dance with her, let alone get to know her except in the most superficial fashion.

King George kept a discreet yet sharp eye on his daughters. After a dance at Windsor Castle when Margaret was eighteen, he checked to see if his daughters were in bed. Finding Margaret's empty he went downstairs to discover her lying on a sofa, with very few clothes on, locked in a passionate embrace with a young Guards officer. The King ordered his daughter to bed and the officer to leave immediately after asking his name and rank. Forty-eight hours later the young man was posted overseas.

Elizabeth seemed both older than her years and also younger and immature. She had little, if any, experience with boys or young men, and probably had never been kissed. She was most certainly a virgin and would act rather coldly whenever young men tried to talk to her. She was seen as a happy, wholesome young woman of some spirit, but rather serious, perhaps lacking warmth and spontaneity, but certainly without conceit. To some in the palace, Princess Elizabeth was almost a saint. And yet she could be stubborn, even imperious, and would sometimes give people a look that sent shivers down their backs. She had also inherited a temper from her doting father as well as his strength of character.

Through the summer of 1945 Elizabeth, then nineteen, saw more of Philip. The following autumn, Elizabeth's teenage dream of love became a reality. The couple spent hours together during Philip's infrequent home leave from his ship, which was stationed in the Far East. They walked on the grounds, talked, dined together, listened to all kinds of music, and, more important, simply spent time alone. The more time they spent together the more Elizabeth knew she was in love and was determined that one day they would marry. And, despite the wishes of her father, she was in a hurry to become officially engaged.

It is not surprising that Elizabeth fell for the dashing Philip. Most of the men she knew were middle-aged, if not old, stuffy and boring, and nearly all worked in Buckingham Palace. The young men she met were always so correct and respectful in the presence of the King's daughter that she never got to know any of them at all well. To the young Lilibet, Philip was invigorating, a self-confident, athletic, good-looking young man who laughed a lot, enjoyed life, was never boring, and who brought excitement into her life, something she had never felt before.

In 1946 the young couple found a secret rendezvous; secret, that is, from her father. They would meet on weekends at Coppins, in Kent, forty miles southeast of London, the home of the Duke and Duchess of Kent, who understood that a teenage romance was going on and thought they should encourage it. Elizabeth took them into her confidence, telling them: "Daddy doesn't want me to see too much of Philip or anyone so please don't tell him." And they didn't.

Both Elizabeth and her father were unaware that working behind the scenes, using whatever friends and relations were necessary, was the man who, as much as Elizabeth, was determined that a betrothal between the two families would take place: Lord Louis Mountbatten. This was his secret ambition, to link his family with the House of Windsor.

Earl Mountbatten, great-grandson of Queen Victoria and an uncle to Prince Philip, was to have a long and deep involvement with the House of Windsor and directly affected the lives of Elizabeth and later Prince Charles.

Whenever they met, Mountbatten would ask his nephew Philip about the romance with the heir apparent, how much time they spent together, what they said to each other, what they did together, and whether Elizabeth talked of a future together. After Philip reported to Mountbatten in July 1946 that Elizabeth had told him she loved him, Mountbatten encouraged him to propose. Philip needed no prompting because he was well aware that young Princess Elizabeth was the greatest "matrimonial catch" among the whole of European royalty, and he was also aware that he was a penniless young naval officer without a home or a proper family.

To some critics, Philip's wooing of Princess Elizabeth, with the assistance of Uncle Dickie, could be seen as cold and calculating. Elizabeth's attraction to his nephew Philip was the opportunity Mountbatten needed to fulfill his secret ambition of linking the

Mountbattens with the Windsors. This unromantic view was encouraged by Philip himself who, when asked about his marriage to Elizabeth, told biographer Basil Boothroyd in 1970:

> "I suppose one thing led to another. I suppose I began to think about it seriously oh, let me think now, when I got back in forty-six and went to Balmoral. It was probably then that we, that it became, you know, that we began to think about it seriously, and even talk about it..." [In Boothroyd's words] Not exactly the words of a young man desperately in love with the girl he wants to marry.

On August 11, 1946, during the Royal Family's summer holiday at Balmoral, Philip, twenty-five, asked Elizabeth, 20, to be his bride. They were walking together in the grounds on a beautiful sunny day when he proposed. Later, Elizabeth told Bobo: "It was wonderful, magical. I just threw my arms round his neck and kissed him as he held me to him, my feet off the ground." Elizabeth knew her father did not want her to become engaged or get married at such a young age, and she told Philip. But she did accept, without first obtaining parental approval, an act completely out of character for Elizabeth, the dutiful, obedient, and loving daughter. She had always been determined to marry her Viking prince, and not even her parents would stop her from doing so.

The night after he proposed, Philip phoned his uncle to tell him of the secret engagement. The delighted Mountbatten had known of course that King George VI opposed the marriage of his daughter, not just because Philip was a member of the Greek royals, without a family, a fortune, or a home, but because, Mountbatten thought, King George's love and devotion for his daughter had become obsessive, even unhealthy.

Mountbatten immediately phoned his other nephew, King George II, newly returned to the Greek throne after a successful plebiscite. He suggested that George leak the news that Prince Philip and Elizabeth of England had become engaged. Mountbatten knew that the betrothal of the heir to the English Crown had to be approved not only by her parents, but also by the government, and he was desperate to secure Elizabeth's hand for Philip officially, before any other contender could be found. George II, for his part, believed and prayed that an engagement between Philip and Elizabeth would seal Britain's obligation to back Greece against the insurgent communists, who sought to overthrow the royalists.

On September 7, 1946, the *New York Times* reported: "Londoners were briefly thrilled today by a report that Princess Elizabeth, who will one day rule over them, was to become engaged to her second cousin, Prince Philip of Greece, but their expectations of marriage were ended by a denial from the Royal Household." Elizabeth's father was furious. First George VI called his wife and inquired whether she knew about the rumor, which she did not. Then he ordered his daughter to come to Buckingham Palace and he asked whether the rumor was true. Dutifully, Elizabeth explained to her father that Philip had unofficially asked her to marry him and that she had accepted. George was angry but said nothing. He did, however, tell her that Philip had ignored all the rules of protocol and had been extremely rude by not asking him first. In his view Philip had behaved disgracefully.

King George told Elizabeth that he could not give his permission or his blessing because the Prime Minister and his government had to be first forewarned of the possibility and their permission obtained. George was very angry, angry with Philip, Louis Mountbatten, and, as he said, "all those bloody Greeks."

Some months earlier, Prime Minister Clement Attlee had alerted the King that the Greek royal family wanted Philip to marry Elizabeth to help their cause. George VI had wanted nothing whatsoever to do with such an arrangement; the future happiness of his beloved Elizabeth was far more important to him than the internal or external politics of Greece. But King George saw the political implications as a legitimate reason to put off Elizabeth's intended engagement, which, he hoped, might provide a breathing space for his daughter to come to her senses and change her mind.

As many a father has discovered, he soon learned that his Lilibet was in love, and there was little he could do. In an effort to postpone the day, King George refused to allow the engagement to be announced officially until all the formalities had been sorted out. Elizabeth could not and did not want to understand the problems; she only knew she intended to spend romantic evenings with the man she was determined to marry, whatever obstacles were put in her way.

Her mother tried to persuade Elizabeth to wait, describing how it took two long years after George had asked her to marry him before she made the decision. Her mother explained she wanted to be sure he was the right man, and by waiting she became convinced their marriage would be happy. The young Lady Elizabeth Bowes-Lyon's marriage to the Duke of York was amazingly successful. He adored her and claimed he could not have lived without her, and many testified that she gave him the backbone to become a much loved and respected wartime King. She was a widow for over forty years and made a magnificent success in her role as Queen Mother, beloved by the entire nation. But behind the smile and the twinkling eyes, and under the floating pastel dresses was a woman of considerable strength. As her staff would comment: "She's as tough as old boots but we all love her dearly."

In 1945 the Churchill government had scheduled a royal visit to South Africa for 1947 to thank that nation for its help and support through the war. Now, that trip came as a godsend to King George, for here was another reason to postpone the engagement. He informed his daughter that the whole family had to visit South Africa and that the trip would last three months. Elizabeth asked her father if it was really necessary that she go, but he was adamant. As he explained, it was the family's duty and duty must come first. Elizabeth had to endure another long, forced separation from Philip, traveling by ship to South Africa, spending weeks crisscrossing Africa with her family. She had little idea of the sort of wild life her husband-to-be was leading back home, but she steadfastly went about her duty, smiling, looking happy, and carrying out the task with self-assurance and much dignity.

She would not have been happy to read the 1947 poll in the tabloid *Sunday Pictorial* that showed 40 percent of readers opposed marriage between Elizabeth and Philip, demanding that if she married she should immediately renounce the throne. The reason: they did not want Princess Elizabeth or the Royal Family involved in any way with the Greek royals, whom they considered not good enough for the English heir.

King George returned to London seventeen pounds lighter and in poor health. Along with conflicts in Palestine and rebellions in India, worry over his daughter's future had taken a severe toll. At a Guildhall banquet shortly after his return the King—with a rasping cough and his voice often inaudible—could hardly finish a sentence.

Elizabeth had turned twenty-one. Prince Philip had relinquished all his Greek titles and had agreed to join the Church of England, renouncing the Greek Orthodox Church in which he had been baptized. King George had finally received formal permission from the British and Commonwealth governments for the heir to the throne to become betrothed. He knew he could not stand in the way of his daughter's wishes much longer, and with a heavy heart he announced his permission in April 1947.

In private, King George gave his permission to Elizabeth holding her face in his hands and kissing her on both cheeks. But tears filled his eyes, which Elizabeth believed were tears of joy for her marriage.

Philip, unable to afford an engagement ring, appealed to his mother, Princess Andrew, now living in Greece as a nun. She sent him the diamonds from her favorite tiara to be made into a ring. By July 1947, Elizabeth and Philip had been secretly engaged for nearly a year, and the newspapers were full of the real-life fairy story of the Princess and her handsome Prince.

King George, unhappy and anxious for his beloved Lilibet, knew the sort of man-about-town Philip had become during the past two years. He feared the Greek would continue his hedonistic ways and, in so doing, break his daughter's heart. Nor did he feel confident that Philip would accept the discipline of royal life. Wary and suspicious of his future son-in-law, King George did not create Philip a Prince or Prince Consort on marrying his daughter. Prince Consort was the title used by Victoria's husband Prince Albert and was customary in all the royal families of Europe. The title Prince Consort showed the man to be married to a queen regnant and simply emphasized a man's official status as the husband of a sovereign. Keeping his title of "Prince," though a courtesy title, showed Philip wanted to maintain his independence. Mountbatten and other courtiers suggested it, but King George would not hear of it. Indeed, Philip was not to receive the title of Prince for almost a decade, though the King used "Prince Philip" as a courtesy title. Philip, however, was never to be Prince Consort.

Prince Philip and his best man, David Milford Haven, were determined that Philip should have a traditional stag party. Philip went tradition one better, and had two, both on the same night. The first, a five-course dinner, was held in the Park Suite at the Dorchester in Park Lane, Mayfair, a stone's throw from Buckingham Palace, with a small select band of twelve men, all from the Royal Navy. Besides Milford Haven, the guests included Mike Parker, Philip's best friend in the Navy, Commander George Norfolk, who had been Philip's captain on HMS *Whelp*, and Louis Mountbatten.

The press discovered the stag dinner and asked permission to take pictures. Philip and Mountbatten agreed, and the photographers trooped in for the last pictures of the bachelor Prince. After they took their pictures Philip asked whether, in return, he and Mike Parker could photograph the photographers. They handed over their cameras, but Philip and Mike Parker immediately jerked out the flashbulbs and smashed them on the floor. The photographers could take no more pictures that night. "Now it's our turn to have the last laugh," Philip said as he ushered the unhappy group of photographers out the door.

After dinner, Philip wanted to thank the chef in person, so Parker and Milford Haven put Philip on a tea trolley and sped him down the long corridors to the kitchens, where an astonished French chef, Jean Baptiste Virlogeux, received Philip's thanks in fluent French.

Philip's second stag party began just after midnight when he, Parker, Milford Haven, and two others went to the Belfry Club, off Belgrave Square, where they drank balloons of brandy and smoked Havana cigars for three more hours. They sang bawdy naval songs, told their favorite risqué jokes, and could hardly walk out of the club when they decided they had drunk enough.

Milford Haven recalled, "Philip and I were staying at Kensington Palace and the next day had to go and see a very senior bishop who was to take us through the wedding ceremony. After breakfast I remember we both had stiff gin and tonics to stabilize us. We were in such a state."

Elizabeth's nuptials were no grand affair as far as royal weddings go because Britain was still suffering the harsh effects of the war. Rationing was still the rule for everyone, including the Royal Family, and King George was anxious that the nation should not think his family any different from them. Because of a shortage of timber for housing no spectator stands were erected along the route from the palace to Westminster Abbey; only a few decorations and flags were flying because of King George's deference to austerity. And Labour

Prime Minister Clement Attlee would not permit the day to be declared a public holiday. As he put it, "We cannot permit the luxury of a public holiday while potatoes are still rationed."

Because of clothes rationing Elizabeth had to be careful with her wedding dress, though she was granted one hundred extra coupons for her trousseau and her eight bridesmaids twenty-three extra coupons each. Her white satin gown shimmered with garlands of stars embroidered in crystals and ten thousand costume pearls had been painstakingly sewn onto the dress to form garlands of York roses and ears of corn. The train was twenty-five feet long.

The day, November 22, 1947, opened with a damp, cold, gray morning, seeming to reflect the nation's mood rather than Elizabeth's youthful happiness. A chill mist hung about the streets of London. Elizabeth, quiet and nervous, didn't speak a word as her wedding dress was fitted by Norman Hartnell, his assistants, and her own maids, who took just over an hour to dress her. And she didn't speak while her hair was being dressed. But she did react when no one could find her bouquet of white orchids, appealing to everyone to search everywhere for the missing flowers. Maids, servants, pages literally ran through palace apartments searching for the missing flowers. With only minutes to go a maid discovered the bouquet in the porter's lodge icebox, put there to keep the orchids cool and fresh until the last minute.

Her sun-ray tiara, a gift from Queen Mary which she wore to hold back her headdress, snapped in half as it was being put on. "Oh no," cried Elizabeth, panicking. But the down-to-earth Queen Mary was in the room at the time. "Don't worry my dear," she said, "there's time and more than one tiara in this palace," and she called for another. Then Elizabeth's double-pearl necklace, given to her by her parents, was missing, until someone realized it had been put on public display with all the other fifteen hundred wedding gifts at St. James's Palace, two hundred yards down the Mall. John Colville, Elizabeth's able private secretary, was dispatched to collect it, but with all the security that day he only just made it back to the palace in time.

Despite the hitches Elizabeth left for the abbey on schedule. She rode with her father in the Irish State Coach, her veil off her face, a royal custom to allow the people to see a royal bride. Along the route thousands, who had spent the night heavily wrapped against the chill night, gathered to cheer and wave, but this was not the wild celebration of VE-Day two years earlier. Many women in the crowd shouted "God bless you. God bless you!" as she trundled past in the coach. Elizabeth looked tentative, hardly smiling, as her father waved regally to the crowd and held her hand.

In the marriage ceremony Elizabeth insisted on including the word *obey*, though she would always outrank her husband from the moment they became husband and wife. Elizabeth believed her promise to obey would help Philip understand that she intended to be a good and dutiful wife. (Philip promised the nonsmoking Elizabeth that on their wedding day he would forever give up cigarettes, which he did, though it took considerable willpower for he had become a chain-smoker during the war.)

Philip, standing tall and erect in his naval uniform, placed the gold ring, fashioned from the same Welsh nugget from which Elizabeth's mother's ring had been made for her wedding in 1923, on his bride's finger. She looked radiantly happy.

Returning to the palace the 150 guests sat down to the wedding breakfast, but the meal was interrupted by a crescendo of noise from the 150,000 people who had broken through police barriers and rushed toward the palace. They kept chanting, "We want the bride!" until Elizabeth and Philip went out onto the balcony, waving at the crowd. Two hours later, after nonstop demands to see the bride once more, Elizabeth and Philip again went onto the balcony.

For King George the wedding of his beloved Lilibet was not a time for rejoicing, for his heart was heavy at losing her. Afterward, he wrote to her, "I was so proud of you and thrilled at having you so close to me on our long walk in Westminster Abbey, but when I handed your hand to the Archbishop I felt that I had lost something very precious. You were so calm and composed during the service and said your words with such conviction, that I knew it was all right.'" He signed it, "Your ever loving and devoted Papa."

To many who attended, the royal wedding has never been forgotten. One of the bridesmaids, Lady Elizabeth Longman, twenty-three at the time, remembers, "The wedding was the first ray of sunshine during that austere period after the war when there was still rationing. The lovely bridesmaid's dresses with the pearl-trimmed satin bows on the skirts made me feel life was on the up and up again. And I still treasure the lovely silver powder compact Philip gave to all the bridesmaids. But it's so precious I never use it."

Elizabeth and Philip honeymooned at Broadlands, the impressive country home in southern England which belonged to Uncle Dickie Mountbatten, the man who had plotted, planned, and worked for eight years to bring the couple together. A more peaceful and beautiful house, set in 5,000 acres of stunning country, could not have been found. But peace was not to be. The press, which would plague much of their married life, discovered their hideaway and were at the gates.

THREE

YOUNG PHILIP

The man who would live a life of absolute privilege, indulged by wealth, and surrounded by pomp, servants, maids, and courtiers was born on June 10, 1921, on the dining-room table of a rented summer villa on the Mediterranean island of Corfu. An afterthought baby, Philip was the son of Prince and Princess Andrew of Greece, the youngest of five children. The only boy, his youngest sister, Sophie, was seven. His mother, Princess Andrew, was thirty-six when he was born.

The imposing Regency-style villa that served as his birthplace boasted balconies and terraces, but lacked gas, electricity, an indoor lavatory, running hot water, or heating of any sort. There was a bathroom of sorts, but water had to be hand-carried to the bath. The only running water—cold—was in the kitchen. The toilets were found at the bottom of the garden. Though architecturally elegant throughout, the villa was in poor decorative order with paint peeling. Philip's parents, though officially royal, were all but poverty-stricken in 1921. They even had difficulty paying the three months' advance deposit on their villa.

Philip was one of the numerous royal descendants of Queen Victoria and her consort Albert, who produced nine children. Today, Victoria and Albert's descendants number nearly seven hundred.

Philip's grandfather was the King of Greece, but he was Danish. He was the second son, born in 1845, of King Christian IX and Queen Louise of Denmark. In 1863 the Greeks were searching for a monarch for their throne, but following years of Turkish rule, only non-Greeks were eligible. They approached young Prince William of Denmark and invited him to be their king.

Prince William, then an eighteen-year-old lieutenant in the Danish navy, did not want to live in such a faraway, backward place whose language he could not speak or understand. His father, however, was adamant and ordered him to take the throne, going so far as to threaten his son with imprisonment if he did not obey. Reluctantly, William was crowned King George of the Hellenes, but soon enough he fell in love with Greece and its people and became a passionate Greek.

Four years after his coronation, George married Olga, the granddaughter of Tsar Nicholas I of Russia, and together they had seven children. Andrew, Prince Philip's father, was the second youngest and was born in 1882.

While Prince Philip clung to many old-fashioned ideas, his grandfather seemed remarkably modern, holding three-hour sessions on Monday mornings in his palace to which any citizen could come to air his or her grievances. His wife, Queen Olga, devoted herself to charities and good works, modernizing hospitals and jails and pushing through penal reform.

Despite his efforts to improve the lot of his adopted people, King George was never universally popular. After several assassination attempts he was eventually shot dead in 1919 at the end of World War I.

Philip's father, Andrew, joined the Greek army at the age of fourteen. His day would begin at 6 A.M. with a cold bath, followed by intensive physical training and education in every facet of war. Five years later, at nineteen, he was commissioned into the cavalry.

In 1903, two years after joining the calvalry, Andrew married the German Princess Alice of Battenberg, a great-granddaughter of Queen Victoria whom he had met at the Coronation of Britain's King Edward VII in 1901. He had fallen passionately in love with the fair-haired young Alice, who was then seventeen, and described at the time as "the prettiest princess in the whole of Europe." Alice's younger brother, Louis, fifteen years younger, would become Earl Mountbatten of Burma and a major influence on Philip, Queen Elizabeth II, and the entire British Royal Family.

Philip's mother was beautiful, indomitable, and strong-willed. She was also deaf but by age twenty could lip-read in four different languages. Prince Philip's father and mother returned to Greece, set up home, and raised a family, but his father spent much of the time away from home, leading the army life he loved. Royal relatives collected a small fortune for them to live on, but it was not to last long.

A dandy, Philip's father sported a monocle and cut a dashing figure in his cavalry officer's uniform. Like his son he enjoyed jokes and making people laugh. He had no income other than the paltry pay of an army officer, which meant that after the wedding gift had been spent, they were always poor and often lived in real poverty. Nevertheless, Prince Andrew insisted on keeping a valet even when there was virtually no money to feed and clothe their five children.

European politics before World War I forced Prince Andrew to leave the army because of his royal connections. When his experience and military acumen were needed against the Turks, Prince Andrew was brought back to action. In 1920 he became a major-general, and later he took command of an army corps. He described the officers and troops under him as "riffraff," "undisciplined," and "ill-trained." He also had little regard for the commander-in-chief, disobeying orders because he believed him incompetent. He even argued openly with the Army Supreme Command when admonished for his arrogance, a trait Andrew seems to have passed on to his son Philip.

Disaster and near death were at hand. In 1922, Andrew commanded the Fifth Army Corps of the ill-equipped Greek Army, then deep in Turkish territory. The Greeks were attacked by the famous Turkish general Kemal Atatürk and forced out of Asia Minor, parts of which Greece had occupied for 2,500 years. Tens of thousands were killed, and a million Greek refugees fled before the advancing Turks. The King, Andrew's brother, was overthrown by a military junta and exiled, while politicians and senior officers judged responsible for the defeat were imprisoned and put on trial. At the first of the trials the six defendants were found guilty and were executed by firing squad the following morning.

Philip's father was told that if he resigned his commission he would be allowed to retire to Corfu and live there with his family. But a month later the junta arrested Andrew, brought him to Athens, and tried him in the Chamber of Deputies with a jury of junior officers. Even before the trial began the jury had decided that Andrew should be shot. Accordingly he was found guilty of disobeying orders, abandoning his position in the face of the enemy, and sentenced to death.

The strong-willed Princess Andrew was determined to save her husband's life. She traveled to Athens and appealed to the junta but to no avail. Then, she wrote letters and telegrams to the Pope and the most powerful crowned heads of Europe—nearly all relatives—asking them to intervene.

Prince Andrew was brought before the Greek dictator Theodoros Pangalos, who asked: "How many children do you have?"

"Five," Prince Andrew replied. Philip was nine months old.

Pangalos smiled and commented quietly: "Poor little orphans."

In desperation, his wife telegraphed her younger brother, Louis Mountbatten, then only twenty-one, and urged him to appeal to Britain's King George V. The chances of help from Britain were slim because Greece, and the Greek royal family, had been pro-German during the Great War and, understandably, feelings were still running high in the early 1920s. But Louis Mountbatten, who was terrified of Alice, not only secured an interview with King George V but actually persuaded him to come to the rescue of his distant relative Prince Andrew. George V called his Foreign Secretary, Lord Curzon, and ordered him to do all in his power to rescue Prince Andrew, even ordering him to send a gunboat to Athens in case it might be needed.

Commander Gerald Talbot, a member of the little-known British secret service, had served as naval attaché in Athens. With false papers and an assumed name, Commander Talbot traveled from Geneva, where he was then stationed, to Athens. He arranged a meeting with Pangalos, a man he had known earlier in his diplomatic career, and informed him in no uncertain terms that if Andrew was not released unharmed, the British government, then the most powerful force in Europe, would view the new Greek government as its enemy.

Pangalos refused, accusing Britain of interfering in the internal affairs of Greece, and saying that Prince Andrew had been found guilty and that justice must take its course. Andrew would face the firing squad the following morning. Pangalos informed Andrew's younger brother, Prince Christopher, who had rushed from Paris to Athens in an effort to save his life, that he was not allowed to see his brother. Pangalos reported, however, that Andrew was waiting philosophically for death.

As Commander Talbot made his final, dramatic appeal to Pangalos, an aide rushed into the room and stammered, "Sir, there is a British warship in the bay."

The Royal Navy ship HMS *Calypso* had arrived at action stations, its mighty guns raised and trained on the government offices. Pangalos was furious, swearing and shouting at Commander Talbot. But, within the hour, the British commander had extracted a promise from Pangalos and the other revolutionary leaders that Andrew would not be shot.

The following day, Andrew was again taken before the court. This time the judge ordered him stripped of his military rank and all royal titles and banished from Greece for life. His honor had been dealt a mortal blow, but he had escaped with his life. That night, Pangalos himself, with Commander Talbot, drove Prince Andrew by car to the waiting HMS *Calypso*, where his wife welcomed him on board.

Word was sent to Mon Repos on Corfu and the entire Greek royal family, nearly all women save for the baby Philip, were told they had only a few hours to pack and leave the island. Philip's sister, Princess Sophie, then eight, recalled later: "It was a terrible business. Absolute chaos. My sisters had to get everything ready. I remember everyone rushing around, packing what they could. Except for Philip it was all women, with Greek ladies-in-waiting, a French governess, and an English nanny. All we took with us was a few suitcases with our personal belongings, the rest we left behind."

The entire family trekked down to the port, with Philip, ten months old, carried in a wooden fruit box. They clambered into a small boat and chugged out to HMS *Calypso*, which had steamed into Corfu harbor.

Princess Sophie went on: "The sea was very rough and nearly all of us were sick. The officers had moved out of their cabins and into hammocks so that the royal exiles could enjoy some creature comforts. We didn't realize what a tragedy it was. The officers put on a concert to entertain us all. It was all very exciting."

Later that day HMS *Calypso* sailed into Brindisi harbor, and the family and their entourage caught a train to Paris in the early hours of the next morning. Princess Sophie was to add later: "On the train Philip was impossible. He would not sit still and crawled everywhere, making himself black from head to toe. He even spent time licking the windowpanes. He was very, very active and no one could control him."

After their dramatic escape from Corfu in the summer of 1922, Prince Andrew and his family settled in Paris, France, where they took a house in the grounds of a larger mansion owned by Andrew's brother George, who had married Princess Marie Bonaparte, a rich heiress. A direct descendant of Napoleon Bonaparte, she was also the granddaughter of the man who founded the famous casino of Monte Carlo.

Like other poor relations of royal families in exile, Philip led a fun-filled life in Paris. He met and mixed with many relatives and, as the youngest of the family by far and the only boy, he was spoiled by his mother and four older sisters. His father taught him to paint and to care for animals. Sister Sophie remembers: "He really loved animals and they loved him."

Andrew spent much of his time with other Greek exiles in Paris plotting their return to power. At the same time, the handsome, dashing, charming Prince, with a military bearing, still in his early forties, found himself most popular with the fashionable ladies of postwar France.

Alice was feeling beleaguered as her errant husband began spending more time away from home and, she suspected, often in the company of other women. She also had to contend with the good fortune of her peers. Many exiled royals enjoyed substantial wealth and were happy to flaunt it. Alice, meanwhile, had to struggle, dressing her daughters in hand-me-downs from some of those rich relations who took pity on her.

To make ends meet, Princess Alice opened a shop in the Faubourg St. Honoré called Hellas, which sold Greek products, from embroidery to honey. The family relied on two stout Englishwomen to look after the children and keep the household together while Alice tended her shop. Nanny Roose cared for Philip in particular while the housekeeper, Mrs. Blower, another intrepid, capable Englishwoman, took charge of the cooking and the housework. To save money, they fed the children on nourishing rice and tapioca puddings. As a consequence, Philip was taught from childhood to be prudent with his money, and despite the wealth into which he married, he has never forgotten that valuable lesson.

The female-dominated household found that the more time Andrew spent away from his family, the naughtier and cheekier his son became. Nanny Roose reported that Philip was a cheerful little boy who liked his own way and frequently misbehaved. He had ferocious energy. His cousin Alexandra remembers holidays at the seaside: "Philip would wander off and return later without explanation with torn clothes, cuts and bruises. He seemed to adore climbing trees, the taller the better."

Alexandra also recalls an incident at home when Philip, then nine, released the pigs from their sties and beat them with a stick to drive them onto the lawn where the adults were sitting enjoying an elegant tea party. The stampeding pigs scattered the ladies and upset most of the tables. The mischievous Philip thought the prank most amusing.

As Philip grew older he became more aggressive, extroverted, and bossy. He loved showing off. He would flaunt the fact he was a prince and told everyone so, but he was never snooty. His English nanny and English housekeeper instilled in him the English way of life, English manners, and, of course, the English language. This background made life much easier for him when he went to school in England, when he joined the Royal Navy, and, more important, when the time came for him to marry the future Queen of England. Philip was a child with no country and no feeling of tradition or destiny. He learned of these traditions from his nanny and the housekeeper who watched over him until he was ten years old.

Nanny Roose was given absolute control over Philip and would quite frequently administer a spanking, either with her hand or a slipper. She spent much of her time trying to control Philip and remembered chasing the naked boy along corridors when he would escape from his bath, persuading him to come down from high trees, bathing him after he splashed through farmyards, and trying to stop his favorite holiday sport—dashing fully clothed into the sea.

Hélène Foufounis was the youngest daughter of a wealthy, exiled Greek family living in Paris and four years Philip's senior. She and Philip became close as children and a great deal closer later in life. Hélène tells of their life together: "At first I was jealous of him because everyone, especially my mother, loved him, with his blond hair and angelic smile. At first, we disliked each other, but later became friends and spent lots of time together, frequently staying at each other's homes when we were growing up. Our nannies were strict with us, spanking us frequently. We were not even allowed to talk at table unless spoken to, which wasn't very often."

Besides worrying about Philip, Alice was also at her wit's end over her four daughters, two of whom in 1927 were in their twenties and no marriages in sight. She had expected her good-looking royal daughters to find substantial husbands, but, as the twenties wore on, the daughters of Europe's old royal families became less wealthy and less of a catch.

After nearly ten years of exile, and with very little emotional or financial support from her husband, Princess Alice suffered a breakdown in 1931. Other exiled royals paid for her stays in various Swiss sanatoriums, which ordered complete rest and relaxation. While she was away there was some good news from the family, who enjoyed some good fortune: within eight months, between December 1930 and August 1931, all four daughters were married, and all four married members of the German aristocracy. The family home at St. Cloud in Paris was closed and the few staff members dismissed.

Meanwhile, Prince Andrew had fallen in love with a most attractive and, more important, wealthy widow, Madame Andrée de la Bigne, a former actress. She owned a small yacht, the *Davida,* which she moored in the sunshine of various Mediterranean ports, usually in southern France. She became Prince Andrew's lover and constant companion; they would spend the summer months happily sailing her boat and the winters living in her villa in the south of France. Any hope of returning to Greece had faded and Andrew, with a growing fondness for fine French wines, was happy to forget the worries of his life and his family; he drifted into a lazy life, happily relaxing in the sunshine with his mistress.

During her years in sanatoriums, Alice discovered religion and, for the rest of her life, wore a nun's black habit. Eventually, she returned to her beloved Greece to found her own religious order, the Christian Sisterhood of Martha and Mary. Finally contented, she devoted herself to good works, forgetting her husband and family of five children.

Prince Andrew and Princess Alice never sought a formal separation or divorce and hardly ever contacted each other. In those days royalty never contemplated such a possibility; divorce was simply not an option.

With Alice living in sanatoriums and his father having virtually abandoned his ten-year-old son, Philip was sent off to Cheam, a centuries-old English preparatory school for the rich, selected because other relatives went there. His father didn't even pay the boy's tuition.

A less-than-average student, Philip excelled at cricket and other sports. He did win one prize, for French (he had spent the first ten years of his life in Paris).

During holidays Philip sometimes stayed at the home of his maternal uncle George, Marquess of Milford Haven, at Lynden Manor, Holyport, a pretty village not far from Windsor. Uncle George became for a time Philip's unofficial surrogate father, paying his nephew's school fees and attending prize-giving days. It was Uncle George who first talked to the young Philip about a career in the Royal Navy.

Philip spent most of his school holidays with Uncle George or with his sisters in their German castles and learned to speak German fluently. As a teenager Philip looked like the quintessential blue-eyed, blond Teutonic boy. Occasionally, his father would visit him during those holidays.

George's wife Nadejda, always called Nada, was a great-grand-daughter of the Russian poet Alexander Pushkin. Nada was a dark, attractive, sexually alluring woman in her thirties and a practicing lesbian. Only a few years before she had fallen in love with her own sister-in-law, the wealthy Edwina, Louis Mountbatten's wife. In the early 1930s she also fell in love with Gloria Vanderbilt. Philip spent much time at Lynden Manor, a great Victorian folly, with Nada and Gloria Vanderbilt and sometimes with Edwina, an uncomfortable environment for a young, pubescent boy.

Uncle George owned one of the most comprehensive pornographic book collections in Europe. The library contained albums of photographs of various individuals and groups having sexual intercourse in every possible position as well as books on sadomasochism, bondage, whipping, thumbscrews, and racks. George also collected odd advertisements for dildoes, vibrators, and condoms, and would apparently sometimes play out his violent sexual fantasies with the lovely Nada.

In 1934, Gloria Vanderbilt was involved in a sensational court case over custody of one of the world's wealthiest children, her own daughter and namesake. Mrs. Vanderbilt's former maid had accused her and Nada of being lesbians, testifying that she had seen them kissing passionately in the Vanderbilt bedroom in Cannes, a charge which Nada emphatically denied. Nada refused to go to the United States to give evidence and, as a result, Gloria Vanderbilt successfully defended against the accusation.

At thirteen, Philip attended Gordonstoun, the Scottish school to which he would later send his own three sons. While staying with his sister at Salem, in Germany, Philip had met the founder of Gordonstoun, Kurt Hahn, an eccentric German Jew. Philip was to say later:

"Even then Hahn was an almost legendary character. Small boys do not normally have much time to be impressed by other boys' masters, but there was an air about Hahn which commanded instant wariness and respect. Apart from that, his famous mannerisms—the stooping gait, the ball of handkerchief in his mouth, the large-brimmed hat and the flashing quizzical eye—all helped to signal the presence of an exceptional being."

Originally, Philip was to attend Hahn's school in Germany and live in Salem with his sister. But after Philip began school at Salem, Hahn was forced to flee Germany, fearing he would be murdered by the Nazis. Despite the brevity of their proximity, Philip had already caught Hahn's irreverence and contempt toward the Nazis. The Nazi salute amused Philip greatly because it reminded him of how English schoolboys had to ask permission to go to the lavatory. To him, the sight of thousands of Nazi soldiers saluting en masse, raising their arms asking to go to the lavatory, struck him as hilarious and stupid. He never forgot.

In 1990, Philip wrote: "None of that family at Salem was at all enthusiastic about the Nazis so it was thought best that I should move out!!" [The double exclamation marks are his]. Hahn found refuge in Scotland and there reopened his school in a house named Gordonstoun near the cold waters of the Moray Firth. When the school opened in 1934, Philip was one of its first pupils.

Hahn's philosophy of education was a mixture of the teachings of Plato, the Boy Scout movement, and the traditions of the English public school system. Hahn was convinced that it was the education provided by the British public school system that had ensured

England's victory over Germany in World War I. Despite its eccentricities Gordonstoun flourished and Philip loved his years there.

Jim Orr, later to become Prince Philip's private secretary, was head boy at the school when Philip arrived. He remembers, "Philip was very friendly, with a sense of fun, and known for his white, white hair."

Both at Cheam and Gordonstoun Philip was a boy with no surname. He was called plain Philip and on formal occasions "Philip of Greece," but to his credit Philip never boasted about his royal connections, preferring to keep his background a mystery. Many of the Gordonstoun boys had little idea of Philip's royal background and saw him as more of an orphan, since his parents never visited the school.

Besides Uncle George, Philip had another surrogate father, his sister Theodora's husband, Berthold of Baden, who was actually his brother-in-law but many years his senior. He befriended the teenage Philip and taught him to fly, fish, and drive a car. "He was a major influence on my character," Philip would comment later.

Uncle George, Philip's principal guardian, developed cancer in 1937 and died a year later. Philip, who had just turned sixteen, was rootless once more, his family dispersed, his parents living separate lives in different parts of Europe, and with no home to call his own. The young man had now lost not only his real father, who had abandoned him, but also the man whom he had respected as his surrogate father.

When Philip left Gordonstoun, Hahn wrote of him: "His best is outstanding; his second best is not good enough. Prince Philip will make his mark in any profession where he will have to prove himself in a full trial of strength." That challenge was fast approaching.

With war looming it was inevitable that Philip should join one of the armed services. His grandfathers had served at sea, his father was a career army officer, and both his father's and his mother's brothers had gone into the navy. Philip loved flying and wanted to join the Royal Air Force, but his uncle Louis Mountbatten persuaded him to find a place in the Royal Navy.

Following the death of Uncle George, Mountbatten began to play a much larger role in Philip's life and invited his nephew to stay at his home. So well did they get on that Mountbatten invited Philip to treat Broadlands as his own home. Mountbatten seemed to want to "adopt" Philip as the son he always wished for but never had. (Mountbatten and Edwina had two daughters: Patricia, born in 1924, and Pamela, born in 1929.)

At eighteen, Philip joined the Royal Naval College at Dartmouth, where potential young officers were trained and, helped by his experience of Gordonstoun life, he enjoyed naval life immensely. He liked the discipline, the formality, and the camaraderie of the officers mess, which he found similar to Gordonstoun. In the Royal Navy proper, Philip felt secure for the first time in his young life.

On June 22, 1939, ten days after his eighteenth birthday, Prince Philip met HRH Princess Elizabeth, then a shy girl of thirteen, for the first time. Her father, King George VI, was aboard His Majesty's Yacht *Victoria and Albert* with his wife Elizabeth and Elizabeth and Margaret when they visited the Royal Naval College, Dartmouth. Captain Lord Louis Mountbatten, Philip's uncle, was in attendance as the King's aide-de-camp. The most ambitious of men, Louis Mountbatten wanted success not only for himself, but also for his newfound surrogate son, Philip.

Mountbatten had arranged that among all the young men at the Naval College that day, Philip—a tall sandy-haired, strikingly good-looking young man—would be selected to show the young Princesses around Dartmouth.

Elizabeth and Margaret's governess Crawfie wrote in her royal memoirs that Elizabeth said at the time of that first meeting: "How good he is!" When Philip jumped over the tennis net, she exclaimed, "How high he can jump!" He and Elizabeth did not play tennis together because she had never been taught to play properly, but they did enjoy a game of croquet which Margaret, then only nine, joined in. Crawfie was less taken with the young show-off. She wrote, "He was good looking though rather offhand in his manner and rather bumptious. I thought he showed off a good deal, but the little girls were much impressed."

When the *Victoria and Albert* sailed from Dartmouth that evening all the cadets took to rowing boats and sailing dinghies to wave goodbye. Prince Philip took a single rowboat. One by one the other boats fell away, leaving just one, manned solely by Philip, striking out far into the sea behind the Royal Yacht. Standing at the stern, Elizabeth watched with a pair of large naval binoculars as Philip rowed on. He was ordered to return but Nelson-like ignored the order. Then he, too, with a wave, turned around his little boat as his young Elizabeth continued her vigil until he was out of sight.

From that day Elizabeth never forgot the handsome Philip. She may have been a very young, immature thirteen-year-old, yet a chord was struck at that first meeting which survived not only a devastating war but long, long periods of separation. In the official biography of King George VI, Sir John Wheeler-Bennett wrote, "This was the man with whom Princess Elizabeth had been in love from their first meeting." When Elizabeth was Queen, she read and approved the manuscript and did not change a single word of that sentence.

Britain declared war against Hitler on September 3, 1939. Philip went on active duty, serving on Royal Navy ships. He was, however, kept out of harm's way because Greece was still neutral and it would not have been diplomatic to have a Greek Prince killed in action on a British ship. Philip was posted as a midshipman to a battleship based in Colombo, Ceylon (now Sri Lanka), but he wanted to see action. He wrote to his uncle, Louis Mountbatten, then a captain in the Royal Navy. In turn, Mountbatten wrote to Vice-Admiral Harold Tom Baillie-Grohman, requesting him to take his nephew, and when Italy invaded Greece Philip was posted to the admiral's battleship, HMS *Ramilles*, in the Mediterranean.

The Admiral recalls: "One day I spoke to the young Philip and told him that as a foreign subject he would not be able to rise above the rank of acting sub-lieutenant unless he became a naturalized British subject. Philip replied that he wanted a career in the Royal Navy. He then went on to say that his uncle had ideas for his future, saying that he thought he could marry Princess Elizabeth. I was totally taken aback and asked if he was fond of her. Philip replied, 'Oh yes, very fond. I write to her every week.'

In the spring of 1940, Midshipman Prince Philip was transferred to HMS *Kent* and then HMS *Shropshire* before Italy invaded Greece in October 1940 and Philip was free to join the war proper. Within months, the Admiralty, with further nudging from Mountbatten, transferred Philip to HMS *Valiant*, one of the Royal Navy's most modern battleships, then on patrol in the eastern Mediterranean.

Philip first saw action in January 1941 when *Valiant* bombarded Bardia on the Libyan coast. A few days later *Valiant* was the target of

German dive-bombers, and Philip wrote about the attack in his logbook with youthful excitement. A few weeks later, in March, during the Mediterranean Battle of Cape Matapan, Philip was in charge of the light used to pick out and illuminate the Italian enemy ships during nighttime battles. He concentrated so intently on his job that he took no notice of the warning shots being fired from the Italian fleet. He wrote in his log, "The result was that the binoculars were rammed back into my eyes and the flash almost blinded me. . . . Luckily the searchlight was not affected so that when I was able to see something again the light was still on target." The Italian fleet, comprising a battleship, eight cruisers, and fourteen destroyers, was routed by the British and, for his gallantry, Midshipman Philip was "mentioned in despatches." His senior officers on board considered the award "well merited."

When Philip had first joined HMS *Valiant* his fellow officers suspected that because Prince Philip of Greece was royal and Greek—he was in fact sixth in line to the Greek throne—he would prove to be a rather effete, highly favored officer. They were surprised to discover his keenness and efficiency and that he employed no airs and graces. With his conspicuous gallantry at Matapan, Philip won his spurs.

A few months later Uncle Dickie had taken command of HMS *Kelly,* a new Javelin-class destroyer with six 4.7-inch guns and two quintuple torpedo tubes, when German Junkers dive-bombers blew the ship out of the water. In his biography of Prince Philip, Tim Heald recounts the story: "As a bedraggled Mountbatten, still covered in oil, came ashore only twenty-four hours after the *Kelly* was sunk in the Battle of Crete almost the first thing he saw was the cheery, grinning face of his nephew Philip."

According to Mountbatten, Prince Philip roared with laughter at his blackened uncle. "You look like a nigger minstrel!" he said. (He would make racist remarks throughout his life.)

Philip was promoted to sub-lieutenant in 1942 and later that year to first lieutenant when he was sent to HMS *Lauderdale,* a Hunt-class destroyer. On that ship he first met Mike Parker, a first lieutenant in the Australian navy. Parker, just a year older than Philip, would become one of Philip's closest friends over the next twenty years. An orphan, Mike Parker would serve as Philip's equerry and private secretary. The fact that neither had any family brought them together. Soon after they met Philip was posted to another destroyer, HMS *Wallace,* escorting the Canadian landings in Sicily in 1943. When that vessel was harbored in Valetta, Malta, for an extensive refit, Philip joined yet another destroyer engaged on convoy duty up and down the east coast of Britain, searching for the dreaded "E-boats," the fast 40-knot speedboats armed with twin torpedo tubes that wreaked heavy damage on British merchant ships.

In 1944 Philip left the European theater to fight the Japanese. Mike Parker now served on a sister ship, and the two were in the Pacific in September 1945 on their respective vessels when they escorted the USS *Missouri* into Tokyo Bay when Japan finally surrendered.

Mike Parker and Philip often took leave together and spent time ashore in North Africa and in various Australian cities. During World War II the world's ports were notorious for drunkeness, brothels, and prostitutes. Respectable young women also loved to be with sailors who were at sea most of the time fighting the enemy. As Mike Parker put it: "There were always armfuls of girls."

Ever since the war Philip has played down any suggestion that he had any sexual experiences while in the navy, although it would be extraordinary if he was entirely celibate from the age of nineteen until he married eight years later.

"Of course we had fun in North Africa," Mike Parker recalled, "but never anything outrageous. We'd drink together and then we'd go and have a bloody good meal. People have always asked, 'Did you go to the local brothels and screw everything in sight?' And the answer is No! It never came into the picture. There was so much else to do." A white lie that Mike Parker always provided for the man who became the consort to Queen Elizabeth of England.

But in Alexandria, Philip and Mike Parker visited nightclubs which were in effect brothels. They would consume copious amounts of Stella beer, watch the belly dancers, and drink with the girls who would come to their tables, sit on their knees, encouraging the young officers to buy high-priced alcohol, and then offer themselves for the hour or the night. Other fellow officers saw Philip and Mike attending these clubs, surrounded by young prostitutes and dancers. The two young lieutenants also visited clubs which featured wild sex shows which often included the most lewd acts involving young women and donkeys. The naked girls carried out all the known and varied sex acts, but it was the animal everyone remembered.

Philip came into his own during visits in Melbourne and Sydney. Mike Parker was Australian and he introduced Philip to society ladies and their daughters who were most impressed to meet a prince of royal blood.

Alexandra of Yugoslavia, Prince Philip's Greek cousin who married the King of Yugoslavia, wrote a biography of him in which she noted, "Philip hit feminine hearts, first in Melbourne and then in Sydney, with terrific impact." Those who knew Philip then recall that the girls were "lining up" to be introduced to the handsome Prince who sported a full golden beard. One hostess, a middle-aged Sydney woman involved in charity work, put it bluntly: "The girls were queuing up to bed him. He was gorgeous, and royal." When asked if Philip did in fact bed any, she replied: "What! Of course he did; he was a real lady's man. He loved his time in Australia. He had a whale of a time."

On occasion Philip would swap identities with Mike Parker when they both wore full beards. Philip loved to play that trick on girls because he wished to know whether the girls wanted him for himself or simply because he was a royal prince. The gamble paid off because Philip scored with the girls he had sought out. That was why he persuaded Mike Parker to repeat the charade on a number of other occasions. It was good for his ego.

On the other hand, Philip had to conduct himself correctly on certain occasions when his ship sailed into port. As a Royal Prince he was expected to attend official cocktail parties and dinners, especially if the British ambassador was in the vicinity. He tried to escape such duties because he much preferred to spend shore leave with his fellow officers. But Philip also knew that at such parties he would usually meet some of the most lovely and eligible young ladies who were looking for escorts, if not potential husbands. And a Royal Prince, even an unknown Greek without a throne, was considered a catch for many of the young women, particularly one with Philip's good looks and sense of fun.

According to brother officers who served with him at the time, Philip had numerous affairs during the war, both in Britain and overseas. On most occasions Philip remained remarkably discreet, but when he did occasionally have too much to drink he would become more open about his conquests. As one fellow officer put it, "Philip always loved to be the center of attention, loved to be surrounded by pretty girls, and loved to be able to take his pick. He could sometimes be arrogant in his approach to girls, adopting a take-it-or-leave-it attitude to which some took offense. But he was hardly ever without a female companion and most were girlfriends in the full sense of the phrase. He certainly loved the girls and they were certainly attracted to him."

Occasionally, Philip would visit Elizabeth when on leave in England. He would occasionally be asked to lunch at Buckingham Palace, and whenever he was in England he would be invited for Christmas dinner at Windsor Castle along with other ex-royals living in Britain during the war.

Philip has always been remarkably reticent about his affair with Elizabeth. Talking to his official biographer Basil Boothroyd in 1970, Philip said:

"I went to the theatre with members of the Royal Family once during the war, or something like that. And, at other times during the war, if I was here [in England] I'd call in and have a meal. I once or twice spent Christmas at Windsor, because I'd nowhere particular to go. I thought not all that much about it, I think. We used to correspond occasionally. You see it's difficult to visualise. I suppose if I'd just been a casual acquaintance it would all have been frightfully significant. But if you're related—I mean I knew half the people here, they were my relations—it isn't so extraordinary to be on kind of family relationship terms. You don't necessarily have to think about marriage."

Even when speaking to Boothroyd, however, Philip, naturally reticent about showing his feelings in public, did not reveal the whole truth about his relationship with the teenage Elizabeth. They used to meet occasionally at Coppins, the country home of the Duchess of Kent, where they would walk together in the grounds and take tea together alone. They would also stay for lunch or dinner, and these secret meetings cemented Lilibet's love for the gallant naval lieutenant. She never tried to find another eligible man to marry. She had in fact made up her mind that she wanted to marry Philip, and she was determined to do so, despite considerable opposition from many people, including her own parents.

Philip later told Boothroyd, "I did not think about marriage until

1946 when I was invited to stay at Balmoral. I suppose one thing led to another. It was sort of fixed up. That's really what happened."

Philip appeared to be the perfect husband for the young teenage girl who would one day be Queen of England. Pictures taken before and after their engagement show a formality between the two which makes their relationship seem strained, if not forced. None of the pictures show a young couple madly in love with each other; nothing in their body language suggests love or even affection between them. In every photograph and film Philip seems on his best behavior, determined to show respect for Elizabeth, as though he should act with the utmost decorum because his fiancée would become the next Queen.

The man who persevered in encouraging the marriage was the irrepressible Lord Louis Mountbatten. He saw in Philip the once-in-a-lifetime opportunity to stamp the Mountbatten name on the oldest and most prestigious monarchy in the world, the British throne. Mountbatten went out of his way to ensure that the young, impressionable Lilibet saw Philip whenever possible throughout the war years. He would speak to her about Philip whenever they met, which was quite frequently in the latter days of the war, after Britain's wartime Prime Minister, Winston Churchill, took the ambitious Mountbatten under his wing and promoted him to positions of considerable power and influence.

Mountbatten would tell Lilibet where Philip was serving, what he was doing, how the war was going for him. And he would provide snippets of information so that Elizabeth's interest and attraction to Philip was sustained despite the months of forced separation. Elizabeth, of course, understood that she had to be patient. She would read the newspapers and listen to the wireless, as the radio was then called, and hear commentators urge wives and girlfriends to wait patiently for their loved ones who were fighting for their country.

Elizabeth also followed the example of tens of thousands of other women. The future Queen of England would spend hours in the evening knitting socks for the young man in her life. Elizabeth was not a prodigious knitter, but with help she managed to make socks good enough to send to the man she dreamed about.

Elizabeth had been educated and trained by her mother and tutors to devote her life to duty above all else: duty to the nation, to the British people, and to the vast British Empire on which, at that time, the sun never set. And Elizabeth believed in her heart that waiting for her Prince was part of that duty.

Throughout the war she kept a black-and-white photo of Philip's face with a full beard beside her bed in Windsor Castle. Her sister Margaret recalled that every night Lilibet would kiss the photograph before going to sleep. Margaret also said her sister diligently wrote every week, telling him that before going to sleep each night she kissed the picture of him.

From the little that Philip has said about his courtship of Elizabeth, their relationship was remarkably formal on his part. It was Elizabeth, excited by the relationship, who dreamed of love and who wanted to be loved by her Prince. For his part, Philip showed great restraint, more a formality of courtship rather than a passion, so very different from all his other love affairs.

Mountbatten advised Philip to act with respect toward Elizabeth, never to take advantage of her in any way; to remember that he was five years older and to treat her like a flower that needed to be nurtured. Mountbatten also made Philip realize that Elizabeth was precious, not just to her family but to the nation. He also told him that if they were to marry, then he must understand that his position as her husband would be one of privilege which he must never forget, for he would be the consort of the Queen, the most important person in the entire kingdom.

Margaret has revealed that she would sometimes see Philip and Lilibet walking together in the grounds of homes where they met when Philip was courting her; that she would see them strolling side by side, talking and occasionally holding hands, but she never saw them kiss or cuddle. She said that whenever the two of them were together on a sofa, both appeared rather distant toward each other, Philip not daring to appear too pushy or overeager. She never saw them rush toward each other, kiss passionately, or hug each other. They always appeared reticent, even awkward, as though fearing that any passion might break the spell of correctness between them.

Philip did not remain faithful to his Princess. As a midshipman, Philip was required every day to fill in the Admiralty Form S. 519, a record in his own words of anything important or interesting that had occurred that day. Whenever one of Philip's ships docked in a port around the world, whether it was in South Africa, Egypt, Cyprus,

Gibraltar, India, Ceylon, Australia, or the Far East, Philip would record many, but not all, shore leaves with an exclamation mark. According to one of Philip's brother officers, that was Philip's sign to remind himself of a romantic liaison in that port.

Philip wrote after leaving Durban in HMS *Kent,* "The fact that many hearts were left behind in Durban is not surprising." But on that occasion there was no exclamation mark.

Whenever Philip had leave in London, Uncle Dickie would try to ensure that he saw Elizabeth, whether just for tea or a meal. There were, however, many other young socialities, as well as ambitious mothers, who were most keen that this good-looking young Prince, Philip of Greece, should meet other girls. He was inundated with invitations to dinners, to house parties, weekend gatherings. No one in London society circles knew at that time that Philip was in fact courting Elizabeth. Nor did anyone know that the teenage Princess had any thoughts as to whom she might one day marry.

Not until 1943, when Lilibet had turned seventeen, did the romance blossom and Philip let it be known that he was indeed courting the heir to the throne. George VI was not at all happy when the Queen told him that Elizabeth was infatuated with Philip. George had no wish to lose his daughter, especially at such a young age, but Queen Elizabeth saw how love-struck Elizabeth had become with Philip and persuaded her husband to allow the romance to continue and "let love take its course."

In 1943 Philip's ship, HMS *Wallace,* went into dock for a refit and Philip stayed in the attic of Uncle Dickie's house in Chester Street, Belgravia, less than a mile from Buckingham Palace. For most of that time Mountbatten continued in command of operations in Southeast Asia while the extremely wealthy Lady Mountbatten worked with the Red Cross. Young Philip had the house to himself.

That Christmas, Crawfie had a chance to study Philip when he came to the Palace. She wrote: "He was greatly changed. It was a grave and charming young man who sat there, with nothing of the rather bumptious boy I had first known about him now. He looked more than ever, I thought, like a Viking, weather-beaten and strained, and his manners left nothing to be desired."

Crawfie added: "Lilibet acted better than she had ever done before. She was animated, there was a sparkle about her."

From that Christmas on, Philip began to correspond openly with Elizabeth, and it was common knowledge to those aboard HMS *Whelp*, a ship of the 27th Destroyer Fleet, then engaged against the Japanese in the Pacific, that Philip's girlfriend was in fact Princess Elizabeth. Understandably, it won him admiration and respect.

Back in London, those close to King George and his wife, along with most who worked in Buckingham Palace and the other royal palaces, knew that Princess Elizabeth had fallen in love and that her intended husband was Prince Philip. Few people, particularly members of the aristocracy and the establishment, could imagine for one moment that the heir to the British throne would be permitted to marry a Greek Prince. It was of no concern to them that he was so good looking or that he was a prince of royal blood. And they ignored the fact he had descended from Queen Victoria. He just wasn't English.

Louis Mountbatten realized that Philip's genealogical background could prove an impediment. He understood that after such a devastating war the British people might not be keen on the young, innocent Princess Elizabeth's marrying a foreigner. Some aristocrats, even distant members of the Royal Family, such as Queen Elizabeth's brother David Bowes-Lyon, described Philip as simply "un-British"; others unfairly described him as "a ghastly foreign fellow." But they had the hugely ambitious and highly intelligent Mountbatten to contend with. He would not let the matter rest and Philip commented, "There was much to-ing and fro-ing about my adoption of a surname and just as much argument about the house name," referring to the Royal House of Windsor, or whatever other name Philip would take if he should marry Elizabeth.

The quick-tempered Philip saw no reason why he was not eligible, as Prince Philip of Greece, to marry the British Princess Elizabeth. He was related to Queen Victoria in just the same way as Elizabeth. He had been proud to be called Philip, Prince of Greece, despite the fact he had lived there only for the first year of his life. He liked the unofficial title because his father had been a member of the Greek royal family, though of course not in any way Greek himself. Now he let it be known that if the British authorities decreed he could no longer keep his unofficial title, then he wanted to be named officially "Lieutenant Philip." But that would not do. The gray men of the Palace decreed that he had to have a proper surname.

Amazingly enough, Home Secretary Chuter Ede suggested that Philip take his mother's official German family name: Schleswig-Holstein-Sonderburg-Glucksburg. The last thing any self-respecting Englishman, particularly members of the aristocracy, or anyone who had just fought in the war, wanted at that time was for Princess Elizabeth to marry a Boche!

Worse, all four of Philip's sisters had married into the German aristocracy. Moreover, two of their husbands had actually fought against the British as officers in Hitler's forces. That was enough for many people, especially the average Englishman, to bar Philip forever from even dating Elizabeth, let alone asking for her hand in marriage. Some believed he should be banished from Britain, and only a few thought he should be permitted to marry into the Royal House of Windsor.

Uncle Dickie suggested that Philip take *his* surname, Mountbatten, the anglicized name of Battenberg. It sounded British and Philip had no objection, especially as Uncle Dickie had done so much of the work behind the scenes to bring about his nephew's marriage to the British Crown.

Those days at the end of the war were a difficult time for Philip. He had no family or home to call his own and spent his time living either at his Uncle Dickie's London home or in the Kensington Palace apartment of his friend Milford Haven. And another problem became evident. He had very little money, surviving on the paltry pay of a Royal Navy lieutenant.

John Dean, Mountbatten's butler, and Mrs. Cable, the cook, spent much of their time on the care and feeding of young Philip, who would arrive looking for a bed for the night or the weekend. Mrs. Cable recalled: "Philip would ring the doorbell and I would find him standing on the front doorstep, sometimes with a suitcase, asking if it was possible to stay the night. I would always ask him if he needed a meal and he would protest that he didn't, but he was only being polite. I would get him something to eat and John Dean would take his clothes, and wash and iron them so he would be presentable the following day. He hardly had any civvy clothes at all, just his naval ones. What I do remember is that he was always polite and considerate and he always carried with him a photo of the Princess in a battered leather frame which he placed by the side of his bed in the attic."

Prince Philip had learned a lot during the war. He had grown up fast, as most young men had during that long conflict, and now he was a mature twenty-five-year-old.

He had enjoyed the companionship of brother officers and a number of women, sharing some of the women's beds as well. Philip, who had accepted the hardship of service life for six years, wasn't sure whether he could endure the discipline of a life married to the heir to the throne. Philip loved parties and being the center of attention, and he loved women, too. He knew he was successful with women, that he could attract women whenever he wanted to, despite the fact he had no money and no home; his good looks and sense of humor had always won through.

Many people, especially those who had fought and survived the war, needed to enjoy themselves, and Philip did too. During those months following the war he was the center of attraction at the society nightclubs he and his fellow officers frequented. But he was discreet and, unlike many of his companions, he never drank too much or misbehaved with any girl in public. He would spend weekends away from London attending house parties, where he was so often the object of attention by many of the young ladies present.

An officer who went out on the town with Philip recalled: "Philip was always a lady's man and he loved their attention. He always had girlfriends but he was most discreet. Occasionally he would wink when leaving a party to escort a girl back home. We had no idea of course if anything ever happened, but we had our suspicions. He was a lad, all right, though he never discussed sex. He kept his love life to himself. When it was officially announced he was to marry Princess Elizabeth, some of us were taken by surprise for he had always played the handsome bachelor role so well. For him to settle down with one woman seemed impossible."

The more Philip enjoyed his bachelor life the more uncertain he felt about spending the rest of his life with Elizabeth. He knew the King objected to his daughter's marrying at such a young age, but Philip also believed King George did not want Elizabeth to marry him personally and assumed it was because of his Greek and German background.

Elizabeth told Philip of the lengths to which her father would go to persuade her to change her mind, hoping that she would fall in love with someone else. She assured Philip she wanted no one else. King George organized dances and balls and dinners at Windsor, Sandringham, and at Balmoral in Scotland to which young aristocrats were invited so that his Lilibet might perhaps take a liking to one of the young men. They, in turn, were expected to dance with her and get to know her. Many of the young men enjoyed the evenings, but most of them became enamored with the lovely, budding Margaret, then sixteen and prettier, more vivacious and flirtatious than her more serious elder sister. The King saw to it that Philip was not invited to those evenings. Naturally, that irked Philip and made him feel inferior and self-conscious whenever he met the King. It also put doubts in his mind as to whether he should indeed continue pursuing Elizabeth.

King George went so far as to order the Special Branch to look into Philip's background and to prepare a detailed dossier on his views, his politics, his allegiance, and his sincerity. They examined his financial stability, his bank account, and every detail of his naval career and war record.

The King's most senior courtiers, as well as members of the aristocracy, persuaded him that Philip should not be permitted to marry his daughter because that would mean that the domineering, conniving Mountbatten would become the power behind the throne. Jealous of his meteoric rise to power and his growing influence in political circles, they all knew that Mountbatten had complete control over Philip.

King George conducted long talks with Winston Churchill about Philip and his uncle, Mountbatten. Fortunately for Philip, Churchill held Dickie Mountbatten in high esteem, admiring Mountbatten as a man of action and determination, and not unlike himself. Indeed, Churchill finally persuaded the King that Philip would be a valuable addition to the House of Windsor, pointing out that Mountbatten and his nephew had been loyal and obedient and that both had exemplary war records. Philip had displayed obedience and courage in the face of the enemy, just the sort of qualities required of the future Queen's consort.

Queen Mary, George VI's mother, believed Philip would make an admirable match, and she informed her son of her views. Herself a German Princess who had married English royalty, she saw no reason whatsoever why a prince of Greece, and in fact a member of the Danish royal family, should not marry into the House of Windsor. She noted: "Three consorts of the same Danish royal family have married into the English Royal Family, supplying wives for James I and Edward VII, and a husband for Queen Anne: why not a fourth?" At a stroke she had removed the single most powerful argument against Elizabeth's intention to marry Philip.

Queen Mary had met Philip quite regularly and confided to her lady-in-waiting Lady Airlie that she found him to be intelligent, polite, handsome, and eminently suitable for her granddaughter. She believed that King George had somehow persuaded his wife to find another, more suitable husband for their daughter. Numerous matchmaking older women were entrusted with the task. A number of eminently suitable young aristocrats had died in the war. Those suitable consorts who were introduced to Princess Elizabeth did not have the slightest effect on her. No matter how hard her parents tried, they were unable to shake her determination and her love for the handsome Philip.

In the summer of 1946 Philip proposed, in secret, to Princess Elizabeth, after taking the advice of Uncle Dickie. Philip knew he should have first asked the King for his permission to marry, but he did not do so because he wanted to make sure Elizabeth really wanted to marry him before formally asking her father. Elizabeth recalled, "He proposed to me by some well-loved loch, the white clouds overhead and the curlews crying." The dream she had nurtured for seven years had come true.

Two days later Philip formally asked the King for Elizabeth's hand, but the King could not, on his own, give permission. In any case, King George still wasn't certain that Philip was the man for his daughter though he was beginning to realize he was having great difficulty finding someone more suitable. The King explained that the government and various Commonwealth governments had to approve the marriage.

King George decided to put his daughter's intended husband to the test to see if he would fit into the family. Philip was invited to spend a month at Balmoral in the autumn of 1946. Philip had a terrible time. He hated the idea that he had to wear a kilt, feeling it made him "look like a sissy." One day, as a joke, Philip curtsied when the King came in for lunch. George said nothing but gave Philip a withering look: Philip had insulted Scotland and Scottish traditional dress.

Philip loathed everything about Balmoral. He hated having to do without running water in his room and complained about his noisy bedroom on the ground floor. He could not bear the formal behavior and felt he was on parade day and night. Of course, Philip knew he was being observed, which he found insulting to his family. The two men just didn't get on. Everything Philip did grated on the nerves of the impeccable George. He criticized Philip's dress sense and noted his scuffed shoes, his ill-fitting dinner jacket, which he had borrowed from Uncle Dickie; the clothes he wore for shooting, turning up in gray flannels instead of knickerbockers.

George believed Philip was not sufficiently deferential, speaking out of turn at table and showing off in front of Elizabeth and Margaret. Philip simply rubbed Elizabeth's father the wrong way. In turn, Philip rebelled. He became outrageous, too cheerful, boisterous, and joked too much, while the King wanted someone more like himself—correct, rigid, Victorian and, above all, quiet. At the end of the month King George was convinced his beloved daughter had made an awful mistake.

Appalled at Philip's behavior and attitude, King George asked for a special, secret report on Philip's lifestyle. The report revealed that Philip lived a carefree life with little or no discipline. His language was peppered with profanity. Philip lived in Kensington Palace with his cousin, David Milford Haven, and their rooms were described as a "disgrace with clothes, shoes and dirty linen strewn everywhere." They smoked all day, lounging about the palace or speeding around London in a small, black MG sports car Philip had acquired. At night they went out on the town, clubbing until dawn, returning home usually half drunk and sometimes not returning at all. During this period Philip seemed arrogant and unpleasant, showing off about his royal connections while seeking the attention of adoring young debutantes who were happy to throw themselves at him.

He was so very different from the girl he wanted to marry. Elizabeth was calm, gentle, sweet, attentive, and dutiful; she spent her evenings at home in the palace with her parents.

The detailed reports made painful reading for George. He believed it his duty to dissuade his daughter, to save her, as he saw it, from marrying such an arrogant, though "damned" handsome, prig. In the autumn of 1946 he insisted that his daughter accompany the family the following year on a ten-week trip to South Africa, secretly hoping the trip might persuade her to change her mind.

As the Royal Family set sail to South Africa on board HMS *Vanguard* in January 1947, King George gave strict instructions that Philip not be allowed to board the ship to say farewell to Elizabeth, nor even permitted to wave farewell from the dockside. It was the same when the family returned ten weeks later. The King had ordered that no one should know of the real relationship between Philip and Elizabeth.

Philip spent those ten weeks enjoying a bachelor life in London, throwing dinner parties at Mountbatten's London home, and frequenting nightclubs. On Elizabeth's return the young couple began to see more of each other and Philip escorted her to the theater, to dinners, and to the more respectable nightclubs. The press began to report that Elizabeth and Philip now acted like any other young couple in love. The newspapers were full of pictures of them together and the royal watchers wrote of an impending engagement.

For Philip, the announcement of a formal engagement would, in one respect, cause him severe embarrassment. He was unofficially engaged to be married to one of the world's wealthiest heiresses, yet he himself possessed no more than a few pounds. When their engagement was finally announced in the Court Circular in July 1947, Philip, the King's future son-in-law, had precisely £6.10s in the bank ($20) and his lieutenant's pay of £11 a week ($30 a week). He had no home and no family. Nearly destitute, his entire belongings could fit into a pair of suitcases. His entire wardrobe consisted of three naval uniforms, one lounge suit, a blazer and a pair of gray trousers, an evening dress suit, and a shooting jacket, plus some underwear. Every sock he owned was darned.

Officially, the royal announcement read: "It is with the greatest pleasure that the King and Queen announce the betrothal of their dearly beloved daughter the Princess Elizabeth to Prince Philip RN, son of the late Prince Andrew of Greece and Princess Andrew, to which union the King has gladly given his consent."

Philip celebrated by joining his friends for a night on the town and became rip-roaring drunk. Now it did not matter that he had no earthly possessions. He would never have to worry again. He was going to be rich and powerful. And he was only twenty-five.

III

MARRIAGE AND MONARCHY

FOUR

BRIDE, MOTHER, AND QUEEN

Elizabeth and Philip spent their wedding night—November 22, 1947—in a magnificent four-poster Tudor bed with an ivory satin padded bedhead, heavy damask covers, and pink sheets. The room had been decorated with Salvador Dalí gouaches. Edwina Mountbatten, Uncle Dickie's wife, had lent them her luxurious suite, which included separate dressing rooms and a lavish bathroom, at Broadlands, the country home she had inherited. Not until the following morning did they see the wonderful picturesque view from their bedroom window, across the Test River valley and the forests beyond.

After attending the wedding, Mountbatten and Edwina were already returning to India, where Dickie Mountbatten had been appointed governor-general, leaving the young couple to enjoy their honeymoon alone in the beautiful Palladian-style mansion. Looking after their every need was the ever-faithful Bobo and Philip's valet, the chatty John Dean. Also on hand were Frank Randall, the butler, and Charles Smith, Mountbatten's valet.

The couple spent early December walking and riding and lounging around a roaring log fire in the Broadlands sitting room. Elizabeth had taken her favorite corgi, Susan, with her, for company. Britain was still in the grip of wartime food rationing, but nothing was spared for the royal honeymooners. They feasted on pheasant, lamb, beef, and veal as well as freshwater fish from the Test, washed down with excellent French wines. They drank champagne cocktails before dinner and Elizabeth insisted that each night they dine by candlelight. Their honeymoon at Broadlands was the only time they were to share a bedroom throughout their entire married life. As soon as they returned to London they were given separate quarters at Buckingham

Palace, and forevermore Elizabeth and Philip have, except on the rare occasion, slept in separate rooms.

Until her honeymoon, Elizabeth's relationship with the press had been idyllic. Journalists had respected her privacy, and she would happily give time for photographs to be taken. But now the Fleet Street newspaper editors decided the nation wanted more of the fairy-tale wedding. After years of death and destruction, they wanted to provide the King's subjects with something that would warm their lives.

Whenever the couple left Broadlands, reporters and photographers pursued them in cars, even followed them on horseback. Because it was winter and the leaves had fallen, photographers climbed trees to get a better view, training binoculars and their "long-tom" lenses on the couple's bedroom.

When the couple attended morning service at Romsey Abbey, more than a thousand people beseiged the church, arriving with ladders, chairs, and stepladders to stand on in order to catch a glimpse of the honeymooners through the church windows. Even headstones on the graves were pulled from the ground so they could be stacked up to give people a better view. After one week Philip had had enough and the couple canceled the last week of their planned honeymoon, returning to Buckingham Palace. Later, they spent another week at Balmoral, hidden from the prying eyes of an adoring public and the lenses of Fleet Street.

Philip was furious. It was the start of his lifelong tempestuous relationship with the press, particularly photographers. During the honeymoon he vented the anger and frustration which was to erupt many, many times over the following decades. On several occasions Philip, his eyes blazing, screamed at the press to go away, and when that didn't work he yelled: "Fuck off, leave us alone!"

King George decreed, in 1947, that Elizabeth and Philip should be given Clarence House,* in the Mall, as their London home, but when they inspected it they were shocked. Clarence House had been left derelict for some years. The rooms were still lit by gaslight, the interior walls were covered with mildew, ceilings had fallen down, bomb damage to the roof and top floor had gone unrepaired, and there

---

*The Queen Mother has lived in Clarence House since the death of her husband in 1952.

was no central heating or running hot water. They were given temporary housing in Buckingham Palace while their first permanent home was being renovated.

After his wartime adventures, Philip found it difficult to settle down to mundane married life. So that he could be near his young bride, he had been given a desk job at the Admiralty, which he hated. He would walk to and from work each day, even in the snow and rain, through St. James's Park to his office. Dressed in his mackintosh and trilby, Philip would travel the mile on foot, unnoticed and unrecognized by the general public. Much of the time he seemed petulant and short tempered at the Admiralty and was no fun at home.

In public Philip seemed to have difficulty coping with his new royal life and resented having to take second place behind Elizabeth. On a visit to Paris in May 1948, when she was three months pregnant, Philip appeared moody, unpleasant, and even rude, while Elizabeth, suffering from morning sickness, nevertheless smiled and put a brave face on everything. But even she looked angrily at Philip when he yelled at a photographer he discovered hiding under a table during an official dinner engagement.

Back in London Philip continued to show signs of frustration, discontent, and even regret. In public he would hardly ever smile and seemed to be stern, even sullen, as he accompanied Elizabeth during official engagements. In private he always wanted his own way, rewriting speeches, trying to cut through red tape, demanding that he be consulted in matters which really were of no concern to him, only to his wife, the heir apparent. He found it difficult to cope, especially when he learned that his orders were not carried out because higher authorities had countermanded them.

Philip, who in the past had asserted his masculine pride so forcefully, hated living in the palace, where he had to conform to all the rules, endure rigid formality, and accept being waited on hand and foot, and where he was prevented from spending much time alone with Elizabeth during the day. It wasn't that Philip was madly in love with Elizabeth. He was annoyed that others—her advisers and senior members of the court—had priority on Elizabeth's time. His pride was bruised.

Though only twenty-one, Elizabeth showed the resilience and obedience to duty that became a mark of her entire life, attending functions, dinners, luncheons, and official ceremonies even when six months pregnant. Philip became so fed up and intolerant of life at the palace that he enrolled in a staff course at Greenwich Royal Naval College, so that he could live with the other officers rather than at the palace with all its petty restrictions.

Fed up, irascible, and moody, Philip turned to his old friend Michael Parker. They would go out drinking together in the evenings to the London nightclubs that were doing a roaring trade in postwar Britain. Only with Michael did Philip seem able to relax, and he poured out his frustrations to his fellow naval officer and comrade in war as well as revelry. Parker knew how to deal with Philip, how to make him laugh as they talked of their times together in the war, their drinking bouts, and the various women they had both loved and left.

Philip discovered that as Princess Elizabeth's husband he was entitled to an equerry, who would be his factotum, secretary, friend, and adviser, all paid for by the Crown. He was determined that Mike Parker should be that man. During the final few months of Elizabeth's pregnancy, Philip spent more and more time with the engaging, fun-loving Mike Parker, cementing even further the bond between them.

Throughout November 12, 1948, Elizabeth's nursemaid, Bobo, spent most of the day with her, comforting her and sitting by her bed holding her hand throughout the early stages of labor. Philip occasionally popped in to see how Elizabeth was progressing but spent most of the day with Mike Parker. At 9:14 P.M., just two hours after going into labor, Elizabeth gave birth to a 7 pound, 6 ounce baby, a rosy, plump, healthy, and bawling little boy. King George VI and Queen Elizabeth arrived minutes after the birth, the King cheering as he walked into the makeshift hospital ward in the Buhl Suite at the palace. Philip, who had been playing squash and later swimming with Mike Parker, arrived with his hair still wet. Parker brought a bottle of champagne and a huge bouquet of Elizabeth's favorite flowers—camellias, lilies, carnations, and roses. He gave them to Philip, who handed them over to Elizabeth. A forty-one-gun salute was fired, the bells of St. Paul's and Westminster rang out for three hours, and bonfires were lit across the country.

Both Elizabeth and Philip had decided beforehand that if the baby was a boy he would be named Charles Philip Arthur George. It had been three hundred years since a King Charles had sat on the English throne, and the name did not evoke memories of past glories. King Charles I was executed in 1649 after losing England's Civil War against the Parliamentarians, King Charles II was renowned for a reign of licentious behavior following the dour years of Cromwell's military rule. But Charles was Elizabeth's favorite name.

For a few weeks Elizabeth insisted on breast-feeding Charles, but it wasn't long before his nurse, Helen Lightbody, took complete charge of the baby. It seems extraordinary today, yet within three months after giving birth, Elizabeth began her strict routine of seeing Charles only twice a day, for an hour after breakfast in the morning and for a further thirty minutes each evening around six. Otherwise, Charles never saw his parents. Helen Lightbody and nursemaids were given absolute responsibility for bringing up the future heir to the throne. It wasn't that Elizabeth didn't love her baby, although many believe that such short daily meetings with him could not have produced satisfactory bonding; it was simply the way members of the Royal Family believed parents should rear their babies—left to someone else to nurse, educate, and train.

That had been the tradition in the Royal Family since Queen Victoria's days, and Elizabeth and Philip saw no reason to alter the royal routine. This unquestioning attitude shows how little Elizabeth had been exposed to everyday life, since after World War II the accepted view was that mothers should bond with their babies, spend time with them, and not leave them to be brought up by nannies and nurses.

Only months after Charles's birth, Elizabeth traveled throughout Britain, visiting her future subjects while undertaking royal cere-monies and exposing her unhappy and truculent husband to the public gaze. Philip would deliberately ignore people or speak to them gruffly, hardly ever smiling or waving to the crowds who turned out to welcome the young couple. Even as time went on, Philip seemed unable to accommodate the idea that his function was to assist his wife as she went about her royal duties. So fed up did he become that he decided to seek re-enlistment in the Royal Navy to escape his role as consort to Elizabeth.

King George was outraged at the reports he received. He believed Philip was behaving disgracefully. His daughter had taken over many of his royal obligations, and yet Philip seemed to give her virtually no support, earning for himself a reputation for tetchiness and truculence. King George also became angry because the fear he had always harbored about Philip's arrogance was proving correct: a penniless young man with little to offer but good looks now strutted around as if the world owed him everything. He complained bitterly to his wife about Philip's behavior, but she tried to allay his fears, saying that Elizabeth still seemed happy and that was all that mattered.

Elizabeth pleaded with Philip not to go back to sea, but he insisted. Then she pleaded with him to stay in home waters so he could be near her and baby Charles. Elizabeth also told him that because her father had become so ill—he suffered from arteriosclerosis—she needed him near her. Philip would have none of it.

Philip demanded to be allowed to return to the navy and further, that he be permitted to serve abroad. Much to Elizabeth's distress he resumed his duties in Malta on November 17, 1949, joining the destroyer HMS *Chequers* as first lieutenant and second-in-command. But Philip was not to put to sea immediately so Elizabeth, with her father's blessing, flew out to the Mediterranean and spent six glorious weeks with her husband at the governor's house. She forgave Philip his selfish behavior. Alone with her bronzed Viking prince under the Maltese sun, Elizabeth felt as though she were on a second honeymoon.

Never more happy and relaxed, she became "a naval wife," having her hair done at the local hairdresser, swimming and sunbathing, and dancing with Philip by moonlight. Elizabeth enjoyed the practical jokes Philip played on her, such as chasing her down corridors wearing a huge pair of false teeth or putting a dummy snake in a powder box. She was so intoxicated with happiness that when news came that Charles, now one, was ill with tonsillitis, neither she nor Philip returned to London. Nor did she return home to be with her son at Christmas. She flew back to London in early January when Philip's ship put to sea. She was pregnant again.

Philip, posted to the Middle East, was happy to be back at sea but complained that, as the husband of Princess Elizabeth, he found it difficult taking orders from other officers, despite the fact they were his seniors. Desperate for command, he pestered Uncle Dickie to secure for him the captaincy of his own ship. Uncle Dickie, then Flag-Officer Commanding the 1st Cruiser Squadron in the Mediterranean, told his nephew he would try but that he had to be patient.

Mountbatten also introduced his nephew to one of the great joys of his life, polo, a game at which Mountbatten was an authority and, when younger, a very good player. Mountbatten played polo throughout his naval career but encouraged Philip to do so when his nephew moved to Malta where Mountbatten had his Mediterranean headquarters. Philip loved the sport and was to play for nearly twenty years.

Finally, on August 15, 1950, Philip learned that he had achieved his lifelong ambition and been given command of his own frigate, HMS *Magpie*. That day he was gazetted a lieutenant-commander and, as luck would have it, his daughter Anne Elizabeth Alice Louise was born.

In command of his own ship Philip was, finally, in his element. Determined to be the best ship's captain in the entire fleet, Philip worked his ship's crew to the breaking point, demanding greater discipline and harder work. In the annual regatta his ship won six of the ten boat events, and Philip himself stripped to the waist, rowing stroke, to lead one of the whalers to victory. It was the life he loved.

Once Elizabeth had finished breast-feeding Anne she flew out to Malta again to spend more time in the sun with Philip. The Admiralty decided that HMS *Magpie* should become a floating embassy, and they made official visits to a number of Mediterranean countries, including Greece, where Elizabeth met some of Philip's relations. The *Magpie* became known in the navy as Philip's private yacht. For two wonderful years Philip was in his element, happy and cheerful, enjoying the naval life he loved, reveling in command of his own ship, playing polo whenever on shore leave, and enjoying the occasional visits from Elizabeth.

Back at Buckingham Palace, concern was growing for the King's health, and it was believed Elizabeth might soon have to take over as Regent. The senior Palace advisers decided Elizabeth would have to assume more of her ailing father's duties and that Philip would have to accept indefinite leave from the navy and accompany his wife during her official assignments.

Back home Philip once again became impatient with staff at the palace, moody and unpleasant. In public he would try to smile and be pleasant on most official occasions, but at Clarence House and at the palace he was rude and offensive to the staff, who tried to keep out of his way.

On January 31, 1952, Elizabeth and Philip set off for a royal tour of Australia and New Zealand. It was decided they would stop in Kenya for a few days to see the wedding present given them by the people of Kenya, the Sagana Royal Lodge, a lovely hunting lodge at Nyeri. On their second night at Sagana Elizabeth was asleep when Philip heard tapping at the window and went to investigate. It was Mike Parker. "I'm afraid I have the most terrible news," he said. "The King is dead."

"My God," said Philip. "Are you sure?"

"Yes, it's been confirmed," Mike Parker replied.

Philip closed the window and woke Elizabeth. She was devastated, at first unbelieving that her beloved father had died, then desperately upset that she had not been at his side at the end. She burst out crying, unable to control the tears.

Bobo, who was polishing Elizabeth's shoes in the next room, heard the crying. She immediately went into Elizabeth's bedroom and held her close, comforting the grief-stricken young woman to whom she had been a second mother for most of her life.

Mike Parker recalls, "The next day I saw Philip, and it seemed the weight of the world had suddenly descended on his shoulders. I never felt so sorry for anyone in my life. He looked awful."

In reality it was the moment Philip had dreaded, for now he wasn't married simply to the heir to the throne, but to the Queen, the sovereign, and he would have to take his place, walking two paces behind her, for the rest of his days. His dreams of returning to sea and to a long career in the Royal Navy had disappeared forever.

As the British Overseas Airways Corporation four-engine Argonaut landed at London airport the following day, Elizabeth saw the line of black limousines waiting and commented: "Oh, they've sent those black hearses" (the name she and Princess Margaret had as children for the royal cars). But this time the limousines not only meant the death of her father but also the end of her own youth.

For Philip, too, that homecoming would end the fun-loving relationship he had enjoyed with Elizabeth and shatter forever the chances of their enjoying a life together with their two young children. The role that Philip would play for the rest of his life became clear even before they had left the plane. As he went to escort Elizabeth down the aircraft steps he was told by Sir Alan Lascelles, the late

King's Private Secretary, that Her Majesty had to descend the steps alone. He could follow a little way behind.

As Elizabeth descended the aircraft steps, she saw her government ministers dressed in black, all looking most somber, as the occasion demanded, standing with bared heads on the freezing windswept tarmac. They had come to welcome home their new monarch. Winston Churchill was the first to greet her. The occasion affected him more than anyone. He could not control the tears that welled in his eyes and coursed down his cheeks as he bowed to the twenty-six-year-old Queen. For Churchill knew the massive responsibilities that lay before her, knew that she was ill-equipped to cope, and that the death of her father meant an end to any prospect of a normal, happy married life for the young woman who walked so lightly toward him.

Elizabeth's realization that she had become Queen did not fully take effect until the following day, February 8, 1952, when she was escorted to St. James's Palace, next door to Clarence House, to meet her Privy Council. Snow fell outside the tall windows as Elizabeth, dressed in black, entered the chamber to join the 192 Councillors arrayed in dark suits before her, headed by Winston Churchill. In a young, clear, high-pitched, childlike voice, Elizabeth read out the declaration of her accession and spoke of the heavy duty laid upon her so early in life.

She was never allowed to forget her duty. During the first months of her reign, four men would spend hours at a time drilling into Elizabeth the gravity of her responsibilities, the burden of her duties, the all-important mantle that had fallen upon her, and the mammoth task that lay ahead of steering the ship of state with the same firm hand and resolute determination that had been shown by her ancestors, her father King George, her grandfather George V, and her great-grandmother Queen Victoria. And those were the words and phrases her advisers actually conveyed to young Elizabeth. It was no wonder she felt so ill-prepared for the job ahead.

Her four advisers were Churchill himself, her father's dear friend and adviser Sir Walter Monckton, Sir Alan ("Tommy") Lascelles, and Uncle Dickie Mountbatten. Mountbatten knew Lilibet, as he always called her, better than all the others, yet he too would spend hours lecturing her.

Elizabeth knew very little about the politics of the nation and nothing about party politics. She had, of course, grown up believing that Winston Churchill, Britain's wartime Prime Minister, had saved the nation from the German army, the Luftwaffe, and Hitler. She revered him as many young people did at that time. Churchill would spend hours with her, drilling her for weeks on some of the intracacies of British party politics, explaining what was happening and what had to be done.

The seventy-eight-year-old Churchill was eager to be the new Queen's teacher and professor, her guide and mentor, informing her of the ways of the world. He was paternal toward his young pupil, and they enjoyed their hours together. Inexperienced, naive, and grossly ill-educated for the task before her, Elizabeth came to depend on the great man for support and advice. As one of Churchill's contemporaries put it, "He believed he was teaching her how to be Queen; he had this sense of history and of destiny and he wanted to be the man who educated her into the job. And, to a great extent, he did."

Churchill in particular was worried that Elizabeth had been poorly educated for her new role as monarch, and constitutional lawyers were brought in to explain every aspect of the monarchy and the sovereign's duties. Elizabeth felt great pressure, overawed by her new role, and desperate to learn and succeed.

Sir Walter Monckton, later elevated to the peerage as Viscount Monckton of Brenchley, in Kent, was an English lawyer who became Attorney-General to Edward, Prince of Wales, in 1932. They had been friends since they were at Oxford together. It was Monckton who acted as go-between during the abdication crisis of 1936, negotiating on Edward's behalf with Prime Minister Stanley Baldwin, and it was Monckton who wrote the King's abdication statement. He attended the later marriage of the Duke and Duchess of Windsor, and after the Duke's exile he continued to advise him. His brilliant mind, integrity, and coolness under pressure earned the respect of King George VI and he became George's closest unofficial adviser throughout the King's sixteen-year reign. Never a week would go by without Monckton's coming to the palace for a glass of whisky and a chat with King George.

Monckton was divorced and remarried in 1947, acts which would have barred virtually anyone else from the palace forever. He had, however, become so important to the King that he was still welcomed as a valued and trusted friend and adviser. George VI told him, "Of course you understand that it may not be possible from now on for you to enter the palace by the front gates, due to the social consequences of your divorce, but I want you to understand that the back door is open to you twenty-four hours a day and I hope you will make frequent use of it."

Upon her father's death, Elizabeth naturally turned to Sir Walter, who was then sixty-one, and sought advice from him on many matters. She felt she could trust him simply because her father had put so much faith in his advice and would see his friend two or three times a week to discuss matters of state. Other advisers included the Archbishop of Canterbury, Geoffrey Fisher, a former headmaster who was then sixty-five and the man who crowned young Elizabeth Queen in Westminster Abbey in June 1953.

For her everyday work at the Palace, Elizabeth's most important adviser was Sir Alan Lascelles, her austere, rather bloodless, bespectacled Principal Private Secretary. He was tight-lipped, impeccable, and precise, but exactly the wrong person to be advising an inexperienced young woman who sought warmth and understanding in her hour of need and even a little humor.

In retrospect, many believe that the absence of young people who might have provided the young Queen some respite from the burdens of monarchy was unfortunate. In particular, the four primary advisers, all old men in their sixties and seventies, were too heavy-handed in their "education" of the young Elizabeth during those months, giving her little chance to settle into her awesome new life.

Elizabeth took her new role as monarch extremely seriously, and not surprisingly, overnight she changed. Prior to her accession, Elizabeth was a happy, sometimes extroverted young woman. At dinner parties or balls with Philip, people noted how much Elizabeth loved him. The Princess always attended polo matches at Windsor Great Park, watching Philip take part; she walked around the pony lines, patted the ponies, fed them lumps of sugar, and took a great interest in the matches, particularly when Philip played. The following season the smiling, fun-loving Elizabeth had disappeared and she wore the look of a grave, even solemn person, straight-faced, unsmiling, almost humorless. It seemed her entire character had changed dramatically within a matter of months.

Photographs taken during those two years show a marked change in her attitude and appearance. Once Queen, Elizabeth seems to have adopted the mantle of monarchy, almost like a shroud. In addition, the court was still in mourning and she was always pictured in black. From that time on Elizabeth came to be seen by the public as a rather glum, unfriendly person who went about her life as sovereign with a grim, some even said a sour and grave, look. Soon after the accession she told a friend, "Extraordinary thing, I no longer feel anxious or worried. I don't know what it is but I have lost all my timidity and somehow becoming the Sovereign and having to receive the Prime Minister for instance has made me feel more self-assured and uninhibited."

The change in Elizabeth of course also affected Philip. He was determined to help his wife in any way possible, but it was very difficult for this macho man to assume an inferior role, even for his sovereign. He adopted a criterion: What could he do to save the time and energies of the Queen, his wife?

For example, he tried to have members of the Royal Household come to him with matters which they would normally bring to a husband rather than a wife, but he had difficulty persuading anyone to talk to him when there was an opportunity of speaking to the Queen herself. In an interview with his official biographer Basil Boothroyd, Philip said, "Because she's the sovereign everyone turns to her. If you have a King and a Queen, there are certain things people automatically go to the Queen about. But if the Queen is also the *Queen* they go to her about everything. She's asked to do much more than she would normally do. Many of the Household of course have to report to the Queen and the fact they report to the Queen is important to them, and it's frightfully difficult to persuade them not to go to the Queen, but to come to me."

Two incidents made Philip realize he would never be accepted by the haughty English aristocracy or the British establishment, who feared a backdoor takeover of the English Crown by the German Battenbergs.

Uncle Dickie's official title had been Louis of Battenberg, which became Earl Mountbatten of Burma. His father, a full-blooded member of the German Battenberg family, was also called Louis of Battenberg. Philip's mother Alice was Uncle Dickie's sister, and also a Battenberg.

On hearing the news that Elizabeth had ascended to the throne, Uncle Dickie called for champagne and shouted a toast, "The House of Mountbatten now reigns!" The plot he had hatched more than a decade before, when he had seen the way the thirteen-year-old Elizabeth looked at his young nephew, had come to fruition and one of his greatest ambitions had been secured. In truth, Philip was just a pawn in the master game that had been plotted since the beginning by his ambitious uncle. According to all the traditions of genealogy he was correct, for Elizabeth had married a Mountbatten. But Dickie Mountbatten's triumph would prove short-lived.

Uncle Dickie now advised Philip that he must send a carefully worded plea to the government for the name *Mountbatten-Windsor* to be used in place of *Windsor* in official references to the Royal Family. Indeed, it was Louis Mountbatten who wrote the letter, which he had Philip sign, and sent it to his old friend, Prime Minister Winston Churchill, the man who had backed Mountbatten throughout the war and had organized his rapid promotion to the very heights of military glory as Supreme Commander of Allied Forces in Southeast Asia, and later as Viceroy of India. Churchill and Mountbatten had been a formidable duo throughout the great conflict, and Mountbatten now hoped Churchill would support him.

Queen Mary, herself a German, heard that Mountbatten claimed at dinners at Broadlands that a Mountbatten now reigned in Britain, a most remarkable feat considering Britain had fought two world wars against Germany within forty years. Mary, a staunch monarchist and a confirmed Englishwoman, could not stand Dickie Mountbatten, whom she constantly referred to as "an ambitious upstart." She was beside herself with fury, realizing that "the upstart's" boast was indeed correct. So she wrote an urgent note to Churchill, informing him of the news and asking him to ensure that a name change would not be tolerated.

Perhaps more than any other single person, Churchill had been responsible for the defeat of Nazi Germany. He became apoplectic at Queen Mary's news. Twenty-four hours later the official letter from

Prince Philip arrived, and Churchill exploded in rage. He called an immediate Cabinet meeting, to take place within the hour.

At the end of the Cabinet meeting the Lord Chancellor, the Lord Privy Seal, and the Home Secretary wrote a letter that was immediately sent by hand to the Queen and Prince Philip. It sternly informed them that by a unanimous decision of Cabinet, the name Mountbatten would not be used by the Royal Family and the official name would continue to be *The Royal House of Windsor*.

Ironically, it was on Elizabeth's twenty-sixth birthday—April 20, 1952—that she signed the authorizing Order in Council, with the stroke of a pen ending once and for all Dickie Mountbatten's ambition. On learning the news that the name Mountbatten would never be used, Philip shouted in fury at Elizabeth, "I'm just a bloody amoeba! That's all."

Dickie Mountbatten called on Lilibet and asked her quietly why she could not order her government to change the name. Mountbatten's faithful secretary for twelve years was in the room at the time. He recalled, "Elizabeth explained to him: 'I tried everything, Uncle Dickie, but they wouldn't let me. They told me I couldn't change it. They told me it was nothing to do with me.'

"Mountbatten asked, 'What do you mean they? Who are you referring to? Who are they?'

"Elizabeth just looked at him for a moment and then replied, 'I don't know. I don't know who they are. But they are the people who tell me what I can and cannot do. I'm always told that "they" say do this or that but I don't know who they are. I've no idea. I never know who they are. I'm afraid there's nothing I can do.'"

"They" have advised Queen Elizabeth throughout her entire reign, and she still does not know who "they" are. In fact, "they" are sometimes the government, perhaps the bureaucrats or the civil servants, rather than the ministers. It is sometimes committees, of which there are hundreds, filled with mostly faceless men who advise and pass on their recommendations and decisions to the Palace. Elizabeth may be the Crown on top of the vast edifice that is the government, bureaucracy, armed services, the Church, and British society, but she has little or no control or, indeed, even influence over the great majority of decisions and recommendations that are all made in her name.

Despite her palaces and castles, her wealth and position, Elizabeth is far, far more restricted than any one of her subjects. It was a lesson she learned very early on in her reign and has never been able to forget or, more important, change.

To Dickie Mountbatten the decision was a bitter blow. He knew he could no longer pursue his goal, that the family name should become the royal name. Still, he had to take care of his unhappy, angry, and dispirited nephew. He invited Philip to Broadlands to discuss the situation. Philip told Mountbatten that this decision was another effort to keep him from the pinnacle of power and influence. He bridled at always having to call his wife "Ma'am" in public, like everyone else. And at having to bow whenever she entered a public room. Both Mountbatten and Philip felt they had been cheated.

Elizabeth understood Philip's anger, but she also knew she could not oppose the wishes of Queen Mary, her own mother, Churchill, and the entire government. Elizabeth discussed the matter with her advisers, Sir Alan Lascelles and Sir Walter Monckton. Elizabeth wanted to do something for Philip and asked them to explore the possibilities. After lengthy talks with constitutional lawyers it was decided Philip could be given a more senior position than consort. Before the State Opening of her very first Parliament in September 1952, the Queen issued a declaration stating she was "graciously pleased to declare and ordain that HRH The Duke of Edinburgh should henceforth have, hold and enjoy the Place, Pre-eminence and Precedence next to Her Majesty."

Elizabeth felt overjoyed that she had been able to do something for her husband. Though only a gesture, it was typical of Elizabeth then. She wanted to please and pacify the man she loved, to make him feel important, not her appendage. And, in a bid to give Philip something significant to do, Elizabeth decreed that he should head the council planning her Coronation.

Philip, however, remained unsatisfied. This restless, energetic, angry young man could not contain himself and set about trying to revolutionize Buckingham Palace. He condemned the place as Victorian and out of touch with reality; he castigated the senior courtiers for being placemen, promoted to office for reasons other than suitability. He was determined to bring the palace up to date by shouting at members of the Royal Household and the royal servants, "This is the bloody twentieth century, not the nineteenth."

He began inspections, as though in command of a ship, trying to instill Royal Navy discipline into the palace staff. He would stride through the corridors finding fault everywhere. He would suddenly storm into servants quarters, into the kitchens, the scullery, and other areas where he should not even have ventured. He would frequently swear at cleaners, footmen, and cooks whenever he found a speck of dust, a dirty window, or a mark on the floor or wall.

He would stop anyone he met and ask, "Why is this done like that? Why don't you do this in another way? Why don't you use your initiative? Why don't you use your bloody brains?" Particularly incensed by members of the Household, Philip would often threaten old retainers: "Buck your ideas up or you'll be out on your bloody neck."

Rumblings below stairs drifted upward as the four hundred royal workers who then worked at the palace took exception to Philip's unwarranted and insulting criticism of their work, their competence, and their traditions. Finally, workers' representatives told senior members of the Household that Prince Philip was going too far and Sir Alan Lascelles was asked to advise him where his responsibilities started and where they stopped—that is, to mind his own business.

Angry, frustrated, yet unbowed, Philip decided to lead his own life and forget about modernizing the palace and the ancient regime which he despised and ridiculed in private, and sometimes in public. He made every effort to free himself of the smothering attendance of royal servants, refusing to let flunkies carry his bags or open doors for him, yelling and swearing at them, "Don't you think I'm bloody well capable of carrying my own case?"

He insisted on driving a car himself, refused to allow the elevator operator to ride in the ancient palace elevator with him, dismissed the projectionist from threading and showing movies he watched, but did the job himself. He had a small kitchenette built in his rooms, equipped with the basic necessities—an oven, gas rings, a refrigerator, a small larder—so he could cook his own meals or make a cup of tea or coffee without having to go through the rigmarole of phoning for something to be sent up from the kitchens, which, he complained, took hours and always arrived cold.

He installed a direct telephone system for himself in the palace so he could talk to anyone, including Elizabeth, without going through the main switchboard, which often took over five or ten minutes to place a call for him.

He would sometimes be seen heaving furniture around, not only his private rooms but also the Queen's rooms and other apartments of state, simply because he was fed up with the way everything was always placed in precisely the same position.

He went further. Angry that he was not permitted to return to active naval service, he went to the extraordinary lengths of having his suite of rooms at the palace converted to look like a ship's cabin. Carpenters used beautiful African mahogany, a present received on one of his overseas trips. The cabin was constructed to his exact orders, with every piece of furniture, the shelving, the wardrobes, and the lighting designed to make him feel he was back in the navy on board ship.

He became increasingly angry, believing that senior Household members were ganging up against him, refusing him involvement in any official matters, keeping him away from the affairs of state, from the monarchy, even from his wife as much as possible. He has, for example, never been permitted to examine the red dispatch boxes— containing all government papers and the affairs of state—that the Queen is sent several times a day.

In a way Philip was right. No one in government, including Churchill and his senior ministers, no senior civil servants, no one at the palace, or any of the establishment figures wanted the forceful, arrogant Philip taking over the reins of power from the young wife who was so obviously in love with him and, some feared, under his spell. They knew full well the ambitions of Mountbatten, whom they regarded as an opportunist, and feared Philip might follow in his uncle's forceful footsteps. Tacitly, they all froze him out of any position of power so that he would have no real influence on the Constitution, the monarchy, or his wife.

The isolating of Philip exemplifies the workings of the British system: no decision was actually taken, no one caused any overt fuss. There was simply a consensus that this individual, even an individual as important as the sovereign's husband, had no right to wield power or influence the Crown, so events unraveled to ensure that he was unable to influence any decisions or policies.

Even today, at over seventy years of age, Philip has never been able to come to terms with the fact that he has never been accepted by the establishment, even after nearly fifty years of marriage to the Queen.

Philip discussed his problems with two people, Uncle Dickie and Mike Parker, who could offer little real help. Uncle Dickie explained how the royal establishment worked, shrugged his shoulders, and told him to be patient. Mike Parker took him out for drinks and they talked irreverently and insultingly about the system and the people who ran it.

Ultimately, Philip decided, for all intents and purposes, to forget his role as a royal prince, abandon any pretense of being consort to the Queen, and instead to concentrate his life and his future on simply being a man with a wife to protect and a family to take care of. Ironically, Philip, who loved to command and who yearned for power and authority, was destined to have none.

Mike Parker would provide some light relief by telling him to look on the bright side. Wasn't he married to the Queen of England, the wealthiest woman in the entire world? In 1953 being paid the equivalent of twenty thousand dollars a year? Didn't he have his own secretary, his own equerry, a valet, a chauffeur, and a few Rolls-Royces to drive around? Couldn't he play polo every weekend, ride, shoot, and fish at will, and didn't he have the run of three or four palaces? As Mike Parker frequently reminded him, "Not bad for a naval lieutenant."

The second incident that made clear to Philip his status as a perpetual outsider arose over the matter of Coronation invitations. The Coronation Council of which he was head gave permission for his three sisters to attend the grand affair but refused to allow any of his wealthy, aristocratic, German brothers-in-law to appear. (One of them had fought throughout the war against Britain.) Before the war, as a teenager, Philip had been very friendly with two of his brothers-in-law and had frequently been a guest at their homes in Germany. Now he was not even allowed to invite them to his wife's Coronation as private citizens. The council remained adamant, and Philip could do nothing to reverse their decision.

Furious, Philip protested personally to Elizabeth, begging her to intervene, pointing out that refusing to invite his own brothers-in-law was an appalling insult to him, to his sisters, to his family, and indeed to their own marriage. Elizabeth took up the matter with her advisers and Sir Winston Churchill, but they insisted that no member of the German aristocracy, some of whom had backed Hitler, could be invited to London for the Queen's Coronation. Elizabeth could do nothing. And they did not attend.

To appease Philip, however, she arranged a wonderful surprise for him, an extraordinary promotion from lieutenant to Admiral of the Fleet, in January 1953. The leap in rank gave Philip both pleasure and pain. Though he loved to wear the uniform and be treated as an admiral in the Royal Navy, he was frustrated once more that he had not earned the rank, as his Uncle Dickie had done, working his way up through the officer corps until he had deserved the promotion. Philip was too honorable simply to enjoy being given an honorary title only because he was married to the Queen.

Meanwhile, Elizabeth had begun to enjoy her newfound royal power. Already basking in the glory of her forthcoming Coronation and her divine accession to the throne, she decreed that the occasion would be the most splendid in British history, despite the fact the nation was still struggling from the crippling war. She ordered that all the ceremonial chairs be reupholstered; magnificent chandeliers taken apart crystal by crystal, cleaned, and refitted; mirrors repolished; all tables french-polished; furniture regilded; and all the livery to be used, examined and reworked. The cost amounted to a staggering $10 million ($100 million in 1994 dollars)!

As Coronation Day approached Elizabeth became more involved with the spiritual and religious side of the ceremony. In her first Christmas broadcast to the nation, in December 1952, six months before the crowning, Elizabeth told her subjects, "Pray for me on my coronation day. Pray that God may give me the wisdom and strength to carry out the solemn promises I shall be making."

The Right Reverend Michael Mann, Dean of Windsor and domestic chaplain to the Queen for thirteen years (until 1988) commented: "The Queen looked upon her Coronation in much the same way as I looked upon my ordination as a priest, or my consecration as a bishop. It is something that is indelible, that is hers, and she feels that she was called to it by God. To give it up would be an abdication of her responsibilities."

On June 2, 1953, the day the crown was ceremonially placed on her head and she was proclaimed Queen, Elizabeth had been on the throne sixteen months. She was still only twenty-seven years of age, in love with her handsome husband, the mother of two children, and the person the nation hoped would bring about a new Elizabethan Age, with its glorious buccaneering spirit personified by the adventures of Sir Francis Drake and Sir Walter Raleigh. One newspaper headline read: THE SIGNS ARE BRIGHT FOR A GREAT REVIVAL.

Elizabeth, backed by her advisers, and the Churchill government were determined to spare nothing to make her Coronation a spectacle never to be forgotten. Hers was the first ever televised, and though not many people in Britain then owned or rented a home TV, thousands were rented for the day by village halls, organizations, and public houses so that the nation could watch the spectacle on the black-and-white screens. In the United States, the networks fought their first all-out battle for supremacy over who would first get to show Queen Elizabeth II being crowned.

Westminster Abbey was closed for months before so that seven thousand tiered seats could be accommodated for those invited guests and those who had a right to attend; buildings along the route from Buckingham Palace to Westminster were freshly cleaned and painted; stands were erected, as were supports for flags and decorations. Her wedding may have been a rather subdued affair, but Elizabeth was determined her Coronation would be majestic.

Elizabeth herself had to rehearse for the great day. Worried about the size and weight of the crown, Elizabeth took to wearing it occasionally while working at her desk in her office. And for some weeks she walked up and down the ivory-and-gold ballroom in the palace, trailing behind her sixty feet of bedsheets that had been sewn together, for that was the length of her official Coronation train. Sometimes the rehersals ended in laughter when Philip, bored with the repetition, fooled around. Occasionally, an irate Elizabeth, half laughing, reprimanded him, "Stop being silly and do as you are told." And Philip obeyed.

The Earl Marshal, in charge of proceedings, had problems with the bishops, who had to march in step as they walked down the abbey. Sometimes, head in hands, he would say: "If you bishops don't learn to march in step we will be here all night. Now come on, concentrate, pretend you're in the army, left, right, left, right." Finally, a Guards sergeant-major was brought in to drill the aged bishops until they marched properly.

Elizabeth ordered the pile of the new red carpet to be cut down because the weight of the train made it difficult for her to walk gracefully. She also feared some of the older aristocrats, resplendent in their long robes, would be unable to walk at all unless the pile was trimmed. In rehearsal, Elizabeth realized the orb and scepter were too heavy for her to hold for any length of time, so the Lord of the Manor of Worksop was brought in to stand near Elizabeth throughout the ceremony and to support her right arm if it should tire under the weight.

Churchill feared the three-hour Coronation service would be too arduous for Elizabeth and kept suggesting parts should be cut back, but Elizabeth would not hear of it. "If my father did it at his Coronation," she would reply, "then I will at mine." And she would chide Churchill, "Don't you realize I'm as strong as a horse?"

When Bobo woke Elizabeth at seven on Coronation Day, she reported bad weather. It was a cold and drizzling morning, and the forty thousand people who had lined the route throughout the night were shivering and wet through. But they had endured the inclemency to ensure themselves the best positions to witness the royal spectacle.

The Lord Mayor of London led the Coronation procession, which represented commerce and the nation's wealth; then followed the ambassadors and representatives of foreign countries who had come to pay homage to the new sovereign. Third came parliamentary leaders, led by Churchill and accompanied by the prime ministers of the Dominions, the Empire, and the Commonwealth. Finally came all members of the Royal Family, culminating in the Queen herself riding in the golden Great State Coach, drawn by eight Windsor grays. Surrounding the State Coach were the Sovereign's Escort of the Royal Horse Guards, whose duty and privilege, by tradition, is to personally guard the monarch.

As Elizabeth made her way up the aisle of Westminster Abbey, eight pages carried her long train and the choir of Westminster School greeted her with the cry, "Vivat, Regina Elizabeth, vivat, vivat, vivat." After kneeling to pray in silence for a few minutes, Elizabeth sat in a chair of state while being formally presented to the people. Around her stood six ladies-in-waiting, dressed in virginal white satin, their heads garlanded.

In a loud voice, the Archbishop of Canterbury, addressing the huge congregation, presented Elizabeth as their Queen, turning to the four sides. All shouted in unison, "God save Queen Elizabeth." After the final response trumpets echoed around the abbey.

The most solemn part of the ceremony, the Coronation Oath, Elizabeth gave in a clear voice, though few could actually hear her words. She promised to rule her peoples according to the laws and customs of their separate countries; promised to maintain the laws of God, the Protestant religion, and the Church of England. Finally, kneeling at the altar steps and with her right hand on the Holy Bible, she sealed her solemn oath: "The things which I have here before promised, I will perform and keep. So help me God." She kissed the Bible and signed the oath as permanent witness of what she had just undertaken.

And then came the anointing of Elizabeth, the most important symbolic gift the sovereign receives at the Coronation, for it is by this act that the sovereign is given God's authority to rule. It is perceived as being of mystical significance, the same as anointments in Old Testament times. The golden ampulla, a two-handled flask for sacred use only, in the form of an eagle, was taken from the altar along with a golden spoon. Four Knights of the Garter held a rich canopy of cloth of gold over Elizabeth's head. A bishop poured oil into the spoon and the Archbishop of Canterbury anointed Elizabeth, tracing a cross on the palm of each hand and on the crown of her head.

A hushed silence greeted his words: "Be thy head anointed with holy oils, as kings, priests, and prophets were anointed: and as Solomon was anointed by Zadok the priest and Nathan the prophet, so be you anointed, blessed and consecrated Queen over the Peoples whom the Lord your God hath given you to rule and govern. In the name of the Father, and of the Son, and of the Holy Ghost. Amen."

Finally, the moment of coronation. Elizabeth walked to a side chapel to be robed in private. First, a long full garment of white linen and lace which reached to her feet. Next, the supertunica, a long, close-fitting belted garment of cloth of gold. Elizabeth was ready.

The regalia handed to her have religious significance. The golden spurs she touched are the emblems of chivalry, of a code of behavior by which justice is done and the poor protected. The five State Swords define the role of the sovereign, though only two are used in the ceremony. Elizabeth should have placed the Great Sword of State on the altar, signifying the submission of her temporal power to God's spiritual authority, but because of its great weight she exchanged it for a jewelled sword. These swords are given to her "to be used as a minister of God."

Three other swords—the Curtana, which has a broken blade to denote mercy, the Sword of Spiritual Justice, and the Sword of Temporal Justice—were laid on the altar. A crimson and ermine royal robe was placed around her shoulders and more regalia handed to her. The Archbishop handed over the golden, bejeweled orb, with the words, "When you see this Orb thus set under the Cross, remember that the whole world is subject to the Power and Empire of Christ the Redeemer." Then the sovereign's ring was given to her as "an ensign of kingly dignity and of defence of the faith."

On her hands, the Archbishop of Canterbury placed gloves before presenting the Sceptre with the Cross in her right hand and the Sceptre with the Dove in her left, signifying that she would rule with justice and mercy. Visibly endowed with all the symbolic powers of authority, the confirmation of actual sovereignty finally arrived with the placing on her head of the Imperial State Crown, with its 3,093 jewels, the supreme sign of the magnificence and majesty of earthly power.

The service inspired admiration and awe. The world saw Elizabeth, small, slight, young and unwordly, dwarfed in her magnificent, overweight monarch's robes, a huge sixty-foot-long train, with a large, heavy, solid gold crown on her head, surrounded by Peers of the Realm resplendent in their robes. All paid homage to someone who a couple of years earlier was just a young woman in love with hardly a care in the world. It was a touching sight, but many felt that Elizabeth was being asked to shoulder too many responsibilities for someone so immature and innocent.

As she stood in her robes, holding the regalia, the abbey erupted in a crescendo of noise, the seven thousand present shouting, "God save the Queen." Trumpets blared and the guns on Tower Hill fired a forty-two-gun salute. That was the signal to everyone in London that

Elizabeth had taken her place in the succession of English sovereigns.

When the noise finally died down the Archbishop handed her a Holy Bible, saying "The most valuable thing that this world affords."

Escorted to the throne Elizabeth sat, wearing the huge crown and holding the two scepters while Princes of the Blood, Peers of the Realm, and Bishops of the Church stood before her and swore allegiance.

Prince Philip's homage to his wife was proclaimed in a hushed silence as he said, "I, Philip, Duke of Edinburgh, do become your liegeman of life and limb and of earthly worship; and faith and truth I will bear unto you, to live and die, against all manner of folks." It was a proclamation that few men would want to make to their wives and it helped increase further the physical divide that Elizabeth was creating with her husband of just five years.

Her journey back to Buckingham Palace was even more triumphal, though the rain never let up for a moment. The procession was led by a selection of Her Majesty's forces from all over the world, the entire route guarded, shoulder to shoulder, by British servicemen. Tens of thousands of people cheered and waved every inch of the way as she sat in the Great State Coach, wearing her crown and carrying her orb and scepter so all could witness her majesty. Elizabeth arrived back at the palace anointed, crowned, acclaimed to reign, and very, very tired. All she wanted was a cup of tea.

In a jubilant mood after her revivifying tea, Elizabeth walked around chatting to everyone, not wanting to take off her crown and robes. She said, "I am so happy that everyone has so enjoyed the day with all the street parties, the pageantry, and everything, but it was different for me. To me it was a solemn religious act of dedication. Do they realize that?"

Dermot Morrah, of the *Arundel Herald Extraordinary*, wrote, "Certainly the sense of spiritual exaltation that radiated from her during the service was almost tangible to those of us who stood near her in the Abbey." And poet and writer Robert Graves commented after an audience with the Queen, "The holy oil has taken for that girl. It worked for her all right."

The great moments of the Coronation in Westminster Abbey provided the young, impressionable Elizabeth yet more proof that her life must be dedicated to the British people and those of the

Commonwealth around the world. She would readily sacrifice herself to that duty, and Churchill described her as "a gleaming champion."

Even at the time of the Coronation there were those who feared Elizabeth would sacrifice herself too generously. A writer for the *Manchester Guardian* commented, "The inarticulate hopes of the multitude are centred on her person, but what should one expect of this girl? One feels that she must on no account be 'victimised.' There will be a temptation for all of us to place too heavy a burden on her for our own purposes, but no human being should be used in this way."

The weight of tradition and responsibility, encapsulated in the Coronation, began to overwhelm Elizabeth. She began to believe that her role as sovereign must take precedence over every other aspect of her existence, including that of being a mother to her two children and a wife to her husband. Elizabeth began to believe in the divine right of Kings, the political doctrine holding that monarchy is divinely ordained, that hereditary right is indefeasible, that kings are accountable to God alone for their actions. At her Coronation she had been anointed sovereign by the Archbishop of Canterbury in Westminster Abbey before the sight of God; in effect, she had married the monarchy. In those first few months and years Elizabeth viewed the burden of monarchy with desperate seriousness.

Elizabeth had been raised in the Victorian belief that the prime reason for sex was to procreate, to produce heirs. Now, believing in her heart that she had done her duty to God and to the British nation by providing two heirs to the throne in Charles and Anne and that her life should now be dedicated, totally and completely, to her role as sovereign, Elizabeth banned Philip from her bed. Her royal duties did not include or necessitate any further sexual activity with her husband.

To Elizabeth this ban did not mean she didn't love or cherish Philip, nor did it mean that he was not head of their nuclear family. It did mean, however, that all her energies, all her strength had to be reserved for her role as monarch to ensure her ability to fulfill her duty to the Crown, the Commonwealth, and the British people.

So overpowering had been the burden of advice from so many people that Elizabeth was unable to cope rationally with the dramatic change in her life from Princess to Queen. The energetic Philip was nonplussed, confused, and puzzled by Elizabeth's change of heart and the argument she put forward to him for banning him from the matrimonial bed and withdrawing conjugal rights. When he tried to argue the point with her she would simply reply that her life had changed since becoming Queen and she now had duties to God, and the nation, not just to her husband.

Unable to make any headway at all through reasoned discussion, Philip turned to Uncle Dickie for advice. Mountbatten cautioned against any dramatic action, suggesting that Philip be patient and hope that in the weeks and months ahead Elizabeth would see the error of her ways and resume their sex life. Philip was not so sure.

He also discussed the matter with Mike Parker, who believed, given time, that Elizabeth would come to her senses. He advised Philip to ignore Elizabeth's present attitude, drop any discussions about the matter, and carry on his life as though nothing between them had changed.

The 1950s proved difficult for Elizabeth, trying to come to terms with her life as a wife and mother and her commitments to her duty as Queen. Many nights she went to her bed alone, worried sick about the huge responsibilities she felt incapable of bearing. Should she dedicate her life to the monarchy, devoting herself to the British people like a nun devoting her life to God; or should she take some time for herself and create the right atmosphere in which to raise a happy family?

Ultimately, Elizabeth could never forget the promises she had made to her father: to serve the people and protect the monarchy. A dutiful daughter, she chose the former and has never looked back. Her Coronation in Westminster Abbey only confirmed her "marriage" to the monarchy, and her whole life has been dedicated to sustaining that "marriage." As a result Elizabeth became a remarkably lonely woman.

Philip understood his wife's turmoil but couldn't find a way to help her. He decided to let Elizabeth and her advisers and courtiers thrash out the problems of the Crown and the monarchy while he looked after the family, carried out his royal duties, and lived his own life.

(It was Uncle Dickie, not Prince Philip, who finally persuaded Elizabeth to consider having another child in the late 1950s, when she talked to him of her difficulties in balancing her family life with the demands of monarchy. She had told Mountbatten of her "sex ban"; he disapproved but he did not push her to change her attitude. Eventually, Elizabeth and Philip had two more children: Andrew in

Elizabeth, with Margaret in the pram, walking with nannies in Hyde Park in 1933. Elizabeth, then eight, would not know for three more years she would one day be Queen of England.

Elizabeth, fifteen, and Margaret, eleven, in 1941 broadcast to the British people during World War II.

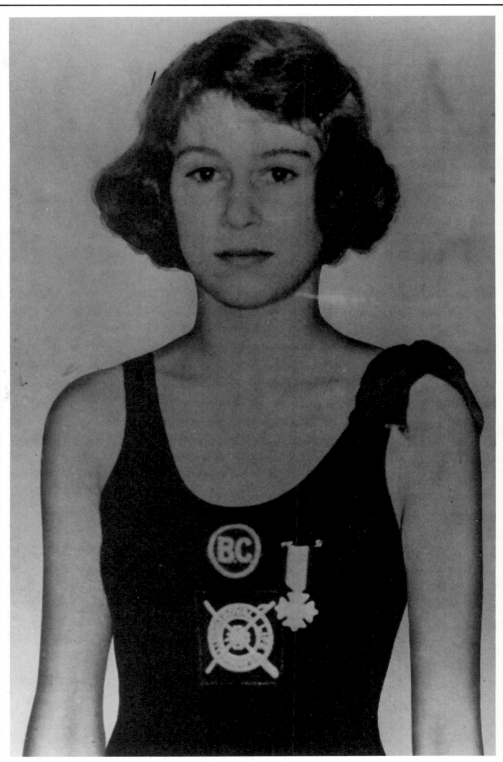

Princess Elizabeth, thirteen, in a bathing costume.

Elizabeth, eleven, and Margaret seven, at the coronation of their father King George VI in 1937. They are waving to the mass of people gathered in the Mall as they stand on the balcony of Buckingham Palace.

Elizabeth, twenty, and Margaret, sixteen, with their mother, Queen Elizabeth, at a Sandringham garden party in July 1946.

The wedding of Elizabeth and Philip in 1947, pictured on the balcony of Buckingham Palace waving to the cheering crowds:

The formal family photograph after Elizabeth's marriage to Prince Philip in 1947.

Elizabeth and Philip on honeymoon at Broadlands, Hampshire, the country home of Earl Mountbatten.

Elizabeth holding Prince Charles at his christening in November 1948. Sitting on Elizabeth's left, dressed in black, is Elizabeth's grandmother, Queen Mary of Teck, who was married to George V. Queen Mary was to have a significant influence on the young Elizabeth's education.

The christening of Princess Anne, with Prince Charles, then two, Philip, King George VI, Queen Elizabeth, and Queen Mary of Teck.

Elizabeth dancing with Earl Mountbatten in 1951. "Uncle Dickie" would become Elizabeth's father figure after the death of King George VI in 1952.

Elizabeth, dressed in black, at the top of the steps of the aircraft that brought her home from Kenya on the announcement of her father's death in February 1952. The first picture of Elizabeth as Queen of England.

The moment of Coronation of Queen Elizabeth II in June 1953 at Westminster Abbey.

Queen Elizabeth photographed by Cecil Beaton on the day of the coronation. She holds the Sceptre and Orb and wears the Imperial Crown, which has the famous Black Prince's ruby in the center.

Elizabeth and Philip on their way to Buckingham Palace in a Rolls-Royce. The young man in front is Lt. Cmdr. Michael Parker, Philip's equerry and close friend.

1960, and Edward, four years later. Apparently, Edward was not planned, but Elizabeth was only too happy when she found herself pregnant again.)

By denying Philip conjugal rights, Elizabeth provided the excuse he needed to live the way he wanted, as a promiscuous man-about-town without the slightest feelings of guilt toward Elizabeth or his marriage vows. Of course he would be discreet—he was husband to the Queen—but that discretion did not mean that he couldn't enjoy himself. He was to share the beds of many women who had signaled their willingness to sleep with him. Following his marriage, Philip had soon discovered that women were even more interested in him than before, perhaps because his wife had become the most important woman in the country. But Philip, arrogant about his physique and his sexual prowess, believed the women came to him for his own attributes, unrelated to his position as the Queen's husband.

For company, Philip had his stalwart friend Mike Parker. They seemed to have the same ideas about everything, competing hard against everyone and each other, in every sphere of their life— swimming, playing squash, table tennis, and even competing over women. They had both loved the navy, the camaraderie, the discipline, the officers mess, and the adventure. They had thoroughly enjoyed the competitive atmosphere the navy offered and had thrown themselves into service life with wholehearted enthusiasm. They knew the Royal Navy had made men of them. Together through the war they had lived life to the fullest and now they would enjoy life in postwar London.

* * *

Footnote. In the early 1950s, CBS and NBC were battling for viewers. NBC, the pioneer, had lost the lead to CBS in radio, and now its lead in television entertainment was being threatened. ABC, then the runt of the litter, was not involved; they decided to transmit Canadian TV's film, scheduled to be shown later that day. The race to screen the Coronation would be won or lost transporting the film across the Atlantic. Full broadcasting facilities were prepared by both networks at Boston's Logan International Airport. It was arranged that a Royal Air Force Canberra would fly from London with the BBC telecast and hand over two copies of the film, one to NBC and one to CBS. Both networks hired private P-51 Mustangs, the American-made World War II fighters, to meet the RAF Canberra in Goose Bay, Labrador, and transport the film to Boston for broadcast.

Determined to win, NBC invested in a secret weapon, hiring a Canberra jet bomber, which was about to be delivered to the Venezuelan air force. The mission would be codenamed Operation Astro.

On the morning of the Coronation, CBS was stunned to hear that NBC would screen the Coronation at 1 P.M., three hours earlier than scheduled.

Over the Atlantic, the secret Canberra developed a fuel leak and had to return to Britain. NBC now had to rely on the official arrangement. CBS's Mustang took off from Goose Bay thirteen minutes ahead of NBC's. Then, NBC's Mustang developed ice problems, arrving at 4:37 P.M., twenty minutes behind CBS's plane. Jubilation reigned in the CBS hanger at Boston, gloom throughout NBC.

Suddenly, Charles H. ("Bud") Barry Jr., NBC's vice president, had a brainstorm. He phoned ABC and agreed to pay all ABC's costs to share their Canadian TV footage. NBC went on air precisely thirteen minutes ahead of CBS. Jubilant, NBC took a full-page advertisement in next morning's *New York Times* to celebrate the victory.

Years later the truth emerged. The NBC Canberra turned back in mid-Atlantic not because of a mechanical failure, but because the two pilots, Royal Air Force reserve officers, were ordered to return by the British Air Ministry. Why? A senior NBC executive had informed BBC friends of Operation Astro. The BBC bosses decided they did not want any American network to broadcast the Coronation before Canadians, members of the Commonwealth, had seen their Queen, their head of state, crowned. They phoned the Air Ministry and explained the situation.

That decision by the Air Ministry revealed the power of the British establishment at that time and the lengths to which they were prepared to go to make sure the world conformed to their principles, above all other considerations. It also showed their narrow-minded attitude, something which Elizabeth would now have to face.

FIVE

EARLY PROBLEMS

To the British people Queen Elizabeth II has been an exemplary monarch, a beacon of steadfastness in a fast-changing world, someone who has won their admiration and esteem by carrying out her duties with distinction. Everyone looks to her as a kind of national conscience, a moral exemplar. Yet the more Elizabeth is exposed to scrutiny, the more one discovers a different woman, one whose world has been filled with sadness and tragedy and whose life has not been without some blemish.

For forty years Elizabeth has perpetuated the same dedication to her people—not just in Britain but throughout the Commonwealth—with which she began her reign. In 1952, following her Coronation, she decided to undertake a grand fifty-thousand-mile world tour so that her peoples could see their new sovereign. Accompanied by Prince Philip, she flew to Canada in November 1953 en route to Bermuda and Jamaica. They boarded a sixteen-thousand-ton liner, the *Gothic*, and sailed through the Panama Canal to Fiji and Tonga before steaming on to New Zealand and Australia.

Everywhere they went the welcome was tumultuous. On the way back home they landed at the Cocos Islands near Australia, Ceylon (Sri Lanka), and Aden before visiting Uganda. Then they flew to Tobruk in North Africa, to be reunited with Prince Charles, five, and Anne, three, who had sailed out on HMS *Britannia*. On the voyage back home the family called at Malta, the island that brought back happy memories for Elizabeth, and Gibraltar, before returning to London and a exultant welcome for the first British monarch to circumnavigate the world.

Throughout that long five-month tour Elizabeth had been anxious about her sister Margaret, then twenty-three, who she knew was in love with a married man, Group Captain Peter Townsend, the handsome former World War II fighter ace, war hero, equerry to King George VI, friend to the family, and adviser to the King. Elizabeth and Margaret had always been close. Elizabeth had always been a responsible, well-behaved daughter, while Margaret was more naughty, mischievous, sometimes willful.

In the autumn of 1952 Margaret personally told her sister that she was in love with Townsend. Elizabeth, who was also fond of Townsend, was torn between happiness for her sister and heartache because of the problems such a marriage would cause. As Head of the Church of England, Elizabeth could not condone her own sister's breaking the Church law against divorce by consenting to her marriage to a divorced man, no matter what his virtues.

The drama of the ill-fated love affair between the divorced Townsend and the young Princess Margaret divided the nation, the government, the House of Commons, the Church, and the Royal Family. The war had changed many people's views toward divorce and remarriage. So many couples had become separated or divorced and so many had remarried that fierce arguments for and against divorce were rampant. The Church, monarchy, and the establishment were desperately trying to stem the tide of divorces, while growing numbers of ordinary people were beginning to accept divorce as an option for couples to consider when they found themselves living a miserable marriage.

Peter Townsend was an extraordinary young man. In one of his books about the royals, Douglas Keay described Townsend as "a mixture of Trevor Howard in *Brief Encounter* and Leslie Howard in *Gone With the Wind*, which meant with women at least, that he could hardly go wrong." King George could have given him no higher praise when he said Townsend, whom he appointed in 1944 on a three-month trial, was the kind of son he would have liked to have had. "He was George VI's favorite equerry, and the King had given him the honor of Commander of the Victorian Order." It is ironic that Peter Townsend became Deputy Master of the Household, as did Elizabeth's great friend Patrick Plunket a few years later.

Townsend's job as an equerry, with its long hours and lengthy travel, meant Townsend hardly ever saw his wife. Eight years after "joining" the Royal Family and ten months after King George VI's death, he was granted a divorce on the grounds of misconduct by his wife. In those days the court always drew a clear distinction between those "innocent" and those "guilty" in a divorce case. Townsend was adjudged innocent and was thus not required to resign his post inside the palace. Indeed, shortly afterward the Queen Mother promoted him to Comptroller, the most responsible position in her household, and he moved into her home, Clarence House, where Princess Margaret, then twenty-three, also lived.

Margaret was a beautiful young woman and from the age of eighteen, if not before, had a host of admirers and eligible young men pursuing her. She partied, she danced, she attended weekend house parties in the country; she smoked, drank, and enjoyed her life to the full, accepted as a very modern young woman. Newspapers were full of stories about the Princess out on the town.

King George and his wife Elizabeth were keen for their daughter to marry a British aristocrat, particularly since Elizabeth had married "a foreigner." At one time or another Margaret was escorted by a number of young aristocrats, including the Marquess of Blandford, the son of the wealthy Duke of Marlborough; the Earl of Dalkeith, son of the Duke of Buccleuch; and William "Billy" Wallace, the grandson of the famous architect Sir Edward Lutyens. But Margaret wasn't really interested in any of them.

In 1948, Margaret, just eighteen, fell in love with Danny Kaye's crazy humor when she met him backstage when he performed for the first time at the London Palladium. Fascinated by his sense of fun, his handsome face, and lithe figure, she then fell in love with the man. At first, King George was amused by his daughter's interest in Danny Kaye, but he became alarmed when informed that Margaret was becoming seriously involved with him. Danny Kaye was not only thirty-five—nearly twice her age—but also married. His wife, the gifted lyricist Sylvia Fine, was staying with him in London.

Kaye returned to the United States and Margaret continued her life of partying. All this time, Margaret had been seeing more of Townsend, who, at that time the King's equerry, spent many hours a day with the Royal Family. He was fifteen years older than the Princess.

In 1951, Townsend wrote, "She was a girl of unusual, intense beauty, confined as it was in her short, slender figure and centres about large purple-blue eyes, generous, sensitive lips and a complexion as smooth as a peach. She was capable, in her face and in her whole being, of an astonishing power of expression. It could change in an instant from saintly, almost melancholic, composure to hilarious, uncontrollable joy. She was, by nature, generous, volatile. She was a comedienne at heart, playing the piano with ease and verve, singing in her rich, supple voice the latest hits, imitating the famous stars. She was coquettish, sophisticated. But what ultimately made Princess Margaret so attractive and lovable was that behind the dazzling façade, the apparent self-assurance, you could find, if you looked for it, a rare softness and sincerity."

This was the young woman with whom he fell in love. She had met and flirted with a number of young men, aristocrats and commoners, but she had never fallen in love with any of them. Only one month after the death of her father in February 1952, Margaret realized she was in love with Peter Townsend. Sometime in 1952 she and Townsend became lovers, eight years after they had first met.

At Elizabeth's Coronation, the press caught one unrehearsed moment which attracted great media attention in America: Princess Margaret was seen innocently flicking a speck of fluff from the uniform of Group Captain Peter Townsend as they stood together after the ceremony. The following day, news of Margaret's flirtation with the handsome war hero made headlines in the *New York Daily News* and the *Journal-American*. The matter was not even mentioned in the British press, for the Palace then had the most remarkable control over the media, something unthinkable today. The episode was repeated in the European newspapers, yet still nothing appeared in Britain until two weeks later, when *The People* repeated rumors of a romantic interest between Margaret and Townsend. The first scandal of Elizabeth's reign was about to erupt.

When Margaret told her sister about her lover that autumn, Townsend went to see Tommy Lascelles, the Queen's sixty-five-year-old Private Secretary and a paragon of the establishment, to inform him of the affair. On hearing the news Lascelles blurted out, "You are either mad or bad." Lascelles believed that another abdication-type scandal would seriously damage the monarchy, and since he understood his job was to preserve the monarchy above all else, he decided to pit his formidable authority against it.

At first, Churchill, then Prime Minister, wholeheartedly supported the marriage, saying, "What a delightful match. A lovely young royal lady married to a gallant young airman, returned safe from the perils and horrors of war!" Palace advisers, however, and his own wife Winnie finally persuaded Churchill to oppose the marriage, for fear of damage to the Crown. He called a Cabinet meeting which unanimously decided the Prime Minister must advise the Queen against such a royal marriage. Margaret was bound by the Royal Marriages Act of 1772, which stipulates that any member of the Royal Family in line of succession to the throne must secure the sovereign's authority in order to marry before the age of twenty-five. Since both Prince Charles and Princess Anne were in line before her, Margaret was convinced that Elizabeth would give her permission.

Elizabeth faced a heartrending predicament. As a young woman who had wanted and won Philip, she understood her sister's craving for Townsend. She desperately wanted to hug Margaret and say, "Yes, yes, yes, I am thrilled for you; I hope you both will be very happy." But she couldn't. She talked to the Queen Mother, who broke down and wept uncontrollably that her own daughter should have fallen in love with a divorced commoner, an exact parallel of King Edward's amour with Mrs. Simpson, a divorced commoner. In anguish, Elizabeth and her mother wept together.

Elizabeth showed remarkable strength of character. She told Churchill, Lascelles, and the Archbishop of Canterbury that she would ask the couple to wait a year. She called them together and gave them the news. Margaret threw her arms around her sister, hugging her: "Thank you, thank you, Lilibet," she said, tears in her eyes. Townsend and Margaret went away believing they would be able to marry "in a year or so."

But other forces were at work. Lascelles, the Royal Household, Churchill, the Cabinet, Church leaders, and many members of the House of Lords were determined to stop the marriage. The majority of the British people, however, supported Margaret and her wish to marry a commoner. Once again the nation was divided over the Royal Family and the love of a commoner. In the left-wing magazine *Tribune* which he edited, Michael Foot, a Member of Parliament and future leader of the Labour Party, wrote:

> This intolerable piece of interference with a girl's private life is all
> part of the absurd myth about the royal family which has been so
> sedulously built up by interested parties in recent years. The laws of
> England say that a man, whether he has divorced his wife or been
> divorced himself, is fully entitled to marry again...If those laws
> are good they are good enough for the royal family.

As agreed, Townsend went abroad, exiled to Brussels as Air Attaché
to the British Embassy, where the press never let him alone. Against
advice from Lascelles, Elizabeth gave the couple permission to write
and telephone each other. Before Townsend left London, Lascelles had
told them, "A marriage is not impossible." But he was deliberately
deceiving them. On her twenty-fifth birthday Margaret waited to
greet the man she still loved and wanted to marry. Now, according to
the law, all she had to do was give notice to the Privy Council and she
would be free to marry.

The new Prime Minister, Sir Anthony Eden, himself a divorced
man, came to see Margaret at Balmoral and told her that some MPs,
including the great Lord Salisbury, had threatened to resign if
Margaret married Townsend. In an emotional meeting during which
Margaret cried tears of rage and astonishment, Eden said that if she
did marry him she could not remain in line of succession and would be
barred from receiving any salary from the government for performing
royal duties. She knew that Townsend would have to retire from the
Royal Air Force on some paltry pension, which meant they would have
virtually nothing to live on.

Elizabeth told Margaret when they met, "You can still marry him
but it will cause the most awful rumpus. They will do everything in
their power to stop you." Then Elizabeth, revealing the superficiality
of her power, added, "You know there is nothing I can do. You know
that I want you to be happy but they are very determined to stop you
marrying him. They will do anything to prevent the marriage."
Elizabeth was referring to the establishment figures, government
ministers, senior civil servants, and members of her own Royal
Household.

Amid a tumult of journalists and photographers, Townsend arrived
back in London in October 1955 and the couple were reunited in

Clarence House. That night they left London and drove to a beautiful fifty-room Georgian mansion, Allanby Park, in Berkshire, forty miles northwest of London. It was their first weekend together under the same roof for eighteen months. As the world press camped outside, Margaret and Townsend spent three days and three nights together. They were determined to marry, no matter what forces were ranged against them.

The Cabinet was informed that the wedding would take place, and Margaret believed she would be permitted to marry the man she loved once she was over twenty-five, when she would no longer need the sovereign's permission. The establishment played its final hand, a trump card. Tommy Lascelles asked Margaret to come see him. He told her, "One fact seems to have been overlooked. If you insist on marrying Group Captain Townsend you will have to go into exile, and live abroad, in the same fashion as your Uncle David was permitted to marry only on the condition that he abdicate and live abroad."

Centuries ago, sovereigns assumed the authority to exile people from their lands, and did so. Whether any sovereign in modern times believes he has the authority to exile anyone is very doubtful. Officially, the Duke of Windsor was not exiled. He abdicated and, in exchange for a handsome settlement, agreed to live abroad permanently.

Margaret was stunned. David's situation had been so very different: he was the King. Finding courage in anger, she screamed at Lascelles, "I'm not the sovereign. There is no chance that I will ever become Queen. How can you compare my position with that of Uncle David? How can you?" (Margaret has never forgiven Lascelles for his hypocrisy. She said, "I shall curse him to the grave." When her relationship with Townsend finally ended, Margaret never spoke another word to Lascelles.)

Margaret stormed out of the meeting with Lascelles to see her sister.

Elizabeth kept shaking her head, telling Margaret of the power of the establishment, the government, the senior members of the Royal Household, Church leaders, all of whom were implacably against the marriage. Margaret went to the Archbishop of Canterbury to seek his support, but he offered no hope.

In October 1955, the *London Times*, then the voice of the establishment and the Church, thundered, "The Queen and her family are a symbol for her subjects throughout the Commonwealth, and the vast majority of these people will not recognise this marriage."

Townsend wrote later, "We were both exhausted, mentally, emotionally, physically. We felt mute and numbed at the centre of this maelstrom." That night Townsend arrived at Clarence House with a piece of paper which he gave Margaret to read.

It said, "I have been aware that, subject to my renouncing my rights of succession, it might have been possible for me to contract a civil marriage. But, mindful of the Church's teaching that Christian marriage is indissoluble, and conscious of my duty to the Commonwealth, I have resolved to put these considerations before any others. I have reached this decision entirely alone, and in doing so I have been strengthened by the unfailing support and devotion of Group Captain Townsend. I am deeply grateful for the concern of all those who have constantly prayed for my happiness."

Together they made their decision that they could not marry but would spend one last weekend together at a friend's house in the Sussex countryside. Twenty-four hours later, when the world expected an announcement of their forthcoming marriage, came the stunning statement from Princess Margaret.

It began: "I have been aware that..."

Elizabeth felt guilt, shame, and sorrow: guilt that she had not been more forceful; shame that she was not capable, even as Queen and head of state, of persuading the establishment; and deep sorrow for her sister. She had learned another lesson she would never forget.

Many biographers suggest that Philip fully supported Elizabeth throughout the crisis, but that is not true. Although Philip and Townsend had been acquaintances for many years and had spent many ferocious, competitive hours on squash and badminton courts, Philip had always been jealous of Townsend. He was jealous of his brilliant and courageous war record, his friendship with King George VI and the Queen Mother, and his popularity with the entire family. Townsend was a most likable man; Philip was not.

Townsend, an elegant, introspective man of genteel manners, found Philip brash, brusque, and overzealous. Philip's behavior can only be understood as the result of his jealousy, for he actually went out of his way to prevent the proposed marriage.

On one occasion during a private dinner with Elizabeth, he turned to Margaret and told her bluntly, "Stop being so bloody stupid and stop this marriage nonsense." Margaret blushed and looked angrily at Philip. Elizabeth said nothing, intimidated by her husband's ferocious attack upon her sister.

Philip considered his wife's sister vain and frivolous. Not surprisingly, Margaret has never forgiven Philip for taking sides against her and, as a result, the two have never been close. Philip's no-nonsense attitude toward Margaret made it more difficult for Elizabeth to cope with Margaret's distress and caused her much personal agony.

A major problem Elizabeth had inherited was the family's relationship with the Duke and Duchess of Windsor, who had been exiled from Britain's shores in 1936 after Edward VIII's decision to marry the American divorcée Wallis Simpson. Elizabeth was only ten years old when her uncle abdicated and her father succeeded to the throne. She had never seen either the Duke or the Duchess since. Naturally, she picked up the bitterness that divided the family, especially from her mother, who never forgave her brother-in-law for forcing her husband into the role of King, something for which he was unprepared and never wanted.

In character, interests, and appearance, young Elizabeth, thirty years her junior, could hardly have been more different from the Duchess. Yet Elizabeth, far more than her mother, showed the Duchess compassion and, later, forgiveness. Throughout her reign, Elizabeth tried to heal the breach between her mother and the Duke and Duchess, but to no avail. The Queen Mother never forgave them, not even in death.

Elizabeth was prepared to grant the Duke's greatest wish—that the title of Her Royal Highness be conferred on his wife—but her mother would not hear of it. Every time the matter was discussed, Elizabeth would listen and say, "It's Mummy that matters. We mustn't do anything that hurts Mummy's feelings." So nothing happened.

In 1962, Elizabeth provided a permanent private office for the Duke of Windsor and invited him and the Duchess to London for the unveiling of a memorial plaque to Queen Mary. But the offer of an HRH was not forthcoming and so the Duke returned with his wife to Paris and to exile.

Ten years later, in May 1972, Elizabeth and Philip paid a state visit to France. The timing was fortuitous, for the Duke, then seventy-eight, was dying of cancer. Elizabeth went to the Windsors' home and, after taking tea with the Duchess, went to see her uncle. He had refused to see Elizabeth in his pajamas, linked up to tubes and drips, and insisted the nurses dress him and prop him up in an armchair. Elizabeth found him sitting in his favorite chair smartly attired in a tie, blazer, and gray flannels. He couldn't stand and could hardly talk. After thirty minutes Elizabeth bade him farewell, kissing him on the cheek. She knew he was at death's door. Ten days later he died.

Elizabeth arranged for his body to be flown, in a coffin of English oak, to London, and from there to Windsor for burial. Mountbatten was asked to attend to the Duchess during her short stay in London. He was the natural person for this task since he had been the special negotiator between the Royal Family and the Duke after the abdication.

The Duchess was concerned about coming to London for the funeral. She told Mountbatten, "I am worried about Elizabeth, the Queen Mother, who never approved of me."

Mountbatten reassured her, saying, "She will welcome you with open arms. She is so deeply sorry for you in your grief and remembers what she felt like when her own husband died." The Queen Mother did welcome her and was polite, but there appeared to be no genuine warmth between the two women.

Standing in St. George's Chapel, Windsor, where the Duke lay in state, the Duchess said, "He was my entire life. I can't begin to think what I am going to do without him, he gave up so much for me, and now he has gone. I always hoped that I would die before him."

Mountbatten commented later, "I must say I feel desperately sorry for her. She is so lonely and sad, and yet kept saying how wonderful the family were being to her, and how much better the whole thing had gone than she had expected."

Nevertheless, some time after she had returned to Paris, the Duchess of Windsor remarked, "The Queen, Prince Charles, and Princess Anne were polite to me, polite and kind, especially the Queen." Then she added, "Royalty is always polite and kind. But they were cold. David always said they were cold."

That was probably a harsh judgment. Elizabeth nearly always appears cool during her official duties as monarch, and to a great extent she has to behave that way. She often seems distant when chatting to strangers but not to those she knows well. And yet it would be untrue to say she is cold and distant, for she can show great enthusiasm and a great sense of fun whenever the mood takes her in her private life, which very few people witness.

After the Duke's funeral Elizabeth went out of her way to make life as comfortable as possible for his widow, who lived the invalid life of a recluse for many years before her own death, in April 1986, at the age of ninety. Elizabeth ordered that her body be flown to England and laid to rest beside her husband in the grounds of Windsor. Almost thirty years earlier the Duchess had persuaded her husband to buy an enormous burial plot in Green Mount Cemetery, Baltimore, because she was convinced the British, and especially the Queen Mother—her archenemy—would attempt to achieve in death what they had failed to achieve in life: their separation. Elizabeth, however, had informed both her uncle and the Duchess that she would provide a burial place for them both at Frogmore in Windsor Great Park, and she kept her promise.

IV

FRIENDS AND LOVERS

SIX

SEXUAL ADVENTURES

Prince Philip is the most fiercely competitive of men and a most macho figure. Yet for nearly fifty years, he has been forced, in public, always to walk at least two paces behind his wife. As if to add further insult to his pride, Philip does not constitutionally exist at all. Nor can he be involved in any way in his wife's role. These factors have only aggravated Philip's natural aggression, leading to irritation, impatience, and, on many occasions, bloody-mindedness.

Philip is forbidden to see state papers, those official government documents filled with state secrets that arrive in boxes two or three times a day at Buckingham Palace for the Queen to read and which contain everything of importance in which the government is involved. Once, shortly after Elizabeth became Queen, Philip was offered the right to peruse them but turned down the privilege on the grounds that it would restrict his own freedom of speech. Since then, it has been tacit policy that Philip never sees or reads the papers.

In fact, however, Philip enjoys having it all. Throughout most of Elizabeth's reign, Philip has always read, and still does read, whichever papers he wishes to, and has readily discussed them with Elizabeth. She respects his opinions and all during her reign has used her husband as a sounding board. Since Philip and the Palace maintain that he never sees government papers, he remains free to comment about any subject he wishes.

When King George VI finally consented to Elizabeth and Philip's marriage, he appointed Philip to the Privy Council, a body of royal advisers which originated in England in 1070 and later became the chief governing body, the forerunner of the Cabinet of ministers. Today its powers, now purely formal, are limited to royal proclamations and Orders in Council, and membership is an honor granted automatically to Cabinet ministers and others who have held high political, ecclesiastical, or judicial offices in Britain or the Commonwealth. Because no discussion ever occurs, Philip has never attended. In fact, the meetings are so brief that no one, not even the Queen or her ever-present representative, ever sits down.

King George also honored Philip in other traditional ways. On the morning of the wedding, King George created Philip Duke of Edinburgh and he was given a new armorial bearing. The arms seemed most appropriate, showing hearts, lions, a cross, and a castle; supporters being a golden lion with a ducal coronet on its head and a naval coronet round its neck, and the hero Hercules complete with bulging muscles, bushy blond beard, lion-skin around his waist, and cudgel. Philip was also created a Knight of the Garter, for protocol's sake, one week after Elizabeth had been given the same honor.

Philip's life changed dramatically that day in February 1952 when King George VI died and his wife became Queen. Philip had been head of the family for more than four years, and by nature he loved being in command of anything, whether captaining a cricket team, a ship of the Royal Navy, a polo team, or his own family. At a stroke his days of leadership were over.

He later revealed his disappointment: "Until that point I was head of the family. Within the house, whatever we did, it was together. I naturally filled the principal position. People used to come to me and ask me what to do. After the King's death the whole thing changed very, very considerably."

It took some years for Philip to come to terms with the fact that, although he was nominally head of the family, he was all but superfluous as far as the Royal Household, government ministers, and the establishment were concerned. And he was given short shrift by many members of the aristocracy who regarded him as "Phil the Greek," or "a German princeling," which, in the years following World War II, was a considerable insult.

Lord Charteris, who was appointed Elizabeth's First Private Secretary in 1949, observed Philip during those awkward early years. He commented: "I think Philip might have tried a little harder to accommodate the views of the Royal Household. Because of the way he was treated, especially before his marriage, he had a certain amount of prejudice against the old order. He thought it was stuffy and needed shaking up. He came to being the consort of the sovereign as opposed to the husband of a princess with a certain amount of antipathy and impatience. He sulked quite a bit."

Philip's great friend from the navy, the Australian Mike Parker noted: "I felt that Philip didn't have many friends or helpers in the Palace. There were people who were in a position to give a helping hand and who, it seemed, were reticent about doing so. Some of the British establishment were hidebound and prejudiced. Some among the senior Household members were affected to find the Duke 'teutonic' and there was also the business of all his German relations. We had just been through a war and Germans were Germans."

Prince Philip never wanted to become Prince Consort, as Albert, Philip's great-great-grandfather, did after some years of marriage to Queen Victoria. The title would have promoted his official status while obviating his human vocation. Philip believed that accepting the title of Prince Consort meant he would be forced to reduce his role to that of a mere symbol. His instincts were to distance himself from the mystery of monarchy and to assert his rights and duties as a husband and father. Furthermore, in the far-off days of the 1940s, when they were married, Elizabeth herself insisted on promising to "obey" her husband in her wedding vows, as virtually every woman who was married in the Church of England did.

It was Boothroyd, Philip's official biographer, who noted in a June 1981 *Times* article, that Prince Philip dislikes having servants bowing and scraping before their superiors, and especially to him. He has always seen himself first as a man, and only secondly as a prince. Sometimes, Philip will chastise a servant for opening a door for one of his sons: "He's not helpless. He's got hands like everyone else!"

It was not only with servants, however, that Philip earned his reputation as the impatient, irascible, abrasive, almost aggressive character the world has come to know. He has given many bureaucrats a tongue-lashing, and exclaimed to many journalists and photographers, "Why don't you fuck off!" He is often rude to strangers, bludgeoning them with a totally uncalled for opening remark, leaving the victim not knowing how to answer the Queen's husband.

Frequently, when meeting black ambassadors from black Commonwealth countries, Philip will ask them, "How are the natives back home? Any rebellions lately?" It is meant to be a joke but is often not taken as one by those on the receiving end of his wit. They are left embarrassed and unsure as to how they should answer the Queen's husband.

He loves to appear to be in control, especially of the Queen. Particularly in his early years, when inspecting factories or shopping malls, Philip would snap loudly so everyone could hear, "This is a bloody waste of time" or worse, "Let's get the hell out of here!" As he intended, Elizabeth would be embarrassed and would usually cast a hard glance at him, indicating he should keep quiet. Sometimes Elizabeth's reaction worked, but on most occasions Elizabeth would smile and the visit would come to a fairly abrupt end. Invariably impatient, Philip didn't seem to care whom he upset, even his own wife.

Easily bored, frustrated, and impetuous, Prince Philip has irritated many people, particularly officials. He will nearly always find fault when accompanying the Queen on official walkabouts, for example, when the Queen gently waves and smiles to those who have turned out to cheer her. He often loudly proclaims, "Get rid of some of these bloody police officers, no one can see us," or alternatively, he shouts, "There's no bloody police officers here. Get the Home Secretary."

Philip has been equally abrasive to those in senior positions in the royal palaces, not just servants. He would sometimes describe royal servants as "a load of arseholes" or "gormless twits" to their faces, knowing that he could get away with these insults because of his position. His coarse expletives, learned in the Royal Navy, have not earned him much respect.

At the same time, however, Philip has often been helpful to his wife, and on occasion they can be an enchanting double act.

Ronald Allison, a former Buckingham Palace press officer, recalled, "I've always admired the way the Duke supports the Queen. They are very close and understand each other perfectly when meeting the people in whatever part of the world. On an engagement together the Queen will be walking down one side and Prince Philip the other. She'll be quiet and smiling and he'll be cracking jokes and livening the atmosphere.

"I believe a good way of seeing how close a couple might be is their desire to share things. A frequent memory I have of Prince Philip is seeing him—if he's spotted something in the crowd—drawing the Queen's attention to it. 'Oh, look there, darling,' he'd say, making sure she had seen it. If you don't like someone very much you don't bother to point things out. You don't care whether they see things or not."

Despite the bad times, and with Philip Elizabeth has experienced many, some in the palace today still believe she needs her husband's constant support. "I dread to think what would happen if anything were to shorten his natural life," commented a bishop who has known both of them well for many years. "She would be absolutely shattered. I am not sure, even with her inner strength, that she would be able to recover."

Soon after becoming Queen, Elizabeth realized she had to find things to keep her mercurial, overactive husband from having too much time on his hands. She knew Philip was a man of action. Unable to keep still for a moment, he had to find a way of releasing his unbounded energy while engaging and challenging his intelligence and intellect. Boothroyd describes his energy as "numbing." Elizabeth also fully realized that, like his father, he was very much a ladies' man and he had the ego, the self-confidence, the good looks, and the natural sex appeal to make whatever conquests he desired. He would not let his natural attributes go to waste.

One of Elizabeth's first ideas about keeping Philip occupied was to put him in charge of modernizing Buckingham Palace, Windsor Castle, and Sandringham, as well as making him Chief Ranger of Windsor Great Park, four major tasks which gave him, in essence, a new career in estate management.

Philip came up with hundreds of new—some good, some zany, and some hopeless—ideas he wanted implemented immediately without discussion or debate. He refused to listen to the opinions of other people who had far greater experience, nor would he take advice. Given this approach, many of his innovations proved to be disasters. Whenever he's in charge, Philip becomes the captain of a ship in the middle of a battle, issuing orders from the bridge and demanding instant obedience. Often, he brushes obstacles aside with a scorn that appears totally arrogant and not very appealing. This approach may work well in the Royal Navy during wartime, but with peacetime civilians it is less effective.

Impatient with those who ran Buckingham Palace, and especially the Queen's advisers, Philip was determined to drag the monarchy into the twentieth century. He believed, sometimes correctly, that the old fogies who ran the Palace were the prime reason the British monarchy of the 1950s remained rooted in the nineteenth century. Philip wanted change, innovation, initiatives, and he worked hard to get Elizabeth to go along with his ideas.

Philip never recognized that Elizabeth herself was also rooted in the nineteenth century, despite the fact she was only a youthful twenty-six when she became Queen. She had lived the life of a cloistered princess, surrounded by royalty, residing in palaces and castles, cut off from the people, never mixing or meeting anyone who didn't first bow or curtsy to her. She had never gone shopping, never been to a market, never waited in line, never been on a crowded bus, train, or subway. Nor had Elizabeth walked through crowded city streets, rubbing shoulders with people. She didn't have the faintest idea how ordinary people lived in their homes. She had never had to do a day's work, never washed a dish or dusted or cleaned or even made a bed or a cup of coffee, let alone prepared a meal or done the laundry. She had no idea of the value of money—there had never been a need to know. Throughout her life she had been surrounded by servants and maids, living exactly the life of a princess in the court of Queen Victoria.

Philip first set about Buckingham Palace, marching through its miles of corridors inspecting everything, including the servants' quarters, the kitchens, the cellars, the bathrooms, the electrical system, and the plumbing, finding ways to modernize, if not revolutionize, the workings of an institution that had barely changed in over a hundred years.

He came up with a hundred and one ideas but found it impossible to implement all but a handful of them. "This bloody place needs a bomb underneath it," he would shout, "and so do most of the people who work here!" The staff would wince whenever Philip went on one of his "inspections," knowing full well it would end with yet more innovations and changes that none of them wanted. He complained one day in a loud voice so a number of senior courtiers would hear, "It's more difficult to get Prince Charles's cot from Windsor to Buckingham Palace than to move an army across the Rhine!"

A senior member of the Household recalled, "Prince Philip would walk briskly along the palace corridors, hands clasped behind his back to prevent round shoulders, long neck thrust forward, face inquisitive, frowning, aquiline, like a fierce quizzical eagle, snapping at servants, demanding answers to impossible questions. He was always challenging, sharp and, the staff believed, dangerous. But most of the time his bark was worse than his bite."

But his efforts to modernize Buckingham Palace, though not sweeping, did produce some results. False ceilings were installed; the central heating was eventually overhauled; rooms were painted in brighter colors. He brought in modern office equipment, like electric typewriters, streamlined the chain of command, and installed an intercom system which saved footmen and pages miles of walking every day. And he did win a cheer for one suggestion which was immediately implemented: that footmen should no longer have to powder their hair!

As was the custom in industry in the late 1950s, Philip decided to undertake a time-and-motion study in an effort to cut staff and make the palace run more efficiently. He called in Sir Basil Smallpiece, a successful British industrialist, and, after several weeks and a full report, about one hundred of the four hundred staff members who worked at Buck House were let go. Many of these were pensioned off because they had, in fact, passed pensionable age (sixty-five for men, sixty for women). Philip commented later: "I don't think it made any difference at all. There still seems far too many people doing far too little work."

A substantial proportion of palace staff are gay. For a good many years, a number of senior advisers as well as those whom the Queen Mother likes to surround herself with have been notoriously gay. The Queen Mum, still charming, delightful, and going strong in her nineties, enjoyed their sense of humor and appreciated their dedication to duty. Philip, on the other hand, was unhappy about having the palace peppered with homosexuals.

One day he noticed that a particular footman had been missing for some time and asked his page where he had gone.

"He was fired, Sir," came the reply.

Philip wanted to know why.

"I'm afraid he was found in bed with one of the housemaids, Sir," was the reply.

"And they sacked him!" an outraged Philip exclaimed. "The man should have been given a medal."

In his haste to create change he sometimes overstepped the mark. To brighten up the stuffy palace he "borrowed" some paintings he found in another part of the Royal Household and put them near the private suites. When Elizabeth saw what he had done, she was horrified. "Those belong to the state collection," she said. "You'll get us shot. We can't touch them."

Philip's next modernizing project was Windsor Castle, which, in the 1950s, was a freezing, drafty place in winter, having no central heating and only half a dozen or so electric fires in the entire castle. Heat came only from coal and wood fires, which were totally insufficient for heating for the huge rooms. Philip had wall lights installed as well as some central heating and a great many more electric fires, mainly in fireplaces. He also installed some modern bathrooms with hot water. So tiny was Elizabeth's original personal bathroom she could only climb into her bath from one end. As another innovation he replaced all the old, metal hot-water bottles—which were religiously put into beds each evening—with modern rubber ones. Philip also wanted to introduce electric blankets, but Elizabeth believed they would prove too expensive.

Philip had more success at Sandringham, in Norfolk, 120 miles north of London, a house owned privately by the Queen which she had inherited from her father. Buckingham Palace, on the other hand, is the property of the state. Philip decided Sandringham was to be run without pomp and ceremony, with no flunkies bowing and curtsying. Sandringham would be the country house where Elizabeth, Philip, and the children could relax and enjoy as an ordinary British family. He fired many of the staff, deciding that the family would "muck in" and sometimes cook and wash up and make tea themselves. He also decreed there would be no servants at table, not even a butler. Elizabeth, of course, had never experienced anything like it. At first she found it all "immense fun"—making tea, getting the children to help serve, and clearing away dishes. But not for long. Soon thereafter the servants returned. So Philip's only real successes with the family at Sandringham were new kitchens, the installation of a dishwasher, and having the family appear for breakfast instead of having it served in their rooms.

Philip went beyond trying to improve domestic arrangements and exerted his energies on efforts with larger implications. One successful project was to introduce modern farming techniques at the Queen's estates. At Sandringham he took a rather run-down farm and turned it into a modern, profit-making enterprise, and he did this despite mountains of official government red tape. The Queen owns three thousand acres which are not let to tenant farmers and which now produce pig for packaging bacon and sausage, turkeys for Christmas, and mushrooms and blackcurrants for market. Everything is now sold, usually at a profit. Before Philip set about reorganizing the farms to operate at a profit, the farm food was reserved for the royal kitchens or handed out to those living in royal houses or apartments. Even one of Elizabeth's favorite personal hobbies, the breeding of gundogs, is run as a profitable operation. At Windsor, Philip introduced efficient production of milk, cream, and free-range eggs. Most of this first-class food goes to Buckingham Palace for Elizabeth and her guests, as well as to a fortunate few senior courtiers.

In 1956 Philip launched an initiative to foster leadership, self-discipline, enterprise, and perseverance among young people from all backgrounds. As with everything he proposed at that time, Philip was not surprised when the Ministry of Education took a dim view. Some described his plan as "square." But he persevered with his program, which became known as the Duke of Edinburgh's Award Scheme.

Philip wanted to give young people, boys and girls from ages fourteen to twenty-three, a sense of purpose in their lives by developing in them a sense of service coupled with fitness. He has personally raised hundreds of thousands of dollars to ensure its success, and even today, this program is the only one that bears his name. Since its inception over two and a half million young people from fifty-five countries, all volunteers, have taken part from all walks of life, from the middle class to the poorest in the land, as well as those who have served time in remand homes, juvenile detention centers, and jails.

Bearing the imprint of Dr. Kurt Hahn, the German founder of Gordonstoun, the Award Scheme permits young people to tackle anything they wish as long as it is different from their ordinary life.

Some win awards, for example, for working a year in a mental hospital, trekking across fifty miles of country in the winter, clearing canals, or helping the sick, the disadvantaged, or the old. Some will win awards for learning to play the flute, passing a car maintenance course, or playing football. The intention is that young people should enjoy the program.

Philip still attends the six award ceremonies every year, still raises money for the program, and loves to talk about it to all the young people he meets. He has always been a great supporter of helping young people mature into well-disciplined, hardworking, responsible adults. Forty years later it is still going strong, and, whereas at the beginning most taking part were young men, the sexes are now evenly balanced. Prince Edward has taken over much of his father's work, but Philip still supplies a constant stream of ideas, advice, help, and encouragement.

Eleven volunteers, ten men and one woman, now constitute the Duke of Edinburgh's Award Scheme special projects group. Chaired by Prince Edward, the committee is a think tank whose function is to devise and run fund-raising events for the awards program. Big business and the government help financially, but most of the money is raised by the committee, by holding various events and through private donations.

Philip also originated a plan to improve Britain's industrial relations. In 1947 he also founded the National Playing Fields Association, and in 1961 he joined the World Wildlife Fund, operated for the protection of endangered species. Both have been hugely successful, in part due to Philip's drive and energy.

Throughout his life Philip has loved serving on committees and, in particular, chairing them. To many he is a very good chairman, but others say he is far too dominant and interfering, demanding to have his own way, rather than letting the committee decide democratically.

He participated in Britain's Automobile Association activities for many years, spouting views which usually brought short shrift from motorists. He has been heavily involved in polo and carriage-driving committees as well as education and universities, housing, and the environment.

"I happen to find myself in rather an individual position," Philip explains. "I am involved in the activities of a great many groups but the sheer number of these groups makes it impossible to belong completely to any one of them. Furthermore in many cases my involvement is as an active or titular head, and that in itself tends both to isolation and objectivity."

Despite a lifetime spent accompanying the Queen on official royal engagements across Britain and around the world as well as his involvement in many causes and committees, Prince Philip has always found plenty of time to indulge his primary passion, women.

The pursuit of women has probably been Philip's principal interest from his days as a young naval officer during World War II, through his polo-playing period and well into his sixties, if not his seventies. Even today, at most functions Philip can be found chatting to one or two of the most attractive women in the room, flirting with his smile and his piercing blue eyes, and laughing and joking.

Two of the women with whom he had affairs early in his life wrote books about Philip. Both concealed their affairs with him while protesting their innocence so strongly that many readers took it for granted both had shared his bed from time to time. The first was Queen Alexandra of Yugoslavia, with whom he had a two-year affair, and the second, the cabaret artist Helène Cordet, the daughter of the Foufounis family, old friends of his mother's who lived nearby during the family's exile in Paris.

Helène remembers that she and Philip used to play doctors and nurses together as children. She also recalls their playing a game called "The King, the Servant, and the Pig." She said, "Philip always volunteered to play the pig. No one wanted to play the king. Philip would refuse to play the king, saying he feared he would have his head chopped off."

Philip loved pigs. At Helène Cordet's home in Marseilles, the ten-year-old Philip loved to spend time with the pigs, walking them around, mucking and feeding them, and even cleaning out the pigsties.

Queen Alexandra's book hints at jealousy as well as strong resentment toward Dickie Mountbatten, suggesting he interfered in her affair with Philip. The lovely Alexandra, his cousin and a member of the Greek royal family who eventually married King Peter of Yugoslavia, met Philip when they were both seventeen. Two years later in 1940, after Italy invaded Greece, their love blossomed. Alexandra wrote, "Suddenly Philip arrived in Athens gay, debonair, confident..."

Philip was to spend a considerable amount of time in Athens, almost always staying with Alexandra's family. She told stories of air raids: "In the evenings the family often gathered either at the Palace with the King or at one of our homes. We never knew when Philip would join us. When the air-raids began we were supposed to go to a shelter...but instead we went to the roof-garden and watched.... Philip contributed a running commentary amid the bark of ack-ack guns, the flutter of searchlights and the roar of bombers."

Philip pursued Alexandra relentlessly, seeking her out after she and her family fled to the comparative safety of Cairo. She wrote, "Philip soon tracked us to Shepherd's Hotel. In his little wasp of a car we went out to the Ghezira Club, swam in the pool or just talked through the long, lazy afternoons when he was off duty. We explored the old bazaars and the magnificent botanical gardens together."

As if by accident, Philip even turned up in Cape Town on board a troopship just weeks after Alexandra and her family had sought refuge in South Africa. The affair was on again. Back in London the following year Philip was a constant visitor to the family house and dated Alexandra frequently. She wrote: "I best remember Philip on furlough, Philip dining and dancing and confiding." They spent weekends at the country home of their cousin Marina. Despite her denials Alexandra was one of Philip's earliest serious passions. He thought she was wonderful.

Helène Cordet, née Foufounis, a petite, attractive, vivacious girl, was his childhood sweetheart. She would become a well-known nightclub singer and television personality of some fame in postwar Britain. Helène had two children out of wedlock, Max and Louise, an act of courage at a time when the middle class of Britain frowned on such "antisocial" behavior. Most middle-class, churchgoing men and women in postwar Britain considered an illegitimate child an absolute disgrace to the family and believed that as a consequence the young mother could never find a husband.

Helène and Philip spent a good deal of time together in Britain during and after the war, and they have remained good friends through the following decades. Today many who knew Philip and

Helène during the war years still believe Philip fathered both Max and Louise, and most certainly Max, although Helène has always denied she ever had an affair with Philip or that either of her children are his. Perhaps the most telling fact is that his great friend, Mike Parker, has never denied Philip's paternity of Max.

Helène Cordet married twice. She first married when she was twenty (Philip just sixteen). She proclaimed happily, "Philip was the best man at my first wedding. He also gave me away. My mother didn't realize someone had to give away the bride so Philip volunteered. He was wonderful." That marriage ended in divorce. Her second marriage took place during the war; the groom was a French Air Force officer, Marcel Boisot, who deserted her just months afterward.

The relationship between Helène and Philip has always remained close. Philip helped pay for her son's education—at Gordonstoun, the school he attended and to which, in turn, he sent Charles, Andrew, and Edward. Philip suggested Gordonstoun to Helène, and there is no evidence that Philip ever helped finance the education of anyone else's children. Philip's normal rule is to keep in touch with his various godsons only until they reach the age of twenty-one; after that they are on their own. However, to this day, Prince Philip still keeps in touch with Helène's son Max, now a successful fifty-year-old businessman living in China. He even saw Max when visiting China on an official royal visit with the Queen and disappeared mysteriously for some hours after taking the traditional walk along part of the Great Wall.

Helène Cordet still keeps in touch with Philip and has occasionally visited Buckingham Palace, taking tea or having a meal there with him. But not when Elizabeth is present. She has met Elizabeth only once, a very brief encounter. Elizabeth smiled sweetly and said, "Oh, I've heard so much about you. How nice to meet you at last." There was no further conversation.

Throughout her life, the ever-faithful Helène has always defended Philip, frequently commenting in her lovely French accent, "Of course he likes women. He is like his father was. I know he has this reputation. But if a man doesn't look at a woman, what happens? Let us not forget that some people say other things, completely the contrary, and that is terrible. What the hell can he do to have a decent reputation? If he doesn't look at women, they say he likes men. He likes women. So what? It's a good thing."

In October 1956, Elizabeth, then thirty, and Philip, thirty-six, were approaching their ninth wedding anniversary and finding life testy and difficult. Rumors circulated, particularly in the continental press, that their marriage was going through a rocky patch. The Queen realized that Philip needed to get away from London. It had already been decided that Philip should open the 1956 Olympic Games in Melbourne. Now, Philip proposed that he visit many other Commonwealth countries on the return trip. Elizabeth, fed up with his aggressive attitude, glum appearance, and bad moods, readily agreed. He was therefore scheduled to leave Melbourne on the Royal Yacht HMS *Britannia* and return via New Zealand, Malaya, The Gambia, Antartica, the Galápagos Islands, and the Falklands. It was a mammoth tour. Altogether he would travel 39,000 miles and be gone four months.

As his private secretary and equerry, friend and confidant, Commander Mike Parker went along too. They were determined to relive, once again, their youthful good times as wild bachelors in the Royal Navy. Philip and Mike Parker were known to be very much alike and to have enjoyed life together during the war and in and around London ever since. They went to parties, traveled the world, played squash and badminton, and often ate together. During his four-month trip Philip missed not only his ninth wedding anniversary, but also Christmas and the winter break with Elizabeth and the children at Sandringham. Nor did he return to be at the Queen's side during the 1956 war over the Suez Canal when Britain, France, and Israel joined forces and attacked Nasser's Egypt.

But Philip did send his wife two dozen of her favorite white roses on their wedding anniversary, and he did talk with her and Charles and Anne on the radio-telephone from the Falkland Islands on Christmas Day. The future president of the World Wildlife Fund also went crocodile shooting and bagged one with his first bullet. Philip then arranged for the six-foot length of skin to be sent back to Buckingham Palace, to be tanned, cured, and made into beautiful leather gifts for the royal ladies.

As Philip and Mike Parker sailed back to Britain, newspapers speculated daily on the state of the Queen's marriage. All the signs pointed to a crisis. Word had leaked out that Mike Parker's wife Eileen was suing for divorce, and now the newspapers sensed Elizabeth's marriage was in trouble.

Speculation about the marriage was so intense that Buckingham Palace chose to issue a denial, an action totally without precedent. Elizabeth's Private Secretary, Sir Michael Adeane, gave a statement to the press which said, in its entirety: "It is quite untrue that there is any rift between the Queen and the Duke of Edinburgh." Naturally, such a statement, delivered with the full authority of the Queen and her most senior advisers, only fueled rumors.

At a Guildhall lunch to mark his return from the long world tour, Philip tried to curry favor with the public by suggesting that his lengthy absence from his family was an act of duty and service to the Crown. He told the assembled guests, "I believe there are some things for which it is worthwhile making personal sacrifices, and I believe that the British Commonwealth is one of those things and I, for one, am prepared to sacrifice a good deal if by doing so, I can advance its well-being by even a small degree."

Then Parker's solicitors issued a statement that said, "We are authorized to state that Lt. Commander Parker has tendered his resignation as private secretary to the Duke of Edinburgh and this has been accepted. The existing circumstances of his marriage make it impossible for him to carry on with his present occupation."

At the time it was suggested that Parker could not remain as Philip's secretary because of his impending divorce. Not so. At that time the Prime Minister himself, Sir Anthony Eden, was a divorced man who had remarried. And another senior Cabinet minister was also divorced.

The newspapers, believing that Parker was taking all the flak, in effect covering up for problems within the royal marriage, scented blood. PARKER OF THE PALACE QUITS; GRIM DUKE SEES OFF HIS FRIEND, PARKER, screamed the headlines. THE DUKE'S FRIEND IN SENSATION. Over the radio-telephone Elizabeth urged Parker to stay on and so, of course, did Philip.

Philip let it be known that he blamed the press for applying so much pressure that Parker felt impelled to quit. In fact it was not the press, however, but the Palace courtiers—members of the Household—who in secret made the decisions that ended Parker's close relationship with Philip.

For some time the Palace had worried that Mike Parker was a bad influence on Philip and feared that once the press began to dig deeper, they might unravel the secrets of Philip's extramarital affairs. By leaking stories to the press that focused the limelight on Mike Parker, Elizabeth's senior advisers believed they could perhaps save Philip's reputation, and paper over the cracks in Elizabeth's marriage. They also kept Elizabeth in the dark about Philip's sexual adventures, since they did not wish to add to her marital problems by telling her everything they knew.

Despite the headlines, however, there was no need for Parker to resign at all unless he and Philip believed revelations of their escapades together might emerge which were so sensational as to bring discredit and embarrassment to Elizabeth, and the monarchy. And the two of them had much to hide.

After his boisterous wartime experiences, Philip simply could not settle down to a boring life confined to Buckingham Palace. He welcomed Mike Parker's suggestion that they join a select secret group, the Thursday Club, so named because the few members always met on a Thursday. The idea was to bring the weekend closer and have a real bash, usually at Wheelers, the fish restaurant in Old Compton Street, Soho, then the heart of London's red-light district. In those days, walking down Old Compton Street invariably meant being propositioned by any number of prostitutes.

Philip and Parker joined shortly after World War II, and Philip was still a member twelve years later when the Thursday Club, fed up with bad publicity and hints of scandal, dissolved itself but reemerged later in Kensington as the secret Monday Club.

Philip had been introduced to the club by his cousin David, the Marquess of Milford Haven, who had remained a close friend since their schooldays in the 1930s. Other club members included the editor of *Tatler* magazine, then an upmarket periodical for the aristocracy; the London correspondent of the *New York Post*; a brilliant young Tory politician, Ian McLeod, who was to become Chancellor of the Exchequer; Peter Ustinov, the well-known actor and radio and TV celebrity; the harmonica player Larry Adler; a British TV personality, Gilbert Harding; and British actors such as David Niven and James Robertson Justice.

Many Thursday Club members came from the press, yet they kept the club a secret from the reading public for seven years. Press members included Arthur Christiansen, editor of the *Daily Express*, the paper Philip was to describe as "that bloody awful rag"; Frank Owen, the legendary editor of the *Daily Mail*; Harold Keeble, a senior executive who worked on several national dailies; Lord Glenavy, better known as the famous columnist Patrick Campbell; and writer Compton Mackenzie.

There were others. One was the infamous Stephen Ward, son of a canon at Rochester Cathedral, a well-known osteopath and portrait artist, who was to cause the biggest political scandal to rock postwar Britain; the other was the famous photographer Baron Nahum. Both men were heavily involved in dubious sexual activities.

Accompanying Philip most Thursdays was Mike Parker. The Thursday Club was all-male, and needed to be. As well as enjoying good food and excellent wine during the three- and four-hour lunches, members would make amusing and risqué speeches, tell stories, usually dirty jokes. Much of the talk would be lewd, the jokes usually sexually explicit, if not plain dirty. The visitors' book was filled with vulgar humor. But the members loved the informal luncheons. There was much loud laughter and revelry. The club survived a remarkable twelve years.

One emblematic incident involved Prince Bernhard of the Netherlands, who was invited one Thursday to attend the lunch. When Bernhard was leaving, a slightly drunk Prince Philip knelt down on the floor, made a lavish, slavelike bow, and said, "Give my regards to Her Imperial Majesty." Philip's theatrics were significant because Bernhard, too, was consort to his wife, Queen Juliana, and shared with Philip the predicament of always being number two, not existing constitutionally, and always having to walk the prescribed two paces behind his wife. This spur-of-the-moment joke spoke volumes about Philip's deeper feelings toward his role.

Sometimes the club members, including Philip, would leave Wheelers and move on to David Milford Haven's luxurious apartment in Grosvenor Square, near the American embassy. Here the fun would usually begin with card playing and then, when the drink had flowed for a good while, girls would be brought in. The eight or so club members would start betting on the women in games with names like "Chase the Bitch" and "Find the Lady." The winner would then go off to one of the adjoining bedrooms with whichever woman he fancied, to the cheers of those left behind. Sometimes the bedroom door would deliberately be left open so that those who wanted could watch the couple having sex.

Elizabeth learned of the nefarious Thursday Club through the tabloids, reading a number of scurrilous stories hinting that Philip and Mike Parker were partying and womanizing wherever they went. She desperately wanted to trust Philip and asked him about the stories. Philip just dismissed them with a wave of the hand as "nonsense." He also suggested that the stories were part of the continuing campaign by those who had opposed their marriage. His argument made sense, and Elizabeth wanted to believe him.

For reassurance, Elizabeth turned to her maid and great confidante, Bobo. Bobo did reassure her, dismissing the stories as "newspaper rubbish" and "tittle-tattle." One of Bobo's famous remarks was "You would think there were more important things for them to write about," and she would often leave it at that.

When more detailed accusations against Philip were made, Bobo would tell her Lilibet, "Don't you worry about such things. We all know that boys will be boys; they will get up to some mischief." More often than not, the naive and trusting Elizabeth would accept Bobo's advice and forget the incident.

Elizabeth, who knew nothing of the opposite sex and had never even had a teenage romance, believed Philip's description of the Thursday Club as just a gentleman's luncheon club that had begun in 1946. It was an occasion for a few chaps to relax, tell a few stories, and have a good meal once in a while. He went along for the relaxation and to enjoy men's company; it was just like being back in the wardroom, aboard ship.

Mike Parker, of course, totally supported his friend and boss in 1956, saying, "We've been given the reputation of being wild, but the truth is that we enjoyed fun and going round with people who knew what was going on. The Thursday Club was a great sounding base, and the idea that it was a drunken orgy was absolute rubbish. People got very merry but never drunk. As far as being wild, not guilty. As far as hanging around women, not guilty."

Parker's first wife, Eileen, wrote *Step Aside for Royalty*, published in 1982, in which she revealed that Philip and her husband habitually slipped out of the palace at night on clandestine jaunts under the pseudonyms Murgatroyd and Winterbottom. She did not reveal what the two got up to, but she had opened a Pandora's box, leaving readers to their own imaginations. Aware of her husband's steamy affair and of the scandalous parties hosted by the Thursday Club, Eileen Parker wrote: "There had been a number of people in high places before Michael whose marriages had ended and who had continued with their careers. My first instinct was to blame sheer panic for Mike's abrupt decision. But on reflection I started to wonder if his resignation was a smoke screen for something, or somebody else."

When asked about the book's allegations, Philip commented, "I had no idea that Eileen had written a book. Now that you have mentioned it, I have no intention whatever of reading it."

One of Philip's close friends was the legendary society photographer Baron Nahum, who reveled in his reputation for bizarre sexual proclivities. He and Philip were, for a time, both on the organizing committee of the Thursday Club. Baron had a withered arm, which forced him to crouch crablike when taking photographs and made him look somewhat sinister. Philip had met Baron through Uncle Dickie, who had wangled Baron the job of royal photographer. It was he who took the wedding pictures of Elizabeth and Philip.

Baron was famous not only for his outlandish dinner parties, but also for very intimate private parties, held at his apartment, at which anything went. The guest list was kept secret, and Philip and Mike Parker were occasionally invited. There was sadomasochism, men whipping girls and girls whipping men, bondage, girls who served drinks and food dressed only in masonic aprons, as well as gays and lesbians and group sex. It was no accident that one of Baron's friends was Stephen Ward, osteopath to the rich and famous who also provided girls, mistresses, and prostitutes.

Philip's passionate interest in polo also brought him into frequent contact with many lovely, beautiful women. As a result his name became linked with numerous women and rumors of affairs were rife. In the late 1950s and early 1960s Philip was playing polo two and three times a week, usually at Windsor Great Park and Cowdray, but also at polo tournaments that always ended with champagne and parties and, often, a dip in a pool. Most of the women he met were married to other players. Elizabeth enjoyed attending polo with the players' wives at Windsor on Sunday afternoons, after lunch at the castle. Occasionally, she would invite the players to Windsor Castle for a swim in the pool and she, too, would change into a one-piece bathing suit and join the men.

Life on the polo circuit seemed to lead to romance. One celebrated casual romance that began at a polo match involved Susie Ferguson, wife of Major Ron Ferguson and mother of the irrepressible Sarah. Undoubtedly, the Ferguson marriage had been shaky, and the beautiful Susie left Major Ron for the handsome Argentine polo player and wealthy landowner, Hector Barrantes, because she could no longer put up with her husband's philandering.

One wealthy patron of a number of polo teams during many seasons in the sixties and seventies recalled, "Philip undoubtedly had affairs with a number of polo wives. How many I don't know, but at least a dozen or more during those years. It was a well-known fact. I would watch him chatting to them after play, perhaps over champagne or a beer. He had them eating out of his hand. They were of course attracted to the macho image of the game, and Philip was always a strikingly handsome man. In his polo gear, even more so. His affairs were well known and yet, to his credit, he was most discreet and, it must be said, the women have behaved impeccably, never kissing and telling."

Philip's favorite tournament was at St. Memse, near Orly airport, held yearly in the 1960s, usually at the end of May. The host was Robert de Balkany, a Rumanian of humble origins who, after a Yale education, made a fortune from real estate and was once married to Maria Gabriello, daughter of Italy's ex-king Umberto. De Balkany had owned a beautiful château with a cobbled yard with stables on two sides. On his estate he built a great polo field where he kept fifty ponies, attended by about two dozen grooms.

A millionaire who attended over the years said, "Four or five teams and their patrons would be invited for the weekend, and I saw Prince Philip there on a number of occasions. Before arriving one would be phoned and asked if we were bringing a lady or would prefer to take pot luck. There was nothing crude. The ambience was relaxed and wonderful, the food was exquisite and the wines superb. The parties were held in this fabulous bar and large room, and we would be given bedrooms above this long hall. There was also an enormous shower room where everyone could shower at the same time and, of course a number of individual bathrooms."

He added, "The ladies on hand were wonderful and always so very sexy and sophisticated. Philip used to enjoy himself, as did everyone who attended. The Queen certainly never accompanied him on those weekends, and I don't remember him ever arriving with a lady. I think he preferred to take pot luck. As far as I remember he spent a lot of time chatting to a number of the ladies. It was all so discreet. I remember that Princess Grace Kelly used to attend the weekends occasionally and would often chat with Philip. But she was only interested in one man, David Niven, the actor. They had a remarkable relationship; David Niven was undoubtedly one of the great loves of her life, she adored him. And when you saw them together it was magic.

"The young ladies who were invited on their own for the weekend were known, of course, most of them friends of friends. The patrons would arrive on Friday, the players on Saturday, and we would fly home on Sunday evening. It was the perfect polo weekend."

Besides the polo wives, there were a number of well-known women with whom Philip became deeply involved. Two of the best known were the actress Merle Oberon and British TV personality Katie Boyle; with both women Philip had passionate affairs which went on for a number of years. Dickie Mountbatten introduced Philip to Merle Oberon in 1956. She was forty-five, ten years Philip's senior, but she looked like she was in her twenties. Petite, with dark, smiling, almond-shaped eyes, an olive complexion, and an engaging personality, she was close to Philip's idea of the perfect woman. From the moment he met her he was smitten, and thought her one of the most beautiful women he had ever met.

Merle Oberon, who died in 1979, was a remarkable woman. Born a half-caste in the slums of Bombay in the days of the Raj, she was determined to end her life of poverty quickly. Her fine features and natural beauty helped, and she told the world she was an army officer's daughter, born in Tasmania. (She took the secret of her humble background to her grave.) In reality, Estelle Merle O'Brien Thompson was the daughter of a mechanical engineer from Darlington, England, and a nurse who was part Irish, part Sinhalese, and with some Maori blood. Her parents nicknamed the lovely Merle "Queenie." While

Merle was still a child, her father deserted his family to return to England, leaving her doting mother to raise the girl by herself.

Merle Oberon got her first film part in 1929, and her career took off in the 1930s after she met Alexander Korda, one of Britain's great moviemakers. They became lovers and eventually married, but like many movie marriages it was not to last. In all, Merle married four times but always kept a soft spot in her heart for her blond prince, Philip.

Secret dates were organized and Philip and Merle became lovers. Merle had designed a magnificent house in Mexico, overlooking Acapulco Bay. A built-in waterfall cascaded toward the swimming pool by the sea, and exotic flowers filled the beautiful, large garden. She named the house Ghalal, the Mexican word for *love*.

At the beginning of the sixties, Merle lived in this house in Acapulco with her husband, the multi-millionaire Italian-Mexican Bruno Pagliai, whom she had married in July 1957. Lord Mountbatten visited with his private secretary John Barratt for a two-week holiday, and Philip accompanied him. Philip and Merle often ate alone under a canopy of tall trees overlooking the bay, one of the most romantic places in the world. When she decided to sell her home in 1973, she commented "Many people are going to be sad about me selling the house because we threw some wonderful parties. When Philip heard the news he phoned to say he felt a pang in his heart at the thought the house was to be sold."

According to John Barratt, "There was obviously great sexual chemistry between the two, and Philip spent most of the time in her company. It seemed her husband was away. At night we would often leave the two of them alone and they would go for walks together in the moonlit gardens. It was a most romantic atmosphere. Mountbatten and I simply assumed they were lovers. They certainly acted as though they were."

Merle Oberon and Philip met quite frequently after that. On one occasion Philip was aboard the Royal Yacht *Britannia* when it sailed into Acapulco Bay. He ordered a five-gun salute fired in the direction of Miss Oberon's house, giving further rise to speculation about an affair.

Katie Boyle, a beautiful blonde seven years younger than Philip, was another passionate love. Born Caterina Irene Imperiali di Francavilla, she arrived in London in 1946, a fugitive after the collapse of fascist Italy. Her mother launched her into London society, and within two years she had married Captain Richard Boyle of the Irish Guards. In 1951 she met and fell in love with her second husband, Greville Bayliss, a wealthy stockbroker, Lloyd's underwriter, and a racehorse owner. They were married in 1955.

But it was to Prince Philip that Katie lost her heart, and the two would spend days together in a Belgrave Square apartment Philip would use for his amours. (He also used another apartment in South Audley Street; various people had keys to these places, which were organized by Mike Parker.) A longtime friend of Philip's, and about his same age, recalled, "Philip's affair with Katie Boyle was very steamy. She was, so I understand, a most passionate woman and they had the most extraordinary times together. When they were able to be together in private, it was, so I understand, nonstop sex. He loved it."

A polo friend of Philip's recalls that on one occasion when Katie Boyle entertained Philip at her London home, she received an urgent message that her husband had returned home unexpectedly and was on his way to the apartment. Philip rapidly exited through the apartment's back entrance just as Katie's husband put the key in the front door.

In the beginning of 1962 Philip traveled 58,000 miles through South America, visiting more than a dozen countries. The official records of that remarkable trip, officially sanctioned to "stimulate British commercial relations," should have been released in 1993, under the government's thirty-year rule, but the Foreign Office has instructed them to remain sealed until 2023. A Foreign Office spokesman said, "The tendency is to release all papers after thirty years, unless things are terribly sensitive."

The trip was a roisterous affair.

Just before Philip arrived in Argentina, the Peronists had won a landslide victory. The military was apoplectic, and all Buenos Aires realized a military coup was imminent. Because of Prince Philip's visit the military agreed to postpone the coup until he had left the country. The British Embassy was informed. Philip was greeted by flag-waving, cheering crowds, managed to play a few games of polo in Argentina, and spent evenings being entertained in the capital. An Argentine polo player commented, "All the beautiful women of

Buenos Aires were at Philip's feet."

Philip's next stop was La Concepción, then the center of Argentina's polo-mad aristocrats, for three days of rest, recuperation, polo, and partying. His hosts were the Blaquier family, the epitome of Argentine high society, combining historical and social credentials with great wealth.

In the early 1960s, La Concepción was owned by Malena Blaquier, a beautiful, stylish widow in her early forties, following the death of her husband Silvestre in a plane crash. Malena was the social megastar of Argentina who threw the most sought-after parties of the social set. She happily agreed to be Philip's hostess for three days and gave him the run of the estate.

The enchanting Malena had an outrageous reputation, and she and Philip spent the three days enjoying La Concepción's famed entertainments. During the day Philip enjoyed polo and lazing around the swimming pool with his hostess Malena; at night, walks through the warm summer evenings, dinners, barbecues, grand balls, midnight swims. "For most of the time Malena was at his side," recalled a guest. So enchanted was Philip that he stayed an extra day at La Concepción.

As a result, the scheduled military coup was in progress and tanks were on the streets as Philip's motorcade made its way to Buenos Aires airport. Such a detail would not normally induce the Foreign Office to insist on concealing the state papers for a further thirty years. The real reason remains a mystery, although it is accepted that Philip is involved.

Details of his long tour are sparse. Most British newspapers at the time, though recognizing his failings, praised him for his flag-waving trip. As the *News of the World* reported in April 1962, "His enemies say he is arrogant, overbearing and has an exaggerated idea of his role in the Monarchy. His friends describe him as loyal, highly intelligent, hard-working, with a deep desire to do the job to the very best of his ability."

The editorial continued, "His friends say he has travelled the world showing the flag. His enemies regard these trips as junkets, highly relished by someone they still regard as an extravagant playboy."

Philip's "bachelor" life came very close to being exposed back home. The man who terrified many wayward husbands was Stephen Ward, who was at the center of the Profumo scandal of the early sixties. Ward, who had been trained as an osteopath in America, became a minor celebrity among the rich and famous for successfully treating their back problems. His list of patients included Philip's cousin, David Milford Haven, Winston Churchill, Averell Harriman, Danny Kaye, and Elizabeth Taylor. But secret areas of Stephen Ward's life were to electrify the nation.

Ward, then in his fifties, would bring pretty young women, some of them call girls, to Cliveden, home of Lord Astor, for weekends of sex and revelry. Ward had been lent a cottage on the estate and would frequently visit during the summer. A talented portrait painter of some repute, Ward was granted the rare privilege of an exhibition at Leggatt's, the Queen's personally authorized art dealers, under royal patronage. Ward's subjects included Labour leader Hugh Gaitskell, Prime Minister Harold Macmillan, Cabinet Minister Duncan Sandys, Lord Boothby, Douglas Fairbanks, and Sophia Loren. As a result Ward went on to paint the Duke of Kent, Princess Margaret, Lord Snowdon, the Duke of Gloucester and, of course, Prince Philip. Ward was on first-name terms with everyone who attended the parties, though they didn't realize that he was the supplier of the enthusiastic young "amateur" hookers.

The nubile girls, including the infamous Christine Keeler and Mandy Rice-Davies, then teenagers, would serve food and drinks to the gentlemen and indulge whatever sexual kicks the Cliveden set requested. Occasionally, Philip attended, but never the Queen.

A City millionaire who attended three Cliveden weekend parties in the early sixties said: "I remember standing by the swimming pool one lovely summer's evening, and this attractive young girl came up to me wearing nothing but a maid's white hat and a tiny apron which did not even cover her pubic hair. Her breasts and everything else were naked. She asked me what I wanted to drink. It was in fact Mandy Rice-Davies. A little later another girl, dark-haired, came out to announce that dinner was served. She was wearing just a little hat and long thigh-high black boots and nothing else whatsoever. In her hand she carried a long whip. Very sexy. And that was Christine Keeler.

"About a dozen men were at dinner and about six or seven girls would serve the wine and the food, the girls virtually naked. It was after dinner that the fun and games began and, of course, most of the girls would end up in bed with one or two of the men. It was accepted practice. The girls would be well paid, I suppose, but I never saw any money change hands. I suspected that for most of the time they did it for fun. They reveled in the champagne, high life."

At one or two of these weekend parties for the rich and famous, John Profumo, then Tory war minister, met Christine Keeler. They had an affair. At the same time, she also had a secret affair with the Soviet naval attaché to Britain, Captain Yevgeny Ivanov, who had also attended parties at Cliveden. In a sensational newspaper article, in 1963, Keeler, for a substantial sum of money, confessed that Stephen Ward had urged her to obtain from Profumo the delivery date of U.S. warheads to the West German army. Nuclear warheads had in fact been in Germany since 1958, according to a secret NATO document, but U.S. officers in Bonn were in charge of them, not the German army. Ward's request to Keeler for information was made at a time when War Secretary Profumo was discussing in the House of Commons the matter of who should be in command of the warheads.

Ward maintained he had become involved with top-level espionage in an effort to stave off a possible nuclear war at the time of the Cuban missile crisis of 1962. Three days after Keeler's bombshell story hit the headlines, Ivanov, who was known to MI6 as a Soviet spy, fled to Moscow, never to return to Britain. Ivanov died in January 1994, a disgraced and alcoholic former secret agent. KGB chiefs never forgave him for his lack of discretion in compromising Britain's War Minister.

A bon vivant and multimillionaire of Italian descent, Profumo had married the ballet dancer Valerie Hobson. He first tried to bribe Christine Keeler to remain silent about their affair, and then he stood up in the House of Commons and denied he had ever had sex with her. He called on Prime Minister Harold Macmillan to tell him Keeler's story was untrue. An angry Ward was determined the truth should come out and began informing London society that Profumo was lying. The establishment decided Ward had gone too far and, in an effort to silence him, arranged for him to be arrested and charged with obtaining illegal earnings from prostitution. Ward's arrest failed to stop the rumors, and two months later Profumo confessed.

Eventually, Ward stood trial for living off immoral earnings, and Keeler, as well as three other call girls, testified that they had given part of their earnings to Ward. Despite the fact that many titled people, a number of Cabinet ministers, and members of the establishment knew him well, no one would speak in Ward's defense. That hurt Ward. He overdosed on barbiturates while en route from jail to court on the very day the jury was to announce its verdict. He never recovered consciousness or heard that he had been found guilty. He would have received about fourteen years in jail.

Since then, suggestions have been made that Ward did not commit suicide but was murdered by Britain's security services, fearful that he might tell all at a later stage about his involvement with MI5 and MI6. Removing him once and for all would not only save the reputation of the security services, but also the good names of many of Britain's rich and famous. At the time, Prime Minister Macmillan wrote in his diary, "Partly by the blackmailing statements of the call girls and partly by Soviet agents exploiting the position, more than half the Cabinet were being accused of perversion, homosexuality and the like." Macmillan went to the grave believing the entire Profumo affair was engineered by the Soviets to remove one of Britain's foremost pro-nuclear ministers.

Elizabeth knew every detail of the scandal from reading the facts in her dispatch boxes and in the newspapers, as the story unfolded. Elizabeth never put all the blame on Profumo, preferring to believe that his only sin was to be found out, not that he had been living an adulterous, scandalous, sexual life with young prostitutes and thereby putting the national security at risk. Indeed, Elizabeth chose to remain on friendly terms with Profumo, and many years later was smiling happily with him when she awarded him a medal, Commander of the British Empire, for charitable work for London's poor.

Some suggest that Elizabeth is incapable of seeing the bad side of anyone's character, that she always gives people the benefit of the doubt, no matter what the judgment of their peers or even of the courts. She also seems to believe that much of life is simply bad luck in being caught out and staunchly believes no one would deliberately put at risk their marriage, their reputation, or in Profumo's case, national security. Perhaps this blind spot results from her knowing so few people well in her life. Those she has known well—her family, her few close friends, and her advisers—she implicitly trusts and believes will always tell her the truth.

Rumors surrounding Philip's alleged affairs with a number of women continued to be the stuff of gossip, though the newspapers were careful never to reveal such tantalizing stories. Sensibly, perhaps, Philip did not confine his search for members of the fair sex to Britain; indeed he seemed to prefer to play away from home, as far away as possible from London, Elizabeth, and anyone who might recognize him.

Occasionally, Philip attended the notorious wild Roman sex parties of the late sixties on which Fellini based his film *La Dolce Vita*. Between one hundred and one hundred and fifty people would be invited to the Palazzo Borganza, a perfect setting for sensational parties, on the first Monday of each month for most of the year. The invitation list read like a Who's Who of the international jet set, people who wanted to enjoy their lives to the ultimate and had the money and the connections to do so. Most of the guests were Italian, French, and American financiers, bankers, socialites, as well as international polo players, tennis stars, and those who had the money to fly to Rome once a month just for a party; many well-known Americans attended, such as Harry Winston and Revlon's Charlie Robson, as well as the Agnellis and a few of the European royals like Prince Philip; the Sicilian Massimo brothers were involved.

A French millionaire who went to a few parties recalled, "I was totally taken aback the first party I attended. I had heard rumors of the goings-on but wow, they were fantastic. There were really two parties going on, the one for men only which was strictly a stag party, and the other for men and women. Sometimes a group of gays would hold their own party upstairs.

"Everyone wore dinner dress and about fifty or sixty men would be chatting and drinking cocktails or champagne waiting for dinner. Just before dinner a bevy of perhaps fifty beautiful young women would walk down the central stairway. They were naked except for outrageous hats, and sometimes masks.

"They would go into the dining room and disappear. Before dinner the men would be invited to take off their trousers and leave them, walking into dinner immaculately dressed, but with no trousers. They would sit down to dinner at this magnificent table, and hidden beneath the cloth were the girls, who spent twenty minutes or so taking care of the men. Outrageous but wonderful!

"After dinner there was gambling. Roulette, blackjack, chemin de fer, poker, whatever; well organized and very civilized. And, naturally, the champagne and wine would flow.

"At the end of the evening the girls would reappear. This was the Rome Olympic competition. Twelve girls, all naked, would lie down on the floor in the beautiful drawing room, and the men would be invited to lay bets, not on the girls but on the men. The competition was to see which man could have full intercourse with all the girls without ejaculating, and, of course, the girls were encouraged to really make love, to be seductive and vigorous in their lovemaking. And each man had to stay with each girl for seven minutes.

"It was hilarious. Most of the men failed after two or three girls, and I hardly ever saw one man complete the task. To enter the competition each man had to put a thousand dollars into the kitty. Whoever completed making love to all twelve girls first won the jackpot. Usually twenty to thirty men took part. At the same time, however, tens of thousands of dollars were wagered on the competition by those simply watching. The trick was to select a man who was not very well endowed and not very young. Experience told. I actually won the pool a couple of times. Today it sounds dreadful but it was great fun. Those parties in Rome had style; they really were the Dolce Vita."

At the end of the evening, after more drinking and hilarity, the girls would join some of the visiting men, either staying the night in one of the many bedrooms or in the visitors' hotels.

The festivities ended in the summer of 1969, after one of the girls who had attended the party was found dead outside. She had indulged in a great deal of intercourse and had died from an overdose of drugs. When the police discovered some of the names of the other guests, the possibility of a scandal finished everything.

Similar parties were also held at Estoril in Portugal, and that too attracted many jet-setters. But these also ceased at about the same time as the Rome parties after a young fisherman's son was found dead on the beach, having been raped. The host was the King of Italy, and the British military attaché to Portugal was recalled immediately because he had attended the party.

Prince Philip is known to have attended at least a couple of the Rome parties, but there is no record of his ever participating in the frolics. Nor is there any record of his attending the parties at Estoril.

With his pal, Mike Parker, Philip sometimes visited the infamous Directors Club in London's Duke's Yard, off Jermyn Street, not far from Piccadilly. A drinking club for the privileged, it was visited by more than half the Cabinet, members of the House of Lords, financiers, bankers, and those members of the aristocracy who liked visiting London for a wild time.

A room had been converted to a small theater with a tiny stage. Late at night girls would arrive to titillate the sexual palates of the members and perform kinky acts onstage to the cheers of the male audience. As a British tycoon commented, "I went there quite often during the late 1960s because the people who frequented the club were among the most influential in the land. But the sex acts were worse than anything I had ever seen, worse than in Marseilles, which had a dreadful reputation. In the Directors Club they even introduced a donkey onstage for the girls. Awful.

"It has always been said that the night the club was raided by the police there were 105 people there; half of them said they were named Smith, and the others said they only spoke German. If they had arrested everyone in the club that night there would have been hardly anyone at the next day's Cabinet meeting, for most of the government ministers were in the club drinking."

Because of Philip's naturally boisterous character and his service in the Royal Navy, it is not surprising that he would occasionally enjoy wild, risqué parties. He has, however, always been very discreet. Indeed, it is remarkable that so little has been written about Philip's rather exuberant life during the past fifty years. Because he did not want to embarrass Elizabeth or the monarchy, Philip's liaisons are also carried on as discreetly as possible, and nearly all his affairs have been with married women, rather than young unmarried women, which is riskier.

Philip has been very friendly with a succession of married women, but that is not to say he has had affairs with them. His name has been linked with Pat Kirkwood, the beautiful British cabaret artist known as the Champagne Girl in the fifties and who was for a while unofficially engaged to the photographer Baron. She denies any involvement with Philip, despite the fact she and Philip were seen dancing for hours on end one night at the Milroy Club, one of London's brighter night spots of the 1950s.

Pat Kirkwood did, however, happily reveal how Philip loved to let his hair down and really enjoy himself. She recalled, "We stayed dancing for ages. He was fantastic, dancing fox-trots, sambas, quicksteps. It was ballroom dancing in those days. We got on like a house on fire. He told me not to bother saying Sir or Prince Philip or Your Highness or anything. The dance floor was packed and everyone was coming on just to see Philip dance so wildly with me, Pat Kirkwood."

Pat Kirkwood's detailed account of her night with Prince Philip in 1949 reveals how Philip loved to escape the confines of his new royal home, even in the early days of his marriage when Elizabeth had no burdens of monarchy to contend with. That night Elizabeth was at Balmoral in Scotland, and she and Philip had been married less than two years.

Pat Kirkwood, Baron, Philip, and another naval officer, Captain "Basher" Watkin, who was also present, stayed at the club until the chairs were put on the tables. Then the four went to Baron's apartment, where he cooked scrambled eggs. The party didn't break up until 5 A.M., when Philip took a taxi home.

News of Philip's night on the tiles reached the newspapers within twenty-four hours, and reports were on the desks of senior members of the Household the following day. King George flew into one of his violent tempers, instructing his staff to have Philip carpeted immediately and to remind him in no uncertain terms that he was now married to the future Queen of England and that he had better learn to behave himself. Within hours a senior member of the Royal Household warned Philip to keep out of nightclubs, away from the limelight, and not to put his, his wife's, or the family's reputation at risk at any time in the future. He was also told that the warning came on the orders of the King, who was appalled at his behavior.

Philip learned fast. Never again was he seen in public acting outrageously with any other woman. Indeed, he learned the lesson so well that despite his incessant womanizing, which went on for decades, only a handful of people knew of it. And they have kept their silence. He and his pal Mike Parker continued to go out on the town, enjoying themselves, but from then on almost always in private.

The affairs continued throughout Philip's married life. One particular affair, however, which has been kept from the public, earned Philip rebuke and chastisement from members of his family. It was an affair that broke Elizabeth's heart.

SEVEN

PHILIP'S DARK SECRET

Perhaps the best-kept secret in the hearts of most members of the Royal Family, including Elizabeth and her children, Charles, Anne, Andrew, and Edward, has been Prince Philip's twenty-year affair with one of Britain's favorite princesses, the lovely Alexandra of Kent, daughter of the late Duke and Duchess of Kent.

The Duke, her father, a handsome and talented artist, is the younger brother of King George VI. King George decided to use that name when he succeeded to the throne following the abdication of his brother Edward. His first name was Albert, named after Queen Victoria's husband, but he didn't wish to be called King Albert. Until the lovely Marina, Alexandra's mother, came along, he had showed a greater sexual interest in men than women. The bisexual Duke would often appear at private dinner parties wearing lots of makeup. He also used to dress up in women's clothes. His sexual appetite was legendary, and he did not much mind if his partner of the night was male or female.

Marina, a snobbish and stunningly elegant woman, was an exiled, penniless Greek princess with Teutonic arrogance, and a cousin of Prince Philip. Marina boasted that she and husband George were the most royal family in the land and would refer to Queen Elizabeth, the Queen Mother, and the Queen's sister as "those common little Scottish girls." The comment was reported to Queen Elizabeth II, who understood the comment as an insult to her mother. She was not amused.

Born in 1936 and fifteen years younger than Philip, Princess Alexandra is perhaps the most natural of all the royals. With her fun-loving personality, she is undoubtedly one of the nation's favorites, endearing herself to everyone with her warm smile and gentle character; she is like the Queen Mother, who always seemed so pleased to meet and chat with everyone. Whenever I met Princess Alexandra, usually out riding in the mornings in Richmond Park, where she lives, she would always wave and smile and say hello.

As a schoolgirl in the 1940s and early 1950s, she had a reputation as a gregarious, happy girl, loved by everyone. She told school friends: "When I marry, he must be rich, madly in love with me, and he must be tall." Alex, as everyone calls her, grew to be five feet, ten inches tall. As for her requirement of wealth, all her classmates knew that Alex was always dressed in secondhand clothes, usually hand-me-downs from her cousins Princess Elizabeth and Princess Margaret. Elizabeth and Alexandra are first cousins.

The man who courted Alex for eight long years, Angus Ogilvy, belonged to one of Britain's most prestigious aristocratic dynasties, the Airlie family. Angus was tall, handsome, and highly intelligent; and he was madly in love with her. Unfortunately, Angus wasn't very rich and never has been, even after a lifetime working in the City, London's financial center.

Angus Ogilvy did not want to become a part of the Royal Family, although his own family had always been senior members of the Royal Household for generations, and still are. He knew the problems of marrying into the royals. Ironically, it was Elizabeth who came to the rescue, declaring that although Princess Alexandra would be expected to continue her royal duties, representing the Queen on occasion and chairing charities, Angus could continue his career in the City. The marriage finally took place, in great splendor, in Westminster Abbey in 1963. More than fifteen hundred guests attended the reception held at Windsor Castle, and Elizabeth herself led a private bus tour of Windsor Great Park.

At the start of their marriage Alexandra seemed very happy and, to friends, appeared to be deeply and sexually involved with Angus. Lord Rupert Nevill, who had become Philip's private secretary following Mike Parker's resignation, gave a great dinner party to celebrate the marriage. A guest recalls: "Alexandra was her charming, smiling self as ever, but all she wanted to do was to leave and take Angus home to bed. She used to say quite openly that they could not stay out of bed."

Angus and Alexandra had two children: James, born in 1964, and

Marina, named after her grandmother, in 1966. Since their father is not a member of the Royal Family they have no titles, which is one of the reasons Alexandra's mother Marina did not want her to marry a commoner. But Alexandra didn't mind at all.

The affair between Alexandra and Prince Philip had begun sometime in the 1950s, when Alexandra was in her twenties and Philip in his late thirties. She had a twinkle in her eye for Philip from the day she was a bridesmaid at his wedding in 1947, when she was just eleven years old. She never lost it.

As she grew into a beautiful, friendly young woman, Alex saw Philip frequently, on royal occasions and at family gatherings. In 1953, when just seventeen, Alex joined Elizabeth and Philip on a rare spring cruise in the Mediterranean on board the Royal Yacht *Britannia*. And every year she joined Philip for Cowes Week, the spectacular sailing festival in the Isle of Wight which the Royal Family has traditionally attended since the reign of George V (1910–36), who loved this week of competitive sailing. The Royal Yacht would drop anchor in the harbor and the festivities would continue every night after the serious business of yacht races was over for the day. The tradition was continued by Mountbatten and by Philip. It was during one of these Cowes Weeks that the friendship turned to romance and Alex and Philip became lovers.

Philip loved messing about in small boats, something he had learned to enjoy at Gordonstoun in the 1930s. He had continued his love of sailing at Dartmouth Naval College and during his years in the Royal Navy, which gave him the opportunity to take part in sailing competitions. Philip was a good sailor and, with his natural aggression and competitive spirit, won many races.

In 1947, the Island Sailing Club of Cowes gave Philip and Elizabeth a Dragon-class yacht as a wedding present. The yacht was dark blue, and Philip christened her *Bluebottle* ("Dragonfly" . . . "Blue-fly" . . . "Bluebottle" was Philip's line of thought). For years he sailed her competitively during Cowes Week with his regular Cowes crew, which included the colorful local boatbuilder Uffa Fox. They made a great sailing team, for Fox knew all the problems of sailing around the island waters. He later persuaded the people of Cowes to give Philip one of the first Flying Fifteens racing yachts, which he had designed. Prince Philip named her *Cowslip*.

Elizabeth went to Cowes for only one year and did not enjoy that experience. She preferred large boats, like the *Britannia*. And it wasn't just the yachting she disliked. A country woman, Elizabeth did not feel at home with the informal sailing clique at Cowes, who spent the entire week either on the water or talking about boats and the races over a drink or at dinner at the end of the day.

Almost every year Alexandra would join Philip on board *Britannia*. In the evening she would act as hostess when the sailing fraternity and the local dignitaries came on board for drinks and dinner. There would be party games and dancing that lasted into the night. Alex was a most popular hostess. She was a tall, good-looking young woman with a sparkling personality who fit into the informality of the yachtsmen. They all loved her and thought it wonderful that the Princess, who never seemed interested in sailing, would come to Cowes for their most important week of the year. Little did they know Alexandra was deeply in love with her cousin's husband.

As Unity Hall wrote in her book, *Philip: The Man Behind the Monarchy*, "In court circles it is common knowledge that they have always been close. . . . It is said that she and Prince Philip have come to rely on each other for friendship and support. . . . Alexandra's husband is said to feel pangs of jealousy at the depth of the friendship between the two of them, but it is accepted in the Royal Family that Alexandra and Philip have a special relationship."

Whenever Elizabeth was away from Buckingham Palace, Alexandra would arrive at the palace or Windsor Castle, where she and Philip would swim together. Alexandra, however, never visited Buck House when Elizabeth was there, and certainly never when Philip was not.

Sergeant Ron Lewis, an ex–Welsh Guards sergeant-major, became the royal couple's baggage master thirty years ago. His job is to make sure that the Queen's and Philip's trunks, suitcases, and bags are at the right place at the right time, no matter if they are traveling thirty miles to Windsor for the weekend or on a world tour. He must know where all the senior royals are at any given time.

Though totally discreet, he was heard to remark on one occasion in the 1970s: "I don't know how those two, Alex and Philip, manage it. They spend so much time together and they seem like two lovebirds." Those who have seen them together note the way they talk to each other, the body language, the intimacy between them.

When it finally became known that Alex and Philip were lovers, the revelation caused a major crisis in the family. Absolutely furious when he heard of the affair, Mountbatten confronted his nephew and ordered Philip to end the affair immediately. Philip refused and told Mountbatten "to mind his own bloody business."

As a result, the two men were never again so close. Mountbatten instead became closer to his great-nephew Prince Charles, with whom he had always had a rather good relationship; now Uncle Dickie virtually took over the role of father figure.

Mountbatten wrote to Philip, "I do hope you will be more discreet in your relationship with Alexandra." He then pointed out that as his second cousin, Alexandra and he were "too close." Mountbatten also cautioned, "If news of this affair should enter the public domain you must realise the reflection this would have on the whole family and especially on Lilibet." (Mountbatten loved his role of surrogate father to the Queen. He was obsessed with Lilibet and would frequently be found expounding her personality or her role as sovereign. He repeatedly declared, "She is intelligent, bright, and undoubtedly the best monarch Britain has had for two centuries.")

How Elizabeth discovered the affair is not known, but the answer lies in the strange ways palace politics work. There are two schools in the palace. The larger one supports the Queen because she is the monarch. A smaller, more aggressive faction supports Philip. Whenever either side uncovers a tasty morsel of gossip that it believes should be passed to their respective leaders, someone is always prepared to put in the knife and deliver the message.

Elizabeth's reaction to discovering the affair is not known, but it can be guessed by what she confessed to Uncle Dickie. Miserable, Elizabeth turned to the only person she could rely on, Mountbatten, for guidance and a shoulder to cry on. She had known of some of Philip's sexual escapades, but the news that Philip was involved with Alexandra, a woman ten years her junior whom she had always counted as a close friend, as well as her own cousin, hit Elizabeth hard.

Mountbatten told her that it was just one of Philip's flings and he expected it would soon be at an end. Elizabeth was not so sure; she had seen the two of them together and sensed they were indeed close. Now she feared for her marriage. Mountbatten assured her there was no question of Philip's leaving her and setting up a discreet "alternative" home with Alexandra.

Elizabeth also turned to Bishop Mervyn Stockwood, who was for many years a counselor and adviser to members of the family, and especially to her. It is not known whether the Bishop also discussed the matter with Philip.

It is extraordinary that an affair involving two members of the Royal Family, one of them married to the Queen, has remained a secret for so many years. To the nation and their beloved Commonwealth, the royals have purported to set an example for all their subjects. Yet the Queen's consort, the man married to the Head of the Church of England whose views on adultery were unwaveringly strict, has been living an adulterous life for most of the forty-five years he has been married to the Queen.

Alexandra's daughter Marina almost revealed the secret in 1989, when she became pregnant. Her parents urged her to have an abortion, and Marina was so angry that she decided to tell all to a newspaper. Fortunately for her parents, and Elizabeth and Philip, caution prevailed and the affair remained a closely guarded royal confidence, known only to a very few.

Time and again those close to the Royal Family have admitted that, according to the royals themselves, the sin is not in doing something morally wrong, but in being found out. Britain's strict libel laws have been instrumental in keeping Philip's adulterous life private. Many newspaper and magazine proprietors also feel that to disclose Philip's behavior would humiliate the Royal Family and perhaps threaten the monarchy. As a consequence they did not want their journalists to inquire too closely or dig too deep, for fear of what they might discover.

In his bid to enjoy his life with as little risk as possible, Philip sought to be invited overseas where he could behave with far more freedom. A favorite jaunt involved the famous Bohemian Grove, deep within the Californian redwoods, sixty-five miles north of San Francisco. Each summer a thousand or more VIPs—the decision makers and opinion molders of the Western world—meet in mid-July to relax, attend lectures and debates, and enjoy themselves for three weeks. For decades the Bohemian Grove retreat was the major social event of America's male power elite and their overseas friends. And for decades those who attended went in secret, another reason Philip, as well as many others, loved to join them. In the 1970s, when Philip visited, members included Ronald Reagan, George Bush, George Shultz, Caspar Weinberger. Former Presidents Nixon and Ford were also members, as well as many of America's wealthiest businessmen, including David Rockefeller, William Randolph Hearst Jr., hamburger king Ray Kroc, and the recluse Daniel Ludwig. Herbert Hoover called Bohemian Grove "the greatest men's club in the world."

The 2,700-acre Grove, on the banks of the Russian River in Northern California, comprises 128 small camps, each operated by 20 or 30 members. These camps bear such names as Wild Oats, Woof, and Toyland. The claim to fame of President Reagan's camp, Owl's Nest, is a gin-fizz breakfast. Another camp nearby boasted a fine collection of erotica. Most of the time members sit around and chat, discuss politics, business, and deals. They also hunt, fish, or just stroll around, going from camp to camp for a drink, a meal, and a chat.

Women are not permitted anywhere near the Grove. Even the waiters and kitchen staff are all male. One reason women are banned is that a number of members "jump the river" when visiting the Grove. They quietly leave the sacred enclave in favor of a trek to nearby Guerneville. More than ten bars await them in this sleepy, rural town, all bursting with high-class prostitutes who come from all over America, and some from overseas, especially for the profitable Bohemian trade.

One of the more notorious such taverns is Northwood Lodge, operated by a Ugandan named Manu Kanani. He freely admits that girls flood the town solely for the three-week bash and earn small fortunes. According to Kanani, "These were high-class girls, no street walkers. These girls were very sophisticated, very experienced." Kanani acknowledged that a photographer staying at nearby Hexagon House had his arm broken by a Texan rancher when he attempted to photograph bar patrons. He also remembers Prince Philip coming to his bar and enjoying one of the girls. "Of course I recognized him," he said. "I'm a Ugandan, I know what the Queen of England's husband looks like. There were pictures of him all over Uganda."

Convicted San Francisco madam Brandy Baldwin revealed how she supplied prostitutes, champagne, and entertainment to Bohemian members. "I did the Bohemian for ten years. They were such beautiful people, very generous. In the beginning I was working out of motels with just a few girls. But it got to be so much fun that I rented a little house in the woods, a beautiful little place. The girls used to bring all their fancy underclothes so they could do little shows and the gentlemen just loved it." But she had no recollection that Philip ever came to one of her shows.

There were other overseas parties Philip loved to attend. John Barratt, Lord Mountbatten's much maligned private secretary for twenty years, told of one club in Nassau in the Bahamas that Dickie Mountbatten and Prince Philip used to frequent. "I would sometimes go with Mountbatten but not always. He liked to go and let his hair down there. He rather enjoyed the raunchy atmosphere. So did Philip. It was a place for wealthy as well as famous people because everyone was so discreet. One had to be a member or be invited. It was high-class dive, with lots of heavy drinking, drugs, and, of course, high-class whores. The girls waiting for wealthy clients were all very good looking, usually white, but there were some coffee-colored girls as well.

"When Mountbatten and Philip were in Nassau they would stay with Sybilla Clark and, more often than not, whenever Philip was in Nassau, Christina Ford, Henry Ford's former wife, would be there. Sybilla was an attractive, vivacious American-Italian, bubbly and bright. With her stunning figure and blond hair, Sybilla was the perfect woman for Prince Philip—exactly his type—and he loved the short miniskirts she wore during the late sixties. Philip thoroughly enjoyed his visits to Nassau.

"I understood from Mountbatten that Philip also had an on-off affair with Christina Ford over a number of years. Mountbatten said she was very keen on Philip."

Yet Philip has been so discreet that he believes he can laugh off any suggestion of infidelity to Elizabeth. In December 1992, Philip gave an interview to the *Independent on Sunday* in which he was asked about long-standing rumors that he had affairs.

He burst out laughing and said, "Have you ever stopped to think that for the past forty years I have never moved anywhere without a policeman accompanying me? So how the hell could I get away with anything like that?" Some noted, however, that the wording was not an outright denial.

Prince Philip's relationship with the press, mainly British newspapers, of course, has been checkered. Prince Bernhard recounted one incident during a dinner in New York when he had to physically restrain Philip from wanting to "sort out" photographers whom he believed were coming too close.

On royal tours overseas Philip would often be testy. When photographers arrived at his meeting with Prime Minister Nehru in New Delhi, in 1959, Philip snapped, "Who are all these damned people?" And in a direct insult to the impoverished Indian economy at the time, he added, "I thought there was supposed to be a film shortage in India!" Later, when touring the Taj Mahal, he shouted at one photographer, "Get on with your bloody business and stop talking."

At a horse show in Lahore, a Pakistani photographer he had never met slipped off a flagpole and fell to the ground. Philip screamed, "I hope to God he breaks his bloody neck!"

At a famous occasion in Gibraltar Philip remarked, referring to the famous apes that inhabit the rock, "Which are the press and which are the bloody apes?" That remark did not go down at all well with the British press corps. They never forget it and never forgave him.

On a number of occasions I have heard Philip, annoyed at photographers taking pictures, tell them to "Fuck off" and "Bugger off," apparently unconcerned who might overhear his abusive orders.

During a state visit to China with the Queen in 1986 he referred to his Chinese hosts as "slitty eyed." He was furious the following day when he learned that his remark, made to touring Scottish students, had been plastered all over the British press and that several editorials had lambasted him for his offensiveness. Elizabeth was furious with her husband for bringing her, the monarchy, and Britain into such disrepute in front of the Chinese leaders, making her look foolish and Philip extremely rude. Philip blamed any unpleasantness on the newspapers that reported his remark.

Sometimes he didn't care whether his "gaffes" were reported or not. In October 1993, at age seventy-two, Philip was attending a cocktail party in Toronto, Canada, in aid of the World Wildlife Fund for Nature. Talking to pretty fashion writer Serena French, he first asked,

"I suppose you'll be looking out for people wearing mink coats then?" She commented that no one would wear fur to a wildlife fund event. Philip quipped, "Well, you never know what they're wearing underneath." Then, putting his hand on the girl's arm he leaned forward and asked, "You're not wearing mink knickers are you?" winking and roaring with laughter at his cheekiness.

Sometimes Philip hurls abuse at the press within hearing range of Elizabeth. She generally responds in one of two ways: either she looks the other way and pretends not to have heard him, or she stares at him coldly. Philip usually bites his lip but never replies.

Sometimes on royal tours, Philip loses his temper with Elizabeth, complaining bitterly about her devotion to duty. Former *Time* photographer Peter Jordan recalls one such moment during the 1985 tour of the island of Grenada. Philip shouted at Elizabeth, "Your bloody obsession with shaking hands with everyone! Why do you have to do it? Let's go." Jordan says that the Queen took not the slightest notice of his outburst and made Philip wait until she had completed her round of farewells.

In return, the British press over the years has shown Philip little courtesy. It has delighted in poking fun at him and deliberately baiting him because they know he will often respond with impatience, irritation, and anger, and frequently a number of choice expletives.

In Trinidad in 1987 he turned on reporters and, to their amazement, snarled, "You lot have ruined my life." Newspapers responded by printing the complaint along with a description of that life: a young man arrives in Britain penniless, homeless, now lives a life of absolute privilege in multiple palaces and castles, with an income (at that time) of $300,000 a year, sixteen weeks holiday a year, and a mass of servants to care for his every whim. Philip looked foolish.

At times Philip totally misjudges his position and the privileges he believes he is entitled to simply because he is married to the Queen. Some of his actions have appeared naive. On one occasion, for example, Philip needed to go from Holy Island in Scotland to Windsor so he could play in a polo match later that day. To get to Windsor in time he demanded, and was provided with, a naval launch, a destroyer, a car, an aircraft of the Queen's Flight, and another car at the other end of the trip. He arrived on time, thanks to the taxpayers, who footed the bill which ran into thousands of dollars.

Philip, who thought those demands perfectly reasonable, was outraged the following day when the newspapers attacked him for wasting so much taxpayers' money to play a game of polo.

Despite all the press criticism, Philip has remained relatively popular with some sections of the British public. In 1969 the Tory broadsheet the *Daily Telegraph* ran a competition to discover whom the British thought would make the best dictator. Prince Philip won handsomely.

In many respects Philip would probably have reveled in the role of dictator, for he would have been able to give vent to his modernizing ideas; his push for greater scientific and industrial advancement in Britain; for more efficiency in all walks of life; for his ideas for the armed forces; on how to bring up the younger generation.

Throughout his entire adult life, Philip has been fettered and, as a result, has become frustrated and angry. Even in the late 1980s, when over sixty-five years of age, he was not even permitted to move some of the royal horses he uses for carriage driving from the Royal Mews at Buckingham Palace, where they are kept for state occasions, to Sandringham, one hundred fifty miles away. He wanted to build an enormous ménage or arena for schooling horses and Britain's carriage drivers. Philip had designed and organized everything, and the money was to be donated by Patricia Kluge, who for ten years was married to John Kluge, one of America's richest men.

Like Philip's, Patti Kluge's life has been a rags-to-riches story. The daughter of an English Arabist, Edmund Rose, and an Iraqi mother, Patti was born in Baghdad and spent much of her youth there. As a teenager she worked as an erotic dancer in a Baghdad nightclub. At nineteen, she moved to London and got a job as a belly dancer at the Labyrinth Club, in London's seedy Bayswater. There she met her future husband, Russell Gay. She not only began posing nude for his soft-porn magazines but also allowed him to write a column of explicit sex advice to readers under her name. In 1973 Patti married her soft-porn publisher.

After three years Russell Gay went to Monte Carlo while Patti moved to New York and the two divorced. In New York, Patti met John Werner Kluge—thirty years her senior and five inches shorter than the statuesque dancer—a man born in Germany who immigrated to America at the age of eight. After attending Columbia University on a scholarship, he became a captain in army intelligence during World War II. As a civilian he began buying and selling small radio stations. In the sixties he started to collect TV stations and founded Metropolitan Broadcasting, which later became Metromedia, and which he sold to Rupert Murdoch for $2 billion in 1985.

Patti married John Kluge in 1981 and began a wild spending spree that continued until the couple separated in 1991. During those ten years Patti was determined to use her husband's enormous wealth—estimated at $5 billion—to achieve her great ambition of becoming involved, in whatever way possible, with Britain's Royal Family.

John Kluge had become a good friend of Armand Hammer, the wealthy American businessman who founded Occidental Oil and maintained strong business and political connections with the Soviet Union. Then in his eighties, Hammer was also a major philanthropist and a friend to Prince Charles. Some years previously Hammer had persuaded Charles to become patron of the United World Colleges, a group of charitable, multinational, multiracial colleges for teenagers which aspire to develop world understanding by breaking down racial prejudice and national barriers.

In November 1985 Hammer organized a charity dinner to raise money for the colleges in Florida. He invited Patti Kluge to become chairwoman of the gala ball, which meant she would meet both Charles and Princess Diana. But just before the ball was to take place, gossip about Patti's past was revealed, and John and Patti Kluge decided to take a world cruise instead. Patti did receive a letter from Charles spelling out his unhappiness and sympathy at the way she was treated. As Charles said then: "I can't see what all the fuss is about."

As if to prove his point Charles accepted an invitation to go aboard the Kluge yacht, *The Virginian*, and spent some time with John and Patti Kluge during his Majorcan holiday in 1987. Diana, however, declined the invitation. Patti Kluge's determination continued apace. She invited one of Charles's best friends, the wealthy Duke of Westminster, and his wife Tally to stay on *The Virginian* when they came for week of fund-raising in New York to aid leukemia research. Another close royal friend, King Constantine of Greece, attended a weekend housewarming party at the Kluges' four-thousand-acre

Virginia estate in 1986. Patti's strenuous efforts paid off when Prince Andrew and Fergie went to lunch with them, and Charles and Diana invited the Kluges to dinner at Highgrove.

In the mid-eighties, Patti Kluge decided to take up competitive carriage driving, a very expensive and difficult sport, one in which Prince Philip himself had first participated only a few years earlier. During those years Philip spent a great amount of time perfecting his driving, schooling his horses, and he saw a lot of Patti. Physically, Patti was Philip's type of woman, a tall, shapely, good-looking, athletic woman with a charming personality, smiling eyes, and a most attractive face.

Patti came to Britain in 1985 and met Philip while discussing carriage driving with thirty-year-old David Saunders, Philip's coachman at Sandringham. During that year Philip and Patti, then in her mid-thirties, became lovers, and Patti volunteered to fund the building of a royal ménage at Sandringham and set up a comprehensive carriage-driving center. Philip was delighted. Patti Kluge bought six magnificent horses and stabled them at Sandringham at a cost of $75,000 a year. Philip decided to move his royal horses from London to the center as well.

As was customary, and necessary, Philip put forward his idea for moving the horses from Buckingham Palace to Sandringham to the members of the Royal Household, who have authority over any ideas involving the monarchy and the state. They rejected his plan, even though it would have cost the taxpayers nothing. They argued that the royal horses had always been stabled at the Royal Mews next to Buckingham Palace and there they would stay, no matter what Philip wanted.

A close friend of Philip reported, "I was involved with development of the idea, and Philip phoned me one day to tell me what had happened. I have never heard or seen him so furious, he was beside himself with rage at the bureaucrats who controlled the Palace. He was fucking and blinding like a trooper. He was outraged. He went berserk."

Eventually he took the problem to the only person who could help—his wife Elizabeth. She told him that she was just as hidebound by the rules as he, and if "they"—those people who ran the Palace—decreed the horses could not be moved there was nothing whatsoever that she could do about it.

To Philip, the decision highlighted once again the total lack of power or authority he has been permitted by the establishment throughout his entire life. Elizabeth, however, may have had another reason to refuse to intervene; she had been informed that Philip was seeing a great deal of Patti Kluge and there were whispers of an affair.

After Philip had been refused permission to keep the royal horses at Sandringham, it was announced, rather surprisingly, that the Sandringham Driving Centre would be closed down and that Mrs. Kluge would take her horses away.

During her affair with Philip, Patti had persuaded her husband John to spend $12 million to buy Mar Lodge, a mansion set in a 77,500–acre estate built in 1896 for Edward VII's daughter Princess Louise. The neighboring estate was Balmoral, Elizabeth's Scottish home. Patti's husband spent another $9 million to renovate the dilapidated mansion and construct a stable yard, complete with a harness room which featured a crystal chandelier. She also persuaded John to fund, for five years, the Royal Windsor Horse Show, which is run every year from the mews at Windsor Castle. Although Elizabeth accepted $75,000 a year from Patti Kluge to sponsor the horse show, she also refused to meet her, shake her hand, or acknowledge her husband's mistress.

In 1988, Patti's team of American grays won the major trophy, the Harrods International Driving Grand Prix. Patti climbed into the Royal Box beside her driver, ready to be officially introduced to the Queen and receive the prize from her. Elizabeth did not even look at her and handed the prize to the driver instead. It was a deliberate and calculated snub by Elizabeth. That snub had nothing to do with Patti's former life as a naked porn star, for if it had, no other members of the Royal Family would have been permitted to entertain her in their homes, nor would they have accepted her hospitality. Elizabeth snubbed Patti because she knew of her affair with Philip.

Prince Philip's adult life can be divided into two rather distinct periods: before 1957 and after 1957. In 1957 Philip had been married ten years, and Squadron Leader Henry Moresby Chinnery replaced Mike Parker as his private secretary. In an interview with the *New York Post*, Parker's estranged wife Eileen said, "My advice to Mrs. Chinnery is that it would be better if she lived in London. Then she would be sure of seeing her husband fairly often."

In 1957 Elizabeth decided to make Philip a Prince of the United

Kingdom. Previously, Philip had been only a Prince of Greece but had been permitted to use the title "Prince" as a courtesy. Queen Victoria had bestowed the same dignity upon Prince Albert some seventeen years after their marriage, and it was now ten years after Elizabeth and Philip's wedding. Henceforth, Philip's official title would be His Royal Highness Prince Philip, Duke of Edinburgh.

As noted earlier, Philip became involved in both the International Equestrian Foundation and the World Wildlife Fund. He continued to travel widely, throwing himself more into his royal duties. Even in 1991, at the age of seventy, Philip spent nearly eight weeks abroad, on numerous royal duties. As James Orr, who later became his private secretary, said of him, "He was a real self-driver. He would go on till he dropped." Today, he still pushes himself hard.

Philip also expected his polo ponies and driving horses to follow his example. During the years he played polo, Philip was renowned for being hard on his ponies, treating them harshly, in contrast to his son Charles, who always treats his ponies with far greater care. Because of an arthritic hand Philip gave up polo at the age of forty-eight and took up carriage driving in the 1980s. He has become remarkably adept at the sport and still pushes his horses hard in his ambition to win.

Philip has always taken a keen interest in Britain's manufacturing and scientific industries, helping wherever possible to expand his country's industrial prowess and exports overseas. He has also shown a keen interest in the Royal Navy. But perhaps his greatest achievement has been the creation of the Commonwealth Study Conferences, which have helped members from all over the world understand better the relationship between industrial relations, the community, and the individual. His enthusiasm and expertise have been overshadowed by arrogance and, as a result, he has not won the respect of those senior advisers who work at the palace, nor of the general public.

Philip runs the most efficient office in Buck House, but even he had to wait until the mid–1980s before being permitted to purchase computers and word processors for his highly motivated staff of three senior officials and four secretaries. Brian McGrath has served as Philip's private secretary since 1982. McGrath, of Eton College, the Irish Guards, and the wine trade, joined Philip at the age of fifty-six. He succeeded Lord Rupert Nevill, with whom Philip had a very close relationship for twelve years as his treasurer and later his private secretary. As a stockbroker Lord Nevill also helped manage the Queen's extensive stock portfolio. Philip also has an equerry, Lieutenant Commander Malcolm Sillars; the administration is in the care of Jimmy Jewell, a former Guards sergeant-major.

Philip's personal library contains nine thousand books, including six hundred books on birds, five hundred on religion, four hundred on horses and riding, and three hundred fifty on the navy and ships. Philip loves reading poetry, and he owns more books of poetry than fiction, which accounts for only two hundred volumes. The library also contains two hundred books on humor. Philip has also collected two hundred cartoons from various artists, every one about himself.

At the age of seventy Philip still loves flying aircraft. An extremely able pilot, he has flown many types of planes, including a Concorde and a Vulcan bomber, putting in more than five thousand flying hours, many at the controls of aircraft of the Queen's Flight. He has also flown helicopters. A keen photographer and talented watercolor painter, Philip believes painting helps to relax him.

Throughout his life Philip has enjoyed being a busybody, invariably telling other people what to do. As a member of the International Equestrian Federation put it, "Many believe it would be better if the Duke simply chaired meetings instead of arguing every item on the agenda and trying to ram his ideas down everyone else's throat."

Yet there is a side to Philip which runs contrary to his brusque personality. He has shown an abiding interest in religion and philosophy which began in the early 1960s after the Right Reverend Robin Woods was appointed to the Deanery of Windsor.

According to Woods, "At first the Duke had absolutely no time for the Church of England." Apparently he did not even want Prince Charles confirmed and during the service read the Bible instead of paying attention. Afterward, the Archbishop of Canterbury, Dr. Michael Ramsey, said, "That was bloody rude of the Duke."

Philip's religious upbringing had been chaotic. He had been brought up in the Greek Orthodox Church, then as a teenager became involved with German Protestantism, and ultimately married the Head of the Church of England, which meant becoming a practicing, believing Anglican. From his teenage years to the 1960s Philip became disenchanted with all religion, even cynical toward church teachings; sometimes he was deeply agnostic, occasionally professing to be an atheist.

Despite Philip's attitude toward the church and religion, he and Woods grew closer as Philip supported a plan to raise $650,000 to convert the existing Deanery college buildings at Windsor into a residential conference center. As a result they became friends, and Woods would drop in at Windsor Castle on weekends for a cocktail before dinner.

On Woods's promotion to the diocese of Worcester, Philip wrote to him, saying, "It has been simply marvellous having you at Windsor and your help and guidance for us and for our children has been invaluable, but frankly I think the Church needs your services more urgently than we do." It was a sincere sentiment built on eight years of friendship. Five years later, in 1975, Bishop Dudley Mann, who was a suffragan to Robin Woods at Worcester, took over the Windsor post.

Philip's involvement with the church continued. As a result of talks with Bishop Mann, Philip wrote a collection of philosophical essays, edited by the Dean, which was published in book form in 1982 and entitled *A Question of Balance*. Philip began with a textual analysis of Karl Marx's *Communist Manifesto*; other chapters included were called "Truth," "Clashes of Interest," and "Community Health."

Two years later he published *A Windsor Correspondence*, in which Philip and Bishop Mann argued in a series of letters about Sir Fred Hoyle's theory, entitled "Evolution from Space," suggesting that science and Christianity might be moving closer together.

His third philosophical work is *Survival or Extinction*, subtitled *A Christian Attitude to the Environment*, which he wrote together with Bishop Mann. In it the two men try to persuade the Church to take more interest in the conservation of nature.

As a result of his dialogue with Woods and Mann, Philip grew closer to the Anglican Church and came to enjoy the discussions of philosophy and religion. His interest is primarily intellectual, however, and he has so far not embraced the faith as a true believer.

As the years have taken their toll on him, Philip—while still crusty and acerbic—has become demonstrably more contemplative and reflective. During his youth and middle-age Philip was restless, impatient, and curious, as well as a man of action. Now he seems to prefer wrestling with questions about the meaning of life and the existence of a supreme being.

Bishop Mann says, "I believe the Duke has acquired a peace of mind that he did not have earlier in his life. But there's a worm inside the man that drives him on. I don't know that he would ever feel fulfilled, though he might feel content.

"The problem with Philip is that he could never accept anything until he had gnawed it and chewed it to pieces. When he's in a corner and he's lost a point in an argument he doesn't stop like other people and say 'yes, well maybe you're right.' He goes shooting off on something else...and usually he will go away and come back later having accepted the point. When you're actually in an argument with him, he will never admit that he's being convinced. You know if he has been convinced if he's changed the subject or changed the line of questioning. He would find it very difficult to say, 'I'm sorry, I'm wrong.'"

Mann believes a person who can admit errors has no need to constantly bulldoze people in discussions and arguments. In 1990, Tim Heald watched Philip at work over a period of months before writing his biography *The Duke*. Heald wrote: "Still he puzzles me. Real humility sits uneasily alongside apparent arrogance, energy and optimism coexist with sudden douches of cold water, real kindnesses are mingled with inexplicable snubs; certainty and uncertainty, sensitivity and insensitivity, walk hand in hand. He is gregarious, he is a loner; he loves argument, he cannot bear to lose one. . . . His apparent inconsistencies certainly make him intriguing, but they also make him exasperating. He is energetic, mercurial, quixotic, and ultimately impossible to pin down—partly on purpose."

He rarely makes jokes at his own expense, but sometimes a little humility does appear. At one time he applied for membership in the Imperial Poona Yacht Club, which wasn't really a club but an excuse among friends to get together for an occasional drink. Philip signed himself "The Maharaja of Cooch Parwani," which translated means "Maharaja of not a lot."

Ultimately, Philip must be judged on how well he has fulfilled the job for which he accepted responsibility when he married Elizabeth, not simply as her husband but, more important, as consort to the Queen of England. Ever since her Coronation in 1953 Philip has been always at her side, photographed on thousands of royal occasions, resplendent in naval uniform or an elegant, well-cut suit or evening dress, as though a fixture, a rock of support for her to lean on. Thousands of pictures testify to this.

He has also single-mindedly pursued knowledge and is not the "ignorant bum" he once called himself. He has organized and chaired meetings, spoken his mind, and involved himself in his interests of science and engineering and whatever else took his fancy. To his great credit, he has never shirked his duty in carrying out prodigious amounts of royal work, engagements, functions, and speech making. He has done more than pull his weight, for years being the hardest-working royal, attending more royal occasions and events than most other members of The Firm, including all the younger ones.

At the end of his biography of Philip, Tim Heald wrote, "The consensus among those I consulted is that the Duke has pulled this off." If Heald had written his biography a couple of years later, however, when the monarchy was plunged into crisis and those he interviewed knew more about the lives of the royals, perhaps the consensus would have been rather different.

Unfortunately, Philip seems to have failed in most of the important aspects of his life: he has not been a faithful husband, indeed quite the opposite; the support he has given his wife in her life's work has been little more than cosmetic; in the one area he was determined to carve out a substantial role for himself, as father to his children, he has been negligent and a disgrace. Away from the flashbulbs and the photographers, Philip has led the solitary existence of a bachelor, doing the things he has always wanted to do, from painting to polo, from sailing to shooting, to carriage driving, not caring how these pursuits affected those who depended on him.

Philip once said, "I am not really interested in what goes on my tombstone." As it happens, his epitaph may not be very flattering.

EIGHT

INTIMATE FRIENDS

Throughout the 1950s Elizabeth found she increasingly turned for advice to Uncle Dickie. He proved a valuable adviser, not only concerning government policies and foreign affairs, but on more personal matters also. At first, most of his advice was professional. Only later, when they became closer acquainted, did Uncle Dickie advise on all matters, particularly family problems.

Mountbatten advised Elizabeth when the Soviet leaders Bulganin and Khrushchev visited Britain in 1956, and he spent many hours with her through the dramatic days of 1956 after President Nasser of Egypt seized the Suez Canal and Britain, France, and Israel sent in troops to recapture it.

As First Sea Lord, Mountbatten was intimately involved with planning the Suez invasion forces, although personally he was passionately against the military operation and told Prime Minister Anthony Eden as much. He explained his opposition to Elizabeth and urged her to try to persuade Sir Anthony against using force. Elizabeth totally accepted Mountbatten's line of argument, took his advice, and, using her right as monarch, advised Eden to take the greatest care before taking direct military action.

Eden went ahead in secret, not informing American President Dwight Eisenhower or Secretary of State John Foster Dulles that the invasion would take place, for fear they would try to stop the action. Eden didn't even inform the United Nations. Only at the last moment did Eden inform Elizabeth the invasion would take place. Of course, Elizabeth had no authority to stop the action and had to accept Eden's decision. Britain, France, and Israel seized the canal, and Nasser promptly blocked it by scuttling ships still in its waters. Mountbatten was furious, fearing a debacle.

Within hours after the invasion, the United States applied the strongest possible pressure to halt the military action, ordered a run on sterling and the French franc, and cut off all credit. Two more weeks and Britain would have been financially ruined. Eden had to back down. The invasion had openly divided the nation, Britain lost power and prestige, and Sir Anthony, mentally and physically ill, resigned.

The Suez debacle cemented the working relationship between Elizabeth and Mountbatten, and through the following years Elizabeth came to depend to a remarkable extent on Uncle Dickie.

Louis Francis Victor Albert Nicholas, 1st Earl Mountbatten of Burma, born in 1900, the great-grandson of Queen Victoria and Albert, was distantly related to Elizabeth, who was Victoria's great-great-granddaughter.

During World War II, Mountbatten achieved a meteoric rise to power and authority, from a senior naval officer in 1940 to Supreme Allied Commander South-East Asia by 1943. He was appointed the last Viceroy of India and oversaw the rapid transfer of power from 1947 until 1952. He then returned to naval service as 4th Sea Lord and Commander of the Mediterranean Fleet. In 1955 he became First Sea Lord. Four years later he reached the pinnacle of power in Britain's armed forces, becoming Chief of the Defence Staff.

Mountbatten was a natural confidant and counselor for Lilibet. He was a relative of both the Queen and her husband, and he had a vast wealth of experience and knowledge which neither Elizabeth or Philip could begin to match. And the rascally, manipulative Mountbatten encouraged the relationship, thoroughly enjoying the power and influence it gave him. From the time of the Suez crisis, Mountbatten, then fifty-six, became a father figure to Elizabeth, then thirty, and the two remained close until his death in 1979.

Mountbatten not only had access to many world leaders and power brokers in many Western democracies, including the United States, he also talked to the common people—shopkeepers, naval ratings, soldiers, people he met in everyday life—and more than that, he listened to what they had to say. From these meetings and odd chats with ordinary people, Mountbatten had his finger on the pulse of the nation and knew how people felt toward the monarchy and the Royal Family; and he would pass on much of this to Elizabeth, who, throughout her entire life, has been kept as far away as possible from her subjects, closeted in palaces and castles.

Indeed, the number of ordinary people Elizabeth ever had serious conversations with during her entire life can probably be counted on the fingers of both hands. It was one of the reasons she clung to Bobo for so long, because Bobo understood what the common people thought—and told Elizabeth so. In that respect Bobo was invaluable.

John Barratt describes Mountbatten's attitude toward Elizabeth through the late fifties and sixties: "In some ways I thought their relationship became too close, he became too obsessive towards her and too possessive of her."

Mountbatten would bring up her relationship with Philip in general terms, asking, "Is everything okay between you and Philip?" More often than not Elizabeth would be noncommittal, but sometimes she would confide her innermost thoughts to him.

Mountbatten had realized quite early on in their marriage that Philip intimidated Elizabeth. Sometimes at dinner Philip would shoot his wife a severe look, and she would be suddenly quiet, dropping the subject she was speaking about. After being married only a few years, Philip would occasionally say, "Shut up," and she would obey immediately, looking embarrassed at being addressed that way in front of the family.

Quite often at night, Philip would stand up and say, "Time for bed," and Elizabeth would immediately leave whatever she was doing and retire with him, without any argument.

Among the family, Philip generally played the arrogant male with his wife, especially during the first years of their married life, but even after she became Queen in 1952.

During open discussions at table, Philip would always state his viewpoint most forcefully, often disagreeing with his wife's argument, telling her bluntly, "Do keep quiet" if he wanted to make a point. He was particularly firm when speaking to Charles, often criticizing him for no apparent reason and deliberately taking the viewpoint opposite to his son's.

Sometimes Elizabeth intervened, defending Charles. That would infuriate Philip, who would tell her, "Mind your own business while I am addressing the children, will you!" And Elizabeth would obey and keep quiet.

Philip also had a rather unpleasant way of putting down his wife, making her feel small, usually in front of the family. John Barratt recalls, "It was as if Philip got some pleasure from treating his wife like that, deriding her, telling her she didn't know what she was talking about, ridiculing her views and her opinions. He intimidated her. He always did. And she accepted the position most of the time. As far as I can recall she always did as he said."

Uncle Dickie didn't like the way his nephew treated Elizabeth, and in the early days he suggested that Philip show his wife kindness and consideration. As time went on, however, and as Philip became involved in more sexual adventures, the less he permitted his uncle to discuss any personal matters with him.

As a result, Uncle Dickie showed more warmth toward Elizabeth. He would be attentive toward her, kind, even gentle, asking her opinions and views and listening to her arguments, something which he knew Philip hardly ever did. Through the sixties Elizabeth and Mountbatten would go for walks together at Broadlands or Windsor, not Elizabeth and Philip. Uncle Dickie would hold Elizabeth's arm as they walked and chatted.

How close Mountbatten and Elizabeth were became evident when Elizabeth became romantically involved with another man, Henry George Reginald Molyneux Herbert, 7th Earl of Carnavon, the grandson of the 5th Earl, the man who discovered the famous tomb of Tutankhamen in the 1920s. Harry first met Elizabeth during her teenage years (he is two years older than she), and they danced together on a number of occasions. And Harry was one of the young men King George had suggested as a prospective husband. Harry's courtesy title was Lord Porchester, and he was affectionately referred to as "Porchy."

Elizabeth and Porchy became close friends in the 1950s due to their keen interest in horse racing. In 1956, Porchy married an American girl, Jean Wallop, eldest daughter of the Honorable Oliver Wallop and Mrs. Wallop of Big Horn, Wyoming. Lord Porchy, a racing man all his life, became chairman, and later president, of the Thoroughbred Breeders' Association, president of the Amateur Riders Association, a member of the Horseracing Betting Levy Board, and chairman of the Jockey Club's race planning committee. In December 1969, Porchy became racing manager to the Queen.

Throughout the late fifties and sixties, Porchester and Elizabeth spent many, many hours together, discussing every aspect of racing: Elizabeth's studs, stallions, broodmares, bloodlines, purchases, sales, race meetings, and of course her string of racehorses currently in training. From Porchy, Elizabeth gained some of her considerable knowledge of the race game of which she is now considered a fine judge.

But there was more to the relationship than racing. In public, Porchester always called Elizabeth Ma'am or Your Majesty and showed her every respect, but in private he called her Lilibet and she called him Harry. Fortunately for Elizabeth, Porchy was not like his father, who boasted of making love to more than a hundred women in his life. The 6th Earl's life nearly came to an untimely end when, at an advanced age, he was found locked in the arms of the Earl of Craven's wife Wilhemina, a gorgeous redhead. Craven burst through the door brandishing a loaded revolver, and Porchester's father beat a hasty retreat through the bathroom as bullets ripped into the door behind him.

Since his father's death in 1987, Harry Porchester has enjoyed the magnificent Highclere Castle, set in six thousand Hampshire acres not far from Broadlands. Harry Porchester's upbringing was typical English aristocracy: educated at Eton, where he was captain of boxing; trained at Sandhurst; served in Egypt with the First Household Cavalry; and released by the army after becoming disabled. He took up farming, but his love has always been racing. He spent a great amount of time and effort on his stud, though, to his credit, he has also spent many years in local government after having failed to gain a seat in the House of Commons in 1953.

Porchy is tall, well built, good looking, and distinguished. Though balding, he looks ten years younger than his three score years and ten. Friends describe him as "charming, polite, with a good sense of humor, and a twinkle in his eye." As a young cavalry officer and the son of the Earl of Carnavon, Porchy was much sought after by ambitious mothers wishing to marry off their daughters to a member of the aristocracy. But Porchy rebelled against tradition and fell in love with a lovely, fresh-faced Wyoming girl who came to England at the age of twenty-one. In a 1989 interview, Harry provided some evidence of his happy domestic life: "We're a very lucky family. My wife and I are very lucky to have our children and grandchildren and each other."

Porchy has also been most fortunate in his close relationship with Elizabeth. For example, she has maintained remarkable faith in him in his capacity as her racing manager, for he has been a downright failure. Throughout Elizabeth's abiding love affair with the race game, she has, like most owners, always dreamed of winning the English Derby at Epsom Downs, the blue riband of racing. But the chances of doing so seem to be drifting further away, not closer. Indeed, during a seven-year lean spell in the 1980s, the Queen did not even have a three-year-old good enough to enter the race, much less win it.

The Queen spends a small fortune, about $500,000 a year, on her string of racehorses and her own stud, and she is in constant conversations with Porchy, who always has a say in which mare to put to which stallion; studying their bloodlines. She also involves herself daily with the more mundane decisions, as which horse should partake in which races. So she, too, is responsible, in her selections of stallions and broodmares, for her lack of success at the very pinnacle of racing. She studies books and computer printouts and constantly educates herself, as well as spending hours discussing with experts the breeding program of the royal stables. She loves knowing the details of all of them, especially if one should go lame or fall ill. Her interest in her racehorses is total. Yet thus far she been unable to breed top-class colts.

During the 1960s Elizabeth began to spend a great deal of time with Porchy and they would frequently meet at Broadlands, where Uncle Dickie would be their host. They would ride together, walk for hours with the dogs, and sit and chat into the night.

Mountbatten became concerned that Elizabeth was infatuated with the handsome Harry Porchester, perhaps even emotionally involved. After much thought Mountbatten took the unprecedented step of writing her a letter of warning.

One of John Barratt's important daily chores was to read all the letters Mountbatten wrote, whether private, public, or official. He said, "Mountbatten would dictate most letters but he always wrote his private ones to Lilibet by hand. He always showed me all the letters he wrote, prior to posting them, so I could check them over and perhaps point out any possible errors.

"I remember very well the letter he wrote to Elizabeth about Porchy. It was in the late 1960s. As usual the letter began 'Dear Lilibet,' and he went on to warn her, 'I urge you to be more discreet in your relationship with Porchy.'" Barratt commented, "Mountbatten had been growing increasingly concerned about the Queen's close relationship with Porchy. He knew what was going on and was worried in case things got out of hand. He saw the way they were to each other, how close they had become, acting towards each other as though lovers.

"I think there was also a sense of jealousy too. However, he was genuinely concerned that she and Porchy were spending too much time together at Broadlands and it was obvious that he believed they were becoming too involved. He told me so; he used to shake his head about it, not knowing how he should tackle the situation. Elizabeth was so animated when Porchy was around, and they got on so well together."

Elizabeth appeared to take little notice of Uncle Dickie's warning for she continued to see much of Harry Porchester, but the couple spent fewer weekends at Broadlands. Later they would travel abroad together on racing business and spend weeks together. Philip hardly ever accompanied his wife on such overseas trips, for he was never a racing man. Since 1975 Elizabeth and Porchy have often visited Kentucky together during the spring yearling sales. They nearly always stay at the Versailles, Lexington farm of one of America's most wealthy and secretive multimillionaires, William Stamps Farish III, a good friend of former President George Bush.

Will Farish's grandfather founded Humble Oil, which later formed the major part of Exxon; his other grandfather was chief executive of Sears, Roebuck. His father died in a flying accident in 1934, when Will Farish was just four. Will Farish married Sarah Sharp, daughter of Bayard Sharp, a du Pont heir and horse breeder. Polo-mad Will and Sarah loved horses and have taken great pride in breeding the finest thoroughbreds in America. As president of the U.S. Jockey Club, Will Farish met Elizabeth during a polo match, and they got on so well he invited her to stay with him and Sarah during the Kentucky horse sales one year. For Elizabeth, the Farish hideaway—Lane's End Farm—was a perfect location, cut off from prying eyes and in the heart of racing country.

During a visit in October 1984, Elizabeth, fifty-eight, became fascinated with a revolutionary computerized bloodstock service installed at Corporate Center in Lexington and spent some time watching the screen as stallions' bloodlines were analyzed and reanalyzed along with those of selected mares to ensure a perfect mating and a good chance to produce foals that would prove winners of Class 1 races. During that visit Elizabeth attended a special meeting at Keeneland, probably America's most beautiful racetrack, where the Queen Elizabeth II Challenge Cup Stakes served as the highlight of the day's racing. Now Elizabeth keeps some of her broodmares in Kentucky, breeding from the plentiful supply of top-class stallions at the Farish and neighboring studs.

One of those neighboring stud farms is owned by Senator Malcolm Wallop, grandson of the Earl of Portsmouth, who owns a magnificent ranch at Big Horn, Wyoming. More important, however, his sister is Jean Wallop, now Lady Porchester, and he is therefore Porchy's brother-in-law. During their 1984 visit Elizabeth and Porchy stayed with him for a couple of nights.

Porchy had every proper reason to accompany Elizabeth to Kentucky, for she needed his advice, but the visit also meant they enjoyed a week together away from the strictures and disciplines of Buckingham Palace. All the people she met during her visits to Kentucky remarked how relaxed and happy Elizabeth appeared whenever she was there. Away from the pressures of life back home, she could revel in never-ending talk of racing and racehorses, the perfect holiday for the horse-mad Elizabeth.

Even today, Elizabeth and Porchy still enjoy each other's company. Most of their business is conducted by telephone, but they do, of course, see quite a lot of each other when planning the Queen's racing calendar and any possible sales or purchases of stallions and mares.

Mountbatten's jealousy over Lilibet manifested itself in odd ways. He kept a most remarkable collection of pornographic books, mainly involving sadomasochism, at Broadlands, though he also kept some at his London home in Kinnerton Street. In one of his favorites, The Riding Mistress, the eponymous heroine, makes her recalcitrant young riders sit astride a wooden horse while she whips. His favorite photographs—transparent colored slides which he would look at through a viewer—nearly always depicted young women, fully dressed for riding in tight breeches or jodhpurs, usually wearing knee-high riding boots and carrying a whip.

Barratt said, "I saw the slides once. There was nothing pornographic about them, however. All the women were dressed and all in riding gear."

Barratt revealed that Mountbatten achieved sexual satisfaction on his ponies, most of which were retired polo ponies. He also disclosed that Mountbatten had a special relationship with one of his grooms, a lovely young girl with a boyish figure named Mary Lou. Her contract stipulated that she was to go out riding twice a week with her employer. Mary Lou was Mountbatten's ideal woman: young, slim, boyish, attractive, and a good horsewoman. The gossip at Broadlands was fed by the fact that whenever Mountbatten rode out with Mary Lou or any of his other girlfriends, he always wore a condom, and all the staff knew this. Mountbatten wore his spurs only when riding out with a woman, but not when riding on his own. He would achieve sexual satisfaction by fiercely spurring his ponies, using the sharp rowels of the spurs, to drive them faster, which frequently caused the ponies to bleed.

One of Mountbatten's great joys was to ride out with Lilibet whenever she visited Broadlands. They would usually go out once or twice together during a weekend. Together they would school their ponies, as all polo players do, riding them in circles and figures of eight. Barratt, however, has no idea if Elizabeth was at all aware of Uncle Dickie's secret sexual proclivities or whether, indeed, any of the girls or young women he rode out with ever knew.

Mountbatten's sexuality has always been a question mark. Barratt, an open homosexual, lived and traveled the world with Mountbatten for twenty years. He swears that His Lordship was never interested in men, young or old, and to his knowledge never had a homosexual relationship nor ever wanted one. He maintains that Mountbatten was openly heterosexual and nearly always attracted to young, slim women with boyish hips.

Philip Ziegler, Mountbatten's noted biographer, is convinced that he was never gay, despite his former naval valet's being madly so and his close relationship for many years with Peter Murphy, a highly intelligent Irishman who had served in the Irish Guards. A noted homosexual as well as a brilliant linguist and pianist, Murphy was denounced as a Communist agent in 1952. His being homosexual and a Communist placed Mountbatten, one of Britain's most senior naval officers, in an awkward position. Western intelligence agencies, particularly the CIA, had become highly concerned about possible Communist infiltrators. Mountbatten asked the British Security Services to investigate Murphy's alleged Communist sympathies and they cleared him of any involvement with the Communist Party. This clearance was passed to the CIA, which accepted that Mountbatten was no security risk.

In his biography Ziegler details a number of Mountbatten's affairs, all with women, both before and after his marriage to the highly sexed Edwina, and he emphasizes that he was always attracted to good-looking, intelligent young women. Both Ziegler and Barratt, however, believe that Mountbatten, though he liked to portray himself as a sexual athlete, was not a very highly sexed man.

In 1975 I helped write a series of articles for the *London Daily Mirror* which revealed details of a homosexual ring centered on the Life Guards barracks in London. A number of young guardsmen informed me that Mountbatten was involved and they gave detailed, signed statements of alleged visits to his Kinnerton Street home. Mountbatten recorded in his diary, "I refused to take this allegation that my name was mentioned in connection with this ring seriously and I said that I might have been accused of many things in my life but hardly of the act of homosexuality." As a result of an internal investigation by the army, five Life Guards officers and thirty-six guardsmen were found guilty of homosexual activities and dismissed from the regiment.

Sir Robert Scott, Permanent Under-Secretary at the Ministry of Defence in the 1960s, and his friend and colleague, remembers Mountbatten saying to him in reference to the same allegations, "Edwina and I spent all our married lives getting into other people's beds." Ziegler claims that Mountbatten exaggerated, believing he conducted only two long extramarital affairs, both with women, to the apparent satisfaction of both parties, but that he was never promiscuous. It was Edwina who was boundlessly promiscuous.

The closer Mountbatten grew to his beloved Lilibet, the further he became estranged from Prince Philip. After spending years working to arrange their marriage, Mountbatten turned against Philip, primarily it seems because he was no longer able to influence his nephew and because he had failed to prevent his persistent adultery. In private conversations with John Barratt, Mountbatten would occasionally say, "Philip can't take this life. There are too many restrictions for him. He can't toe the line. It would have been much better if he had gone off and married some rich American lady. Then he could have had the time of his life without risking himself or Lilibet to public shame."

It was on the advice of Uncle Dickie that Charles went to Gordonstoun, the school of which Mountbatten was a governor and the alma mater of Philip. Heated discussions, even rows, raged for months about Charles's education. The Queen Mother, however, strongly believed Charles should be sent to a traditional English public school. Elizabeth did not know how to evaluate the differing side because she herself had never been to school.

The argument against Gordonstoun was that it would promote radical ideas which might manifest themselves later when Charles became Prince of Wales. The Queen Mother feared that Charles might take after his uncle, Edward VIII, whom she scorned after his decision to abdicate and go off "with that Simpson woman," or that he might become a freethinking, extremist reformer or even a radical philosopher. She and other senior members of the Household preferred schools like Eton or Harrow, fearing the effect of Gordonstoun on a child like Charles, who did not have his father's strong, rebellious character.

Elizabeth's only other emotional involvement was with Patrick Plunket, probably her favorite courtier. She loved having Patrick around the palace, not simply as a highly intelligent adviser but also as a friend and a soul mate. Patrick Terence William Span, 7th Baron Plunket, was two years older than Elizabeth and came to royal service when appointed equerry to King George VI in 1948. From the start Elizabeth responded to Patrick's sweet nature, and when she succeeded to the throne in 1952, Patrick continued as equerry until she promoted him two years later to Deputy Master of the Household, a post he held until his tragic death from cancer in 1975 at the age of fifty-one.

Patrick Plunket never married. When he first arrived on the scene in the late 1940s, he became so popular with the King and Queen, indeed the whole family, that there was a hope he would marry Princess Margaret. A slender, good-looking man with thinning dark hair and an aristocratic profile, Plunket inherited his handsome looks from his mother, the daughter of Fanny Ward, the famous American actress known as the Eternal Flapper. His grandfather, Joseph Lewis, became a celebrated diamond magnate in the Transvaal, South Africa. An aunt brought up Patrick after his parents died in an air crash when he was fourteen. Plunket enjoyed the arts, from opera to classical music, the theater, the cinema, and particularly the world of fine arts. He was never very interested in women, but he wasn't interested in men either. Despite rumors, gossip, and innuendo, the people who knew him well believe that, at heart, Patrick Plunket was asexual.

His relationship with Elizabeth began after the war, in which he served as a lieutenant colonel in the Irish Guards before being wounded. They would go riding together, a pastime which they enjoyed frequently together throughout the next twenty years. Patrick not only rode with Elizabeth, but also frequently went shooting with Philip, fishing with the Queen Mother, and occasionally escorted Princess Margaret before her marriage to Tony Armstrong-Jones.

Charming and witty, he came to be treated almost as one of the family, but he became very, very close to Elizabeth. The whole family showed him warmth and true friendship, which gave him emotional security and a feeling of belonging. In return, Patrick gave dedicated service. An aristocrat by birth and inclination, educated at Eton and Cambridge, Patrick brought a touch of elegance, taste, and a detestation of the second-rate to everything he did. Elizabeth found his personality warm and their friendship very different from her relationship with Philip.

Elizabeth needed someone of Patrick's warmth, generosity of spirit, and lightheartedness to counteract the forceful nature of Philip's full-blooded nature and meteoric changes of mood. Patrick had a knack for diffusing awkward situations and bringing harmony where there was so often discord and argument. Elizabeth appreciated this enormously because she was often fed up with Philip's never-ending ranting and bad temper.

Patrick also had a genius for entertaining, and the family often asked him to join their parties. He would make everyone relax and enjoy themselves, something which many members of the Royal Family find surprisingly difficult. Elizabeth would frequently roar with laughter at Patrick's antics, throwing back her head, tears of pleasure streaming down her face. He was one of the very few men that could draw that reaction from Elizabeth, and she loved him for it. The family nicknamed him "Master of the Revels," for he understood better than anyone how to mix informality with splendor.

Patrick had yet more talents. He had a sure sense of decoration and an instinctive appreciation of quality in sculptures, antiques, and paintings. Patrick enjoyed molding Elizabeth's rather philistine understanding of anything artistic, an effort she appreciated. She had never shown any real interest in the arts, her education had utterly disregarded them, but she did want to learn more, primarily because she had found someone she trusted and liked and who made art fascinating. Patrick, more than anyone, inspired and developed the Queen's Gallery at Buckingham Palace, which has proved such a success.

Patrick's relationship with Elizabeth became remarkably close, and he was a stabilizing influence in the palace for a quarter of a century. In private he would greet her with a kiss on the cheek, which she welcomed. In full view of members of the Household, Patrick always addressed her as Ma'am, though she invariably called him Patrick. Philip was not in the least jealous of the relationship; indeed, he seemed to welcome having Patrick around nearly as much as Elizabeth because it relieved him of all the duties he was unsuited for, such as being pleasant, understanding, comforting, and cheerful.

For over ten years, through the late 1960s and early 1970s, Elizabeth and Plunket would go out secretly together, to dinner, to the cinema and, occasionally, the theater. They would have supper and enjoy a glass of champagne, no one aware of their identities. Frequently on a Monday evening, Elizabeth and Plunket would leave the palace in Elizabeth's old Rover, she dressed in a coat with a scarf over her head, to conceal her identity.

They would often visit a cinema, usually the Odeon in King's Road, Chelsea, two miles from Buckingham Palace. Plunket would pay, always securing two seats at the back of the auditorium, though at that time there were no assigned seats. After the show they would sometimes walk across King's Road to Raffles Club, a highly respectable dining and drinking place which was decorated like a library and not frequented by the aristocracy. They would ask for a table at the back of the dining area, the darkest spot in the club. Together they would enjoy a light meal and a glass of champagne or wine before driving back to the palace around midnight. Apparently no one recognized Elizabeth, perhaps because they never expected to see the sovereign in such places.

These secret outings were an absolute joy to Elizabeth. They were the only moments in her life when she could be among ordinary people, unrecognized and unknown, enjoying mundane life like everyone else.

Occasionally, Elizabeth and Patrick would take long walks together in Windsor Great Park, sometimes alone, but more often than not with the corgis. They particularly loved the beautiful, secluded Valley Gardens, overlooking Virginia Water, which sported white delphiniums and peonies. These flowers became Elizabeth's favorites. After Patrick's death from cancer in 1975, Elizabeth placed a wooden seat in his honor in the Valley Gardens, which today still holds a special place in her heart.

Some have suggested that Elizabeth and Patrick were lovers, but I have found no evidence to support this contention. Their relationship was almost certainly asexual, but in many respects Elizabeth loved Patrick Plunket in a way that she never loved anyone else. She responded to his warmth and kindness, his patience and sincerity. And she felt closer to him than any other man in her life, including Porchester and Prince Philip.

Elizabeth not only liked having Patrick around her most of the time but relied on him greatly, not just for advice but for moral support. He was a kindred spirit who understood Elizabeth better than anyone else, and probably far more so than Philip.

Patrick Plunket was not, however, simply fun to have around. Elizabeth sought his advice in many areas. He was astute and articulate; he understood people and their politics, whether the politics of members of the Household or the politics of government. Perhaps his greatest attribute was his understanding of people and their motives, which proved invaluable to Elizabeth, since recognizing people's baser motives has always been foreign to her nature.

Without personal ambition, Patrick seemed happy as a courtier with a remarkable degree of objectivity, perhaps one of the great criteria for counselors to the powerful. In return for the happiness Patrick brought to Elizabeth's structured life of service, she showered on him those rewards and honors which were in her personal power to grant. In 1955 she made him a Member of the Royal Victorian Order, Commander of the Royal Victorian Order in 1963, and Knight Commander of the Royal Victorian Order in 1974, when she knew he had not long to live. Elizabeth could give no higher personal honors to anyone.

In 1971 Patrick learned he had cancer and told Elizabeth he had been informed that it was incurable. His illness put such a strain on Elizabeth that she, too, became run-down and ill. She was due to undertake an extensive forty-seven-day tour of Southeast Asia with Princess Anne but decided to postpone it to stay in Britain with Plunket. He would not hear of it and persuaded Elizabeth that she must carry out her duty. The trip was not a success, the heat was unbearable, and Elizabeth suffered from stress. She phoned Plunket every day.

Patrick fought his four-year illness with humor and courage. When he became seriously ill Elizabeth was always a frequent visitor at his bedside. When he died in June 1975 she wept openly.

Another man close to Elizabeth through the sixties, seventies, and eighties was Sir John Miller, Crown Equerry from 1961 to 1987, and appointed an extra equerry when he became seventy years old. No man made Elizabeth laugh so much and no man seemed to get into so many scrapes.

Sir John Miller served as an officer in the Welsh Guards throughout World War II and stayed on to command the 1st Battalion, the Welsh Guards, from 1958 to 1961. Horses were his lifelong fascination, and his love of them cemented a strong and lasting relationship with Elizabeth. Since retiring from the army in 1961, Sir John has been president of many British organizations, societies, clubs, and associations, all concerned with various aspects of horses, ponies, riding, and carriage driving. He has also been in charge of every royal ceremonial procession for nearly thirty years.

Sir John summed up his thirty-year career as Elizabeth's equerry in characteristic fashion: "I am what they call the Crown Equerry, which means I am in charge of all the horses and carriages. The cars as well come to that. I've got a lot to be blamed for."

The Queen has often been exasperated with the ever faithful Sir John. Elizabeth's typical cry, heard frequently in the intimate royal circle, is: "Where, oh where, is John Miller?" or "That man always disappears when he's wanted." And yet another variant: "You make me so cross, John."

When called, Sir John would emerge, as if by magic, perhaps from under a carriage or from behind a horse, resplendent in his black bowler, his pince-nez on the end of his nose: "You called, Ma'am," he would say, and on most occasions Elizabeth could only smile and shake her head. He is a lovable, thoroughly charming character whom many see as the quintessential English aristocrat and member of the Royal Household.

Unmarried, Sir John has devoted his life to Elizabeth and to royal service, accompanying her whenever she left home to stay anywhere in Britain, on hand for every eventuality. They would often have supper together, and Elizabeth used him for many years as a sounding board. Elizabeth knew she could rely on this rather pompous man with a dreadfully limp handshake to state his views honestly and openly, saying exactly what he felt. There were never many such people with the courage to do that in Buckingham Palace.

In the 1960s, gossip linked Sir John romantically with a lady-in-waiting at Buckingham Palace. Sir John's answer was typical of him: "When you're a bachelor you have to take someone to a dance. I have known this young lady for many years. But talk of an engagement is absolute bunkum and rubbish."

Another loyal servant, but of totally different character, is Sir Matthew Farrer, the private lawyer to the Queen since 1965. Elizabeth has come to depend more and more on Sir Matthew's opinions and advice, and as a result, she made him both a Commander of the Royal Victorian Order and, in 1983, a Knight Commander of the Royal Victorian Order.

Sir Matthew is an extremely able lawyer held in the highest repute. His family firm, Farrer & Co., founded two hundred fifty years ago, has been the sovereign's advisers for generations. Many of the nation's aristocratic families and members of the establishment come to Farrer & Co. to sort out their legal matters.

The Farrer who currently holds all the Queen's secrets is the most retiring, if not secretive, of men. For example, no official photograph of Sir Matthew exists in the public domain.

Born in 1928, he now flits between his homes in London and Sussex, his office in Lincoln's Inn Fields and, increasingly of late, through the gates of Buckingham Palace. He usually goes by bus rather than by chauffeured Rolls-Royce. And none of his neighbors in London or Sussex have ever met him, although he has lived in the same houses for decades. Over the past fifteen years, as problems have mounted over the marriages of the younger royals, Elizabeth has turned more and more to Sir Matthew Farrer, the lawyer she has come to regard with admiration and who many believe is now one of her principal unofficial advisers.

It is not without irony that Farrer & Co also carry out vast amounts of legal work on behalf of those members of the British press which have exposed the Royal Family to so much embarrassment—those newspapers owned by Rupert Murdoch's News International: the scandal tabloids *The Sun* and the *News of the World,* and the broadsheets *The Times* and *The Sunday Times,* which have of late espoused a degree of republican sentiment.

Sir Matthew has been responsible for seeking solutions not only to the marital problems of Diana and Fergie, but before that also of Princess Anne and Princess Margaret. He was intensely involved during 1992 and 1993 in Elizabeth's decision to pay income tax and spent many weeks in high-level discussions with the Queen as well as her senior courtiers.

Elizabeth's close relationship with Sir Matthew goes back to the time of her sister's separation from Lord Snowdon in 1976, over which the Queen spent many sleepless nights. It was not the first time her sister had caused such heartache. Elizabeth had shared a remarkably happy and carefree childhood with Margaret. Privileged and pampered, cut off from the world and ordinary people, their mother Queen Elizabeth, a stout, warmhearted woman from Scotland, had been determined, and succeeded to a great degree, in allowing them extraordinary freedom.

That freedom has seemed all the more precious to Elizabeth as her childhood recedes with time. Ever since she became Queen, Elizabeth's life has been dictated by protocol, duty, and service, as well as those never-ending boxes of papers she must read, day and night, seven days a week, fifty-two weeks a year.

V

BEHIND PALACE
GATES

NINE

A FAMILY DIVIDED

For better or for worse, Elizabeth's life has been dominated by one man, Prince Philip. The teenage Elizabeth fell in love with her blond, handsome Prince and, despite her father's objections, married her dashing young naval officer. She never imagined at the time that he would be a cantankerous, unfaithful husband and heartless father.

Yet Elizabeth has managed to come to terms with Philip's character and double standards. Very few wealthy, rich, powerful women would have put up with the pain and anguish which Elizabeth has managed to do for nearly fifty years.

She has shown remarkable discipline about her own personal life under the most severe strains imposed almost solely by her husband. At the same time she remains genuinely fond of him, although she admits, "Sometimes he riles me" and on other occasions that "he infuriates me."

Philip's affair with Princess Alexandra, however, caused their marriage to reach a breaking point.

John Barratt recalled, "According to what Mountbatten told me, that was very nearly the last straw. Elizabeth was beside herself with rage and anguish. She was deeply hurt and upset. She felt humiliated and scorned, yet there was nothing she could do."

As Head of the Church of England, she could not divorce her husband. Her only recourse was to ignore him for days and weeks and months. "She gave Philip the cold shoulder treatment," commented a senior courtier in Prince Charles's office. "Elizabeth made him squirm but it didn't put a stop to the affair, which went on for many, many years."

The affair became known throughout the Royal Family, including the household of the Queen Mother and eventually of Prince Charles. Commented John Barratt, "As soon as one royal household hears something juicy, everyone knows within hours, if not sooner. And then of course it's the duty of the senior person, usually the private secretary, to inform their boss of what they have heard on the grapevine. And, invariably, whatever we heard was indeed true."

Elizabeth had known that Philip chased other women. Dickie Mountbatten helped put it in perspective for her, telling her of his own marriage, in which his wife, the wealthy, gifted Edwina, had openly enjoyed liaisons with both men and women, including the Indian leader Pandit Nehru. Mountbatten talked to her of the pain he had suffered at his wife's hands before her early death in 1962.

One of the earliest lessons of Elizabeth's married life was learning to adopt the same attitude to Philip's affairs as Mountbatten had to his wife's. He told her he used to say to himself, "Oh, let her get on with it."

Mountbatten also explained to Elizabeth, "Philip knows what side his bread is buttered. Don't worry, he'll be back." Mountbatten knew how Philip thought because they had had many talks together in the days when Mountbatten planned his nephew's marriage to the future Queen.

When Elizabeth feared losing whatever love Philip had to give, she would seek Mountbatten's advice. On those occasions Mountbatten would discuss Philip's personality and character. He would remind her that Philip was only manifesting his natural sexual aggressiveness and that he was not capable of falling deeply in love.

John Barratt recalled, "Mountbatten knew Philip so well. He knew Philip was just sowing wild oats with no real emotion attached. He would say to Elizabeth, 'Don't worry, he'll get over it.'"

Mountbatten was right, but Philip's affairs took a considerable toll on their marriage and, inevitably, on Elizabeth's love for him. He didn't appear to care what effect his affairs had, for he didn't stop for nearly all his married life.

In those first happy years while Elizabeth was still a princess, Philip did take a strong line as head of the household. He was in his element making decisions, whether choosing the colors for their home or bossing the servants. He enjoyed that role. During those five years

Philip dominated Elizabeth, who seemed happy to be subservient and let the man she loved take responsibility.

But everything changed dramatically on the sudden death of King George in 1952, when Elizabeth became the Queen and Philip was relegated to the role of consort. The sudden change proved difficult enough for Philip, which was to be expected, but the reversal of roles also proved extremely difficult for Elizabeth, the more so because of Philip's aggressive attitude to everyone and everything.

Those close to Elizabeth have often heard Philip shout at his wife, even in company. During the 1970s at Broadlands, John Barratt was in the room with Mountbatten, Elizabeth, and Philip when Philip said to his wife, "I'm thinking of going out for a stroll. Care to come along?"

Elizabeth replied politely, "No, thank you, I think I will stay in. But you go if you wish." Barratt recalled, "Philip gave Elizabeth a piercing look of anger and stormed out of the room, shouting at her, 'Don't come, then. Go to hell.'"

On another occasion, during a royal tour, Philip turned and yelled at Elizabeth, "For God's sake, come along. I'm not prepared to stand here waiting for you any longer. What the hell is wrong with you!" Elizabeth gave him a cold stare, but she obeyed him.

Philip frequently uses the language he learned in the Royal Navy: *fucking* this, *fucking* that, and the word *bloody* most of all. He seems to think swearing is a manly virtue, but Elizabeth, though she puts up with it, finds his language coarse. On occasion she, too, has been known to swear, but very infrequently. The worst she ever says is *bloody*.

Those who have known both Philip and Elizabeth say that in any discussions or arguments between the two, nine times out of ten Elizabeth gives way. She learned early on that Philip not only is obstinate but also hates to lose any argument on any subject with anyone, including his wife.

Philip as consort differs markedly from the model of Albert as consort. Albert believed his individual existence should disappear into that of Victoria; "He should aim at no power by himself or for himself, should shun all attention, assume no separate responsibility before the public, but make his position entirely part of hers and fill every gap which as a woman she would naturally leave in the exercise of her regal functions."

Philip believes nothing of the sort, although when he and Elizabeth are among anyone other than the family, he always acts with the utmost decorum toward Elizabeth, treating her more as the Queen than as his wife. He will stand behind her, never in front; he will usually heed her conversation when in company, rather than speak his own mind; he will always act as if on duty when others are present. On one occasion at Balmoral, where the family was on holiday, he arrived late for drinks before dinner. Only ten guests were present, yet Philip bowed to his wife on entering the room and said, "I'm very sorry I'm late," before going and helping himself to a drink. And he would never leave a room before Elizabeth, even when on holiday.

Nevertheless, within the Royal Household Philip has demanded that he be treated as "Head of the Family," particularly in regard to the upbringing of their children.

It is not known when Elizabeth allowed Philip back into her bed, but, in 1960, seven years after the Coronation, Andrew was born, and four years after that, their youngest son Edward. Philip had been raised without a real father, as his was away during the critical years of his childhood and youth. He was therefore determined to be a strong father figure in his own family. Prevented from continuing in the Royal Navy by the death of King George VI, Philip felt limited in his choice of jobs. Given Elizabeth's many duties and responsibilities, Philip decided that he should be both father and mother to their children.

To equip Charles, his firstborn son, for his role as the next King of England, Philip wanted him to become a man's man, and the best way to achieve that was by his becoming a naval officer. He also believed that a normal schooling, instead of a cloistered existence, cut off from the outside world, as Elizabeth had experienced, would help Charles understand his fellow citizens.

Philip failed, however, to take into account Charles's character. Prince Charles is far more sensitive than his father, instinctively shy and retiring, and has none of Philip's brash self-confidence. Yet Philip disciplined his son, from a very young age, as though he were a junior naval rating rather than a beloved firstborn child. Philip's attitudes toward child rearing verged on the Victorian: Charles was to remain quiet at all times, unless asked to speak; sent to his room for the least misdemeanor; and threatened with a good "thrashing" for the slightest infraction.

Philip frequently administered corporal punishment to his young son, usually his hand on Charles's backside. Later Philip used a slipper or a tennis shoe to beat Charles. Philip once gave him a spanking for sticking out his tongue in public, another time for slipping an ice cube down a servant's neck, and in yet another instance for being rude to guests. And he was always beaten for not immediately obeying his father. All of these beatings took place before Charles turned six.

Charles's first governess, Miss Catherine Peebles (nicknamed "Mipsy"), a good-hearted, kind, no-nonsense Scotswoman, arrived at the palace when Charles was five. She believes that Prince Philip was partly responsible for the boy's nervous, oversensitive personality. Charles was nervous about coming forward and afraid to say anything out of fear of his overbearing father. Mipsy recalled, "If you raised your voice to him, he would draw back into his shell and for a time you would be able to do nothing with him."

At first, Elizabeth tried to intervene to protect her firstborn from Philip's strict discipline, but he would say, "The child must learn to obey, and I intend to teach him."

Mipsy did, however, also have some kind words for Philip. She said, "The Duke of Edinburgh was a marvelous father. He used to set aside time to read to Charles and Anne, or help them put together those little model toys. And he taught them practical jokes, like putting dead birds in guests' beds or feeding visitors tadpole sandwiches."

Charles believed his father was brave, good, and invincible. He imitated his walk, holding his hands behind his back, hoping to please him, and he yearned to grow up to be just like his papa. He desperately wanted his father's confidence and his love. But from the beginning Philip resented the life Charles would lead. Instead of encouraging him, Philip subjected his eldest son to a regime of obedience, trials, and punishment. The man who should have been proud of his son's achievements hardly ever praised him, and whenever he failed at anything Philip was quick to condemn him. Throughout Charles's childhood and teenage years, Philip ignored his son's needs because he was driven to prove himself right and clever. While it is true that Philip taught Charles to stand on his own two feet, it was at a great price.

He refused Charles help when he needed it, refused Charles advice when he asked for it, and, more important, turned his back when Charles yearned for paternal love. The adoration and love Charles bore his father gradually turned to estrangement and fear in the face of icy contempt.

In recent years, Charles told one of his close friends, "I can never remember my father ever telling me he loved me; I can never remember him ever praising me for anything; I can never remember him putting his arms around me and giving me a hug. It was all very sad. It has taught me that I must never be like that with my sons. I want them to know that I love them and to let them feel that I do."

In his determination to bring the British monarchy into the twentieth century and make it more open, Philip persuaded Elizabeth and the Queen Mother to send both Charles and Anne to ordinary fee-paying public schools so they would meet and live among more ordinary children. Charles attended junior schools and what the British call "preparatory" schools. At thirteen, after much fierce argument in the family, Charles was sent to Gordonstoun, which Philip was convinced would "make a man" of him. Philip even instructed headmaster Robert Chew to treat Charles with more severity than the other boys.

Charles received canings and other disciplinary measures from Chew and his housemaster, and he was alternatively teased or ignored by the other boys. Charles would tell his grandmother, the Queen Mother, that during his first year at Gordonstoun he cried himself to sleep most nights. In an effort to bring some comfort to his miserable life, the Queen Mother took to inviting Charles frequently to Birkhall, her Scottish home on the Balmoral estate, not far from Gordonstoun. There, Charles, suffering from homesickness and loneliness, found a sympathetic and comforting shoulder to cry on. The Queen Mother has always had a soft spot for Charles and understood the ordeal of this quiet child in an alien world.

"He is a very gentle boy with a kind heart, which I think is the essence of everything," she once said. The Queen Mother believed Charles would have been happier and more confident if he had gone to Eton. She also knew that Elizabeth would have much preferred Charles to attend that quintessentially elite school because it was close to Windsor Castle, but Philip and Uncle Dickie had won the argument, and Charles went to Gordonstoun.

Charles enjoyed his three years at Cambridge, for at university he could behave as he wished and was able to strike up a number of happy relationships with people of different ages. Moreover, he was spared the school discipline his father believed would be the making of him. Charles also enjoyed the Royal Air Force, where he learned to fly, and later, piloted jets and helicopters.

Philip, backed by Dickie Mountbatten, then decreed that he must spend some years in the Royal Navy. In November 1971, at age twenty-three, Charles joined the guided-missile destroyer HMS *Norfolk* and found life on board with thirty-three stuffy British officers so miserable that he confessed to spending many nights in his tiny cabin, once again crying himself to sleep.

One officer on HMS *Norfolk* who became a close friend recalled, "He really was so very unhappy during the nine months on *Norfolk*. He felt alone and miserable. It is not an exaggeration to say he hated his time in the navy. Most of his life, particularly at school, he felt people didn't want to chat with him or become his friend because he was heir to the throne."

Charles had hoped his fellow officers would be able to cope, but they feared adverse effects on their naval careers if they as much as argued with him.

Chief Petty Officer Michael Colborne, who later became the comptroller of Charles's private office, saved Charles's sanity during those first five years in the Royal Navy. Charles admired his honesty, common sense, and understanding of life and people. There was a natural empathy between the two men, even though Colborne was fourteen years older. Unlike any other older man he had ever met, except perhaps for Mountbatten, Colborne was warm and open, honest and straightforward, all the qualities Charles admired but never found in the people around him. His friendship with Michael Colborne would become one of the most important relationships of Charles's life.

By the side of his bunk Charles kept only one photograph, that of Princess Alexandra, who had always shown him kindness and friendship. It was an odd choice, since he certainly knew of her ongoing affair with his father.

Elizabeth turned over almost all parental authority to Philip, allowing him to raise their four children. She gave Charles and Anne the same type of upbringing she had experienced, seeing them only twice a day, thirty minutes in the morning at around nine and another forty-five minutes in the evening before bedtime. They spent the rest of the time with nannies.

Times had changed by the 1960s, and Andrew and Edward suffered much less discipline than Charles or Anne. They were given more freedom, and their relationship with both Elizabeth and Philip was more open, although they were still cared for primarily by nannies.

After the war, Britain's aristocratic families were crippled by escalating taxes and death duties. It was primarily the impact of severe taxes on Britain's rich and aristocratic families that changed their child-rearing practices after World War II. Some families had to pay tax on unearned income at 83 percent. They were also forbidden to claim tax relief on any household employees. As a result, the number of people they employed in their homes cut a deep swath in the army of domestic servants they had employed previously. This resulted in wealthy parents becoming more involved in rearing their own children, rather than handing them over to nannies and maids to take care of their offspring.

The Royal Family never paid direct taxes, or death duties, and Elizabeth continued her life in the time warp of Buckingham Palace, where the royal lifestyle had not altered in decades. Servants, footmen, pages, maids, and cooks continued to populate the various royal residences, though today their numbers are somewhat reduced. Despite the family's wealth, no comprehensive central heating existed in Buckingham Palace, Windsor Castle, Sandringham, or Balmoral until the 1960s.

From the moment Charles was born, in November 1948, Elizabeth was all too happy to have others care for him, and even more so when Anne came along two years later. Elizabeth never changed a diaper or bathed any of her children; they were always brought to her sitting room shiny clean at the appointed time, and she would hold and talk to them while their nanny would report on their progress. Then

Elizabeth would politely hand them back. Her children were only a small part of her life. Elizabeth spent more time caring for her beloved corgis than for her own children.

Once they became teenagers, a standing joke among the four children has always been how difficult it is for any of them to see their mother on her own, and impossible to see her without the dogs being around.

Yet when all her children had grown up Elizabeth did confess, once, "I came to the throne when I was very young, and I never had the opportunity to bring up my children. The Crown separated them from me. It is something that I have regretted all my life, and I am determined that Charles shall not be put in that position. I want him to be a father to his children, because I was never allowed to be a mother to mine." Elizabeth was being less than honest, for when Andrew arrived in 1960, eight years after she came to the throne, and Edward four years later, Elizabeth was once again happy to have them cared for by nannies and maids, though she had more time to herself.

On one occasion Anne was asked if she left her children with her mother when she had to be away. Anne replied, "Leave the children with Mother, you must be joking. That's the last thing she would want."

Charles's relationship with his mother has been described by family counselors as "unhealthy" because he was expected, even by Philip, to treat Elizabeth as the Queen rather than as an ordinary boy would treat his mother. Throughout his life Charles has shown his mother the utmost respect. Adhering to all her wishes and demands, he believed she could do no wrong. He was brought up never to argue with his mother, never to be critical, and to accept all she said. It was a point that Diana could not bear. Time and again Diana would have violent arguments with Charles because he would refuse to disobey his mother or even argue with her. Diana became infuriated because Charles would not express his own opinion but would agree with his mother's point of view even if it was diametrically opposed to his own.

Throughout the early years of his life Charles worshipped his father, despite the discipline meted out to him. The adult Charles shares many interests with his father. Both men are talented watercolor painters. Both are avid readers and are deeply interested in philosophy. (Charles, however, loves music and the opera, whereas Philip does not.) In different ways, both are highly intelligent men, though neither would suggest for a moment that they are intellectuals.

Charles also tried to emulate his action-minded father, to the point where it began to annoy Philip. Charles tackled everything, and more, that his father did. They both sailed small boats and captained Royal Navy ships; both played polo well; both shot deer and birds and fished expertly; both flew aircraft and helicopters competently.

But Charles excelled in some of these activities where his father was only competent. Charles was a far better pilot than his father, particularly with choppers; Charles flew fighter jets at speeds exceeding Mach 1 and parachuted from aircraft, neither of which Philip ever did. He also skied downhill much better than Philip, snorkel dived, team raced on horseback, and hunted deer and fox with hounds, all things Philip hadn't done.

In their baser interests, however, they are extremely different, particularly concerning the opposite sex. All his life Philip has felt the need to prove himself with women, chasing, flirting, and bedding them. Charles has had far deeper, meaningful relationships than his father.

Those very few who know both Philip and Charles well believe that the father's attitude toward the son has been dictated by a deep-seated resentment that the son, as King, would be accepted, respected, honored, and legitimized in a way Philip could never achieve. Some believe his jealous bullying was to have a disastrous effect on Charles's life.

Although Charles was not privy to the great majority of his father's sexual escapades, he did learn of the long-standing affair with Princess Alexandra. It hurt him that his father should have subjected his mother, whom Charles adored and respected, to such humiliation. Father and son did not speak for some months. For Charles, who had hero-worshipped his father in his younger days, it was perhaps the single most important event that changed forever Charles's relationship with Philip for, at a stroke, he lost his respect for him.

Princess Anne was much like her father, a girl with guts and courage, a forthright attitude, a no-nonsense approach to life which Philip greatly admired. Anne would be rude to people in public and stubborn in private. Philip would laugh and forgive her, although Elizabeth tried to control her wayward daughter, who was far more challenging than Charles had ever been.

During her teenage years at Benenden, a girls' school housed in a Victorian mansion in Kent, forty miles from London, Anne had on occasion been rude and difficult to the teachers, but she had also made some firm friends. She was spirited, vigorous, and, some complained, even pushy. But she spoke her mind and stood her ground whenever challenged. At sixteen she became captain of her house and house-mother, both positions of responsibility.

If Anne were not a royal, she might be described as a "plain Jane." At sixteen Anne felt awkward in public and lacked confidence in herself. She thought herself ugly, with a protruding nose, eyes too close together, and overweight. And she hated her hair, which her mother said made her "look like a sheepdog." Anne would use her beautiful, thick, long hair as a shield against the none-too-friendly world, brushing it forward over her forehead.

Philip told her that character and personality were far more important than looks. Anne would remember this dictum when the beautiful Diana arrived on the scene. Her father talked to his polo-playing friends with children Anne's age and suggested she would enjoy their company. A flood of invitations—to balls, dinner parties, weekends away, and barbecues—arrived, and at eighteen, Anne finally began to enjoy what had been difficult teenage years.

Philip wanted to be a responsible father and would take Charles and Anne away once every month or six weeks for a weekend on their own, usually to Sandringham. Later, Andrew and Edward would also join his family weekends. Elizabeth, however, hardly ever attended these occasions, which were reserved for Philip and the children. They would eat together, go for walks, sometimes shoot, ride, play games, watch a film, and, more important, talk together. The purported purpose was to resolve problems that might be unique to royals. Most of the time, however, Philip would lecture, telling his children what they were doing wrong and how they should behave in the future.

Philip intended the weekends to be fun, an opportunity to relax and enjoy each other's company away from the strictures of Buckingham Palace. He wanted his children to live like ordinary youngsters for those two or three days. Instead he spent the time ridding himself of tensions, demanding the children's obedience and absolute attention. These weekend retreats went on for years until Charles and Anne reached their late twenties and decided they no longer wanted to go. What is surprising is that the children attended as long as they did.

Philip also insisted that his offspring learn to appreciate their privileged life, pull their weight, and not just carry out royal duties. During his bachelor days Charles would take a dozen or so people to Sandringham twice a year, usually for a few days or a weekend shoot in September and January. He would have the run of the place, shooting during the day followed by boisterous dinners where the wine flowed.

Philip decided in the early 1970s that his son should bear the cost of such treats and ordered Charles to pay the going rate (set by Philip) for the shoots. Charles's friends had no idea that he had to pay to use the family home, but in the late 1970s and early 1980s, he would contribute $2,000 to $2,500 to the Sandringham coffers for a weekend shoot. Eventually he gave up the parties, not because he couldn't afford them but because he was outraged to be forced to pay for the privilege: Sandringham was one of Elizabeth's personal homes and had nothing to do with the state. But Philip wanted to be sure his children realized they had to pay their way in life, that nothing came for nothing.

In 1977, when Charles was twenty-nine, Philip simply stopped talking to his son. During the 1970s Philip saw Charles become a likable, well-rounded young man who was respected and liked by the British public. Eventually, Charles's privileged life and popularity consumed Philip until he could no longer could contain the deep-seated jealousy.

Philip's phone calls to Charles ceased and, what was worse, he would not accept calls from Charles. He ordered his own staff to stop liaising with Charles's office unless absolutely necessary for logistical reasons. When entering a room Philip would deliberately avoid Charles, never looking in his direction, pretending he wasn't there. Only in public would he address Charles, but his smile was glacial and he spoke no more than was necessary.

From 1977 onward Philip went out of his way to avoid being with his son so they never had to speak. There are virtually no photographs showing the two men alone together in that period, although 1977 marked the Queen's Silver Jubilee, celebrated by walkabouts throughout the land, with Elizabeth, in her way, pressing the flesh of her subjects surrounded by her ostensibly loving family.

Charles simply could not understand why his father had turned against him. In vain, he tried to speak to him, to ask why his father acted as though he no longer existed. The only response was silence. When Charles tried to raise the subject whenever the whole family met at Windsor weekends or Balmoral holidays, Philip would simply ignore Charles and speak only to his other three children.

Charles asked his mother if he had done anything to upset his father. Apparently not recognizing the deep-seated resentment Philip felt toward Charles, Elizabeth told her son, "You know what he is like. He will get over it soon enough." But Philip didn't get over it.

Charles would ask his staff and friends about their relationships with their fathers, whether fathers cut off sons for no apparent reason. The answers indicated that while fathers varied greatly, no other father completely cut a son out of his life.

Once again Charles turned to Uncle Dickie. Mountbatten was open and straightforward. He told Charles it was jealousy, that he would be the next King no matter what happened, and that Philip had never been able to succeed in a career because he had never been allowed the chance.

Elizabeth also talked to Uncle Dickie and asked him to try to persuade Philip to rethink his attitude to Charles. She said, "I have tried to talk to him about it but he won't listen to me."

Mountbatten urged Philip to rekindle the relationship with his son, but Philip refused, saying, "It is none of your business. Mind your own business and keep your nose out of my family affairs." As a result of this further setback in Philip's relationship with Uncle Dickie, they drifted still further apart. By the time of Mountbatten's assassination, in August 1979, the two hardly ever spoke.

The effect of his father's behavior has been emotionally devastating to Charles. To this day, he has been far more wounded than most people know.

Elizabeth had always known of Philip's jealousy of Charles. She saw it when Charles was a child, how Philip deliberately criticized his son, rarely displaying affection or offering praise for anything. She noted how Philip pushed Charles, ridiculing him while withholding the encouragement and support the boy craved from his father. Elizabeth was aware that when anyone made a fuss over Charles, Philip would instantly become critical of him.

Worried that Philip's attitude would cause unbreachable divisions in the family, Elizabeth remained concerned about Charles throughout his childhood and teenage years. She had known Charles was not strong but hoped Philip's treatment would help him grow up with the determination and strength of character he would need as King so that the monarchy would survive in the next century.

Elizabeth always wanted to know how Charles was faring. She asked schoolmasters, senior officers, polo players, friends, and colleagues whether her eldest son was coping and enjoying his life. In the words of a polo patron, "She was a bit of a mother hen with Charles. She worried about him, even asking if his ponies were fast and safe. She asked whether his flying was competent or whether it was wise to permit him to fly helicopters or particular aircraft. She even worried when he went skiing and hated the idea of him parachuting. Yet she never wanted to stop him actually doing anything. And I always noted that whenever the Queen did ask me such questions, Philip was never around."

In the early 1980s when Charles was having marital difficulties, he lost interest in his royal duties. He had become disillusioned with everything and everyone. He still absolutely respected his mother but there was little affection. None had ever really existed. His father had turned his back on him, and Charles had lost all respect for him. Dickie Mountbatten, always a source of consolation and affection, had been murdered by the IRA in 1979. His death was a tragedy not only for Charles, but for the entire Royal Family.

Because Princess Anne was a girl, she did not encounter the same pressures from her father as the three boys. Most people who know the four children well say that Anne seems to have more macho instincts than any of her brothers. Some believe her intelligence, sense of humor, down-to-earth approach to life, and natural aggression would make her an excellent heir to the throne. Philip adored his only daughter.

After shaking off her teenage lack of confidence, Anne enjoyed the company of several young men before meeting her husband-to-be Mark Phillips. She had affairs with the former Scottish racing driver Jackie Stewart and the young English polo player Sandy Harper. Irreverently Sandy used to tell the story of Anne's knickers because she never wore frilly, dainty, or sexy panties but always the same style: big, unflattering, white cotton, schoolgirl knickers.

Anne had wanted to marry Sandy Harper, but he didn't want to become involved with the Royal Family and the two drifted apart. As a polo pal put it, "Sandy was worried shitless of what he was getting involved with, the royals and everything; he didn't want to know. But Anne and Sandy had a jolly good dingdong going for some months."

Louis Brown, the late owner of the Valbonne night club in London's West End, would tell of the nights Anne and Sandy Harper visited his club. "Understandably, they would always ask for a table in the darkest part of the club, and I always tried to make sure their privacy was respected. They would indulge in the most passionate embraces most of the night as they had a meal and listened to the music until the early hours. It was an opportunity for the Princess to let her hair down."

Both Elizabeth and Philip were surprised when they finally met Captain Mark Phillips, for he wasn't at all the sort of young man with whom they imagined their daughter would fall in love. Elizabeth found Mark quiet and unassuming and knew immediately that Anne would be the dominant partner. Philip found Mark dull and boring and told everyone so whenever they discussed the marriage. The Queen Mother, on the other hand, believed the couple were a perfect match, suggesting even that a computer would have selected them.

Mark is shy and inarticulate, whereas Anne has the quick-witted intelligence of her father. When the couple appeared on a television talk show at the time of their engagement, Mark barely got a word in edgewise while Anne controlled the interview. The Royal Family nicknamed Mark "Fog," suggesting he was not very bright.

After an affair that began over their love of horses, Anne, twenty-three, and Mark, twenty-five, were married in November 1973, just a year after her parents' silver wedding anniversary.

Anne had won the admiration of her parents, and her spurs, eventing horses, winning the 1971 European Championship on Doublet, a pony Elizabeth had bred to join Philip's string of polo ponies. Doublet became a brilliant eventer instead. Mark Phillips had been a member of the British eventing Olympic Team in 1972. Their lives were horses.

Mark insisted he did not want to join The Firm under any

circumstances and turned down a title the Queen offered. Anne was pleased because it meant their children would grow up as commoners, only distantly related to the Royal Family, far down in line of succession and uninvolved with the myriad duties of royalty. She believed they would be happier and freer. By refusing a title Mark Phillips would not have to undertake any royal functions, and the newlyweds happily went off to live with their horses in the country, in a lovely Gloucestershire home, Gatcombe Park, which the Queen gave Anne as a wedding present.

Mark recognized that Philip thought little of him, and in return he made it known he disliked visiting Sandringham, Windsor, or Balmoral for family weekends and holidays. In contrast, the best holidays of Anne's life are spent at Balmoral with the family. Philip did not care if he ever saw Mark, but Elizabeth became upset when her son-in-law wanted to be on his own. The fact that Mark spurned his wife's family did not augur well for their future.

At first Anne and Mark were inseparable, either at equestrian events around the country or working together at Gatcombe Park. But after the birth of their son Peter, in 1978, Anne and Mark began drifting apart. Anne fell in love with her detective, Sergeant Peter Cross, and became involved in a passionate two-year affair. When Mark learned later of this affair, it was the beginning of the end.

In 1983, when Anne told her parents that her marriage was all but over, neither expressed much surprise. Philip had never believed Mark was an ideal husband for Anne, and Elizabeth felt Mark had never made the effort to get to know the family. Elizabeth told Anne, "I think it will be terribly sad for Peter and Zara." (Zara was the baby Mark Phillips suspected had been fathered by another man.)

Peter had become Elizabeth's favorite grandchild. She used to walk slowly along the corridors of Buckingham Palace holding his hand, even when he was only three and four years old, pointing out to him the names of the men and women in the huge portraits hanging in the palace corridors. She would spend twenty or thirty minutes explaining the relationship of the various people, as though giving him a history lesson. And Peter, who obviously had no idea what Elizabeth was talking about, was happy to toddle along holding on to his grandma's hand.

Anne, who has always been open about her mother's lack of

maternal feelings, commented, "The first time I saw them together I couldn't believe my eyes. There was my mother with my child behaving as though she was really enjoying herself with Peter. I've never her seen her ever spend more than a minute with any child."

After his parents' divorce, Peter Phillips spends even more time with Elizabeth, and they get on extremely well.

Understandably, both Philip and Elizabeth were easier on their younger sons, Andrew and Edward. Both were given much more freedom of expression and behavior than their older siblings, though Philip made sure they were obedient to both him and their mother. Rumors have spread suggesting that Andrew, or Edward, or both, were fathered not by Philip but by men such as Porchy or Patrick Plunket. I have researched these claims as far as is possible and can find nothing at all to substantiate them. They are the stuff of royal gossip, with no substance in fact.

Prince Andrew rebelled more against his mother than his father. He was less deferential than his elder brother Charles, but he quickly understood that he had to obey his father. Andrew would even be playfully rude to his mother, but would not be chastised as Charles was when he was a child. Of all his children, Andrew resembled Philip most: aggressive, strong, and opinionated. Andrew also emulated many of his boorish habits. Elizabeth takes it for granted that at least one of her sons would be like their father.

Andrew also took after his father in his aggressiveness with women during his late teens and twenties. Whereas Philip was always discreet, Andrew became unpopular with many he tried to date and bed because they knew he viewed them as only a notch on his belt. The actress Koo Stark was typical of the sort of girl who attracted him: sexy, raunchy, daring. Their relationship was destroyed by the press because she had appeared in soft-porn movies. Although unsuitable for a prince of the House of Windsor, she was in fact intelligent and most pleasant. She also helped educate Andrew sexually, and he was so smitten that he wanted to set up home with her and, so he said, eventually marry her.

Philip, members of the Household, and the media thoroughly disapproved. Philip intervened personally, advising his son that although Koo Stark was a lovely girl, she was not quite right for him, the family, and especially not his mother. A friend of Philip's commented, "It was as if Andrew had to be reminded that his mother was the Queen."

Andrew was determined to enjoy himself and did so, just like his father a generation before. His romantic escapades were frequently the stuff of gossip in the press. Once he turned up unexpectedly on his birthday at the home of a girlfriend, Katie Rabett, a lovely young blonde who, unknown to her parents, was working as a nude model. Katie Rabett's parents, who lived in an ordinary, sober, middle-class area of London, entertained Andrew with a meal and drinks. The next day newspapers published pictures showing Andrew and Katie kissing good night on the doorstep, accompanied by raunchy pictures of her in the nude. Her father, who had had no idea his daughter was a nude model, protested angrily: "If she has not told me the truth, I shall smack her bottom."

Andrew also attended School Dinners, a London club whose members were punished by attractive young waitresses dressed in maid's black dresses, white aprons, and black stockings. The dresses were very short, revealing black suspenders, lots of bare thigh, and panties. The waitresses would punish the members—all men—by making them bend over and caning their backsides. Andrew loved it.

Both Elizabeth and Philip were informed of the treatment Prince Andrew received at the hands of his fellow officers on the aircraft carrier HMS *Invincible*, as it steamed toward the Falkland Islands in the spring of 1982. Prince Andrew, who piloted a Sea King helicopter, had joined the British task force sent by Prime Minister Margaret Thatcher to evict the Argentines occupying the British base in the south Atlantic.

An officer on board *Invincible* recalled, "Andrew was being a real pain to everyone, throwing his weight around as though he was the ship's captain rather than just a twenty-two-year-old sub-lieutenant, a helicopter pilot, like the rest of us. After we had sailed more than halfway towards the Falklands many of us were heartily fed up with him. One night, after a few drinks, he was invited on deck and we beat the shit out of him. So that no one would get into trouble a number of us had a go at him. We had just had enough of his bragging, treating us like dirt."

The punishment meted out to Sub-Lieutenant Prince Andrew

seemed to work wonders for the young man. *Invincible's* captain found out, and secret messages were flashed back to London and eventually passed on to Elizabeth and Philip. (Andrew has never been told his parents were informed of the incident.) The captain reported that Andrew seemed to be suffering no ill effects and commented later, "It was the best thing that happened to him. After that he was a different chap. He took it and learned the lesson. As far as I understand no hard feelings. He knew he was being a pain."

Like many mothers, Queen Elizabeth has always treated her youngest child, Prince Edward, as her perpetual little boy, causing him many personal problems. Philip treated all his children, from earliest youth, as though they were adults. It was the same with Edward, who, to a great extent, had the same shy, retiring nature as Prince Charles.

As a result, Elizabeth felt more maternal toward Edward than the rest of her children. Edward was a delightful child, always smiling and loved by everyone. Philip, however, determined to make a man of his youngest son the way he had with Charles. Philip believed that because Edward appeared weak and quiet, even an introvert, he had to work harder to make a man of him.

Prince Philip, who knew from experience, once said there weren't many options open to his sons other than the armed services, and that if they did not make a career there the Church remained the only option. For Philip, entering holy orders meant retreating from life.

Like Charles, Edward was unhappy at the spartan Gordonstoun. He would have been far happier at Eton or Harrow or any other major public school which put less emphasis on the hard life of cold showers and morning runs through snow and ice dressed only in singlet and shorts. But Philip decreed that he must follow in his footsteps and those of his two elder brothers.

Philip was honored to be invited to become Honorary Captain General of the Royal Marines, one of Britain's toughest and most respected fighting arms, similar in pride and skills to the U.S. Marines. He decided that as Charles and Andrew had both seen service in the Royal Navy, it would be an excellent idea for young Edward to join the Royal Marines instead. Philip could not have chosen anyone less suited to the rigors of such a life. To succeed in the marines a young man needed the aggression and confidence of a man like Philip. Edward at twenty-three was shy and rather weak. He had enjoyed his three years at Cambridge University, like Charles; there Edward became involved in amateur dramatics and felt at home with music, the opera, theater, ballet, and dance. He wanted a career in the arts, preferably in the theater, and what he definitely didn't want, after the ordeal of Gordonstoun, was a life in the armed services.

One of Philip's proudest moments as a father took place in October 1986 when Edward began his training at the marines headquarters. By Christmas Edward confessed to his brothers that he found the course "too hard and too rigorous," the discipline "too strict," and much of the training "mindlessly boring and juvenile." He also told his father that he did not belong in the marines and had no intention of making the Royal Marines his career. Philip tried to understand, believing his son was just going through the usual doubts of young men when they enter an extraordinarily tough regime. He had no doubt that by the end of the six-month course Edward would thoroughly enjoy the experience and look back on the training as "not all that bad."

Philip had failed to notice that his son was looking nervous and tired and that his spirits were low. But Elizabeth had noticed, and she was worried. She worried that Philip refused to understand the character of his son and tried talking with him about Edward's unhappiness. Stubborn as ever, Philip would not hear of Edward's withdrawing. "I am absolutely determined that he'll finish the course," he said. "It'll make a man of him. Edward needs a bit of toughening up."

So Edward, stamina flagging and feeling miserable and alone, returned to barracks. A month later, in January 1987, Edward quit the Marines in a blaze of anguish and acrimony from his father. Edward had tried to complete the training schedule, which even the marines admit is "bloody tough." More important, Edward had wanted to prove to his father that he was indeed a real man, but the rigors of the training and the mental anguish had been too much for him.

In the bitter family row that followed, Elizabeth seemed determined to challenge her husband. When Edward arrived home, Philip shouted at him, calling him all kinds of obscene names, accusing him of letting down the family, of being a "quitter" and a "coward." For three hours, Philip raged while Edward cried and stammered, trying to explain why he had walked out. Philip didn't want to know.

In turn, Elizabeth was angry with Philip. A member of the Household heard one of the violent arguments between them and recalled, "I had never heard Elizabeth raise her voice like that before. I had never heard her challenge her husband in that way, accusing him of being responsible for Edward's decision to quit because he had never bothered to try and understand his sons. She let Philip have it with both barrels."

The following weekend Elizabeth's anger with Philip boiled over, this time in public. They were attending a pheasant shoot for local farmers at Sandringham. Elizabeth decided to show Philip, the man who prided himself on being great at everything he touched, that he wasn't the Mr. Wonderful he thought he was. In a loud voice, so all could hear, Elizabeth accused him of mishandling the gundogs and of being "ignorant"; she accused him of failing to arrange the shoot properly, telling him that the shoot had been his responsibility. Never before had anyone witnessed Elizabeth criticizing Philip in public, ridiculing his competence in front of his social inferiors.

Philip, embarrassed at being made to look incompetent in front of local farmers, shouted angrily at Elizabeth, "What the fuck are you complaining about? I know what I'm doing. Why don't you fuck off!" Elizabeth, her face filled with fury, strode away from the shoot, leaving Philip fuming and angry.

The drama over Edward made Elizabeth realize how wrong she had been to leave the children's upbringing to such a narrow-minded man and not being involved herself as they grew up. She was angry with Philip and with herself, but she also felt helpless and alone. She saw how much more difficult life had become since the death of Mountbatten, who had been so understanding, not just to her but also to the children. There was no one to whom she could turn for advice. She believed her mother, then eighty-seven, and her ever-faithful Bobo, eighty-three, who were so helpful in the past, were too now old to trouble with family problems.

She determined to take a closer interest in her children. But she feared it was too late, the damage was done, although in 1987 the full extent of its repercussions could never have been imagined.

TEN

STORM CLOUDS

Most of the major crises that have plagued Elizabeth and the monarchy throughout her more than forty-odd years on the throne have not been political, constitutional, or affairs of state. To her great embarrassment, they have been personal family matters involving all that she finds deeply disturbing and abhorrent: adultery, separations, divorce, and remarriage. These problems have given her much heartache and personal grief and, in her view, undermine the monarchy and the role people expected the Royal Family to play in the affairs of the nation.

Elizabeth has been held in the highest esteem by the great majority of the British people, and no one can point an accusing finger at the way she has gone about her life's work. But there is a feeling throughout the nation that she has been let down personally by her immediate and extended family. And in nearly every case, it has always been "sins of the flesh" that have caused the embarrassment and the problems which she has tried to solve, virtually alone.

Throughout much of her reign Elizabeth has been seemingly engaged in a titanic struggle to stop, or certainly to slow, society's changes in attitudes and practices. Since 1950 in particular, her subjects have manifested fundamental changes concerning the values of matrimony, divorce, "living in sin," and having children out of wedlock. Elizabeth has valiantly fought these great social changes by promoting the Christian and Victorian principles she was brought up to believe are sacrosanct and which, in her view, are necessary to a healthy, stable society.

At the start of her reign her attitude toward divorce reflected her grandmother Queen Mary's profound belief that it should never be tolerated under any circumstances. Now Elizabeth is simply sur-rounded by divorces: a third of British marriages end in divorce, and in her own family marriage after marriage has ended in disaster. Elizabeth knows that Queen Mary would never have tolerated such behavior, but she is no longer able to pretend that these changes have not occurred.

In the early 1980s *The Sunday Times Magazine* in Britain published an alphabet of "The Greatest" people in the world at that time. Under *Q* the magazine selected Queen Elizabeth II, explaining, "So much dignity in presiding over the dissolution of the Empire... the demonstrations of loyalty at her Silver Jubilee in 1977 and the unrivalled interest aroused by her and her family all over the world."

The Queen's policy of a slightly more open monarchy seemed to have hit a rich vein at the beginning of the 1980s; after a fairy-tale romance, Charles had married Diana, the young woman who had captured the hearts of the Western world and presented the Royal Family with an heir, Prince William.

In her celebrated biography *Elizabeth R*, published in 1982, Elizabeth Longford wrote:

> The monarchy has grown smarter, the courtiers shrewder, and the megastar status of the royal family has given it immense interna-tional interest and prestige. With so much popularity—and with the royal income automatically adjusted through the Civil List—the monarchy has made itself virtually invulnerable to politics and politicians.
>
> But the true measure of Elizabeth II's extraordinary achievement is that, for all the changes which have happened in her reign, she has surrendered nothing of the essence of the royal myth which she accepted as a sacred trust from that dedicated king, her father....
>
> As a human story and a super-human dream remorselessly conveyed throughout the world by all means of modern mass communications, the monarchy is more than ever indispensable, and probably immortal....
>
> At the same time the Queen's younger children have shown themselves impressive additions to the "Royal Firm," Prince Edward teaching for two terms in a New Zealand school and Prince Andrew establishing the traditional connection between the monarch and the people in time of war. Prince Andrew's performance in the Falklands task force on HMS *Invincible*, where his Sea King helicopter was used as a decoy for an Exocet missile, proved to be an

irresistible mixture of the heroic and the human.....

Whether or not Elizabeth II speaks her mind on any particular occasion, the nation is fully aware of her standards and deeply felt religious beliefs. After thirty years she is intuitively understood and wholeheartedly respected. Against the hurly-burly of national life her thoughts have become a kind of ideal voice-over, no less moving and effective for being often unspoken.

This idealized, perhaps idyllic, view of Elizabeth, her character, and her close family, was shared at that time by the great majority of the British people, from the highest to the lowest in the land. The following decade, however, would see a series of scandals that struck at the very heart of her family and would radically alter people's perceptions of the monarchy and the role of the royals. The scandals even brought into doubt the nation's loyalty to the Crown itself.

But it wasn't only during the 1980s that the House of Windsor suffered disruptions and divorces. Since she became Queen, scandals involving the royals have plagued Elizabeth. Although many influential people have been well aware of their existence, until now the public has not known about them.

From the moment she became Queen, Elizabeth wanted her family to be the epitome of a loving, caring nuclear family, a moral examplar to the British people. She wanted to emulate Queen Victoria, regarded as a paragon of virtue for the nation. Elizabeth understood that two disastrous world wars had weakened the people's moral fiber as well as their sense of duty, obligation, and observance of the values of the earlier half of the century.

Throughout her reign Elizabeth hoped and tried, by her example, to restore that sense of responsibility, of bounden duty to family life. Certainly before World War II, divorcées were treated by the Royal Family like lepers and ostracized by the court. Once again, it was the strict moral code of Queen Mary, George V's wife, who had laid down the Royal Family's rules on morality, sex, and divorce. During her twenty-six years on the throne, divorced people were never allowed in the presence of the monarch. Moreover, any divorced person, man or woman, or even the wronged party in a marital dispute, could not be presented at court or meet any members of the immediate Royal Family. Queen Mary was the most powerful force within the Royal Family at that time, and so strict was her adherence to the sanctity of marriage that divorced men and women were even forbidden entry to the Royal Enclosure at the races.

It was Wallis Simpson's status as a divorcée that ultimately cost King Edward VIII his crown. His mother, Queen Mary, made clear her moral disapproval of her son, heir to the throne.

The 1960s brought dramatic changes in society. This was the Swinging Sixties, the time of the Beatles and the introduction of the contraceptive pill and its revolutionary effect on the sex lives of the younger generation as well as their marital practices. Divorce and infidelity became widespread.

Elizabeth tried desperately to hold the line against social change, and her attitude to divorce was still unforgiving as late as 1967, the fifteenth year of her reign. In a remarkable demonstration of her belief in the principles of the old moral code, Elizabeth acted with dramatic, if not draconian, fashion toward the divorce of her own cousin, with whom she had been on close family terms for most of her life.

In 1967, the beautiful, famous concert pianist Marion Stein divorced her husband George, Lord Harewood, Elizabeth's first cousin. Marion was the daughter of Erwin Stein, a World War II German-Jewish refugee and one of the world's most respected musicians. Before marrying Marion in 1949, Harewood, then eighteenth in line to succession to the throne, had to obtain permission from the Queen. (Even today everyone in line to succession must obtain the monarch's permission to marry.)

The Harewood marriage disintegrated when, in 1959, Lord Harewood met Patricia Tuckwell, a beautiful Australian model known as Bambi because of her dark, doe eyes. They fell madly in love and Bambi had a son by Harewood in 1965, although the world knew nothing about the child until Harewood's divorce from Marion in 1967.

Harewood went to see Elizabeth, explained the situation to her, and asked her permission to divorce Marion and marry Patricia Tuckwell, the mother of his two-year-old boy. At first, Elizabeth refused outright, suggesting in the strongest possible terms that Harewood should leave his mistress and return to his wife. Harewood replied that his marriage to Marion was over and had been for some years.

Elizabeth never cared for the young Countess Marion Harewood, her title upon marrying Lord Harewood. She once said of her, "Marion is the only woman I know who can make me feel like the cook!" Nevertheless, Elizabeth was determined to save the marriage, and she called in Prime Minister Harold Wilson and the Archbishop of Canterbury in an effort to gain their support. She was adamant that no close member of the Royal Family should be allowed to divorce. It was a principle, she said, the House of Windsor would always uphold.

After much discussion, Elizabeth was finally persuaded that, under the circumstances, it was perhaps better to agree to the divorce, mainly because the woman Harewood intended to marry had already borne him a son. But she warned Harewood in a stinging meeting before granting him the divorce that he would be banished from court.

And Elizabeth kept to her word. She used Harewood's banishment as a warning to the rest of the Royal Family, as well as the aristocracy and others, that divorce would not be tolerated in the House of Windsor. Those wishing to divorce would have to accept the consequences, and she made certain that her cousin suffered. It was a prime example of Elizabeth's iron determination to remain loyal to the moral principles she had learned as a child from Queen Mary and her own mother when her uncle had decided to renounce the throne for the love of a divorced woman.

Harewood's total ostracism ended much of his public life. On instructions from the Queen, neither the wretched Lord Harewood, nor his wife, was invited to the funeral of his uncle, the Duke of Windsor, in June 1972, which hurt Harewood deeply. Nor were they invited to Princess Anne's wedding in November 1973.

On Elizabeth's explicit instructions, Lord Harewood was forced to retire early from his position as Chancellor of York University and even as artistic director of the famous Edinburgh Festival. Both institutions were persuaded to honor the Queen's principles by her advisers at the Palace.

But Elizabeth's punishment of Harewood for disgracing the Royal Family could not prevent the changes demanded by the general population. In 1968, much against Elizabeth's wishes, the politicians recognized that they had to bow to the inevitable. After much debate Parliament passed the 1969 Divorce Reform Act, which permitted much easier and quicker divorce with no blame attached to either party.

The Divorce Act meant that for the first time in Britain, a petition for divorce could be presented to the court by either party to a marriage on the sole ground that the marriage had irretrievably broken down. As church leaders feared, and sociologists suspected, the 1969 Act was the catalyst for a dramatic upsurge in the number of divorces. By the 1990s, one British marriage in three ended in divorce, and 25 percent of all live births occurred out of wedlock.

Elizabeth made her cousin suffer for ten long years before finally relenting. In 1977 Elizabeth deemed Harewood had completed his penance and allowed him back into the royal fold. He, and his second wife, were invited to take part in the Silver Jubilee celebrations. Elizabeth felt she had no option but to forgive her cousin, because in 1976 she had been forced to agree to her own sister's separation from her husband. She, who abhorred adultery and divorce, found her life and family enveloped by both.

Princess Margaret had married Anthony Armstrong-Jones, a commoner, in traditional royal splendor at Westminster Abbey in May 1960, the first great family occasion since the Coronation seven years before. The procession of horse-drawn coaches down the Mall was greeted with great cheers and flag waving. Two thousand people attended the wedding and Margaret and Tony, now Lord Snowdon, were lent HMS *Britannia* for a honeymoon cruise. A year later, their first child, David, arrived, and in 1964, Sarah.

Margaret and Tony's marriage was hectic, laced with passion, violent rows, and remarkable individual freedom. In an extremely candid discussion between the two sisters at Buckingham Palace in 1971, Margaret told Elizabeth that she and Tony had been unhappy together for some years. They had an "open" marriage and had both taken lovers from time to time during the past few years. Elizabeth was shocked that her own sister could behave in such a manner, but Margaret saw nothing wrong in what she was doing.

Elizabeth also feared that Margaret's indiscretions would became public knowledge and that the Royal Family's stance on adultery, morals, and extramarital sex would be held up to ridicule.

In fact, Elizabeth had no knowledge of the life Margaret had led ever since the gray men in the Palace had forced her to end her relationship with the love of her life, Group Captain Peter Townsend.

When Margaret realized she could not marry the man she wanted because of her position as sister to the Queen, she became determined to enjoy her life nevertheless. And so she did.

Margaret and Tony Armstrong-Jones appeared ideally suited, and their marriage seemed happy for the first five or six years. But problems soon emerged as Margaret's rather raffish, even bohemian love of life, led her to seek out intimate relationships with other men. The gospel of London's Swinging Sixties sophisticates was free love, and Margaret wanted to live life to the full.

Decades ago, Kenneth Tynan, the brilliant theater critic and writer who died tragically young of a rare disease, told me of blue films Princess Margaret had asked him to arrange and screen for her. Tynan said, "There would only be eight or ten of us at each showing, and she would have a few drinks and smoke cigarettes, with that remarkable long holder which became a sort of symbol of her rebellion. The films were quite raunchy, everything, including lesbian scenes and sadomasochism, and of course masses of straightforward heterosexual gyrations. She loved it all. And when she was leaving she would always say on the way out, 'We must do that again, it is most exhilarating.' And she would disappear into her chauffeured car with whoever was escorting her. Sometimes she would even become a little tipsy but never drunk."

By the middle 1960s both Tony and Margaret had been involved in full-blown extramarital affairs and agreed to make sure that their children would not suffer and that their indiscretions would not become the stuff of gossip columnists. They both knew serious repercussions would occur if Elizabeth heard of their affairs.

They were being naive. As a matter of security, their private detectives had to report back to their superiors the names and, if possible, the addresses and backgrounds of all their friends and acquaintances. More important, it was de rigueur that the detectives would pass on to their superiors the names and relevant details of lovers, or potential lovers, because they could always pose serious problems when members of the Royal Family were involved. Neither Tony or Margaret seems to have reckoned with that channel of communication when they decided to actively enjoy an open marriage. Some suggest they had decided to live the life they wanted to and damn the consequences.

Princess Margaret became involved with a number of men. One of the first was Anthony Barton, a tall, dark, handsome wine importer who had known Tony at Cambridge. Margaret and Tony and Anthony and his Danish wife Eva became close friends and they would all holiday together. Anthony Barton stood godfather to the Snowdons' daughter Sarah. Then Margaret, who found Barton handsome and very sexy, fell in love with him. The two became lovers in the mid-sixties.

A close friend said, "Margaret told me that she had fallen in love with one of Tony's best friends and couldn't keep her hands off him. They would go out to secret lunch and dinner dates together and spend the rest of the day in bed. Margaret had always loved the physical side of life and liked to spend hours making love. She found Anthony Barton irresistible."

Margaret inexplicably phoned Eva Barton to confess: "I have to tell you what has been going on because I feel so guilty." Eva had been totally oblivious to her husband's affair. Naturally there were no more combined family holidays, but Margaret and Barton continued seeing each other for a while longer.

Holidays had always been one of the problems between Margaret and Tony. At first they had both enjoyed commiserating when expected to holiday at Sandringham or Balmoral, and they contrived to avoid such events whenever possible. Margaret preferred lying around in the sun on hot beaches far from England, while Tony, who never liked sunbathing and swimming in faraway places, preferred quiet holidays in the English countryside.

Silly, frivolous rows over where to spend their holidays and weekends proved to be one of the main reasons their marriage drifted apart, perhaps as much as the extramarital affairs they seemed to need.

Meanwhile, in 1966, Tony had found Old House, a ramshackle, uninhabitable cottage on a thirty-acre estate near Nyman's in Sussex, about forty miles from London, which had been handed over to the National Trust some years before. Old House, which had originally been woodsmen's cottages, dated back three centuries. Tony planned to modernize the building, which had no running water, and to create a lake and an island with a pagoda which would be reached by a replica of a gondola.

While his new holiday home excited Tony, Margaret was annoyed that he could spend so much time, and nearly all his savings, on the

Old House. They fought relentlessly about his project. Margaret was to say later, "Tony was responsible for breaking up our marriage by insisting on buying and living at the Old House as much as he did. We had agreed to build a house at Sunninghill where we could water-ski together, but without even discussing the matter with me, he simply went off and bought those dilapidated old cottages. I knew nothing until after he had bought the place. That was stupid and it was the beginning of the end."

But Tony remained adamant, determined to keep his independence. During the first few years of marriage, many believed Tony was just a royal hanger-on, enjoying an easy life of luxury, occasionally accompanying Margaret on official functions, and walking, just like Prince Philip, a few yards behind his wife. Because he was a relaxed, happy character most people believed he loved the role. In fact, he hated it.

The more time Tony spent at the Old House the more Margaret socialized in London. She rekindled an old flame, Robin Douglas-Home, whose uncle Alec Douglas-Home had been Prime Minister of Britain in 1963. Robin, a gifted pianist, and Margaret shared a love of classical music and ballet. Again, Margaret indulged in a passionate love affair which most of London's society knew about because of the time the two spent openly in each other's company.

Margaret seemed capable of falling in and out of love quite easily and was sometimes accused of playing on men's emotions. Robin Douglas-Home, who had one failed marriage, repeatedly pleaded with Margaret to divorce Tony and settle down with him, perhaps even marrying at some later stage. It was obvious that Margaret and Robin had much in common and were very close, but Margaret's good sense prevailed.

Margaret told a friend, "I can't even think of divorcing Tony, my sister would simply not tolerate it. Whatever happens between Tony and I she would expect us to stay married for the sake of the monarchy." As a result of Robin's demands to live together, Margaret realized she had to end her relationship with Robin. Emotionally unstable and madly in love with Margaret, Robin could not get over their affair. He would write her endless love letters which, in the end, Margaret threw away unread. Robin began talking openly of suicide and in 1968, one year after Margaret had finally spurned him, he killed himself at his country cottage. Margaret was devastated.

Margaret had been trying for over a year to put her marriage back on track. She had returned to Tony and they tried to make the marriage work. They still found each other sexually exciting, and Tony was able to satisfy her sexual demands, but he continued to insist on his independence. He wanted to prove himself as a great photographer and spent more time pursuing his career and gaining a worldwide reputation, often to Margaret's annoyance.

The film actor Peter Sellers, a close friend of Margaret's, suggested they travel to the Costa Smeralda in Sardinia for a long summer holiday with his beautiful young Swedish wife, the actress Britt Ecklund. They would be accompanied by Kirk Douglas and his wife Anne. Tony would come too, as well as Princess Alexandra and her husband Angus Ogilvy. It was a great success and Margaret and Tony seemed happy again.

That holiday convinced Margaret that she wanted a private, sun-drenched holiday home to which she could escape and enjoy herself. She loved to laze around in her swimsuit, smoking and drinking, swimming and water-skiing, and spending the afternoons and even-ings relaxing, usually with a large gin and tonic. At the time of their wedding, a wealthy British socialite friend, Colin Tennant, offered her the gift of a home on the tropical isle of Mustique in the Bahamas. Now she decided the time had come to accept the proffered gift, and she contacted Colin, who would become Lord Glenconner, an old friend from her bachelor-girl days.

He agreed to a site above Gelliceaux Bay. Margaret had asked Tony, who had studied architecture at Cambridge, to design the house, but he steadfastly refused, telling her it was a stupid idea to have a holiday home so far from Britain. This disagreement led to yet more rows between the two. Tony's uncle, however, Oliver Messel, a well-known theatrical designer who for reasons of health lived in the Caribbean, agreed to take over the project. When it was completed, with its stunning views over the sea, Margaret named it Les Jolies Eaux.

By the late sixties, the couple spent more time apart, Margaret escaping to Mustique whenever possible and Tony living at Old House, where, after a few visits, Margaret refused to visit, let alone stay for a night or a weekend. Tony, who had become a keen shot under the tutelage of Philip, decided to end relations with the Royal Family, and he stopped shooting. It was obvious to their friends that they were living separate lives and were so open and outrageous about their various liaisons that they appeared to be vying with each other for attention.

Among a coterie of friends were various gay men whom Tony would occasionally entertain at Kensington Palace and also at the Old House. Margaret would frequently ridicule Tony about them, calling him a "pansy" and a "faggot."

One night in the late 1960s, Margaret arrived home to find Tony dressed in one of her ball gowns, dancing on the dining room table with three of his gay friends. Margaret virtually chased the men out of her home, and a ferocious row took place in which Margaret called her husband a "queer" and Tony called his wife "a drunken slut."

At the time, the young social set considered Tony a man-about-town, the husband of Princess Margaret, and a man with an eye for a pretty girl. He had numerous liaisons, some with former debutantes as well as young career women working for the glossy magazines. Tony was enjoying his independence.

Tony's neighbors at Old House were the Marquess of Reading, a wealthy aristocrat stockbroker, his wife Margot, their two sons, and their lovely daughter Jacqueline, then in her early twenties. Tony frequently visited his newfound friends, and in 1970 he and the lovely Jackie, as everyone called her, became lovers. Tony had become so cocky that he would take Jackie to parties and dinners at Kensington Palace at which Margaret was also present.

For more than a year Tony and Jackie Reading continued their outrageous affair all over London. Tony was flattered by the passionate love of young Lady Jacqueline, and she was hopelessly in love with the famous royal photographer and husband of Princess Margaret. Jackie told a close friend in 1971, "I love Tony; I love him with all my heart. And he loves me; he wants to marry me."

When news of the affair hit the front pages of British and American newspapers early in 1971, Lord Reading called Tony to his house, Staplefield, and demanded an explanation. An extraordinary scene took place, almost a recreation of a set piece from a bygone era. In his drawing room, Lord Reading, apoplectic with rage, accused Tony of seducing his daughter, of ruining her chances in life, and of acting like an absolute cad. He banned him from ever entering his house again or setting foot on his estate. He also warned him never to see his daughter again.

Margaret, who had spent the last months happily entertaining such men as Peter Sellers, her cousin Lord Patrick Lichfield, the royal photographer, and others, including her old friend Jocelyn Stevens, became angry, because she felt her husband's affairs made her a laughingstock. In the meantime Elizabeth's advisers had been informed that Tony Snowdon was bragging that he could obtain a divorce whenever he wished.

Unhappy in her marriage and hating to look foolish due to her husband's behavior, Margaret went to her sister to discuss the possibility of a separation. Elizabeth told her it was out of the question for someone so close to the monarch. Elizabeth also told her to arrange a reconciliation because attacks being made on her marriage were damaging the influence of the Crown, which Margaret must realize was vital to Margaret as well as the Queen.

Margaret felt trapped in a loveless marriage and became alternately angry and miserable that she could not separate from, or divorce, her errant husband. She saw nothing wrong in the illicit affairs she had indulged in during the marriage. So Margaret continued to enjoy herself, but with as much discretion as possible. She had affairs with other men, such as Dominic Elliot, an old friend, and others. But Margaret needed not just a man, but a man to love.

Enter Roderick Llewellyn, the younger son of former Olympic horseman Colonel Harry Llewellyn. In the early 1970s Margaret met Roddy, a happy-go-lucky minor socialite who tried to become an upmarket gardener to the rich and famous. Roddy had also tried his hand as a pop star, and for a while was involved in a hippie commune at Surrendal in Wiltshire, a hundred miles west of London.

Margaret took a distinct fancy to young Roddy, with his raffish clothes, long shaggy hair, and soft voice. She was also flattered that an attractive man eighteen years her junior showed such a physical interest in her. She liked his sense of fun, his humor, and his refusal to be subject to the usual boring social constraints. In a matter of weeks the two became lovers. There was another, more personal reason for this affair. Tony spent more time apart from his wife and children, leading a very independent existence.

Ostensibly, Tony still lived with Margaret at Kensington Palace, but they rarely shared a bed together. Both were drinking heavily, and Margaret feared Tony was in danger of becoming an alcoholic. Margaret had just turned forty, drank too much, and had become a heavy smoker. She craved companionship and, because of her age and the fact that she was gaining substantial weight, she luxuriated in the friendship of young people around her, particularly a handsome young man who adored her and wanted to be her constant companion and lover.

It didn't seem to bother Princess Margaret that once again she was courting scandal. Eyebrows were raised, as they had been when she was courting Group Captain Peter Townsend, when she married Tony Armstrong-Jones, and now when she dated a hippie gardener.

Elizabeth cautioned Margaret to tread carefully for fear of further scandal. She would phone her sister and gently try to influence her. Margaret told one of her close friends, "My sister keeps trying to rule my life, telling me what I can and what I cannot do. I have to listen to her, of course, but I don't have to take her advice; I have to lead my own life."

Margaret had always been headstrong; Elizabeth knew that only too well. Margaret continued the life she wanted to lead. Throwing caution to the wind she even visited the hippie commune, sometimes secretly staying the night. In Britain, as elsewhere of course, commune life in the 1970s was associated with free love, nakedness, flower power, and marijuana, all of which were celebrated by Roddy's group. Indeed, Margaret seemed to get a nefarious thrill whenever she visited the commune, everyone eating, drinking, smoking, and chatting together, and watching topless young women gardening. Nights in the commune reverberated with the noise of couples making love.

Ignoring her sister and the Palace advisers, Margaret was determined to enjoy her new young, virile lover and pay no attention to the press and the paparazzi. The more her life with Tony fell apart, the more Margaret seemed to need the emotional and physical security she found in Roddy. Their affair became public knowledge, but newspaper editors had no proof of what they felt certain was another royal scandal.

Then Margaret invited her Roddy to Mustique in January 1976.

They were "snapped" eating lunch together in the sunshine of the lovely tropical island. It was an innocent enough picture, but to the British, suffering that January in snow and frost, the picture conjured up sun, sea, golden beaches, and, more important, sexual innuendo. Margaret Rose was not a popular royal in the 1970s. She was seen as a spoiled princess, with every privilege and no responsibility, prepared to live off the taxpayer and giving very little in return.

For many years some newspapers had viewed Princess Margaret as a legitimate target whenever royal finances, called the Civil List, came before Parliament for reappraisal each spring. After marrying Tony Armstrong-Jones, Margaret received $25,000 a year, which had to pay the wages of her staff of nine. In fact, Elizabeth had been secretly funding her sister, paying for all her clothes and airfares. Her ten-room apartment in the Clock House at Kensington Palace was provided gratis. In 1972, the government put forward plans to increase her allowance to a more respectable $55,000. Some Members of Parliament proposed to axe Margaret's allowance completely because they felt the Queen's sister wasn't earning her keep, wasn't carrying out enough royal duties. The motion was eventually defeated 148 votes to 34. In the 1970s Margaret received $75,000 a year, and this sum was steadily increased, mainly due to inflation, to about $100,000 by 1978 and $125,000 in 1980.

During 1979 Princess Margaret made only 113 official public appearances, while the Queen, with a much greater workload of official business, had undertaken 325 royal functions. Prince Philip had carried out 243. Some newspapers criticized Margaret for "not pulling her weight" and "dereliction of duty."

As the argument on her allowance raged in the press and the House of Commons, in 1979 Margaret said in private, "The increase of $20,000 this year hardly pays for the postage stamps. Don't people realize that all my income goes on the staff that I have to employ."

At that time Margaret employed a first-class private secretary, a former Guards major, Nigel Napier, whom she paid a miserly $15,000 a year; a butler, John Leishman; a housekeeper, Mrs. McIntyre; a lady's maid, Mrs. Greenfield; a chauffeur, Griffin; a cook, two daily maids, and her personal lady-in-waiting Lizzie Paget, all of whose wages she had to meet.

Many in Britain would argue that Margaret had no need for so many staff to care for her needs, but she believes that, as the Queen's sister, she should be entitled to privileges, including sufficient staff to make her life comfortable. In Margaret's estimation, she certainly does not have too many staff; in fact, hardly enough to keep her in the style she believes the sovereign's sister should be expected to live.

The winter that Margaret's photograph was taken with Roddy, the public found itself gripped by a fit of moral indignation aimed directly at the Princess. They believed that in return for her life of privilege and luxury she should at least follow the dictates of conventional morality and remain loyal to her husband, especially since she was a member of the first family of the land who were meant to set an example. Here was Margaret flouting those conventions by taking as her lover a man eighteen years her junior and openly disporting herself at her tropical Caribbean island hideaway. Feelings were running high, which Palace advisers faithfully reported to Elizabeth. They also advised her that if she permitted Margaret's flagrant disregard of the moral codes to continue, the Crown would be brought into severe disrepute.

The picture of Margaret and Roddy, splashed on the front page of the Murdoch Sunday paper, the *News of the World*, made Elizabeth realize the scandal she had long feared had arrived with a bang. Elizabeth was upset and angry. Urged on by her advisers, Elizabeth issued her sister an order for the first time ever. She told her to fly back to London immediately and to leave the wretched Roddy on the island. From the tone of her voice Margaret knew that this time she had to comply with her sister's orders. She flew back alone.

Elizabeth did not know what to do about these unseemly events. As in previous scandals involving her sister, she hoped the matter would soon disappear from the headlines and be forgotten. She kept reminding herself, as the papers also noted, that Margaret was not likely ever to ascend to the throne and therefore her sister's disreputable behavior was not that important to the monarchy. But worse was to follow.

Margaret's husband saw the scandal as a golden opportunity not to be missed. For some time Tony had wanted out of the marriage and had openly boasted to friends that, despite the strict ban on members of the immediate Royal Family ever divorcing, he believed that one day he could leave Margaret permanently. Margaret's stupid indiscretions with Roddy had played into his hands. The day following the *News of the World* photograph, he telephoned Elizabeth and asked to see her.

Elizabeth met her brother-in-law a few days later in her drawing room at Buckingham Palace. Elizabeth had hoped to persuade him to overlook this latest escapade, pointing out that to do so would be for the great good of the family. But Tony had other ideas. Elizabeth was rather taken aback that Tony seemed so determined.

He told her, "I have been made to look a fool. I have put up with her behavior for some years. You must have known what's been going on. But I cannot take any more. The world believes I am just a cuckold and it is ruining me, my reputation, and my photographic work. The time has come for us to separate."

Tony went on, "I am sorry, terribly sorry that our marriage has come to this, but I am left no alternative. Please can you sort something out."

Elizabeth was sympathetic and said she would think about it. Tony had the final word: "You will have to think of something because I won't go on like this."

Elizabeth raged at what she saw as her own sister's stupidity, and she told her so when they next met. Elizabeth knew Tony was using the bad publicity for his own ends. She said nothing to him, but Elizabeth knew the fault was not exclusively her sister's, for she had been kept informed throughout the marriage of Tony's sexual adventures.

Reports of that extraordinary meeting show that Elizabeth repeatedly asked her sister, "How could you? How could you do this to me, to the family, to the monarchy? How could you have been so silly?" Elizabeth buried her head in her hands.

Elizabeth implored Margaret to try to save the marriage. She asked Tony to come to Buckingham Palace and appealed to him, for the sake of the Royal Family, The Firm, to give the marriage "one last try." She assured him that Margaret was willing to give the marriage "another go," a true reconciliation. But Tony remained adamant. He had had enough and was determined to take the opportunity Margaret had presented. Tony sat on a sofa, shaking his head and saying, "It won't work. It's over. It's unfortunate, but it's finished."

Elizabeth knew she had no option but to give way. After calling in royal advisers and lawyers, she gave Margaret and Tony permission to separate, but she was adamant on one point. No divorce.

Tony, however, was not being totally honest and Margaret knew it. Some months before, Tony had told her of his affair with Lucy Lindsay-Hogg, a brunette divorcée in her thirties who lived in a small apartment just five minutes' walk from Kensington Palace. Tony had fallen in love with Lucy during a film trip to Australia in 1975, when she had spent weeks with him in the outback as his photographic assistant. Lucy had been married for four years and her divorce, some years before she met Tony, had been amicable.

After a discreet lapse of time—a couple of months—the Queen gave permission for the official announcement. On March 18, 1976, three months after the scandal became public knowledge, a simple statement from Buckingham Palace read:

> Her Royal Highness The Princess Margaret, Countess of Snowdon, and the Earl of Snowdon have mutually agreed to live apart. The Princess will carry out her public duties unaccompanied by Lord Snowdon. There are no plans for divorce proceedings.

Tony was given $150,000 from Princess Margaret's small personal fortune to enable him to buy a London home, and the couple were allowed the freedom and the independence they both wanted. Tony celebrated with champagne and Lucy, while the wretched Margaret felt lonely and cheated. Tony had ended his relationship with Margaret as a highly successful, world-acclaimed photographer, and he was considered one of the world's ten sexiest men. He had been given a lovely home and the woman he wanted to share his life. Margaret had been all but forced to give up young Roddy. She commented, "The only consolation I have at the end of my marriage is a bottle of gin and packet of fags."

But the feeling of humiliation was Elizabeth's alone. From those far-off childhood days when Uncle David had renounced the Crown for a divorcée, poor Elizabeth had remained steadfast to the stern words of old Queen Mary that divorce would never be tolerated in any circumstances, and especially in the Royal Family. Elizabeth has always considered divorce a curse more than a failure. She saw her sister's separation as a visitation, a warning of dire punishment to come for the family and the Crown. To uphold the monarchy was the one principle, above all else, she was determined to perpetuate, and now the specter of divorce had arrived at the very gates of Buckingham Palace.

Prince Philip tried to encourage his unhappy and dispirited wife, pointing out that both Margaret and Tony were independent, wayward individuals. He urged Elizabeth not to blame herself because her sister and Tony had refused to subordinate their own selfish wishes.

After the heat of the separation had died down, Margaret began dating Roddy Llewellyn once more, and for the next two years they were treated as a couple. But Roddy was never accepted in royal circles, and his career continued to go downhill. His gardening ambitions turned to naught, and his new career, as a pop singer, with enthusiastic support from Margaret, proved painfully unsuccessful. The press once again pointed the finger at what they saw as Margaret's "lack of dedication" and her "love for a worthless young layabout."

In May 1978, Princess Margaret announced that she would seek a divorce from Tony but had no intention of remarrying. Seven months later Lucy discovered she was pregnant; she was thrilled and delighted because doctors had always told her that she could never have children. Without a second thought Tony immediately asked Lucy to marry him. Weeks later, on December 15, 1978, they married quietly at Kensington Register Office, and a daughter was born the following July.

Tony's shotgun wedding and the news of the baby upset and angered Margaret. She thought it disgraceful that Tony had told her neither about the forthcoming child nor his intention of marrying Lucy. And, as Margaret argued, he hadn't even told their own children, David, then seventeen, or Sarah, fourteen. Tony's behavior surprised his friends, who would have expected him to break the news of his marriage to his teenage children rather than let them learn about it, and the expected baby, from reading the newspapers.

Margaret sought solace with Roddy and tried to persuade Elizabeth to allow Roddy to accompany her, even when she was staying at royal palaces. Elizabeth adamantly refused, informing her private secretaries that Mr. Roderick Llewellyn was not to be included in any royal party nor invited to any royal occasion.

One day Elizabeth did meet Roddy, but under the most embarrassing circumstances. As Nigel Dempster related in his biography of

Princess Margaret, *A Life Unfulfilled*, Elizabeth, staying at Royal Lodge, was chatting with Nanny Sumner. Suddenly, Roddy burst in on Nanny to have a button sewn on. He was dressed only in shirt and underpants. On seeing Elizabeth standing in the room, Roddy went a bright red and stammered, "Please forgive me, Ma'am, I look so awful," as he froze to the spot, not knowing how to hide his embarrassment.

"Don't worry. I don't look very good myself," she replied, and put him at his ease by smiling as she left the room.

The next day they were formally introduced by Margaret after church in Windsor. Roddy was still not invited to any royal occasions. Though Margaret accepted her sister's ruling that Roddy must not be invited to royal palaces when the Queen was in residence, Margaret would sometimes risk taking Roddy with her on the odd occasion. He would keep discreetly out of the way though the servants all knew he was staying overnight. Margaret was more embarrassed than Roddy when her sister accidentally met her lover in the nanny's room for Roddy was not meant to be staying at Royal Lodge that weekend.

This decision proved to be a wise one when torrid revelations of Roddy's past were revealed later in a series of articles in the *News of the World* by his older brother Dai. Dai recounted Roddy's numerous suicide attempts and his indulgence in homosexual affairs. Roddy and Margaret were naturally incensed that Dai could sell such embarrassing family secrets.

But Roddy, then thirty-three, was changing. In the early 1980s he met an old flame, Tania Soskin, a free-lance travel writer, and found himself falling in love with her. Eventually he summoned up the courage to tell Margaret he intended to marry Tania. Margaret was said to have commented, "I was shocked to start with but I welcome the news with a sense of relief. I have spent so long mothering that boy. In any case I couldn't have afforded him much longer."

Margaret even threw a lunch party for them at Kensington Palace and would have attended the wedding in June 1981 if possible, but on that day she was away on royal duties.

Following Roddy's marriage, Margaret felt free once again and began enjoying her more lonely but independent life. She also hoped Charles and Diana would start a family soon after their wedding, demoting her further down the line of succession to the throne, and still further out of the royal limelight. Since her hedonistic days, Margaret has lived a quieter, more serene life but has never found another man she would want to settle down with.

In 1980, just two years after Margaret and Tony were officially divorced, Elizabeth faced yet another major sex scandal. Her only daughter Anne was having an affair with her police bodyguard. Sergeant Peter Cross had bright blue eyes and a great deal of charisma. He was a handsome, blond, but balding man in his late thirties, two years older than Anne. Sergeant Cross's own marriage ended a few months after he became her bodyguard, because, as his wife explained, he was never at home, working day and night at Anne's Gloucestershire home, Gatcombe Park.

Mark Phillips sensed that his wife was becoming emotionally and sexually involved with her bodyguard and decided to have Sergeant Cross removed from duties at Gatcombe Park. Anne had changed toward him during those few months, becoming more hypercritical of whatever he said or did. And he had noticed how Anne and Cross talked to each other and acted toward each other whenever they were together. Mark may have been nicknamed Fog, but he was nobody's fool.

Mark informed Commander Michael Trestrail, the Queen's personal bodyguard and the man in charge of Elizabeth's immediate Royal Protection Squad. Other officers were ordered to investigate the complaint and phone calls to and from Gatcombe Park were tapped. Because Anne was then sixth in line to the throne, Trestrail informed the Queen that the affair had been going on for some months and asked if any action should be taken. The Queen asked for a watch to be kept on the couple and for Trestrail to keep her informed. When Mark reported back that he feared the affair had begun, Elizabeth, without informing her daughter, agreed that Sergeant Cross should be transferred immediately from Gatcombe Park and all royal duties.

Elizabeth was ruthless because she feared her headstrong daughter might decide to take the fateful step of divorcing Mark Phillips, and once again, she dreaded the possibility of another marital rupture, another scandal affecting the family.

Assistant Commissioner Wilford Gibson, the officer in charge of overall Royal Protection, summoned Sergeant Cross to Scotland Yard while Anne was abroad on royal duty. Commander Trestrail was also present. Cross was told that his "conduct did not come up to the standards expected of police officers who guard the Royal Family." Gibson also told him he had been drinking on duty.

Amazed by this accusation, Cross replied, "Everyone drinks on royal duty when invited. But I've never been drunk on duty."

Gibson continued, "I didn't say you had been drunk, only that you had been drinking." Of course drinking on duty was considered a serious offense in the police force, but Gibson raised the matter for technical reasons, just in case Cross should object to his immediate transfer. To make sure that Cross understood that the authorities knew about his affair, Commissioner Gibson told him, "We've heard rumors that you have been overfamiliar with the Princess."

Gibson informed Cross he would be transferred immediately to Croydon, a small town south of London, as station officer, a dramatic demotion which some considered insulting to an officer of Cross's ability and past record. Princess Anne returned home two days later to be informed that a new personal bodyguard had been appointed to her and that Sergeant Cross had been transferred.

She was furious and immediately phoned Trestrail at Buckingham Palace. In an outraged voice, Anne said, "I would like to know why my personal bodyguard, Sergeant Cross, has been transferred and on whose authority?"

Later in the conversation Anne shouted, "How dare anyone remove my bodyguard without my permission and without any reason being given whatsoever!"

She slammed down the phone after telling Trestrail, "Do not believe this is an end to the matter."

That night Anne turned on Mark and accused him of telling tales behind her back. Mark stumbled and stammered, but Anne knew that her own husband had initiated the complaint that had led to her lover's forced removal. She appeared to feel no guilt for her behavior, and despite Mark's attempts to quiet her anger she remained in a fury over what had happened.

Without a doubt Anne had fallen in love with her personal guard who seemed so much more a man of action to her than her own husband. She would not give up her lover without a fight, no matter if her own mother had ordered him transferred.

One month after Cross's transfer, Princess Anne found herself

French actress Helene Cordet (née Foufanis) with whom Prince Philip enjoyed a love affair, pictured in 1954.

Showbiz star Katie Boyle, with whom Prince Philip enjoyed a passionate affair, pictured in 1953.

Prince Philip chats with Princess Alexandra, Elizabeth's cousin and Philip's mistress for twenty years, while Elizabeth watches them closely. They were attending the Royal Command film performance *Les Girls* in November 1957.

Queen Elizabeth and Prince Philip pictured with the Tongan Queen Salote during their tour of Commonwealth countries after Elizabeth's coronation in 1953.

Elizabeth enjoying her favorite pastime: horse riding at Ascot in 1961. She is considered a highly accomplished horsewoman.

Elizabeth, forty-eight, with "Porchy" Porchester, her racing manager, after her horse Highclere won the 1000 guineas at Newmarket in 1974.

Elizabeth, forty-eight, with Lord Porchester after her horse Highclere came third in the King George VI and Queen Elizabeth Stakes at Ascot in 1974.

The handsome and elegant Lord Patrick Plunket became Elizabeth's favorite courtier and only intimate friend. (Photo courtesy Desmond O'Neill Features).

Elizabeth, sixty-five, with her mother Queen Elizabeth and racing manager Lord Porchester at the Epsom Derby in 1991.

Elizabeth, forty-nine, with Lord Mountbatten attending polo at Windsor Great Park in 1975.

Elizabeth, forty-nine, and Prince Philip, fifty-five, at Balmoral with one of Elizabeth's favorite corgis in 1975.

Elizabeth, forty-eight, and the Queen Mother, seventy-four, enjoying the country life, at the Badminton Horse Trials in 1974.

Elizabeth, sixty-two, with the Queen Mother, eighty-eight, at Windsor in 1986.

Elizabeth, forty-five, at her desk at Buckingham Palace in 1971.

Elizabeth, fifty-two, with her favorite grandchild, Peter Philips, Princess Anne's son, pictured at Windsor Castle in 1978.

Elizabeth, fifty-nine, pictured in spectacles at the British Museum in 1985.

Elizabeth, sixty-one, at the Royal Windsor Horse Show in a favorite silk headscarf, in 1987.

Elizabeth, sixty-two, at the Royal Windsor Horse Show, in 1988.

Elizabeth, sixty-five, in gleeful mood, chatting with political leaders at the Commonwealth Day reception of Lancaster House, London, in 1991.

Elizabeth, sixty-five, wearing a hard hat on an industrial tour in 1991.

The year is 1992. Elizabeth called it her "Annus Horribilis", the worst year of her long reign. The strain on Elizabeth's face shows all too clearly as she tours the Chelsea Flower Show.

Elizabeth, fifty-eight, surrounded by her family in 1984, after Trooping the Colour, the annual celebration of the Queen's official birthday. They are watching the fly-past of planes of the Royal Air Force.

Elizabeth, fifty-seven, dressed in the Most Noble Order of the Garter of St. George at the annual garter ceremony at Windsor Castle in 1983.

Queen Elizabeth and Prince Philip waving to crowds as they enter St. Paul's Cathedral for the Silver Jubilee Service of Thanksgiving in 1977. On the left is Prince Charles in ceremonial uniform of the Household Cavalry.

pregnant and had no idea what to do. The odds were that Peter Cross was the father. For three months Anne toyed with the idea of saying nothing, pretending the unborn baby was Mark's. But she realized that would be unfair to Cross and dishonest to herself and their love. When she had discovered her pregnancy, Anne tried to shake off her love for her ex-bodyguard but she found that impossible. She acted like a lovesick teenager around the house, unable to concentrate on anything except her exiled lover.

That Christmas Anne sent her lover a signed photograph through a police friend, Inspector Colin Hayward-Trimming of the Royal Protection Squad. Later, Anne sent a message through the same officer, asking Peter Cross to visit her at Gatcombe.

Cross waited in the library. Anne walked in, looking heavily pregnant.

Anne said, "How lovely to see you. I thought I ought to see you to explain before you read about it in the papers. You can see I'm pregnant, five months."

Peter Cross said nothing, waiting for Anne. He looked at her and raised his eyebrows, not wanting to embarrass her by asking whether he was the father of her baby. Anne nodded her head, and Cross went over and put his arms round her.

Anne took the initiative, asking whether he wanted to continue where they had left off. He replied that he very much wanted to see her, if she felt that would be possible. Peter Cross had resigned from the force shortly after being transferred and was therefore absolutely free to visit Anne whenever she invited him. But he did not know whether Anne, the Queen's daughter, would want to continue an affair with a mere police officer. Though taking great risks, Anne wanted to be as discreet as possible and so she would use Cross's police confidant to pass messages to her lover.

In the autumn of 1985, four years after Anne's blue-eyed, blond daughter Zara was born, a series of articles in the *News of the World* gave some details about Cross's relationship with Princess Anne. For a substantial sum of money Cross had agreed to tell something of their relationship, but he revealed no details of their intimate relationship. He did tell the readers, however, that within minutes of giving birth Anne phoned him to say she had a beautiful daughter.

He told of how their close relationship began in early 1980 after he had worked as her bodyguard for just a few months. "I well remember the first evening Princess Anne and I began to confide our real problems to each other. Mark was away and I was doing my last chore of the day, setting the security alarms.

"I was in the kitchen of the Gatcombe Park house. Suddenly I was aware Anne had come in and was going round turning off light switches. I had to smile. She might be a member of one of the richest families on earth, but the Princess had a real thing about saving electricity.

"We started to talk. Then, somehow, we were sitting together on the back stairs, which led from the kitchen to my room. We sat there for two hours. I was on a higher step than Anne. Her arm, I noticed, was leaning against my knee. But that didn't concern me.

"I was too busy that evening thinking about my personal problems, for my private life was in turmoil. I'd left my wife Linda and our two girls because our marriage was over. I had an Iranian girlfriend with whom I shared an apartment in London, on my off-duty times, but that relationship too was running into trouble."

Peter Cross went on to say that he often had such conversations with Anne, and she told him that she talked to her mother, the Queen, about how well she and her bodyguard got on, confiding in each other.

Then he described how their relationship began in the summer of 1980. "One night Mark and Anne both had to go to Salisbury, Anne to attend a dinner and Mark to train for the Olympics. As usual we were late starting and Mark drove like the wind. I found it really difficult to match his speed, driving my car, for I was meant to be escorting them.

"Later Anne told me she asked Mark to slow down because I couldn't keep up. He apparently retorted, 'Who are you worrying about—the car, or the man driving it?'

"After the dinner Anne and I drove back to Gatcombe. When we arrived, we stood chatting in the hall. I was acutely aware of our closeness. It seemed we were standing there for hours. . . . Then we sat down, I flopped down into the armchair and she sat on the carpet at my feet. . . . Suddenly she turned and looked at me, our hands brushed and for a few seconds we were like statues looking directly into each other's eyes. Then suddenly we kissed. Within minutes we moved to the library and there we embraced."

After Zara's birth, Anne and Peter Cross continued their adulterous affair, occasionally spending afternoons making love at the home of a friendly police officer in Surrey and romantic nights at an unused cottage on the Gatcombe estate. Princess Anne took the most enormous risks, but she loved Peter Cross and was prepared to risk excruciating scandal for herself, her children, her husband, her mother, and the entire Royal Family.

Anne would phone Cross where he worked as an insurance salesman, using the name Mrs. Wallis. (It was Anne's mischievous idea to use the name of the most famous adulteress known to the House of Windsor, Wallis Simpson.)

Their affair ended in 1983 when Peter Cross told Anne that he had fallen in love with another woman, a dental nurse. Unhappy, Anne realized their secret affair could not continue without something dramatic occurring. In her heart she knew they could never share a life together.

But the affair spelled the end of her marriage to Mark Phillips. For some time Mark had worked hard to build up a bank balance for himself, for he never liked to think he was sponging off his wife or the Royal Family. To maintain his independence Mark had always refused a royal title, which meant the children were the first royals of the House of Windsor to go untitled. Anne was happy with that, for she did not want her youngsters brought up as royals.

As a former Olympic Games rider, Mark had an excellent reputation as a horseman, and he began to give riding exhibitions, mostly abroad. He also lectured at equestrian weekends and was sponsored by the famous British four-wheel drive car company, Land Rover. He also ran Gatcombe Park's farm, often working sixteen hours a day.

Between April 1988 and April 1989, Anne, then thirty-nine, and Mark, forty-one, spent exactly forty days together as a family with their children. It was a sign that the marriage was going nowhere. But it was not only Mark who was away working. After the birth of Zara and the ending of her affair with Peter Cross in 1983, Anne threw herself into royal engagements. She had been criticized in the press over the years for her attitude, her relationships with the press and with people, her rudeness, and her lack of dedication to the Royal Family. Some sections of the press suggested that she was so negligent about her royal responsibilities, it was tantamount to taking money from the taxpayer under false pretenses.

Like her father, Anne's relationship with the press had become prickly. When annoyed by ever-present photographers Anne would readily tell them to "Naff off," and as a result the press gave her a hard time. She decided to start a new life and eagerly accepted the job of president of Save the Children Fund, a major British charity involved with starving children across the world.

The job proved a watershed for Anne and her relationship with the press and the public. She was frequently shown on TV dressed in a shirt and jeans, helping, encouraging, inspecting, and working in the field. She visited the famine areas of Africa, India, and many Third World countries, actively helping aid workers as they cared for starving children. Overnight, the public's image of her changed and she won almost instant praise.

This was no temporary change in Anne's behavior. She has proved a remarkable president for the charity, spending many weeks every year overseas, traveling tens of thousands of miles, heavily involved with the world's underprivileged children. She also spends many weeks a year raising money for Save the Children. The press, too, changed their attitude, their criticism becoming praise. Anne became the first royal to clock up five hundred engagements in a year, and she then increased that to six hundred.

Elizabeth was proud of her. Anne had realized all her mother's dreams, surmounting her greatest expectations. Anne showed the nation that the Royal Family worked hard for good causes; that they did not sponge off the nation but gave of themselves, selflessly, for charities. In recognition of her work Elizabeth bestowed on Anne in 1988 a title she believed she had earned, that of Princess Royal. Until Elizabeth gave her the new title, Anne's correct form of address was an absolute mouthful: Her Royal Highness The Princess Anne, Mrs. Mark Phillips. Now she would be called Her Royal Highness The Princess Royal. The title also means that, at any time in the future, Elizabeth can bestow titles on Anne's two children.

The title made little difference to Anne. Her life at Gatcombe had always been the same: down to earth with no ostentation. Her home, like other working farmhouses, has chickens running everywhere, dogs in the kitchens and the courtyard, and the main hall cluttered with dirty boots, weatherproof Barbour jackets, and old macs. The grooms, most of the staff, and Princess Anne walk around all day in jeans, sweaters, and sneakers.

No royal house is less formal than Anne's home, and she likes it that way, so very different from the surroundings in which her mother lives at Buckingham Palace or Windsor. Gatcombe is comfortable, the food ordinary, with no fancy cooking. Monday's lunch or dinner is often a cottage pie, the mince left over from Sunday's roast.

Anne happily accepted the title her mother offered for another reason. By making her daughter The Princess Royal, Elizabeth elevated her daughter to the second lady in the land, immediately beneath the Queen herself and above Diana, Princess of Wales. Until then, Diana had been the second lady, but only because she was married to the Prince of Wales. Now, Elizabeth had promoted Anne above Diana, and her rank was her own; Diana had her title from her marriage to Prince Charles. Anne relished the title and its preferment, for she found Diana to be an "obnoxious upstart" whom Charles should never have married. (Anne and Diana can't stand each other, but whenever they are together in public, they pretend to be on friendly terms.)

In 1989, less than a year after accepting her new exalted title, Anne was once again the center of a new scandal, another love affair.

Her marriage to Mark ended quietly, in 1989, in contrast to the dreadful rows, acrimony, and shouting matches Margaret and Tony Snowdon perpetrated, or the storms that erupted between Charles and Diana, and then Andrew and Fergie. Mark did not argue or shout. Whenever Anne tried to pick an argument he would say nothing and then leave the room or go out to work on the farm. The two simply drifted apart.

Most of the family, including Elizabeth, recognized that the marriage between Anne and Mark was over in all but name months before the press wrote about it. But Elizabeth, like many other royals and aristocratic families, hoped that the couple would come to an arrangement, going their separate ways but appearing together for occasional royal functions. Elizabeth believed she could rely on her only daughter to abide by the unwritten Windsor rule: no divorce.

The Queen had occasionally talked to Anne about divorce, particularly during the time of Margaret's separation, and Anne seemed to have understood the damage royal divorces inflicted on the family and on the respect the nation gave to the royals.

In 1988 Anne, then thirty-eight, confided to her mother that she was involved with a young naval officer, Commander Timothy Laurence, then thirty-three, five years Anne's junior. A tall, handsome man, Laurence had been equerry to the Queen since 1986.

An equerry's job is roughly the male equivalent of a lady-in-waiting. He is a member of the Royal Household, a cross between a secretary, attendant, bodyguard, and confidant. The position invariably goes to an officer from one of the three armed services and lasts for just three years. Considered a position of privilege, it nearly always ensures rapid promotion after the three-year stint. Laurence, tall and slim, looked the quintessential equerry in his naval commander's uniform, an important element of his role as a young man always on show, walking one or two paces behind the monarch.

On royal occasions a tall, elegant man in naval uniform, complete with sword and medals, appears considerably more distinguished than a fellow in a lounge suit. Laurence had come to the Queen's attention when he was on duty on the Royal Yacht *Britannia* some years before. When the call from the Palace came in 1986, Laurence was in command of his own vessel, HMS *Cygnet*, a coastal patrol craft. He followed in the footsteps of Major Hugh Lindsay, killed in the avalanche that narrowly missed Prince Charles at Klosters in March 1988. So Laurence became part of the Royal Household and Anne caught his eye.

Elizabeth knew only too well the attraction of equerries. She had tried to comfort Margaret thirty years earlier when her sister had fallen in love with her father's royal equerry, Group Captain Peter Townsend. She cautioned Anne about becoming too involved with Commander Laurence, a quiet, respectful, unassuming man. She hoped their relationship would not mean that Anne would decide to end her marriage to Mark, for the sake of the two children and, more important, for the well-being of the monarchy.

In April 1989, however, the nation awoke to news of a fresh scandal. Four letters had been stolen from Princess Anne and handed to the royal correspondent of the Murdoch-owned *Sun* tabloid by a mystery man. The letters had been written to Anne over a period of eighteen months and had been taken from the briefcase she kept either with her or at her private suite at Buckingham Palace. Because they were stolen property, they legally belonged to the writer. The editor of *The Sun* immediately returned the correspondence to Princess Anne and agreed not to divulge the contents.

The Sun then checked to see whether the letters were genuine, and upon discovering the writer was Commander Timothy Laurence, equerry to the Queen, they decided to splash the story on the front page. *The Sun* changed its mind when they discovered the writer was an equerry to the Queen and therefore someone they judged to be in the public domain, a legitimate subject for a newspaper to write about, as the other person involved was Princess Anne.

Buckingham Palace immediately issued a statement: "The stolen letters were addressed to The Princess Royal by Commander Timothy Laurence, the Queen's Equerry. We have nothing to say about the contents of personal letters sent to Her Royal Highness by a friend, which were stolen and which are the subject of a police investigation."

Before issuing the statement Elizabeth phoned her daughter to ask about the letters. Anne immediately went to see her mother and explained that her relationship with Commander Laurence was serious and she believed the two of them might have a future together.

Elizabeth's heart sank. She said, "You do realize what all this means, to all of us? You do realize what effect this could have on the family?"

But Anne told her mother that her marriage to Mark had been over for some years and that they only stayed together, not just for the sake of the children, but because it seemed the correct way to behave. Furthermore, neither of them had met anyone they seriously wanted to settle down with. Three times during their conversation Elizabeth asked her daughter, "You are sure about Commander Laurence?" Three times Anne replied, "Yes."

Elizabeth had feared something like this but had hoped and prayed nothing would come out into the open.

Minutes after her meeting with Anne, Elizabeth called her Private Secretary, Sir Robert Fellowes, and instructed him to issue the statement to the press. She had hoped Anne would be able to continue her relationship with Commander Laurence and remain married, but it was obvious that Anne had determined that she wanted an open, honest life, and that meant bringing Commander Laurence and their relationship into the public domain.

During his two-and-a-half-year tour of duty as her equerry, Elizabeth had found Commander Laurence a most likable young man, who had not only carried out his duties impeccably but had also endeared himself with his tact and friendliness to various members of the family. So very different from Mark Phillips.

Once again Elizabeth realized she had to face the facts and had to agree to her daughter's divorcing her husband of fifteen years. She had been unable to have a relationship with Mark, whom she believed had never wanted to be part of her family and, indeed, had gone out of his way to ensure he spent as little time as possible in the presence of his in-laws. He would never holiday with Anne and the children at Balmoral, always finding excuses to stay away. Elizabeth had noted that rebuff. She took it as an insult not only to her and Philip but more especially to Anne. Elizabeth believed that if Mark wasn't prepared to put himself out in any way whatsoever, refusing to spend any time with his in-laws, then there was something strange, if not odd, about him. Elizabeth believed his attitude and his actions revealed a total lack of respect to the monarchy, the family, and her personally, which she never forgave and would never forget, although she always behaved correctly toward Mark.

None of these personal thoughts worried her now. She was far more concerned about the effect a divorce in her immediate family would have on people's attitude. Only forty years earlier, Elizabeth had tried to comfort the distraught Margaret when she was forbidden from marrying their father's divorced equerry. Now she knew that if Anne was indeed in love with Tim Laurence, then she would demand a divorce from Mark and remarry quickly. Elizabeth was well aware that Anne's remarriage would be historic, the first time that anyone so close to the throne had remarried after divorce since the days of Henry VIII in the sixteenth century.

Elizabeth told Anne she must wait a respectable length of time before announcing a separation from Mark, so as not to appear affected by the embarrassing revelation of the love letters. But Anne was impetuous.

In August 1989, only four months after the love-letters scandal broke, an official announcement came from Buckingham Palace that Princess Anne and Captain Mark Phillips had formally separated. Nothing was said of divorce, and Tim Laurence, having completed his three years as equerry, had apparently returned quietly to naval life, commanding the coastal craft HMS *Boxer*. He did not remain in the background for long. That same August, Laurence was seen at the Queen's side while on holiday at Balmoral, when there was no need for Laurence to have been in attendance at all. The gossip writers scented further scandal.

Absolutely discreet, Laurence had a knack of quietly disappearing from public view for months at a time, while, unknown to Fleet Street, his affair with Anne was intensifying. Finally, in the spring of 1992, Elizabeth gave her blessing to her daughter to appear publicly with her commander. Pictures taken at the Royal Caledonian Ball showed a very happy Anne dancing the eightsome-reel with the new love of her life, Tim Laurence.

Anne's second wedding, in December 1992—the year of Annus Horribilis—was a stark contrast to her first in 1973. Instead of a magnificent theatrical tableau in Westminster Abbey, televised around the world as a showpiece of British pomp and royal tradition, Anne and Tim Laurence were united in the tiny, plain Scottish Presbyterian kirk (church) of Crathie, near Balmoral.

Anne had wanted a strictly private wedding ceremony, held at the private chapel in Balmoral Castle, away from the cameras, the photographers, and the public gaze. Elizabeth, however, would not allow that because she did not want the Royal Family to look ashamed of what was happening, or to seem to pretend the wedding had never taken place. Anne finally relented but insisted the ceremony remain simple and private. Elizabeth agreed.

There was another reason, however, that a Presbyterian church in Scotland should be chosen. With no Episcopal hierarchy overseeing its ministers, the Church of Scotland had for years taken a more liberal approach to second marriages and tended to leave the decision to the discretion of individual clergy. On the other hand, the Church of England, of which Elizabeth is the governor and head, still frowned on marrying divorced persons, although many Anglican parish priests were happy to do so. For Anne to have married in an English church would imply that Queen Elizabeth, Head of the Church of England, was condoning divorce.

Another alternative would have been a civil ceremony, but once again only in Scotland. The Royal Marriages Act of 1772 debars a child of the sovereign from a civil wedding, as does a law from Victorian times which forbids any member of the Royal Family from marrying in a register office in England and Wales.

On the advice of the Archbishop of Canterbury, Dr. George Carey, who in turn had taken soundings from other senior bishops, Elizabeth decided that Anne should marry in Scotland. Crathie Church was the perfect diplomatic solution.

Permitting Princess Anne to remarry was a major landmark in the royal attitude toward that once taboo subject: divorce. By that time, both of Elizabeth's married sons, Charles and Andrew, had separated from their wives. She was also aware that one day they were likely to want to remarry.

By allowing Anne to divorce and remarry, Elizabeth, and the senior bishops of the Church of England, had permitted a vital precedent that would be of dramatic and significant importance if Prince Charles, the heir apparent, ever contemplated remarrying. The precedent also helped the Royal Family skate over the once sacrosanct idea of marriage for life.

The marriage of Anne to Commander Laurence was even more interesting than it first appeared. For Tim Laurence is of Jewish descent. It was a remarkable coup de theatre for two reasons: Tim's paternal great-great-grandfather was Joseph Levy, the son of Zaccaria Levy, a merchant of Venice who changed his name to Laurence in 1826. And Tim's paternal great-grandfather was a Church of England clergyman, the Reverend Percival Laurence. Tim's Jewish connection is an unusual addition to royal genealogy, but not the first. Lord Snowdon's mother was a Messel, descended from Aaron Messel, a famous banker of Darmstadt.

Princess Anne became Mrs. Timothy Laurence on December 12, 1992, after the simplest royal wedding in modern history. It lasted only twenty minutes. Elizabeth was happy too. Nearly twenty years ago Anne had arrived at Westminster Abbey in a horse-drawn, glass state coach; 45,000 spectators cheered her procession through the streets of London; 1,500 guests packed the abbey; and millions had watched the ceremony on television.

At Crathie, just thirty family members and friends attended Anne's second marriage, and no more than three hundred spectators turned out in freezing weather to see the couple. The bride, the Queen's only daughter, traveled not in a state coach but in a four-wheel-drive Range Rover. Anne, forty-two, and Tim Laurence, thirty-seven, promised to stay "loving, faithful, and loyal...until God separate us by death." After the ceremony, Tim and Anne drove off in their Range Rover, with Anne's children—Peter, fifteen, and Zara, eleven—in the back. Behind them in the kirk remained the busts of Queen Victoria, King George V, and Anne's grandfather King George VI staring down stonily on the empty church from the plinths near the stained-glass window. Nobody was guessing what the stern Empress Victoria would have said; the sight of a divorced Princess Royal remarrying in a Scottish church would have been beyond her comprehension.

The wedding breakfast was also a quiet, rather quick affair, held at Craigowan Lodge on the Balmoral estate. After champagne, a light snack, and the cutting of the cake, the guests left within the hour.

Among the guests was every member of the immediate Royal Family except Princess Diana and Sarah, Duchess of York. Both had decided earlier that year to walk out on their royal husbands. That royal wedding day Diana was photographed, a lonely, solitary figure flying to London and looking distinctly glum. She did not even smile for the cameramen.

All Elizabeth's compassion and diplomacy had been called upon in yet another royal scandal. In 1987, Princess Alexandra's daughter Marina, a talented pianist, then twenty-one, fell in love with Paul Mowatt, a young photographer, twenty-four. For the first three months they were dating, Paul had no idea that his girlfriend had royal connections.

Marina had always been the royal rebel, headstrong, self-willed, and extremely independent. As a teenager she had a strong social conscience and was dedicated to helping youngsters in trouble with drugs and crime. In her teens she worked as a shorthand typist to raise the $3,000 needed for a trip to the West Indies where she helped build a new school. She worked for the money because she refused to ask her parents to finance her life.

She called herself M.O., short for Marina Ogilvy. A tomboy, she enjoyed roughing it, attending Outward Bound Schools and dressing in jeans and sweaters. She shunned royal protocol, calling it "stuffy."

In December 1988 they started living together in part of Paul's mother's semidetached house in Kingston-upon-Thames, only a few miles from her parents' lovely country home, Thatched House Lodge in Richmond Park.

Alexandra and her husband Sir Angus, wanting to show they were modern parents, turned a blind eye to their daughter's new arrangement. Marina auditioned and won a place at the prestigious London Guildhall of Music to study singing and piano. After eight months, however, she quit, telling her parents she wanted to spend more time with her live-in lover and that she was dedicating her life to rock music.

The real shock came in October 1989, when Marina told her parents she was pregnant. She was determined to have her lover's baby but had no intention of getting married. Marina, a cousin to the Queen and twenty-fourth in line of succession to the throne, was to give birth to the first royal baby born out of wedlock for one hundred fifty years.*

Alexandra broke the news to Elizabeth by calling the Queen at Balmoral, where she was holidaying. Elizabeth told Alexandra and Angus to sort the matter out with as little fuss as possible. But the stubborn Marina wasn't open to calm, rational argument.

In a newspaper article before the baby was born, Marina claimed that her mother told her, "You have two options: either get it aborted right away in Harley Street or get married by special licence."

Marina said, "My mother gestured with her fingers in front of my face and told me, 'It will only be about that big. You are a healthy young girl and you will conceive easily again.'

"I couldn't believe she could talk like that, so coldly about my baby,

---

*Scores of royal children have, of course, been illegitimate, or what the English politely called "born on the wrong side of the blanket." Very few, however, were officially recognized. Usually the scandal was hushed up and the mother paid a handsome maintenance allowance. The last officially recognized illegitimate British royals were the ten children of King William IV and his mistress Dorothea Jordan, a famous actress. In 1830 William gave titles to all ten children.

and her grandchild. Paul and I were horrified. And she said the same the next night when Paul was with me. I am still shocked about it. My father was furious and my mother's mouth turned into a kind of snarl. I have been scared on a few occasions that my father might hit me. I have always been a bit frightened of him.

"I asked him what came first, 'Your daughter or Queen and country?' He replied, 'Queen and country.'"

Marina claimed that her parents cut off her allowance of $400 a month after she refused to either have an abortion or a quickie wedding. She said, "All of my life I have heard my parents talk about the image they must have before the public. My mother has this public image of being serene and composed. But I know she was desperate for this not to come out."

Shocked and angry, Marina wrote a six-page letter to Elizabeth which began, "Dear cousin Lilibet." She asked for her help, wise advice, and her guidance. She explained everything that had happened between Paul, her parents, and herself, her love for Paul, their desire to marry one day, and her parents' ultimatum. She said in a newspaper article, "I wrote to her hoping that she could make my parents see sense and help us reach a compromise. I know the Queen likes me and I like her. The Queen is a warm, caring person and I know she will listen to my plea for help."

What worried Alexandra, Angus Ogilvy, Elizabeth, and Philip was the danger of Marina's telling the world the royal secrets of which she was fully aware: her mother's lifelong affair with Prince Philip; the breakdown in her parents' marriage; their sham marriage while actually living apart for years; her father's drinking problem.

Elizabeth knew that any revelation of these royal secrets would cause irreparable damage to her personally and to the monarchy. Deep down, she was furious with the recalcitrant young Marina for what she perceived as nothing short of treachery, accepting $150,000 from the Murdoch's tabloid *Today* to humiliate her parents by revealing their "abortion or marriage" threat.

Elizabeth also knew she had to use her influence with Marina to bring her back into the family and stop her talking to the press. She told Alexandra and Angus that whatever she arranged they must go along with, whatever their private thoughts.

The Queen called Marina to Buckingham Palace. She knew the only chance of heading off potential disaster was to talk woman to woman. And that is what she did. She persuaded Marina that it would be best for herself, her unborn baby, and the Royal Family if she would agree to marry Paul, the man she loved, before the baby was due. After much thought and many comforting words from a sympathetic Elizabeth, Marina agreed.

In February 1990, Marina walked down the aisle on her father's arm in St. Andrew's Church in Ham, Surrey, near her home. She was dressed all in black, with a slight bulge under her long velvet dress. There were no flowers and no bridesmaids, so very different from her mother's glittering wedding at Westminster Abbey in 1963.

Giving his daughter away was about the only thing Sir Angus did for his daughter that day. Both he and Alexandra refused to attend the small reception afterward. Marina wanted to invite one hundred fifty people to the wedding breakfast but her parents refused. And when Marina asked that some relatives be invited to the wedding, Alexandra refused, saying, "Don't be silly, they'd be far too embarrassed."

The Royal Family also shunned the wedding. Only Fergie contacted Marina. They spent time chatting about problems with the family and also about babies, because Fergie was also pregnant at that time, with Eugenie.

The crisis for the Royal Family had passed. The Ogilvy family feud continued. After Marina's daughter Zenouska was born, Princess Alexandra went only once to see the baby, for twenty minutes, during the first two years.

In June 1992, Marina said in a newspaper article, "I have everything a woman could wish for. I have a husband I adore and who loves me in return, a beautiful daughter who is healthy and happy, and my career as a musician. I know the family consider Paul to be the 'wrong sort.' But what is the right sort? I'm sure my parents would have been happier if I had married into the aristocracy, but it just wasn't for me."

Elizabeth survived the Marina problem, but the personal lives of the younger royals continued to cause untold anxiety and trouble for her and the family.

ELEVEN

A WORKING WOMAN

At seven-thirty every morning of the week, a tap on the door of Elizabeth's private bedroom heralds the start of a new day for Her Majesty. It is one of her personal maids, dressed in a black maid's dress with a small white apron, bringing her morning tea. The tea is served in a sterling silver pot, with milk and a bone-china cup and saucer. In the saucer is a sterling silver teaspoon.

"Good morning, Ma'am" are the maid's only words as she enters, and Elizabeth's response is nearly always the same each day, a plain "Good morning." Having placed the tray on a side table, the maid may comment on the state of the weather as she goes to the huge windows and draws the long drapes, bringing light into the room. No further conversation takes place then because Elizabeth has already started her day listening to the radio—which she insists on calling "the wireless"—sitting up in bed. Each morning she turns on *Today*, the highly acclaimed BBC Radio 4 news program.

Meanwhile the maid draws a bath in a large Victorian-style white enameled bathtub, resplendent with large brass taps, then retires, leaving Elizabeth to get up at her leisure. While she listens to the radio, Elizabeth usually has two cups of tea, bathes, and dresses. The previous evening she has selected the clothes she is to wear the next morning. Her clothes have been laid out in her large adjoining dressing room, which is lined with cupboards, drawers, and a number of walk-in wardrobes.

Elizabeth's bedroom is only sixteen feet by twelve feet and is dominated by the blue-counterpaned, queen-size bed and a beautiful Georgian chest of drawers, on which stand silver-framed photos of her children and grandchildren. Crisp white cotton sheets are changed daily, and traditional pure new wool blankets have never been replaced by a duvet.

Nearly all her married life Elizabeth has slept alone, while Philip occupies another set of rooms farther down the first-floor corridor, both suites of rooms overlooking Constitution Hill and the Green Park. Philip is wakened at the same time, but he is served coffee not tea, and he, too, listens to the *Today* program. If neither of them has any engagements necessitating early departures, they usually meet in the breakfast room.

Philip always used to enjoy a typical English breakfast of bacon, eggs, sausages, and toast, but more recently he has joined Elizabeth in taking fruit juice and toast with marmalade. Elizabeth takes more tea while Philip, who has never liked tea, sticks to coffee. There is virtually no talk at breakfast, both preferring to read the selection of newspapers laid out immaculately on a separate table. All the national newspapers are there, including the screaming tabloids, *The Sun*, the *Daily Mirror*, and the *Daily Star*. Though they may flip through the sensational newspapers, they read the more serious journals with a keen interest. Usually, the Queen spends half an hour reading the *Sporting Life*, Britain's daily racing bible, a must for every horse owner. It is her favorite newspaper.

Having finished her breakfast before nine, Elizabeth returns to her private rooms, brushes her teeth, and then makes her way to her suite of offices on the same floor overlooking the Green Park. Whenever she goes from one floor to another, she usually walks down the sweeping staircases and only occasionally takes the slow, ancient elevator, with its mirrored walls and wood paneling.

By 9 A.M. each day her senior advisers, who have their offices on the ground floor, have held their first meeting and decided on what items are to be given priority. Then it is time for her Principal Private Secretary Sir Robert Fellowes, who is married to Princess Diana's sister Jane, to have his first meeting of the day in the Queen's office.

The pattern of her day has hardly altered since she was a young woman. Elizabeth's office, which is in effect her private sitting room, has an elegant though homey atmosphere. There are nearly always fresh flowers—usually pink carnations, or in season, lily of the valley—in a vase on her large antique desk and bowls of sweet-smelling potpourri. She sits on a stunning Chippendale elbow chair with a tapestry seat, and the room has exquisite, delicate furniture, although it is all functional and not merely for display; this is very much a working room. Her desk is a mass of silver-framed photographs of different sizes, nearly all of members of the family but some of horses and dogs. The walls of her sitting room, as would be expected, are hung with fine paintings, some lovely horse paintings by Hondecoeter and others given to her personally by friends.

Like all her staff, Sir Robert always calls Elizabeth Ma'am, but he invariably refers to her in conversation as Her Majesty. Nothing is ever less formal on any occasion, because one of the rules is that the dignity of the monarch must never be jeopardized. Elizabeth, however, calls all members of the Household by their first name from the first day of their appointment because she wants a happy, relaxed, friendly atmosphere in the Palace.

Elizabeth goes out of her way to provide an atmosphere in which her senior staff enjoy working. Words such as *fascinating*, *inspiring*, and *hard work*, as well as *privileged*, are often used to describe what it is like being in the Queen's senior employ. There is a feeling of camaraderie, though Elizabeth will be curt with anyone when things go wrong. All seem to agree she is a most compassionate woman. If any members of staff have personal problems or anyone in their families is ill, Elizabeth will always give advice, consolation, and help in whatever way possible.

Sir Oliver Millar, who was appointed Keeper of the Queen's Pictures in 1972, said, "She is an inspiration. When one talks to her about one of a variety of things, one is always sharply impressed by an astonishing mixture of common sense and an extreme niceness. No time is wasted, but everything is friendly and unpretentious. I always leave wishing I could see more of her."

Other courtiers speak of her strong dislike of snobbery and the fact that she deliberately shows no favoritism to any member of her court. Others talk of the Queen's sense of dignity. Lord Charteris, one of Elizabeth's former Private Secretaries, recalled, "I've known the Queen for forty years and I've never seen her lose her dignity, ever. Whether she's coming into the house wet and covered with mud from deer stalking, or coming down the steps of the aircraft in her dressing gown to give me a message, she's always the Queen." Charteris believes Elizabeth would have made a very successful businesswoman.

She will not put up with tardiness. She considers it a cardinal sin.

Mountbatten would recall the day he feared he might be late for an appointment. "I left home knowing I would be late. I told my driver to go like hell and he drove the wrong way round a traffic island and the wrong way down a one-way street in a bid to save vital minutes. We arrived in a cloud of dust, and I ran up to her room, arriving about ten minutes late. I was huffing and puffing when I arrived. The Queen looked me up and down and said rather curtly, 'Nice of you to decide to turn up, perhaps we can meet another day,' and walked out of the room. I felt so small. But never again was I ever late."

For the Queen to treat Dickie Mountbatten that way shows how strict she can be.

Unless something arises of the utmost importance, Elizabeth's first working conversation of the day will involve the press, radio, and TV reports of that morning. On her desk she will have found reports and newspaper clippings, and these will be read, reread, discussed, debated, and, if necessary, acted upon. Elizabeth knows that the press, which she often calls "the dreaded press," is the nation's link with the monarchy.

The other reason for this priority is the power and influence of the press in Britain. Unlike the United States, Britain has a strong national press. There are five serious, quality newspapers each day as well as six tabloids of varying seriousness and flippancy. All of these are distributed and sold the length and breadth of Britain, all available by breakfast time. These eleven newspapers are read by over twenty-five million people a day, 70 percent of the adult population, a remarkable reader profile for a national press. That is why Elizabeth rates the media as so important.

Most mornings the decision is taken, usually by Elizabeth, not to issue any press statement concerning reports in the media. Even when stories are untrue, libelous, or worse, the Queen issues no denials or even permits any off-the-record comment. The reason is simple: if the Buckingham Palace Press Office issued a denial for every piece of incorrect tittle-tattle published, it would be forced to issue a never-ending string of comments. Moreover, if the Palace failed to comment, the press and the public would believe that unrebutted piece of information was wholly accurate.

The Royal Family never sue the media for libel (and undeniably they could have done so during the recent past) because it might necessitate the cross-examination in open court of the particular wronged royal, perhaps even the Queen herself.

Only on one occasion has the Queen taken legal action against a newspaper. In February 1983, *The Sun* printed an exclusive story about the antics of Prince Andrew and his girlfriend at the time, the actress Koo Stark, revealing how she had run barefoot through the corridors of Buckingham Palace and romped in the State Apartments. The source of the allegations was a former employee, a junior storeman who had quit after two years. More revelations were promised. All royal employees, from the highest to the lowliest, must sign an undertaking not to disclose any information they may acquire while employed at the palace, and the storeman had broken that rule. The Queen applied for an injunction in the Royal Courts of Justice to prevent any further revelations being published. Because the storeman had broken his agreement, the Queen was granted the injunction and no further stories appeared. The story, incidentally, was probably true.

The next most urgent matter for Elizabeth is the daily report, prepared specifically for her by the Vice-Chamberlain of the Household, on the previous day's parliamentary proceedings. She will sometimes make a note to remind herself to discuss a particular matter during her weekly Tuesday evening chat with the Prime Minister.

Early in the day the menu book is presented to her. This is a small, leather-bound red book with a pencil that runs through the front which acts as a latch. The book contains the chef's suggestions for the day, written in French, although nowadays there are no French chefs in the kitchens. She crosses out the dishes she doesn't fancy for lunch and dinner. Every day Elizabeth makes the selection, never leaving it to the chef's discretion. Her preferences are simple and straightforward. She does not enjoy caviar and foie gras and never drinks champagne for dinner. Elizabeth would think all three an absolute waste of money. Most of the food Elizabeth likes is modified nouvelle cuisine: nutritious ingredients, perfectly balanced, and attractive to the eye as well as the palate.

She is extraordinarily fussy about her food. Virtually every piece of food is cut to the same size: each slice of carrot will match the next; each sautéed potato will be of equal thickness and diameter; all cubes of deep-fried potato are identical in size. The food is always decorated with greenery, and no piece of fish is served without garnish. All the food is prepared by chefs who have all trained at Buckingham Palace so they know exactly what the Queen likes and dislikes.

By mid-morning Elizabeth will have been briefed by her duty lady-in-waiting. Over the past few years, Lady Susan Hussey has become one of Elizabeth's principal advisers and now wields astonishing power inside the palace. She speaks with the same authority as Sir Robert Fellowes, and those who work near the Queen realize that a word from Susan Hussey carries nearly the authority of the Queen.

But Susan Hussey's rise to one of the most powerful positions at court seemed at one time to be doomed. According to palace rumor, Philip and Susan Hussey were "having a dingdong," the phrase courtiers, and the Royal Family, use to describe an affair. Nevertheless, Susan Hussey has became the Queen's most powerful adviser, the only woman to attain such prominence and influence since Bobo herself.

Until only a few months before Bobo's death in September 1993, Elizabeth still occasionally sought advice from her old nanny, despite the fact that she was in her late eighties. Bobo MacDonald began her royal service as Elizabeth's nursemaid and later became her dresser. Bobo enjoyed a remarkable intimacy with her sovereign and was one of the major influences on her life. Elizabeth always treated her as a member of the family and discussed everything with her, especially her children.

A redhead who later turned gray, Bobo was slim, capable, and determined. Her relationship with Elizabeth was based on total trust. She never broke Elizabeth's confidences and some in the palace believed the two women were almost telepathic.

Royal biographer Robert Lacey wrote in 1977, "She [Bobo] is prepared as none of the Queen's servants is, to tell her mistress when she has made a poor showing on television or has not spoken her best. Unsentimental and severe, she has come to provide a unique sounding board."

Bobo would accompany Elizabeth wherever she traveled. She had her own suite at Buckingham Palace, Windsor Castle, Balmoral, even on board the Royal Yacht *Britannia*. Bobo would accompany Elizabeth even at weekends when staying at friends' houses. As a result, everyone throughout the palace, including all of Elizabeth's children, treated her with the utmost respect, and often with envy. The rest of the Palace staff always referred to Bobo as "Miss MacDonald."

Bobo believed her principal task was protecting Elizabeth in every way possible. Throughout her life, she acted as Elizabeth's eyes and ears, informing her of things she would otherwise not have known, as well as making sure Elizabeth kept up with all the palace gossip.

A woman of remarkable power, Bobo would decide whether a royal servant was not up to scratch, lazy, or not sufficiently deferential toward Elizabeth. If she came to that decision, the servant would be removed from the Queen's immediate retinue and frequently dismissed.

At some time during the morning the letters need to be read. More than one hundred thousand arrive each year addressed to Her Majesty The Queen. A task force of seven is required to read, sift, and reply to them all, as well as to decide which should be sent through to the Private Secretary or to Her Majesty to read herself. Private letters to Elizabeth are always carefully initialed by the sender in the bottom left-hand corner of the envelope, and these are sent through unopened. Because of the ever-present threat of terrorism nowadays, however, a team of three men, equipped with the latest X-ray machinery, like that used at airports, checks every item of mail that comes into the palace.

Elizabeth invariably begins by reading mail from personal friends. As well as the personal letters, she will, given the time, peruse twenty to thirty letters from the general public every morning, deciding at random and from experience which to read. These provide her with a cross-section of opinion.

One of Elizabeth's little foibles concerns thank-you letters. She is most particular about who writes them. After each and every gathering she attends Elizabeth insists that every letter of thanks arriving at the palace be read personally by her. As a former lady-in-waiting commented, "She simply wants to know, for future occasions, who has written to thank her and those that have not. And, let me say, she knows the names of those people who have not written. My advice to everyone who is ever entertained at Buckingham Palace or anywhere else by the Queen, is to write and say thank you." If no letter of thanks is sent, it may be a very long time before that person is invited again.

Throughout the day Elizabeth never escapes the endless supply of official boxes, the leather-covered briefcases inscribed in gold lettering with the words *The Queen*. They are called "red boxes" because originally they were all red, but nowadays they may be any color—black, blue, or green, or indeed red. The boxes contain government papers, including papers from No. 10 Downing Street, the Cabinet Office, government departments, ambassadors, government ministries, as well as incessant requests to visit factories, hospitals, shopping malls, business parks, museums, and charities. The boxes arrive throughout the day and night at the palace or wherever the Queen is in residence.

Briefing papers on particular matters, such as necessary backgrounders on foreign affairs, will also be sent to her. As monarch, Elizabeth is the only person other than the Prime Minister who receives all information from every government department. She also receives the same type of information from every Commonwealth nation, which the British Prime Minister does not. She spends many hours of arduous, boring reading each day. The same material is also sent to Prince Charles.

The tradition of the monarch's being given access to all state papers goes back to the Bill of Rights of 1689, which established parliamentary supremacy in England by transferring most political power from the sovereign to Parliament. Agreement was reached, however, that the sovereign be informed of everything carried out by his ministers.

Britain has no written Constitution but is governed by an accumulation of customs and precedents which have arisen through history. Traditionally, the role of the monarch within the unwritten British constitution was outlined by Walter Bagehot over a century ago in his famous book *The English Constitution*, published in 1867. He wrote, "To state the matter shortly, the Sovereign has three rights—the right to be consulted, the right to encourage, the right to warn." These three rights are customarily assumed to include the right to know.

For the first two hundred years after 1689, very little government business was conducted, Parliament hardly ever sat, very little legislation was passed, and information from overseas took weeks to arrive by ship. The sovereign had very little paperwork to read. In this century, the explosion in information technology, the speed of transmission, and the amount of government work has meant the number of paper forwarded to the monarch has risen tenfold.

Every year Elizabeth receives three times the number of boxes her father George VI did. Many people believe she does not in fact bother to read many of the boxes sent her because reading everything would be too time-consuming, that her private secretaries sift through the boxes selecting the more important items for her to read.

In fact, Elizabeth is diligent. She regards keeping herself informed as an important part of her job. By reading the government papers she possesses a unique knowledge of what is happening in all the most important matters of state, including the armed forces and the secret services, MI5 and MI6 (the equivalent of the FBI and the CIA). A former Private Secretary said, "A box of work sent up in the evening, even as late as 10 P.M., is invariably read, signed where necessary, and back waiting on one's desk with comments first thing in the morning."

The principal reason Elizabeth devoutly reads so many government papers is because it is her duty to do so. She was instructed as a teenager, and later when she became Queen, that it was her daily duty to acquire as much knowledge as possible about government affairs in order to "encourage or warn" her ministers. That knowledge is contained in the red boxes. What Elizabeth believed forty years ago about her duty she still believes today. And she prides herself on the knowledge she had accumulated over the decades. Some Prime Ministers have been caught out when they discovered Elizabeth knew more about some matters than they did.

As Lord Charteris said, "In forty years of doing business with her I have never seen her enthusiasm waver. She wastes no time but gets on with the work in hand. She is a very quick reader and very quick to spot possible mistakes in planning."

He went on, "Her transparent honesty is so encouraging. You need have no hesitation about telling the Queen about anything. Never need to wrap anything up, whether it's about her children's behavior or whatever. All you say is 'Ma'am, this is what people are saying.' She listens carefully and is glad to be informed, usually."

Many ask, "What real power does the Queen hold today?"

The quick answer is very little, but that is an oversimplification.

Elizabeth is the head of state but cannot order or command her Prime Ministers to do anything. She is Commander-in-Chief of the

Armed Forces but cannot declare war or, indeed, take part in any battles without permission from the Prime Minister. She cannot levy taxes, create her own private courts, maintain her own standing army, or suspend obedience to acts of Parliament.

Elizabeth can, however, exert enormous influence behind the scenes, through senior members of her Household, who have powerful friends in every area of society but particularly in government, industry, Britain's financial center, and the aristocracy, who still retain the great majority of the nation's wealth.

Normally, Elizabeth has read through her first box of the day by 10 A.M., and her first appointment begins between 10 A.M. and 12 noon. Unless she has to attend a royal engagement, most of her appointments now take place at Buckingham Palace. She also likes to review, on her computer, everything being carried out that day by all the other members of The Firm so she knows who is doing what. Until computers were installed in the late 1980s, no one really was able to monitor exactly what any other member of the family was up to, which sometimes led to chaos as well as misunderstandings.

Elizabeth will usually eat a light lunch, often alone but occasionally with Philip or one of her senior advisers. The meal will often consist of fish or an omelette, or perhaps a salad with cheese, and she will drink only still Malvern water, and certainly no alcohol at lunch.

When she hosts a luncheon party, for perhaps ten people, then lunch is a much more formal affair. The guests are "commanded" to arrive at 12:30 P.M., and windshield stickers are provided so cars can pass gate security. A footman escorts them to the cream-and-gold Bow Room, where they meet a lady-in-waiting and an equerry who put guests at their ease over a pre-lunch drink. After everyone has arrived, the Queen walks in quietly, usually with a number of corgis at her heels. She will meet everyone in turn.

Lunch is served promptly at 1:10 P.M. The palace steward slips into the room, catches Elizabeth's eye, and announces, "Luncheon, Your Majesty." A seating plan is posted outside the dining room, the 1844 Room. The Queen always sits at the middle of the table, opposite Philip or Prince Charles. The most important guest is on the Queen's right, and if a lady is present, she will sit on Philip's right. During the first and second courses the Queen will chat to the guest on her right; during the third and fourth courses, to the person on her left. Toward the end of the meal she will talk to others around the table. No one is ever neglected.

At these luncheons lamb cutlets are popular; so are escallops of veal and salmon on a bed of rice. Nothing messy or difficult to eat is ever served, to spare any possible embarrassment to her guests.

Weather permitting, Elizabeth usually takes a walk after lunch in the palace gardens, often with some of her innumerable corgis, all of which she knows by name. After lunch she will sometimes take a short half-hour nap or lie down on a sofa with her feet up, reading the *Sporting Life* or studying her favorite subject, horse breeding. She is forever studying the breeding manuals, books, and bloodlines, of which she now has a quite remarkable and extensive knowledge. She still hopes to put together a combination that will achieve her greatest ambition, to win the English Derby.

At some point during most mornings or afternoons, the Queen will have to meet officially (*receive* is the official royal word that is always used) some dignitary, official, ambassador, or some representative, and probably a number of them. She may also have appointments with groups of people, from a drove of diplomats to a gaggle of Girl Guides. These meetings usually take ten to fifteen minutes at the very most, and the Queen always tries to involve everyone in the conversation, though the topics are invariably extremely dull.

On several occasions throughout the year the Queen will hold investitures at Buckingham Palace, when those who being honored are invited to the palace to receive their award from her personally. Usually around one hundred fifty people receive honors at a time, yet she will chat to each individually for a moment or so without giving any impression of being hurried.

When meeting groups of people, Elizabeth will have been briefed on the group she is to meet and will ask basic questions of them. She will often ask diplomats, "How long will your stay in Britain last?" and she will usually ask whether they have brought their families with them. There will often be a remark comparing London's weather to that of the diplomat's own country.

When meeting groups from Britain she will ask about their work, their role in the organization, and their length of service. She deliberately avoids contentious issues which might draw the monarchy into a question of politics.

The Queen has an astonishing ability to appear animated and interested when she must often be totally bored with those she must chat to. She has trained herself always to appear enthusiastic and concerned.

Humor seldom interrupts such occasions, but when something untoward occurs Elizabeth will often have difficulty smothering a smile. On one occasion at Balmoral, a Privy Councillor was walking away from her backward, when he knocked into a table, sending a book flying. Elizabeth went red in the face. Later, the Councillor apologized to her. "I could hardly contain myself," Elizabeth told him, "I wanted to burst out laughing."

Virtually without exception, everyone who meets Elizabeth is impressed, and the vast majority leave her presence with the same words: "She is really lovely, so interested, so knowledgeable. She made me feel great."

Each day Elizabeth spends at least an hour discussing her future diary with her Private Secretary, planning dates and times of official visits, functions, and meetings, all of which must be attended to with military efficiency. Elizabeth pays great attention to overseas visits, particularly visits to the fifty Commonwealth countries. She is not head of this great family of nations by right of succession, as she is Queen of England. She was appointed to the position by common consent of the Commonwealth nations, which fills her with pride, and which she takes most seriously.

It is said that Elizabeth is "wedded" to the Commonwealth and believes she is the personalized symbol of all that unifies it. It is accepted that there could be an elected president of the Commonwealth, but that the Queen, being nonpolitical, does the job better.

As former Prime Minister James Callaghan (1976–79) commented, "She really does know much more about heads of Commonwealth than any prime minister, because she has traveled so much and over such a long period. She really knows them, and about them."

Another former Prime Minister Lord Home (1963–64) commented: "The Queen does a great deal to make the Commonwealth work."

During every biennial Commonwealth Conference, which Elizabeth always attends, she has private discussions with each and every leader of all the countries attending. Leaders remark that those discussions are "informed and sympathetic."

Elizabeth's diary is not as heavy as it was during the early years of her reign. Still, in the 1990s she continues to average about four hundred official engagements a year, and that figure does not count overseas tours. Philip also continues to participate prodigiously in royal duties, and now the younger members of the family share the workload as well.

At 5 P.M. there is tea, which Elizabeth usually takes in her main drawing room. The tea itself is a special blend, a mixture of China and Indian teas designed by R. Twining & Company of the Strand in London. Anyone can buy this blend at Fortnum and Mason in Piccadilly. The Queen takes her tea with cold milk but no sugar, and most afternoons she used to eat thinly sliced cucumber sandwiches and occasionally her favorite Dundee cake. Often hovering around, hoping for tidbits, are a few of her favorite corgis.

For some years now, however, Elizabeth has been *banting*, the word she and other members of the family have always used instead of the more common *dieting*. The term derives from the surname of a nineteenth-century English undertaker and dietitian named William Banting, whose treatment for obesity was abstinence from sugar, starch, and fat. When asked if she would like a slice of cake Elizabeth will usually answer, "No, thank you very much, I'm banting."

She will often challenge friends if she sees them munching sandwiches at teatime with a slight admonishment, coupled with a smile: "Are you supposed to be eating that? I thought you were banting."

Elizabeth watches her weight at all times and becomes quite angry with herself when putting on too many pounds. Her reason is not vanity but health, for she is determined to live as long as her mother, who was still going strong into her nineties.

After the thirty-minute interlude for tea and relaxation, Elizabeth feeds her dogs, which have on occasion numbered thirteen. The ever-present corgis spend the time yapping and squabbling between each other, as well as fighting for favor from the royal hand, be it a stroke, a pat, or something to eat.

So many of them look identical, yet Elizabeth knows the names and ages of each, and every one has a special place in her heart. Not all are corgis. She also owns what are called "dawgies," an unplanned cross between corgis and dachshunds. Elizabeth adores them all, despite the fact they can be infuriating little animals, difficult to discipline.

Elizabeth, the Queen of England, the crowned head of the greatest surviving monarchy in the world, considers the afternoon ceremony of feeding her pet dogs one of the most important events of her day. Liveried footmen are called in when Elizabeth rings the bell and tells the maid it is time for the dogs' evening meal. First the footman put down a green plastic sheet over the rather threadbare carpet and then return and place the line of dog bowls, each inscribed with a dog's name, on the sheet in a long row. Meanwhile, the excited dogs, keen for their food, scamper around Elizabeth's legs, barking and yapping. A great bowl is brought in and handed to Elizabeth, who then goes to the end of the row and begins to scoop food into each bowl. Every dog knows its bowl, and the footmen stand by in case a greedy one tries to steal another dog's food rather than waiting in turn. If that should happen Elizabeth issues a cross word, and a footman steps in, picks up the offending animal, and, at the risk of being nipped, holds the dog until its bowl has been filled. Only then is the wayward canine permitted to eat its food. One footman confessed on camera, "When [the dogs] occasionally fall upon one another, whoever is present on duty is expected to haul them apart at whatever risk to hand and foot."

Elizabeth always tries to be on hand to feed her dogs personally every day. In fine weather the ritual takes place on the terrace, and after the dogs have been fed, it is time, weather permitting, for a walk in the garden. Elizabeth leads them downstairs, all yapping with excitement, and out into the beautiful garden where they run, fight, chase tennis balls, and spend their "pennies and tuppences," as the Queen delicately puts it, while she walks around playing and chatting and talking to her beloved animals.

Generally speaking the dogs are quite well behaved, mainly because of the rigorous training they received as puppies at Sandringham. Occasionally, however, massive fights break out, during which one poor dog is virtually torn to pieces by the others.

Piles of dirty towels are always kept on radiators or left on the floor near the Garden Entrance into Buckingham Palace, the Queen's personal front door. The footmen use them to clean the fifty-two tiny muddy paws of the thirteen corgis. Throughout the day Elizabeth likes to have three or four of the older, better-behaved corgis in her suite of offices, lying around and waiting for a word or a pat from their mistress. They seem to comfort her, and she loves their company, often chatting away to them while tending to the affairs of state.

It is indeed most unusual if two or three corgis are not with her. Those privileged ones go everywhere with the Queen, walking down corridors, up and down stairs; lying around while she reads a newspaper, watches television, or talks to her advisers. Sometimes they lie under the royal table waiting for Elizabeth to secretly feed them the odd morsel.

Through the years the number of dogs has, of course, varied. In 1993 Elizabeth had only seven as her constant companions: Pharos, Phoenix, Myth, Kelpie, Fable, Diamond, and Spark. On weekends, it is customary for all the dogs to pile into the Rolls-Royce, in the back with Elizabeth, for the thirty-mile ride to Windsor Castle. Like Elizabeth, they also enjoy the weekend away from "the office." They know that at Windsor they will have more "walkies" with their royal mistress, and, with luck, occasional long walks in Windsor Great Park.

And yet, alongside what many people would consider rather eccentric behavior, which the public and her subjects never witness, is a strict belief in protocol. Elizabeth is adamant that everything must be carried out correctly, with the preservation of the monarchy and the House of Windsor the paramount objective.

For this reason she is very particular about the staff she employs, and not merely the senior staff and her personal advisers. Save for the lowly jobs, such as secretaries, footmen, junior clerks, kitchen staff, cleaners, and gardeners, Elizabeth interviews most prospective employees herself, despite the fact they have all been checked out beforehand by other senior staff. At the end of a successful interview for most of the senior jobs, as well as for positions with regular personal contact with her, Elizabeth will usually say, "Let's give it a try for a year. Then if we decide we can't stand each other we can let it go at that." The perfect escape clause that applies to both parties.

Elizabeth is, in fact, very good at finding ways to exit situations for every aspect of her life. The satirical TV show *Spitting Image*, featuring grotesque puppet caricatures of public figures, can be most cruel toward Elizabeth because she is such an easy target.

For decades the single word she uses repeatedly when talking to people is "interesting." Whatever question or answer was put to her, Elizabeth would answer, "Interesting," or perhaps she would vary the reply by prefixing it with "Very." Then she would pass on to the next person and say the same thing. It did make life easy for her but very boring for everyone she spoke to. As a direct result of *Spitting Image*'s mimicry, Elizabeth now tries never to use the word. Even today, however, it still occasionally creeps in, particularly at the end of a busy day of meeting hundreds of people.

Elizabeth also has a wonderful way of avoiding situations, awkward questions, comments, anything that might cause embarrassment in any given situation. During a conversation in which she does not want to answer a question or make a statement, Elizabeth will suddenly say, "Isn't it a lovely day?" Or conversely, "It's not a very nice day, is it?" Another favorite, which she employs as a polite dismissal, is "I think I had better take the dogs out for a walk." Anyone talking to her knows the conversation is at an end and she does not wish to continue it a moment longer. If someone persists, Elizabeth simply turns and walks away, sometimes leaving people in midsentence. Since she is the Queen no one dares challenge her right to leave without answering, a right she uses wherever and whenever she wishes.

As one of her former advisers said, "She never likes to say 'yes' or 'no' to anyone or about anything so that she can never be accused of commenting on anything that might be political or cause offense or give any impression that she is anything but above politics. She never forgets she is the Queen, never. It is ingrained in her."

Elizabeth loves hearing the palace gossip, about love affairs, marital rifts, scandals, accidents, or anything amusing or funny. She hears all this chatter from those staff close to her who are not of senior rank: her dressers, pages, footmen, bodyguards, and chauffeur. She has two special pages, officially called Pages of the Back Stairs, who act as the Queen's official go-between with everyone else in the palace, running errands, taking messages, or delivering and collecting documents. They are usually responsible men in their thirties and forties and, more often than not, gay. They are always extremely discreet.

One footman arrived to see a senior footman, John Davis, standing outside the Queen's sitting room, talking volubly to Elizabeth about the plight of a housemaid whose love affair had gone horribly wrong. He said, "They looked like a couple of neighbors chatting over the garden fence. I waited and listened to Her Majesty wanting to know all the intimate details. She was fascinated and told him to keep her informed."

There is one important phone call she makes without fail each day—to her mother, the Queen Mother, who lived at nearby Clarence House. They chat for fifteen minutes or so. Elizabeth is indeed quite addicted to the phone. She has one in every room she uses and has four on her office desk: one direct line to No. 10 Downing Street, in case of emergency, an internal phone linking her with everyone in the palace, a scrambled line for personal calls, and another private outside line.

Elizabeth's day never officially ends, but she tries to leave her office at around six, after the dogs have had their run and she has received her final briefing of the day as well as read some of the more important letters that have been written in her name or on her behalf. A few, usually the personal ones, she writes herself.

She will try to watch the BBC six o'clock news or listen to the news on the radio to keep abreast of the day's major events. She takes a keen interest not only in what has happened in Britain but around the globe. That is why she also enjoys listening to the BBC World Service programs, because they give a more global view of the day's events.

Often, and more so during the past few years, she and Philip will dine together in the small drawing room. They always dress for dinner. She will wear a smart short dress, and Philip will wear a smoking jacket and a bow tie.

Occasionally a friend and his wife are invited to dinner. The evening is informal, although there are footmen and a butler, and the food is usually plain. The first course will perhaps be smoked salmon or a little terrine, the main course lamb, and always proper puddings, such as apple pie. Most evenings Elizabeth does not drink at all. If she does drink at dinner, it is usually a little dry white wine.

Like every other couple of pensionable age throughout Britain the two, more often than not, will sit and watch television, but only after completing their dinner. Elizabeth will never eat a meal in front of the television set.

The Queen and the Duke are television fans, and some would

suggest they have become addicts during the past few years. Elizabeth sees it as her one true relaxation after a day's work. Besides watching various news shows, she loves comedy shows and some old films. On occasion Philip becomes angry watching "the box" and will hurl abuse at the screen: "What a load of bloody rubbish" is a comment Elizabeth has heard him make a thousand times. Philip's TV interests are more serious, political, and practical. He will often go to his study and watch what he prefers on another set. Sometimes they will spend the evening watching the latest film release, for Elizabeth in particular is quite a movie buff.

When their evening TV viewing is over, they will not see each other again until the following morning. Elizabeth may go to bed early, either to read a book, or peruse the contents of last official box of the day. Elizabeth does not spend so much time nowadays reading but is still sent books by Hatchards, the booksellers in Piccadilly, whose executives make a selection of current titles for her and send them to the palace. Those she wants, she keeps; the others are returned. Elizabeth's reading interests are varied and conservative. She prefers biographies, thrillers, and current award-winning novels, and she has no particularly favorite author except for Dick Francis, whose specialty is thrillers revolving around horse racing.

For much of the year Elizabeth works tirelessly for what she sees as her duty to the nation. Most women of sixty-seven have already retired, but Elizabeth continues her arduous schedule with the same sense of duty she first showed as a young monarch of twenty-six. Indeed, there are those in the palace who believe she now works harder than ever.

She had hoped that by 1990 she would have been able to shift most of her royal duties to her children. The traumas of the failed marriages has meant that Elizabeth has had to continue her duties far longer than she believed would be necessary. Today, she still attends every royal engagement she should without complaint, not even to any of her ladies-in-waiting.

As she undertakes her royal duties, she often meets, shakes hands, and passes the time of day with the same people at the same places in the same circumstances as she has done each and every year for decades. Yet she appears to enjoy herself more than she did in the 1950s and 1960s. Not only has she learned to relax but, more important, she has also learned to smile. For years Elizabeth was considered glum, dowdy, far too serious. Unfairly, people attributed her apparent melancholy to the fact that her bloodline is principally Teutonic.

A great amount of work goes into a royal visit, no matter whether it is a grand royal tour to Australia or Canada or opening a new building two hundred miles from London. The schedule must run like clockwork, not just for Elizabeth, who reveres punctuality, but also for the local dignitaries, for the hundreds who might turn out to see and cheer her; so as not to disturb or disrupt the daily lives of others for the sake of security. The Palace can never forget the assassination of Mountbatten.

Elizabeth herself always checks the plans, and the invitation list, before final details of the visit are authorized and put into operation. She reads through the usually thick file of names and brief descriptions, including their jobs, of the people to whom she will be introduced. A note will be made if she has met them before. Buckingham Palace always asks those providing lunch or dinner for the Queen to submit three menus, and Elizabeth must make her final choice three or four months in advance. However she feels, she will never change her mind or ask for anything else on the day of the visit.

Her selection of the clothes will be made a week or so in advance, in regular meetings with her dresser. Elizabeth ignores conditions imposed by weather. She rarely changes her mind about the outfit she has picked out, and she will never change the schedule because she will not disappoint those who have turned out, often in their best clothes, just to catch a glimpse of her. The palace wet-weather program—a number of umbrellas—is always at hand. Fortunately, Elizabeth rather likes rain, far preferring it to hot weather.

Elizabeth enjoys traveling on the royal train, which she uses frequently and which costs the taxpayer about $2 million a year. Often, she will travel by night, sleeping on the train in a siding somewhere en route to her destination. The dark train, crimson lined, has a carriage with sitting room, bedroom, bathroom for herself, and a smaller compartment and bathroom for her dresser. It is lavishly equipped: the bedrooms are large, the sitting rooms comfortable, and the bathrooms well-appointed. Elizabeth will take her chef with her and eat extremely well; the train is secure and easy to guard, and she can work, reading her boxes or planning future engagements. Courtiers accompanying her have their own coach with sleeping and working quarters. There are also two coaches for police and servants, footmen, and pages. At the back is a spare engine, just in case.

She sometimes takes an aircraft of the Queen's Flight, which costs the taxpayer another $10 million a year or, if the engagement is near enough, she will travel by Rolls-Royce. The Rolls is accompanied by a single patrol car and motorcycle outriders, but their sirens remain silent for Elizabeth cannot bear their screaming. Her car usually travels at reasonable speeds so that the Queen never feels shaken or uncomfortable.

Those who meet the Queen are advised as to what to wear. The Palace suggests they dress comfortably. They can also wear a hat if they wish, and gloves. The Queen always wears gloves, which means no sticky, sweaty hands, either from nerves or from eating ice cream. Elizabeth herself invariably wears a hat but does not encourage other women to do so.

Today, Elizabeth still draws sizable crowds wherever she goes in Britain. Although the crowds are not so large as they were at the beginning of her reign, most Brits still believe it a privilege to stand in line, meet, chat, and shake the hand of Elizabeth. Afterward, they will talk of meeting the Queen for days and weeks, as a highlight of their life.

Because her daily life has hardly altered in forty years, Elizabeth cherishes her weekends away from Buck House. She has always tried to escape the confines of her office, either by spending forty-eight hours at Windsor, the place she calls home, or a weekend with friends somewhere in the country, but never in London.

In the 1960s and 1970s, when Dickie Mountbatten was alive, she loved to spend weekends at Broadlands; she spent more weekends there than at any other country home. She would usually arrive on a Friday morning and would often go riding with Mountbatten through his five-thousand-acre estate. They would return for a light lunch, perhaps a soufflé and salad, and afterward take Mountbatten's Labradors for a long walk. Or they would fish in the River Test during the afternoon, depending on the weather.

Tea would be held in the Wedgewood Room, a quite formal

occasion, with a spirit heater keeping the silver teapot and hot-water jug gently simmering. They would usually have toasted, buttered buns. Elizabeth loves a good tea after an abundance of country air all day.

After tea she would rest or perhaps read for an hour, and Philip would usually arrive in time to change and dress for dinner. Even at Broadlands Elizabeth and Philip never shared a bedroom.

At 8 P.M. everyone would gather in the drawing room dressed for dinner, the men in black ties and dinner jackets, the ladies in long dresses. All would be waiting for the Queen. No one is ever permitted to arrive late.

Elizabeth will usually take a weak whisky with water before dinner and may drink a glass or two of vintage wine during dinner. She has never appeared tipsy in anyone's presence, and no one has ever seen her the worse for drink.

In private Elizabeth, who has a good sense of humor, can see the funny side even when things go dramatically wrong. John Barratt tells the story of one dinner party at Broadlands when the butler, Frank Randall, well into his seventies, had taken a drop too much to drink. "It was an informal dinner but everyone was dressed as usual, the men in dinner jackets and black tie and the women in long dresses. Poor old Frank Randall, slightly the worse for wear that night, had been given the task of serving the soup, and he spilled an entire bowlful right into the lap of the Queen. There was a gasp around the table, and then Elizabeth looked up at Frank who was now in a terrible bother, and she roared with laughter. You have to have a good sense of humor when your lap is full of hot soup."

Elizabeth loves after-dinner games, where she can be seen throwing back her head and laughing. The more childish the games the more she seems to enjoy herself. Charades remains a favorite. Others include a tricky game played with string to which a cork is attached. The objective is to put out a lighted candle placed on the floor. The string is tied around the player's waist so that the cork dangles at the ankles. Each person bends over and tries to extinguish the candle in the shortest possible time. Old Sebastian Ferranti, a friend of the Royal Family, used to chirp up whenever the ladies took their turn: "Take care you don't get singed," and everyone, including Elizabeth, would roar with laughter.

Another favorite party game is Pass the Orange, in which everyone sits in a circle, man-woman, man-woman, and must pass on the orange by holding it under the chin. No hands can be used. Anyone who drops the orange is out and must leave the circle. Elizabeth, who became a skilled player, frequently wins, and she still loves to play this game today.

When everyone has had enough of party games the group splits up, some going to play billiards or snooker, others to work together on a difficult jigsaw puzzle, which Elizabeth enjoys. Some watch television or a movie. Elizabeth usually goes to bed at eleven, even if the party is in full swing.

At seven o'clock sharp the following morning a maid brings Elizabeth her tea tray and breakfast is at eight, served at Broadlands in the Shooting Room. This was thought to be a very adventurous undertaking. Trestle tables would be set up with folding wooden chairs for the guests and everyone, including the Queen, would eat off plastic plates and drink tea or coffee from plastic cups, like school-children enjoying a picnic in the garage at home. The food included bacon and eggs or her favorite kedgeree—rice, fish, and hard-boiled eggs mixed together. For decades Elizabeth, who enjoyed these breakfasts, would always start Saturday at Broadlands with a picnic in the Shooting Room.

Afterward she would take a walk with one of Mountbatten's Labradors, which were related to the Labradors Elizabeth keeps at Sandringham. Then the party would take off for the day's shoot and Elizabeth would always join in. She would not shoot a gun herself, but she loves to work the dogs, springing the birds, and collecting them after they fall to the ground. Elizabeth has been trained to work gundogs by the staff at Sandringham and takes great pride in handling them efficiently.

The midday meal at the house usually begins with sloe gin. A frequent visitor to Broadlands commented, "Lunch was always full of laughter and merriment with everyone joking about what had gone wrong, pulling each other's leg about something or other. Sometimes the Queen would chide Philip for losing his temper over some minor matter during the shoot. Lunch would be a good stodgy meal like Irish stew, followed by apple pie and custard."

Rain or shine the shooting party would venture out by two-thirty for the third stand of the day. All would return by four-thirty for tea, once again in the Shooting Room, everyone standing around in their Barbours and muddy boots. After tea Elizabeth would go to her suite for a bath and a rest; then she would look though some boxes that had arrived during the day, to check if anything of dramatic importance had arrived. After a four-course dinner, always served with a good vintage wine, Elizabeth would usually choose a film, almost always something light. She would ask everyone in the room, "I would rather like to see this one unless anyone has any other ideas." No one ever had any other ideas.

Sunday would start with the same routine: tea at seven followed by the picnic breakfast in the Shooting Room, followed by church, the family visiting Romsey Abbey for the morning service. Sometimes the house party would break before lunch. Elizabeth always wanted to be back in London at Buckingham Palace by the early evening, fully prepared for work the next day.

Now on most weekends Elizabeth takes off for the thirty-mile drive to Windsor Castle, the place she calls home, where she spends more than thirty weekends each year. She spent many of her formative years there during the war, and that is where she feels at peace. She arrives by car from London in time for afternoon tea on Friday, followed by a long walk with the dogs. Despite the nearly one million people a year who visit Windsor Castle, Elizabeth feels a far greater sense of privacy there than at the palace, where no tourists were permitted. At Windsor, the areas to which the public are admitted are isolated from the private areas where the family lives.

After a light, informal dinner Elizabeth and Philip will often watch television or a film. Early on Saturday, before breakfast, Elizabeth usually rides in Windsor Great Park. Sometimes, after a hearty breakfast, she will ride again or visit estate workers and their wives in their homes, chatting to them about personal problems or about their work. She will always take the dogs for a good long walk and reserve at least an hour for her boxes.

On a lovely summer's day both Elizabeth and Philip will spend the afternoon lying on loungers, enjoying the sun. If it is not warm enough they will go back inside to read or browse through the newspapers.

Around teatime, other members of the family will often drop by.

Charles used to be a frequent visitor, though not so often nowadays, and Anne as well. During the past few years Andrew and Edward have spent many Saturday evenings with their parents, Andrew practicing his golf on the nine-hole private course on the grounds.

Occasionally on Saturday evenings Elizabeth will organize a dinner party to which she invites between ten and twenty people, friends, members of the Household and their wives, sometimes MPs, Cabinet ministers, or members of the church. She prefers familiar faces for her Saturday dinners, people with whom she can relax and have fun. Usually swing music or gentle standards from her favorite musicals are played.

Even when Elizabeth is the hostess, she never greets her guests. They stand around and wait for her to appear, usually at seven-thirty, perhaps an hour after they have arrived. Within the space of a few seconds, Elizabeth can look around a room and register which people she knows and which she doesn't. Indeed, she can do this when meeting more than a hundred people at a time, and more often that not, she will remember where and when she met them. She likes to have people around her so that she can to listen to news from the gossip grapevine.

On Sunday morning the Queen never fails to attend the morning service at St. George's Chapel, inside the castle walls. Whoever has stayed the night is also expected to appear.

After church is a traditional Sunday lunch, sometimes attended by one or two children, and perhaps grandchildren, an afternoon walk in the park with the dogs, and most important, reading the thick wad of four quality broadsheet newspapers and the three robust, sexy tabloids, which most weeks carry the latest stories and scandals surrounding the royals. At 6 P.M. most Sundays, Elizabeth says farewell to Windsor and returns to the palace with her dogs for another week at the office.

As well as Buck House and Windsor Castle, Elizabeth has two other homes she has known since childhood and where she likes to relax. Sandringham House in Norfolk and Balmoral in Scotland were inherited from George V by his heir, David. When he was forced to abdicate, Elizabeth's father bought them from him for $1.5 million. They were to become beloved playgrounds for Elizabeth and Margaret, and they have always been special for the Queen.

Elizabeth spent her first Christmas holidays at Sandringham, and she continues to spend every Christmas there. It was at Sandringham that Lilibet enjoyed many happy hours with her father. King George took his daughter wildfowling on the marshes, and they would take long walks together in the cold, crisp December air.

She remembered her childhood Christmases at Sandringham where the family would all meet to lay out their presents on the dining room table on Christmas Eve, forbidden to open them until after Christmas dinner the next day. The tradition has never changed. Elizabeth has also continued the royal tradition of making everyone give unusual, even odd presents, never spending much money—under twenty dollars a present—but making all concentrate on thinking up suitable gifts.

Nothing has changed at Sandringham since Elizabeth's childhood, and she intends to keep it that way. In fact, nearly everything is the same as when it was first built at the beginning of the century: the country-style, old-fashioned furnishings; the net curtains on the windows, even though Sandringham House is isolated in the middle of the countryside, overlooked by no one; the central heating that barely works; the big cold bathrooms. The same jigsaw puzzle that Lilibet first played with sixty years ago can still be found in the Saloon. Every Christmas the family spends time putting it together.

Elizabeth's father died in his sleep in the early hours of February 6, 1952 at Sandringham. Her grandfather George V also died at Sandringham, in January 1936. Elizabeth seems to want to keep alive her happy childhood days at her Norfolk home, where she still spends her six-week Christmas break.

A special pleasure awaits her black Labradors and cocker spaniels whenever Elizabeth sets foot there. Elizabeth's relationship with her dogs is almost uncanny. The gundogs spend most of their days in the care of their trainer Bill Meldrum, but they seem to know whenever the Queen arrives at Sandringham. The dogs want affection, and Elizabeth loves fussing over them and giving them tidbits. Gundog trainer Martin Deeley, who has watched Elizabeth working her dogs, recalled: "Observe her facial expressions and listen to her voice, and you realize that here is a lady who is at home with animals. She knows how far to let them go, she can see when they are trying to please her or themselves and is at one with them at work or play."

Sometimes Elizabeth is asked to judge novice and open Retriever Trials at both Sandringham and Balmoral, but she finds the job nerve-racking and only occasionally will she agree to participate. It's odd that this intelligent woman, with a considerable knowledge of animals, should be so nervous judging them, while all the highly knowledgeable gundog breeders watch and wait for her decision.

Balmoral is the turreted, fairy-tale castle in the Scottish Highlands, close to Braemar, where Elizabeth takes her long annual break which stretches ten weeks from August to October. With its 11,750 acres of grouse moor and five beautiful glens spread across 50,000 acres, it has a magnificent estate which the Queen adores to ride across most days during her long stay, enjoying the spectacular views as well as the peace and quiet of the countryside. She looks forward to that holiday to escape into another world.

Unlike Sandringham, Elizabeth has changed a good deal about Balmoral. Queen Victoria had a mania for tartans, and Elizabeth has replaced them with homey, country-style decor and furnishings. There is always a special tang of wood fires, stag's heads, and heather at Balmoral which visitors find relaxing. There is a wonderful ballroom, but no magnificent state rooms, as can be found at Buckingham Palace. Balmoral is where Elizabeth goes to enjoy life.

She will invite friends to stay for a night, a weekend, or sometimes for an entire week. But the seven-day stay is usually reserved for members of the family or very special guests, such as senior ladies-in-waiting or old family friends. She always invites the current Prime Minister—plus spouse—to visit Balmoral for a weekend. Sometimes, Prime Ministers from Commonwealth countries come there to enjoy the quiet.

Elizabeth's bedroom is a haven of peace. It is filled with photo-graphs of her parents, children, grandchildren, and other relatives at various stages of their lives. In earlier years during the long summer break, the castle would ring with the laughter and chatter of children, and Elizabeth's grandchildren, whom she encouraged to use the castle as their family holiday home.

No matter where she is, however, the official red boxes keep arriving. Yet the few people who know the Queen well report that she does enjoy her life and, despite the many family crises, has learned to relax at weekends, away from the pressures of office.

TWELVE

A COUNTRY GIRL AT HEART

Shy and retiring, Elizabeth would have far preferred a quiet life away from the center of attention and the spotlight that has followed her since her childhood. But when her uncle, King Edward VIII, abdicated in 1936, her father was suddenly thrust from obscurity to become King George VI. The dramatic change was a shock to him, but he responded with remarkable courage.

For Elizabeth, only ten years old then, her change in status was less traumatic. She did, however, realize that since her father was now to be King, she would one day become Queen. Before then, she had believed she would marry a wealthy aristocrat, live in some fine stately home, raise a family, and lead the quiet life of a privileged lady in the heart of the country.

Her passion for country life has never left her. "I love to go to Balmoral," she has often told people, "where I can relax in the beautiful country air and go for walks for hours on end and not meet another soul."

This side of Elizabeth is one the public occasionally glimpse and which this author has witnessed when she has taken walks in Windsor Great Park and attended house trials. Dressed in a full-length, dark green, weatherproof "dry-as-a-bone" waxed coat, which reaches below her knees, a bright silk scarf on her head, and green Wellington boots on her feet, Elizabeth relaxes as she walks through a wet field with a couple of black Labradors at her heels. She doesn't mind if it's raining or cold or damp and misty.

At Balmoral Elizabeth can lead the country life she envies. The castle has always represented freedom for Elizabeth, a precious commodity for someone whose life has been so rigidly ordered and disciplined. It was there that Elizabeth and Margaret, as young princesses, rode their ponies over the moors alone, without a groom accompanying them. It was at Balmoral that their mother, sometimes accompanied by their father, would take them on picnics, both before and after the war. Elizabeth particularly liked to eat off plastic plates and would happily wash the dishes in a sparkling burn or stream before packing up the picnic hamper and heading back to the house. Since those idyllic childhood days Elizabeth has always ridden, and especially at Balmoral, with its rolling acres offering freedom, peace, and solitude.

It was at Balmoral that Elizabeth began her lifelong interest in stalking and where she shot her first stag, at the age of sixteen. Since then she has brought down many deer, but she prefers stalking them. Every year Elizabeth spends days and weeks out stalking in the glens during her holidays at Balmoral.

The royal party will bring along a gillie (Scottish for *attendant*) with a telescope, binoculars, rifles, and a pony boy with a Haflinger pony, to carry the carcass down the mountain. As they walk up the slopes of the glen, Elizabeth is often the first to spot the herd of deer at the foot of a ravine. Together with the entire hunting party, she will immediately drop down and make her way to the nearest boulder to hide and check the herd through her binoculars. If necessary, to prevent the deer from seeing the stalking party, Elizabeth will crawl on all fours through the rain-soaked heather.

To ensure a clean kill, during the annual cull the hunters often leave their initial hideaway and make their way to a new position, sometimes walking for more than two hours. As the party moves through the heather and rocks and across streams, they are barely visible as their tweeds blend in with the background. When in place, the gillie will confirm which stag should be killed, usually an older one. He loads the rifle and passes it to Elizabeth, who takes up her position to shoot. The rifle shot reverberates like a thunderclap around the glen, and the stag lies where it falls.

Elizabeth's reputation as a crack shot is legendary, and she takes a special pride in it, one reason being that her beloved father taught her to stalk and shoot. If ever a stag is not shot cleanly, the party will not give up until the stag has been followed and killed. But as one gillie said, "Her Majesty is a dead shot. I cannot recall seeing her miss, though there will have been times when she did."

Neither Elizabeth or Philip are bloodthirsty about their shooting, nor are they sentimental. They know that deer have to be culled because if deer are not properly farmed the weak will suffer from malnutrition. Charles, Andrew, and Princess Anne all enjoy stalking, but neither Diana nor Fergie hunted deer more than a few times, nor did they want to actually try to shoot one themselves. In the end, fed up after a day of hard walking across glens and through burns, often in filthy weather, they preferred to stay indoors.

On a fine day Diana and Fergie would arrive in time for the family picnic, even if the skies were overcast and threatening, because they knew they were expected. Rugs would be laid down, and most of the party sat, happy to take the weight off their feet after hours of walking. The Windsor clan looked like something out of the last century in their plaids, tweeds, and checks. Only Diana and Fergie appeared on the moors without traditional dress, preferring blue jeans and bright sweaters. Sometimes the whole family would be there, including Margaret with her children and Anne with hers. But those days have mostly passed.

Since Charles's separation from Diana, both Wills and Harry still visit Balmoral in the summer holidays with their father, who is already teaching them the rudiments of stalking and shooting. The two boys understand the discipline of the guns, and they happily join in helping to pick up the fallen birds. They also have their own toy guns, which they love to take to the heather and pretend to shoot, just like Papa. Charles intends to teach both boys to shoot, and he expects them to become expert horsemen. He will certainly encourage them to hunt foxes and deer on horseback. Charles has always remembered his own youthful reaction to hunting. He recalls, "The sound of a horn or hearing the hounds sent tingles down my spine as a child. I just knew I would have to do it one day." His sons share that enthusiasm. It is something which Diana wishes Charles would not encourage, but it is too late. Already, they love the idea and the excitement of the chase and cannot wait till they can join their father riding to hounds.

Young Harry is proving a better, more daring rider than his elder brother. After one fall when he was only six, Harry said, "I went into the mud face first and I got a bloody nose as well—quite a sight they all seemed to think." He went on, "It probably served me right 'cos I jumped straight into a bog and the horse turned about three somersaults."

His fearless approach to riding was also evident when he said on another occasion, "You throw yourself over obstacles. You don't know what's coming—you have to shut your eyes and take a deep breath." No wonder Diana worries about him.

Charles's numerous injuries on the polo field have taken their toll, and in the spring of 1993, at the age of forty-four, he all but gave up his beloved sport. During his twenty-five years of playing the game, Charles had reached the top level, enjoying high-goal polo with some of the world's top players. At the highest level the game requires great physical ability and fitness. During polo matches in 1991 and 1992 Charles would often be seen, between chukkas, lying in agony on the ground trying to find relief from severe back pain. His recurring back problem finally caused him to hang up his polo boots. But it was a severe wrench for him. Without a doubt, polo was for many years Charles's abiding passion. Depending on the condition of his back, Charles has now decided to limit his polo to the occasional charity match.

To Elizabeth, Charles's decision to cease playing competitive polo came as a great relief. During the last few years he had taken some hard falls from his ponies, the most severe when he broke his arm in two places.

During the past three years, he has turned his riding abilities and interest more toward hunting, which is becoming a passion. Sometimes Charles will hunt four times a week from November through March, riding with the Beaufort or the Berkeley near Highgrove; in Leicestershire with the Belvoir (pronounced Beaver); and on Mondays and Fridays with the Quorn. Charles's newfound enthusiasm for hunting began when he and Diana informally separated in 1988, four years before the world realized they were living apart.

Diana has always hated hunting and in the early years of their married life tried desperately to persuade Charles to give it up. To keep the peace in the home he did for a while. But as their relationship became more difficult and they spent more time apart, Charles returned to the hunting field and renewed his love affair with the sport. Diana made it clear that she not only disapproved of hunting but found the great majority of people who went hunting not very good company. She once said of them, "They are so frightfully snooty. If someone doesn't like hunting they think they should belong on another planet they're so stuck up."

Charles knows that many people believe hunting to be cruel and understands that those who oppose hunting want him to set an example. "I do not enjoy the killing but I know it has to be done," he has said. "I wish the anti-blood-sport people could realize how much more painful and more horrible all other known methods of fox control would be."

Elizabeth is happy that Charles likes hunting and shooting because she knows there are few sports in which the heir to the throne can participate. She knows riding, shooting, stalking, fishing, and polo are good ways to relax. And she openly encourages Wills and Harry to follow in their father's footsteps.

Diana once found herself arguing with her mother-in-law at dinner about hunting. Diana said she believed it was morally wrong and that she didn't want her sons indulging in such sports that would soon be banned in Britain. Elizabeth took up the pro-hunting argument, explaining why it was necessary to hunt and shoot, to keep the foxes down and to cull the deer. Diana kept interrupting her, unable to control herself, until she finally shouted emotionally at Elizabeth, "You don't realize how many people in this country hate hunting and shooting because it's so cruel!" Her voice reached a crescendo as she screamed, "Would you like to be hunted and shot at?"

Elizabeth looked at Diana, turned away, and began another conversation, leaving her daughter-in-law angry and embarrassed that she had lost her temper.

When Philip and Charles took part in the same shoot—which nowadays is very rare—the two embarked on a definite but unspoken competition to see who could bag the most birds. Nicholas Soames, a close friend of Prince Charles, said, "Most people realize they are very competitive. Prince Philip always had a reputation for going for a big bag and Charles does the same. Neither want to go home with the smaller bag. No one said anything of course, but the competition was sometimes intense. The Duke seemed to have to prove himself."

Elizabeth and Philip have always taken their main, ten-week-long summer holiday at Balmoral. Philip will spend hours fishing and painting while Elizabeth prefers to ride or stalk or take long walks with her gundogs. As a result Elizabeth is a remarkably fit woman for her age and she takes pride in keeping in shape.

For most of the year, however, Elizabeth relaxes quietly at home most evenings. At the end of the day, unless she must attend a dinner or some other royal occasion, she likes to put her stockinged feet up and lie on a sofa in front of a fire reading a book or watching television. Just the way most of her subjects do.

In many ways Elizabeth is a straightforward woman with few complexities in her character. In most respects she appears a quite ordinary person, especially in her everyday habits, her likes and dislikes, her demands and preferences. She may be the wealthiest woman in the world, yet she hates wasting a single cent. She will go to great lengths to save even a few dollars. She orders curtains to be darned rather than buy new ones; she refuses to get new sofas and chairs when the upholstery is worn out and orders slipcovers instead. Even then, if she believes the slipcovers are too expensive, she will have the old slipcovers darned. When bedsheets wear thin and housekeepers ask permission to purchase new ones, Elizabeth usually refuses, telling them to resew them by exchanging the middle parts for sheeting at the edges. Carpets are hardly ever replaced but are simply sent away to be expertly patched and then put back again. Fitted carpets are resewn so that the old, worn areas are moved to the outside, providing a few more years' wear. And she usually orders carpets underlaid with canvas instead of the more expensive backing which the rest of the Western world uses.

For decades every single light switch throughout Windsor Castle was marked with a small notice: PLEASE TURN OFF THE LIGHT WHEN YOU LEAVE THE ROOM.

Her frugal ways even extend to food. Leftover food from one meal will, if possible, be used the next day. She will always expect meat left over from a roast joint to be minced for a dish the next day, and leftover smoked fish will be used in a kedgeree the following morning. Jam and marmalade left from one meal will be put back into the jar for use another day.

And Elizabeth has no generosity of spirit either. Lord Charteris, Elizabeth's first Private Secretary, from 1949 to 1978, knows her character and personality, her foibles and failures. "The Queen is courageous, honest, humble, truthful, but mean," he said. "She is not a good giver and she doesn't particularly like saying thank you. Her mother is cornucopia. The Queen no. I don't know why. It may be shyness, but she doesn't get any pleasure out of saying thank you. I'm telling you this because the Queen, like everyone has faults. She has fewer than most in my estimation, but that is one of them."

She did, however, say to Lord Charteris when he finally left her service, "Thank you for a lifetime."

"That was enough for me," he said later. She also gave him an exquisite silver salver and two signed silver picture frames.

Elizabeth is stingy even with her own family. Prince Charles tells of one occasion after he moved out of Buckingham Palace into an apartment in nearby Kensington Palace, where many other royals also live. Since he had no furniture he asked the storekeeper at Buck House if there was any to spare that he could have.

He was told the palace basement contained storerooms filled with furniture, most of it antique, which would be ideal for his new apartment. Charles asked his mother's permission. "No," she told him bluntly. "You can't have it, any of it."

Telling the story, Charles said, "I was flabbergasted that she refused. That stuff had lain in the basement for decades, just gathering dust, but my own mother refused to let me have one piece. I argued, but it was no good. Buy your own she told me, that's mine."

Elizabeth extends her tightfisted ways to herself as well as her children. The children were expected to wear hand-me-down clothes, and Elizabeth would then hand over the clothes of the youngest to Margaret's children or any other member of the family who wanted them. She believed it wasteful to throw them out, or even to give them to some deserving children's charity.

While Elizabeth has few real freedoms compared to the average man and woman, she also faces no financial restrictions in choosing and buying clothes. Many women would adore to be in Elizabeth's position, able to spend a fortune on clothes. But not so for Elizabeth, Queen of England.

She once set fashion trends. As a small child she wanted her nursery painted primrose and the British middle classes flocked to follow her lead. On her sixteenth birthday she appeared for the first time as colonel of the Grenadier Guards, and her green beret-shaped felt hat, the top jutting forward over a small peak, was immediately copied and sold in shops across the land.

In 1948 Princess Elizabeth visited France, then the fashion center of the world, and according to her nanny, Marion Crawford, her "wardrobe sent a ripple of excitement through the fashion capital." Christian Dior himself said, "She is magnificent; I never knew from pictures that she could be so lovely or wear her clothes with such distinction."

Three years later Elizabeth and Philip toured Canada. They went square dancing, Elizabeth dressed in a brown-and-white checked shirt and steel-blue dirndl skirt, Philip in jeans, loafers, and a hastily purchased checked shirt (it still had the price tag on it). Such informality surprised their Canadian hosts, but the students at McGill University in Montreal cheered the Princess on: "Yea, Betty, yea Windsor, yea, yea Betty Windsor, rah rah rah." Elizabeth flushed with embarrassment. She had never received such rapt enthusiasm for the way she dressed and behaved.

Later, Elizabeth and Philip flew to Washington. The *Star* proclaimed, "The Princess ought to be told the simple truth...that she has charmed and captivated this city to such an extent that our oldest inhabitants, searching around their memories, are hard put to remember the name of any past visitor comparable to her." Those were the days before Elizabeth took on the duties of monarchy.

In postwar America, Elizabeth had to be careful. Coming from Britain, a country recovering from a devastating war, she did not wish to stun New York society with her outfits, but neither did she want to disappoint. Her day wear was based on a modified New York look: coats that flared, skirts at midcalf length. Elizabeth worried about what the British people might think. The nation was still in a state of shock, recovering from the appalling effects of World War II. Clothes rationing still existed. Elizabeth did not want to appear expensively dressed in the lastest high fashion while the vast majority of the British people were suffering such strictures. For glittering evening occasions she chose embroidered dresses, tiaras, and stunning royal jewelry. Dignity and comfort during the day, glamour at night—the formula Elizabeth has clung to throughout her public life.

As a child and as a teenager, Elizabeth had never selected any of the clothes purchased for her. Each morning her nanny laid out what she was to wear. She accepted the fact that her clothes would simply appear, and it never crossed her mind to choose anything for herself. Crawfie, her first governess, wrote, "The Princess was always conservative about her dress and content to wear whatever was laid before her. Choosing a wardrobe was taken out of her hands by her dressmaker, shoemaker, and milliner. The exact colour of the main garment was given to the tradesmen and then the accessories arrived, perfect, beautiful, and costly, without the personal effort which makes shopping so large a part of the whole intriguing adventure of a young woman's life."

Occasionally Elizabeth did protest, but Crawfie was always on hand to advise. "The princess had to remember," she wrote, "that however she might long to wear a certain colour, she could not do so if it was a shade that would tone in and get lost among a large crowd and make it hard for her to be easily seen by the loyal crowd who congregated wherever she made a public appearance."

Crawfie added, "There were also times when, in the interest of trade, she was asked to wear a certain dress material or shoe style to give a boost to the fashion so the whole world would buy it."

Elizabeth's teenage years came during the war and its immediate aftermath, when the British government rigorously controlled all purchases of clothing by issuing coupons to each and every member of the public, including Princess Elizabeth and the rest of the Royal Family. Determined to set an example, King George and his wife Elizabeth were never seen in lavish dress, nor did they permit Elizabeth or Margaret any excesses. These restrictions occurred from the time Elizabeth turned fifteen to her twenty-fifth year, when most young women love to experiment, and to some degree they account for the Queen's pragmatic approach to her wardrobe and her lack of any real interest in fashion.

During those years some of Elizabeth and Margaret's dresses were made out of material from their mother's old, discarded clothes— including evening dresses and ball gowns, since the severe style of the late 1940s needed much less fabric.

In 1952, British designer Norman Hartnell made Elizabeth's first-ever party dress, when she had already turned twenty-six. Afterward he said, "She accepted the fitting as part of her official duties, but one did not feel that she was interested in clothes as such or in creating or even following the latest fashions. Princess Elizabeth was happiest, one felt, in country tweeds or very simple things and always would be; even when choosing her trousseau she made few suggestions."

Elizabeth never indulged herself even after she ascended the throne in 1952 and government restrictions on clothing were lifted. Most of the time she relied on Bobo MacDonald, then in her fifties and never with any flare for fashion, to be her honest critic. Elizabeth would never decide on any new outfit, any new idea, unless Bobo approved. Indeed, Elizabeth insisted "darling Bobo" be on hand whenever she had to have new clothes made, rather than the designers who came to advise.

Bobo made sure no one dressmaker became too powerful, distributing patronage carefully among a number of leading designers. If a couturier tried to make suggestions as to the Queen's hats, handbags, or shoes to complement a certain outfit, Bobo would always intervene, telling them in her Scottish accent, "Ye know, ye're here for the clothes and not the accessories."

If Bobo disapproved of an outfit it would be put away, never to be worn. Bobo was the only person who openly criticized Elizabeth's outfits, even in front of other staff or the designers. Elizabeth would take the criticism without comment, virtually always accepting Bobo's dress sense. Some regretted Bobo's influence on Elizabeth's fashions, because their joint policy on clothes was always one of minimum fuss.

For a while the young Elizabeth imitated her mother and dressed in fussy hats, decorative trimmings, floating panels, and soft pastel shades that did not suit her or her character. For most of her life the Queen Mother was dressed by the House of Hartnell, first by the late Sir Norman and then by his successors. Most of her outfits consisted of soft fabrics, such as chiffon, georgette, organdy, silk, and lace. They followed a generous basic pattern that allowed for freedom of movement as well as comfort. Pastels always dominated: blues, pinks, yellows, greens, lilacs, and mauves were constantly repeated. Her famous veiled hats never seemed to change from decade to decade, nor did her shoes, with their slight platforms and four-inch heels, even when the Queen Mother was in her nineties.

Elizabeth was gently advised that her mother's styles did not suit her, and so she reverted to her more traditional, less colorful clothes. Then she met criticism for looking more like forty-five than twenty-five. Elizabeth dressed older than her years because, she believed, it made her look more dignified, formal, and elegant.

Even the fashion trade saw that the young Queen had a problem. As a young woman she was expected to enjoy clothes and dress in a casual, informal way, but as Queen, formality was essential to her role. She couldn't win. Normal everyday wear totally defeated Elizabeth, and she continued to look frumpish, boring, and ordinary.

In evening dress, however, Elizabeth looked regal. The dazzling richness of her gowns outshone anyone who tried to compete, especially since no one could rival her stunning jewelry in quality or quantity. In uniform, Elizabeth always looked splendid, with her straight-back, low-bosom figure. In country and riding outfits she looked happy, relaxed, and confident, and any picture on horseback shows an accomplished rider of real ability.

Through the years Elizabeth has spent a fortune on clothes. But of course she must. Each day she probably changes her clothes three times and occasionally four or five. Indeed, if she were fascinated by fashion, as her daughter-in-law Diana is, simply choosing her wardrobe, let alone buying items, would consume most of her life.

Not until the 1960s did Elizabeth discover the classic simplicity of line which suits her best. But even when she occasionally became a slave to fashion, she would save money by making her outfitters adapt and alter her existing clothes.

As the *London Evening Standard* reported in 1971, "Up and down go the hemlines; while we plead with women to wear what suits them, they usually follow fashion...even the Queen appeared at Smith's Lawn, Windsor, garden party at the weekend in a raspberry-coloured suit which clearly had two hemlines—the old and the new. The skirt was originally made to reach the knee. But it had been let down by about three inches!"

The critics became bolder. In May 1972 *Women's Wear Daily* asked scathingly, "Why does the Queen dress so badly? Why must she be the nice Queen in the nice little Chanel copy? And why does she need a dumb handbag? Is she trying to suggest that she's just like other women who have to carry money and identity cards?"

The same year, the usually royal, loyal *Daily Express* commented, "Even the most ardent royalist must grudgingly admit that some of the hats which have rested on the royal head are, to be polite, rather strange creations. Her shoes, somebody once said, were only suitable for retired school marms. All clump and no glamour."

Over the years Elizabeth grew accustomed to being attacked by the media for her fashion sense. In June 1979, the *Daily Mail* suggested the Queen's carefulness with money was really meanness, explaining, "The Queen wore a make-do-and-mend dress for the opening of Royal Ascot, with 24 inches cut off the hemline of a dress she wore in Saudi Arabia in February."

The following day the *Daily Mail* returned to the subject: "Our parsimonious monarch was at it again yesterday—she turned up at Royal Ascot in a printed chiffon dress in grey, pink and lavender, with a matching loose coat and lavender straw hat, created by Hardy Amies for the state visit to Denmark last month."

Sometimes she won praise for being down to earth. In 1979 the *Daily Mirror* commented, "The chill winds of economic reality are blowing through the strangest of places these days—even the Queen's personal wardrobe. In what is obviously an attempt to cut down on the high cost of her clothing—the annual bill is huge—she has just had four of her Norman Hartnell outfits (costing about US$750 each) copied. In these inflationary times when things are so expensive it is probably very sensible of her."

Elizabeth gives more attention to her outfits for overseas tours and royal visits, when she is the object of minute scrutiny by the media. Throughout royal overseas tours, daily press briefings and handouts include a description of the clothes worn and the name of the designer or couture house. Even during her early years as monarch, Elizabeth always tried to appeal to the local people. For example, during a 1957 visit to France she wore an evening dress for the gala opening of the Opera House in ivory satin, thickly encrusted with pearls, topaz, and gold, with fleur-de-lys, poppies, and a tiny gold bee—Napoleon's symbol of industry. It was a subtle form of flattery which the French loved. To the same end, decisions on colors, fabrics, and styles are taken after consultation with the host nation so that no one is embarrassed or any local customs offended. Great care is taken particularly when Elizabeth tours Muslim countries or visits the Vatican.

Elizabeth has devised certain rules for overseas visits. For example, outfits already seen in Britain are not normally worn on formal occasions in foreign countries. A dress worn for an important occasion in one major city during a tour will not be worn again in another city on the same tour. This practice also holds true with different countries and different continents. Clothes worn on an important North American tour will never be seen on a tour of, say, Australia. But in order to save money, such outfits can reappear on tours to less westernized countries.

During overseas trips, the Queen wears clothes that make her look confident, attractive, but, most important, slightly distant. Overexcited foreigners rushing up for a kiss would never do. On the other hand, her appearance must not be too formidable. Adherence to protocol must be tempered by a degree of friendliness and accessibility.

The planning, preparation, and choosing of everything to do with overseas visits, not least the selection of all her clothes, requires enormous amounts of time and energy. Dresses and coats travel in large wardrobe trunks, dark blue, and labeled THE QUEEN. Accessories are placed in separate trunks: hats are hung on suspended ribbons secured to the sides of trunks to prevent their being dented; shoes and umbrellas are packed separately.

For major tours, Guards Sergeant Ronald Lewis, her baggage master, has at his disposal a separate aircraft which takes all the luggage in advance. In addition to the clothes Elizabeth intends to wear, alternatives are packed against unforeseen emergencies, such as torrential rains.

Once the tour begins, the Queen's dressers are responsible for preparing every outfit—pressing, brushing, and checking each item before each occasion. They lay out all the items required for each costume change, from underwear to jewelry. Packing lists and lists of ensembles are essential. The contents of all trunks, cases, and hatboxes are written out in duplicate, one copy kept by the dressers, the other glued to the inside of the container's lid. To keep creases to a minimum, masses of tissue paper are used for each outfit; shoulders and collars are padded with tissue, and every fold is interlined with several more tissue sheets. Important evening dresses and state gowns travel separately on their hangers, shrouded in cotton wool and dark tissue paper (to prevent tarnishing) and zipped in plastic protective covers before being placed in individual containers. Such attention to detail keeps ironing to a minimum on arrival.

Some overseas newspapers like to criticize the Queen when she visits their country. During a state visit to Canada in 1984, for example, the *Toronto Star* took Elizabeth, then fifty-eight, to task for her "unflattering round necks, long coats, and awful hats" as well as "her safe and round hairstyle, which makes her look like a grand-mother." Elizabeth *was* a grandmother, and had been for seven years.

A year earlier, differences between the elegant, fashion-conscious, emerging glamour girl of the Royal Family, Princess Diana, and what many saw as the fuddy-duddy Elizabeth, evoked comparisons and criticism. The *Daily Mail* commented, "Princess Diana is said to be having a marginal effect on the Queen's terrible clothes. In time, hopefully, she will persuade her to reject the double-breasted coat, the felt hat, the sensible costume, the bow-tied blouse. So the next time she goes through her mother-in-law's wardrobe, we suggest she persuades her to chuck out those frumpish stoles the Queen is partial to clutching to her diamante-encrusted evening gowns."

Newspaper attacks compared Elizabeth's fashion sense with the fashion-conscious Diana. "There ought to be someone around," said the *Sunday Express* in 1983, "to save the Queen from wearing silly things. . . . half Britain must have cringed with vicarious embarrass-ment when they saw on TV and in the papers the outfit the Queen wore on Sunday at San Diego. Her fussy blue and white suit was bad enough, but the matching sailor cap she wore with it was gruesome. She ended up looking like a matronly cinema usherette, circa 1940."

Occasionally Elizabeth's fashion advisers urged her to try to stun her audience with high fashion. It never seemed to work. In March 1984, she attended a San Francisco banquet dressed in a froufrou dress of taffeta and lace ruffles, cut with a voluminous skirt flounced from a dropped waistline. A flurry of gold lace ruffles decorated the sleeves, and giant candy bows perched on each shoulder. Along with a glittering tiara, she wore 110-watt diamond drop earrings. It was a dreadful mistake which embarrassed Elizabeth and which she has, sensibly, never repeated.

People often wonder about the Queen's handbag. She has rarely been photographed without one, not even when strolling across her own front lawn. The handbag is invariably leather, highly polished, neat, and buttoned up. But what is its function? The answer, quite simply, is psychological. She needs it. She feels an attachment for her handbag. A handbag is something to clutch when nervous, something to busy the hands during long, awkward moments. It also gives a feeling of security and contentment, and it is as private to any woman as a love affair.

Her handbags are usually copious, always in top-quality heavy calf for daytime and silver fabric for evening, often black, and occasionally white, and never without a loop to hang over her wrist. She has never considered a clutch bag or even a shoulder bag. Her handbags have ignored every fashion change through the decades and have been a frequent subject of criticism, if not open amusement.

And in her handbags? A lipstick, a small gold compact, her spectacles, a handkerchief, and occasionally her favorite gold-plated camera. Nothing more. And never money. She never needs it.

It is the same with her gloves. The Queen regards gloves as essential, not only as a mark of formality but as a practical defense for a woman who has to shake so many hands. Elizabeth has deliberately perfected a rather limp handshake in order to protect her fingers. Her handshake is, in fact, the absolute opposite of Philip's very firm, manly grip. The gloves also help to protect her hands from excessive hand shaking. Most of her gloves are not leather or suede but an artificial suede which can be easily washed, removed, and dyed. That was Elizabeth's idea because the fabric is far less expensive than real leather or suede.

One particular aspect of Elizabeth's royal life bores her to death: the endless hours being fitted for the thousands of clothes she needs. Many people are surprised to learn how many times in one day Elizabeth must have a complete change of clothes, even when not on a royal tour. Depending on what official functions she must attend, Elizabeth may have to change costumes three or four times a day, a real chore for someone not keen on fashion. She tries to make her hours with the dressmakers as relaxed as possible and has been known to perch on a chair, chatting and munching a Mars bar. She needs to have good relationships with her dressmakers because she sees them far more often than she does her children, her husband, or indeed her personal maids.

All testify to Elizabeth's relaxed attitude and her understanding that since she has to have so many fittings, she should enjoy them as much as possible. She usually takes along two or three of her favorite, well-behaved corgis, whom she merrily talks to while the designers and dressmakers get on with their work.

Even in this informal setting, however, Elizabeth insists that strict palace protocol not be breached. The dressmakers are not, for example, permitted to speak unless spoken to or to turn their backs in the royal presence under any circumstances. Whenever leaving the room, the designers and dressmakers must walk backward and bow to the Queen when they reach the door, though she may be standing on a chair munching a cookie. And no one is ever permitted to sit during these fittings, not even on the floor, when working on a royal outfit.

The rewards and the privileges are not great. When the fitting session is over, Elizabeth departs and the fortunate workers are sent tea and cakes to enjoy; if the fitting is before lunch, a single dry sherry will be offered.

Elizabeth has her favorite dyes and, despite her age, can still look remarkable in bright, strong colors. She is not fond of navy blue and keeps black for mourning, despite the fact that she apparently looks stunning in black velvet. She has phases with colors, sometimes yellows, sometimes greens, and frequently the "royal" color, blue. When offered pastels Elizabeth will nearly always comment, "We must be careful with pastels; they won't see me."

The Queen's designers have two main problems: to create the illusion that Elizabeth is taller than her five feet, four inches, and to minimize the fact she is a "clinger." Due to her own personal static electricity, her favorite fabrics—silk crepe de chine and chiffon—tend to cling to her, which is why she hardly ever wears them.

For the record, Elizabeth takes an American size 14 dress; her weight fluctuates between 120 and 130 pounds and is at the upper limit after her long vacation at Balmoral each summer. She keeps dress and skirt hems one-and-a-half inches below the knee, and she maintains the shape of her long slender legs by regular horse riding. And she wears nothing but beige stockings and tights. Shoes are usually black with chunky heels, for comfort during long spells of standing still.

For relaxing in the country, however, Elizabeth invariably wears tweeds, warm sweaters, and sensible walking shoes.

Elizabeth doesn't mind if others appear at a gathering wearing the same color dress she does. Members of the Royal Family do not confer with each other, nor do their dressers, to ensure a variegated color scheme. Shortly after joining the Royal Family, Diana worried about appearing in the same color as the Queen and raised the matter with Elizabeth's ladies-in-waiting. She was told Elizabeth wouldn't mind whatever color she wore.

Prime Minister Margaret Thatcher once attended a function wearing the same color dress as Elizabeth, which didn't bother Elizabeth. The following day however, Mrs. Thatcher wrote Buckingham Palace suggesting that in the future their offices should confer over choice and colors of dress in order to avoid possible embarrassment. Back came a stinging snub from the Palace, obviously with Elizabeth's blessing: "The Queen does not notice what others wear." Mrs. Thatcher was livid.

Elizabeth enjoys nothing more than a day at the racetrack, especially if one or more of her horses are running. Royal Ascot, near Windsor, held for four days every June, is the most stylish day of the year at the races. The highlight is still the processional drive down the course in open carriages before racing begins for the day. Those invited to stay at Windsor Castle feel especially privileged.

The day starts with a ride across Windsor Great Park for all guests invited to stay overnight at the castle. Those who ride end up on the adjoining Ascot racetrack, where they compete in a special, private royal race. The Queen usually wins.

The thirty or more guests will meet for pre-lunch drinks followed by a brisk, simple meal before stepping into a fleet of Rolls-Royces to be driven to the track. The royal party appear in the carriages at 2 P.M. Everyone admitted to the Royal Enclosure at Ascot must dress formally, men in top hats and tails, ladies in their best summer frocks, usually silk. Even detectives and officials wear the Ascot rig, and the ladies-in-waiting wear elegant summer wear.

Officially, anyone can gain access to the Royal Enclosure, but every application must be accompanied by a recommendation from someone who is already a member and the possessor of one of the prized enclosure badges. The Royal Box itself is off-limits.

Elizabeth spends the afternoon literally running from the TV set at the back of the Royal Box, where she watches the early part of a race, to the front of the box itself for the final two furlongs, which she views through binoculars. Her face reveals the excitement, the ecstasy that grips her at great race meetings and tight finishes. She jumps up and down in excitement during the race. Bets are laid on her behalf but, as far as is known, never more than twenty dollars at a time. She is excited and happy when she wins and despairing when she loses.

Between each race Elizabeth and other members of the family will make their way to the paddock to inspect the horses before they run. It is a nightmare for police and her personal bodyguard, since Elizabeth walks though a thousand or more people, many of them total strangers, who stand inches away from her. On many occasions, especially when terrorist activity is at its height, Elizabeth has been warned not to take such a risk, for she would be an easy target for a committed assassin. But she is adamant: no change to her schedule. "If I cannot enjoy my day at the races," she says, "I may as well never leave the palace."

In her own family Elizabeth is the only one passionate about racing, an interest she inherited from her mother, who attended as often as she could even into her nineties. Philip cannot abide racing and attends only under durance. Elizabeth insists that he ride with her in the open carriage down the course. He indicates his annoyance by never showing his face in the Royal Box throughout the entire afternoon. In fact, he refuses to watch the horses run and instead sits in a room below the Royal Box watching cricket on another TV set.

Prince Charles is no race fan either, and when his mother orders him to attend, he is permitted to leave early to take part in polo matches which follow the end of Ascot racing each day. Andrew, Edward, and Princess Anne have no real interest either.

Indeed, Elizabeth and Philip have very little in common. Even when they are in the country, Elizabeth will go riding while Philip fishes; Elizabeth will read a book, perhaps by one of her favorite authors, Dick Francis, whose novels are usually set in the horsey world, while Philip prefers more serious literature. Elizabeth will go for a walk alone with her dogs while Philip will sit and paint, mainly in watercolors.

Neither Elizabeth or Philip enjoys the theater, ballet, or opera, and hardly ever attends. Occasionally, Elizabeth will attend the National Theatre, but she is not an enthusiast. Those concerned with the arts in Britain have given up trying to cajole Elizabeth to be more involved. They argue that even if she is not terribly interested in the arts herself she could, and should, show more enthusiasm and give greater encouragement than she does, perhaps by making public donations or providing patronage. Elizabeth responds that there is no point in feigning interest in something that does not arouse one's natural enthusiasm.

Elizabeth would never claim to be an intellectual, but she is certainly an intelligent woman. At heart she is a country woman, interested in country pursuits. She does not really care for the cultural activities that cities can best offer.

She has no real interest in fine art either, despite being the present owner of the most magnificent private collection in the world which has been handed down through the family over the generations. Occasionally, Elizabeth will purchase a painting for her collection—a Turner or another classic—but mainly because she is advised its acquisition will help fill a gap or supplement a certain part of the collection, not because she is enraptured by a particular work or artist.

Britain's struggling or even successful modern painters have been totally ignored by their monarch, so very different from years gone by when a reigning sovereign became the patron of a nation's aspiring artists. Sir Oliver Millar, Keeper of the Queen's Pictures, commented, "I think the sadness as far as pictures is concerned is that the momentum which began in the early part of her reign, even on a small scale, of purchasing pictures by contemporary British artists, has not gone forward. It is a criticism ever since Prince Albert's day that there has not really been a royal involvement with good modern painting, either significant foreign or British work. But if you don't want to buy modern pictures, why should you? You can't do it as a duty. It has to be something that springs from the heart."

Prince Philip, on the other hand, who paints as a hobby, has bought some modern art and he does support local artists. Every year during the past twenty years, he has privately purchased a number of paintings by Scottish artists at the Royal Scottish Academy.

What seems extraordinary is the loneliness of the life Elizabeth and Philip lead. After a lifetime of meeting people, they now have hardly any close friends with whom they like spending time. Elizabeth has some friends in racing circles with whom she loves to chat about the sport. For female companions she relies on her ladies-in-waiting. Susan

Hussey is always on hand, spending most of her life at the palace and often attending lunches or dinners as a guest while carrying out her duties and acting as a listening post.

There is also the lovely Philippa de Pass, whose husband Robert, now in his seventies, served as aide-de-camp to Earl Mountbatten. Uncle Dickie suggested to Lilibet that Philippa would make an ideal lady-in-waiting, and in 1988 she became the official Lady-in-Waiting to the Queen, not just an ordinary lady-in-waiting. This title means that the Lady has become one of Elizabeth's principal advisers and unofficial close friends. Philippa, now in her fifties, held the job for five years before handing it over to Lady Susan Hussey in March 1993. Both women remain close to Elizabeth, and she values their advice and their friendship. They are her eyes and ears and she sounds them out on controversial matters, but neither woman feels they are really close friends.

Elizabeth hardly ever sees her family now. Gone are the days when she could summon her children to Balmoral for an eight-week holiday every year. It was difficult to relax; the children all had to behave as though they were on parade, with set times for lunch and dinner and set games every night. Throughout the holiday they still had to treat Elizabeth more as the Queen than their mother. Nowadays, the children will drop by to visit their parents for the odd week or so, but none stays around as they used to do for the obligatory eight weeks in the cold, rainy isolation of Balmoral.

Philip has few close friends. The good pals he enjoyed in his youth, such as Mike Parker and Rupert Nevill, have not been replaced. Philip has acquaintances with whom he enjoys passing the time of day, such as those he meets when carriage driving, shooting, or sailing. During the last few years Philip has preferred to spend more time by himself, reading, painting, fishing, or watching television.

Today Elizabeth, now sixty-seven, and Philip, seventy-two, spend more time together, like other couples of pensionable age. But unlike most pensioners, they lead extremely busy and full lives. Very little has changed for them. Elizabeth has the never-ending discipline of the boxes, and, like Philip, she still carries out hundreds of official royal engagements every year.

Philip has mellowed, exploding less frequently and less ferociously. Those in the palace marveled through the years at Elizabeth's patience towards her irate husband, but many missed the point. To some extent, Philip was Elizabeth's "bad" surrogate, providing the missing dimension to her ordered life in which no one would dream of losing his or her temper, shouting, or swearing in her company. For much of the time Elizabeth found her husband a breath of fresh air in a remarkably stuffy atmosphere, though he sometimes overstepped the bounds and annoyed her. Elizabeth is by no means a weak woman; she could have cut off his lava flow of rudeness and expletives in midstream, but she chose not to. Most of the time Elizabeth simply ignored Philip and continued whatever she was doing, impervious to his protests.

On occasion he did upset her, when she felt he was being willful and bloody-minded, or childish. When that happened Elizabeth would let Philip know he had exceeded what she could tolerate by fixing him with one of her icy stares. Philip soon got the message and learned when he had to curb his tongue. But Elizabeth was never frightened of Philip's anger; she accepted his tantrums as part of his character.

What Elizabeth could not tolerate was the women in Philip's life, but she even came to an understanding over them. In the early years of their marriage, any suggestion of Philip's cheating filled Elizabeth with horror and disbelief and, according to Mountbatten, resulted in many tears and sleepless nights. But the discipline which ruled her life helped Elizabeth come to terms with her errant husband. In the end she simply ignored his affairs, pretending not to know what had been going on and, more important, not wanting to know.

To some critics that was the easy way out, but in Elizabeth's unique position, there was no other way out of the situation. She could never contemplate separation or divorce, whatever sins her husband may have committed. She married him the way she was "married" to the monarchy, "until death do us part." Elizabeth has always lived with those disciplines, and whatever her unhappiness or anger at Philip's behavior, there was never the slightest impulse to discard him in any way.

For some years during their marriage, after the birth of Edward in 1964, Elizabeth and Philip lived almost separate lives, rather like "ships passing in the night." In that respect Elizabeth was fortunate. If the mood took her, it was very easy not to see her husband for days and weeks at a time. To Elizabeth, separate bedrooms (as well as dressing rooms and bathrooms) is the normal arrangement for couples in her social stratum. Even today it is not uncommon for Elizabeth and Philip not to eat together from one week to another for a variety of reasons. By deliberately ignoring him, Elizabeth can demonstrate not only her strength of character but also her discontent and dissatisfaction with Philip.

Elizabeth has never been alone during her entire life, unless she wished to be. She always has her courtiers, her personal staff, footmen, pages, ladies-in-waiting, and dressers on hand 365 days a year. When family relations were easy, she kept in daily contact with her mother and could phone any of her children any time she felt like it. When away at Windsor, Balmoral, or Sandringham, she is happy walking with her dogs or riding or pursuing other country activities. Her life is so full and busy, even today, that she has no need for the constant companionship of a husband.

Only on holidays are Elizabeth and Philip truly together, and then their lives are reversed. When they are out stalking or shooting, it is Philip who strides ahead, with the guns and the gillies, and Elizabeth who walks behind, in control of the gundogs and picking up the dead birds. She loves that role. The monarchy was thrust on her, she never asked for it, and sometimes she prefers to lead the more normal life of a woman with a determined and self-confident husband.

When holidaying together, Elizabeth and Philip give dinner parties and invite guests to stay for long weekends. People who attend these events report that during the past few years, as they used to do during the early years of their marriage, Elizabeth and Philip laugh a lot together. Is there any better test of a good marriage than a couple's still being able to laugh together, especially a union of over forty-five years?

THIRTEEN

ALL THE QUEEN'S MEN

On weekdays, life begins to stir in Buckingham Palace at around six, when the first of the three hundred people who now work there arrive at the Queen's official London residence. In reality the palace never rests, for men of various royal regiments take turns to guard their sovereign around the clock. Visitors see them at various palace entrances, and they provide the picturesque daily tourist attraction of the Changing of the Guard, when a troop of the Household Cavalry, resplendent in their bright uniforms, with their horses matched in color, ride down the Mall every weekday morning.

Officially, three separate royal bodyguards have different responsibilities for protecting the queen. The oldest is the Yeomen of the Guard, the most ancient military corps in existence anywhere in the world. It was founded in 1485 after the Battle of Bosworth, in which Richard III was killed, the last English monarch to die on the field of battle.

The Yeomen of the Guard's original duty called for the protection of the sovereign, especially when he went into battle. They were also responsible for the more mundane protection at the royal palaces. Today, the group consists of retired officers, warrant officers, and noncommissioned officers from the army and Royal Air Force. On official occasions, Yeomen stand closest to the Queen and, by tradition, there are always six present.

Once they numbered six hundred; today there are only sixty-six. Most of today's Yeomen would be incapable of defending anyone, let alone the sovereign, for the minimum age for a Yeoman is fifty, and most are nearly seventy, the compulsory retirement age. Another requirement is that they be over five feet, ten inches tall, so they still look impressive in their official scarlet-and-gold doublet, with breeches and red stockings, black buckled shoes, a ruff at the neck, and a black velvet hat with ribbons of red, white, and blue around the crown. They also carry a ceremonial sword which, by tradition, is never drawn.

They may look picturesque and odd, but they have literally saved the sovereign's life in years gone by. Their most recent act of gallantry occurred during the reign of King George III, around 1800. He survived three serious attempts on his life, all foiled by the quick thinking of the Yeomen of the Guard. How much quick thinking would occur today is open to question, but their presence on state occasions has become part of the tradition, and the more professional Guards of the 1990s hope the Yeomen will never be required to actually save the sovereign's life.

Today, the physical protection of the Queen is undertaken by a much more highly specialized group, officers of the Royalty Protection, who provide twenty-four hour security for every member of the Royal Family. (The American equivalent is the Secret Service.)

The Royalty Protection Squad is divided into two sections: (a) those who wear uniforms, numbering around sixty, and are responsible for security within Buckingham Palace; (b) the plainclothes officers, numbering around one hundred, who serve as royal bodyguards.

The Buck House police are based in a special bombproof police station built shortly after a man broke into Elizabeth's bedroom early one morning in July 1982. For nine long minutes Michael Fagan, mentally disturbed and in a state of severe emotional distress, sat on Elizabeth's bed pouring out his problems to her. The nation was shocked that an intruder could so easily gain access to the Queen's bedroom.

Fagan, thirty-five, was having domestic problems involving his wife, their four children, two stepchildren, and Fagan's own parents. Because of abnormal behavior due to his mental condition, his wife wanted to leave him and take the children. For some reason that Fagan himself cannot fathom, he decided he had to make front-page news and share his troubles with the world. He figured the best way to attract the attention of the authorities was to slash his wrists in front of Queen Elizabeth. He was also under the delusion that he was the son of Rudolf Hess, Hitler's one-time right-hand man who parachuted into Britain at the start of World War II, allegedly in an effort to bring peace to both countries. Hess wanted to appeal directly to King George VI, but he was never given permission for an audience and spent the war in a British jail. Fagan decided to fulfill his "father's" ambition and see the sovereign in his stead.

At 6:45 on the morning of Friday, July 9, 1982, a man was seen climbing the palace railings by an off-duty policeman who telephoned the palace police. Two officers went to check but discovered nothing. Then the alarm in the Queen's Stamp Room, which had a reputation for being unreliable, sounded once. The duty seargeant switched it off. A few seconds later it sounded again and the unnamed sergeant grumbled, "There's that bloody bell again!" Again he switched it off, not bothering to check if an intruder had somehow gained access to that room.

Having entered the Stamp Room simply by climbing through the ground-floor window, Fagan found the door from the Stamp Room into the palace interior was locked, so he climbed back out of the window and searched for another way in. The on-duty police who had failed to discover any intruder went back to their room and had a cup of tea. Having tried other ground-floor windows and finding them all locked, Fagan shinnied up a drainpipe to see if any first-floor windows were open. It was broad daylight, and the palace was starting to buzz with all the staff coming on duty. No one noticed anything amiss.

Finding a first-floor window half open, Fagan climbed the nearest drainpipe, and within a couple of minutes was inside the palace. For some unknown reason, he removed his sandals and socks before padding along the corridor leading to the Queen's private apartments. He picked up a heavy glass ashtray and smashed it against the wall, keeping a large jagged piece so that he could ceremoniously slash his wrists before his sovereign. No one heard a sound. The armed police officer who patrolled the corridors around the Queen's private apartments had, as usual, gone off duty at 6 A.M.

While Fagan was walking along the corridor in his T-shirt and jeans, holding the shard of glass, the Queen's personal maid was cleaning up in a room adjoining her bedroom, and the footman on duty had taken the corgis for their early morning walk in the gardens.

Fagan popped his head into several rooms until he saw the Queen lying asleep in bed. Quietly, he slipped into the room and closed the door.

At 7:18 exactly, as the Queen was to report later, she awoke as the long drapes were being drawn, not by her usual maid but by Fagan. She sat up in her nightdress and asked Fagan who he was and what on earth he was doing in her bedroom. Then she noticed his disheveled, unshaven appearance and the jagged glass. Fagan, dripping blood from a cut on his thumb when he smashed the ashtray, walked over to the bed and sat down just a few feet from Elizabeth.

She sat motionless, watching Fagan toy with the jagged piece of glass. "I've got terrible problems," he said. "I've got to talk to you."

Elizabeth said later that she realized as soon as the man sat down that she had to keep her nerve because he was emotionally unstable. "I realised that I had to keep him talking, to keep his attention. I thought that if I kept him talking he wouldn't become violent."

The man didn't seem to know what he wanted to say, so Elizabeth asked him about his problems. As he began to speak more calmly, she put her hand down by the side of the bed and pressed the emergency night-alarm button connected directly to the police control room. She expected that within a minute or so, police would rush into her room. Nothing happened. The bell wasn't working.

Patiently Elizabeth waited, unable to understand why her alarm call had not been answered. She managed to keep Fagan talking about his problems as the blood from his right thumb dripped incessantly on her bedclothes. After a couple of minutes, as Fagan continued his rambling, incoherent story, Elizabeth decided to try another bell, the one she always pressed for her maid to answer. This bedside bell rang outside, down the corridor, and Elizabeth knew her duty maid would arrive within seconds.

No one came. The duty maid failed to hear the bell because she was in a side room farther down the corridor. Elizabeth became alarmed after the only two ways she had to contact anyone outside her room had failed. She wondered whether Fagan had somehow turned off both bells, in which case she feared her predicament was more serious than she had first thought.

Fagan continued to talk, telling Elizabeth about his "father, Rudolf Hess," and explaining why Hess had flown to Britain in an effort to stop Germany and Britain from declaring war on each other. Elizabeth was extremely adept at small talk, practiced at discussing with such a variety of people matters of concern only to them. She kept asking Fagan questions and at one point commented, "Then Prince Charles is a year younger than you."

Recognizing that the intruder was seriously disturbed, Elizabeth knew she must not frighten or alarm him since his reaction could be instant violence. Throughout the ordeal, she kept one eye constantly on the jagged piece of glass Fagan gripped in his right hand. She had worked out that if he tried to strike at her, she would throw the bedclothes over his arm and make a dash for the door.

As the minutes ticked by, Fagan began to relax and Elizabeth decided to risk another tack. She asked if he would like a cup of tea. He said, "Yes." Elizabeth picked up the telephone to order the tea. The call went directly to the duty palace operator and she asked him to send tea to her room, immediately. The Queen, of course, had never before phoned the palace operator to ask for tea. Bemused, the operator thought it must be some joke and didn't immediately react. To be safe, however, he put a call through to the Queen's maid. Once again there was no reply; her maid heard nothing.

Elizabeth was now seriously worried when neither the tea nor the maid arrived. "I kept wondering where on earth everyone was," she said later. "I kept wondering what was going on outside. What possible reason could there be for no one answering any of my calls."

After a few more minutes elapsed and Fagan continued his rambling stories, Elizabeth decided she had to make one more effort to contact someone, anyone. Under the pretense of demanding tea again, she phoned the operator once again and asked him to send up not only the tea, but also a policeman. She told later how her heart had beat even faster when she had quietly spoken the word "policeman" into the phone. Fagan apparently did not notice. The operator thought the Queen's request odd and phoned the police control room, telling them, "Her Majesty would like a police officer to go to her room."

The request was most unusual, but not realizing it was a call of alarm, the duty officer said he would notify someone when more officers came on duty.

Throughout her entire life, Elizabeth had only to ring a bell to ask for something, and within seconds her wish would be instantly fulfilled. Maids, footmen, police would come running immediately. Yet here she was in the most extraordinary and dangerous situation in her entire life, with a mentally deranged man armed with a jagged piece of glass sitting on her bed, and no one answered her pleas for help. She began to worry if there was some sort of plot, that something had happened that she didn't know about. She felt cut off, isolated, and, more important, highly vulnerable.

Elizabeth knew that if no one came to her rescue, she had to get out of the room—quickly. She had to presume the man could become violent at any moment. Why else would he enter her room armed with broken glass except to threaten her, or worse, to use it? She was surprised that he let her make two phone calls, and she tried one last ploy. She asked if he smoked. She prayed that he did because smoking might give her a chance of escape. She inquired if he would like a cigarette while waiting for his tea to arrive.

"Yes," he said.

Elizabeth saw her chance. Remaining calm and cool, she told him, "I'm sorry, I have none in this room. I will have someone bring some for you. Will you wait a moment?"

With her heart thumping, Elizabeth tried to remain as calm as possible as she slipped out of bed, all the time watching Fagan as he paced around the room, still holding the broken glass. He was showing increasing signs of agitation. She put on her dressing gown, tied the belt, and walked slowly out of the room. In the corridor she met her duty maid and told her to ring immediately for the police and tell them a stranger was in her bedroom.

"Bloody hell, Ma'am," her maid exploded. "He oughtn't to be in there."

Elizabeth replied, "Shush, do as I say, and quickly." And the maid went to phone for the police.

At that moment the footman returned, surrounded by eight of Elizabeth's corgis, all of which ran to their beloved mistress, barking and jumping. Hearing the commotion, Fagan ventured out into the corridor, to the shock of the footman. Elizabeth, retaining her composure, and fearing Fagan might strike out at the footman, told him to get some cigarettes for her "guest." The footman called Fagan to the nearby pantry, gave him a cigarette, and, with trembling hands, lighted it.

Having seen the footman and the maid, and with the dogs yapping and barking, Fagan began to show signs of panic. He still held the broken glass in his right hand as he nervously puffed at the cigarette with his left and watched the Queen try to calm the dogs. He began to look around him, but the footman, hoping the police would arrive at any second, enticed Fagan back into the pantry with the offer of food.

Seconds later the police ran down the corridor, and Fagan was pinned to the floor, arms outstretched.

Unbelievably, it had taken nine minutes from the time Fagan entered Elizabeth's bedroom and awakened her until the police arrived. Immediately after his arrest, Elizabeth returned to her bedroom and suddenly began to shake, her hands sweating at the realization of her narrow escape. She had faced at best a weirdo, at worst a mentally ill maniac armed with a large, jagged piece of glass. She almost fainted when her maid led her to her bloodstained bed to recover. For twenty minutes Elizabeth lay quietly, shaking nervously as she regained her composure. Tea was brought and she began to feel better.

More than anything Elizabeth wanted a bath, to somehow wash away the feeling of this man who had sullied her bedroom. After that she felt well enough to dress and have some breakfast. Immediately afterward she phoned her mother to tell her of the incident while explaining she shouldn't worry, that she was fine.

This was not the first instance of Elizabeth's physical bravery and moral courage in the face of a serious, potentially dangerous situation. It also demonstrated her remarkable presence of mind, taking command of the situation and defusing it entirely by herself.

Prince Philip's suite of rooms is just down the corridor from Elizabeth's. When news of the incident was announced, Buckingham Palace reported that Philip was in his rooms, but no mention was made of his part in the affair. That morning, despite the yapping dogs, running policemen, and the commotion caused by Fagan's arrest, Philip apparently heard nothing. Subsequent reports suggested that Philip had stayed at one of his London clubs that night, but none of his friends ever knew him to do so and described him as always returning to Buck House.

The Fagan incident showed how extremely lax security was at Buckingham Palace. Inquiries were ordered by government ministers,

Scotland Yard, and the Royal Protection Squad. Some heads rolled, some police officers were transferred. One change made the next day called for an officer to remain outside the Queen's bedroom until she went to breakfast. Following time-honored tradition, those responsible decided to throw money at the problem, so a new $2.5 million police control room, bristling with the latest electronic gadgetry, was built on palace grounds.

Under questioning, Fagan informed police this was actually his second visit to the palace. He had been there a month earlier, on June 7, and had drunk half a bottle of wine before climbing out of a window and walking away. A butler confirmed that a half bottle of wine had been found around June 7 and in the exact place Fagan had told police. No one in palace security had even known of this incident until Fagan was arrested.

The law of trespass did not permit Fagan to be prosecuted for his "intrusion," so he was accused of burglary over the bottle of wine. The jury acquitted him but, after psychiatric reports, Fagan was sent to a mental hospital.

The Fagan debacle had a sad outcome for one of Elizabeth's favorite police officers, Michael Trestrail, her personal bodyguard and a man who had become a friend during the nine years he served her. Trestrail, a man in his fifties, was gay, and for twelve years he had had a serious affair with another homosexual. Following the Fagan break-in, his male lover tried to blackmail Trestrail, despite the fact that the bedroom incident had nothing whatsoever to do with him. Honorable to the end, Trestrail informed Elizabeth of the blackmail attempt and said he had no alternative but to offer his resignation. Reluctantly, Elizabeth accepted it, knowing she had no other option, even though ignominy would follow for him.

During his nine-year stint, Trestrail had traveled everywhere with Elizabeth, on all her overseas trips and throughout Britain, accompanying her on virtually every royal occasion. Elizabeth treated Trestrail as a friend and confidant, not just as her bodyguard; she appreciated his impeccable manners, his wit, and intelligence, and she chatted with him, sought his advice, relied on his good sense. And his conversation was more amusing than Prince Philip's. There is no suggestion of anything more than close friendship between the two, who were of a similar age, but undeniably Elizabeth felt personally let down that someone whom she had grown close to should have allowed a situation to arise which meant he could no longer continue in the job, thereby putting their relationship at risk. Throughout the forty years of her reign, Elizabeth has been able to count only a few people as confidants and friends, and she and Trestrail had been remarkably close.

Elizabeth told one of her ladies-in-waiting, "I feel so sad for poor Michael. He was so kind and considerate and yet so very good at his job. With him at my side I always felt safe."

As a result of the Fagan incident, the entire approach toward security of the Queen and all other members of the Royal Family was dramatically upgraded.

Another more pertinent and far more dangerous reason for introducing change was the Irish Republican Army, which had carried out two audacious bombing atrocities in London in July 1982, in Hyde Park and Regent's Park. Both bombings were directed at members of the armed forces, and both were close to Buckingham Palace and other royal residences. If the authorities needed further warning of the dangers to which the Queen and other royals were exposed, these bombings concentrated their minds.

Prime Minister Margaret Thatcher ordered a general tightening of security. Britain's crack SAS (Special Air Service) was called in to advise on security. As a result, every room in every palace and royal residence was photographed and the pictures filed in the palace control room and SAS headquarters, so that if it was ever necessary to carry out a raid or rescue mission, SAS troops would know the exact layout of any room and the position of all furniture.

Fagan and the IRA bombers had demonstrated how easily determined bombers could penetrate royal security. Margaret Thatcher recognized what an extraordinary coup the IRA would achieve if they managed to assassinate the Queen or any close member of the Royal Family the way they had murdered Earl Mountbatten in August 1979.

As a result, electronic equipment, which relays information instantly to the Buck House control room, was installed not only at the palace but at all the other royal residences, including Highgrove, the country home of Charles and Diana, and Gatcombe Park, Princess Anne's Gloucestershire home. Now, even if main lines of communication should be bombed or blown up, other backup systems ensure the royal homes are never cut off. As a further measure, every royal car was fitted with an electronic homing device so that the control room knows, at any precise moment, exactly where the cars are. But for an open monarchy like Britain's, virtually nothing can be done to stop an assassin from shooting or throwing a bomb.

The Fagan incident was more worrying, and severely embarrassing for the authorities, because it occurred only thirteen months after a serious attempt on Elizabeth's life in broad daylight. This previous incident also reflected great credit on Elizabeth's courage and presence of mind.

It was on June 13, 1981, during the Trooping the Colour birthday parade, just two years after the IRA had murdered Mountbatten. An unhappy seventeen year old tried to shoot the Queen as she rode down the Mall on her black mare Burmese, a nineteen-year-old charger presented as a gift from the Royal Canadian Mounted Police. Television viewers heard a number of shots ring out; they saw Burmese instinctively break into a canter; they saw Elizabeth lurch backward as she moved to control Burmese—she was riding sidesaddle, as she did on all official parades, making it much more difficult to control her horse.

Suddenly, those watching the brilliant pageant on TV in their homes shouted, "The Queen's been shot . . . the Queen's been shot . . . shot at . . . shot at!"

They saw Elizabeth turn a little pale; they saw her reach forward and pat Burmese on the neck to reassure him; they saw Philip and Charles, on their horses, drop back to form a barrier around her; other mounted officers spurred their horses forward to shield her; and they saw police and members of the public dive on a young man who disappeared in a melee of arms and legs.

Later that day Elizabeth told guests at a Garter ceremony at Windsor Castle, "It wasn't the shots that frightened Burmese but the sight of the cavalry, everyone rushing to shield me."

In her Christmas message that year, which was the Year of the Disabled, Elizabeth played down her own courage while praising others: "There is courage with its bold physical face, the courage of firemen and servicemen," she said, "but above all there is moral courage." In this way she included the unshakable will of the handicapped to endure. "The golden thread of courage" she said, "has no end."

As a result of the scare, members of the Household, senior police officers, and Cabinet ministers prevailed on Elizabeth to abandon riding in public, urged her to stop riding in slow, horse-drawn carriages, and to start adopting more modern forms of transport which were less vulnerable to an assassin's bullet or a bomber's aim. Many urged presidential-style protection, the Queen riding in armor-plated cars with outriders and Royal Protection agents in close attendance. The debate raged throughout the media.

Elizabeth would have none of it. "If my people cannot see their monarch on such occasions," she said, "then there is no point in having a monarchy. The debate is at an end." The youth of seventeen, who had armed himself with six blank cartridges in a replica pistol, was jailed for five years under the Treason Act of 1842. His reason: he wanted to be noticed.

The 160 members of the Royal Protection Squad, like the Yeomen of the Guard, all volunteer for the unit and are handpicked. They have to endure a rigorous selection system, and only one in twenty volunteers is accepted. They must be fit, agile, and crack shots, as well as trained in unarmed combat. They all carry handguns but also have immediate access to automatic weapons. The Queen's personal bodyguard, as well as all royal bodyguards, are under orders never to allow their charges to go out alone. Stories about Princess Diana driving off by herself are untrue because, no matter what the royal demands, the bodyguards are under the most strict instruction never to allow their personal royal out of their sight. And they never do.

Many of those who work in the nation's palaces carry out duties that have been performed by royal servants for centuries. They take great pride in the fact that they are part of such privileged traditions and thoroughly enjoy their rather unusual jobs.

The duties of the colorful Yeomen known as Beefeaters are symbolic, although they do have a function. They are Yeomen Warders, created by William the Conqueror in 1066 to guard state prisoners in the Tower of London, while the Yeomen of the Guard protected their sovereign on the field of battle. Today they have no prisoners to watch over, but they do look after some two million visitors a year who flock to the Tower, and their photographs are taken hundreds of times a day.

There is also the Honourable Corps of Gentlemen-at-Arms, founded by Henry VIII in 1509 as a personal mounted guard. Their number has never altered—ten officers and twenty-seven so-called gentlemen, all handpicked—but now they perform their ceremonial duties on foot. In Scotland, the Royal Company of Archers, founded in 1676, escorts the sovereign on visits to Scotland. Even today the four hundred men must be proficient with a bow and arrow, up to a range of one hundred yards.

Buckingham Palace became the headquarters of Britain's Royal Family in 1762, when George III bought the mansion from the Duke of Buckingham for $100,000 as a suitable London home for himself and Charlotte, his eighteen-year-old wife. In 1822, King George IV commissioned the famous architect John Nash to redesign the original building. It now has 19 magnificent state rooms, 52 bedrooms, 188 staff bedrooms, 92 offices, and 78 bathrooms—in all, a grand total of 429 rooms.

It is here that Elizabeth, following the tradition of British sovereigns since George III, conducts the business of a constitutional monarchy. It is also where the Queen receives foreign heads of state, representatives of the diplomatic corps, her Privy Council, and where she entertains groups of people at small, intimate lunches or holds magnificent banquets for over a hundred guests.

Until August 1993, Buckingham Palace was a unique constitutional royal palace because it never opened its doors to the general public. Since that date, when Elizabeth agreed to open Buckingham Palace to visitors for two months each year, however, anyone can now pay twelve dollars for the privilege of viewing the magnificent interior. (See appendix for a full description of what is on view.) Paying visitors use a different entrance from visitors with appointments to see senior members of the Household on official business.

Private, nonpaying visitors are welcomed in a time-honored fashion. On arrival at the massive gold-topped gates at the entrance to the palace grounds, the invited guest is directed to the North Centre Gate by a police officer. One officer checks your identity and telephones a footman inside the palace to ensure that you do indeed have an appointment. You then make your way across the gravel forecourt to the Privy Purse Entrance, which is on the right when viewed from the Mall.

The steps immediately in front of the Privy Purse Door are carpeted, even though they are exposed to the rain and snow throughout the year. Just as you arrive on the steps, the door is opened by a liveried footman dressed in a dark green frock coat, black trousers, white shirt, and striped waistcoat. The footman addresses you by name and invites you to wait in a tiny adjoining room furnished with gilt chairs covered in lime-green silk. There are two small, exquisite writing tables, an umbrella stand, and another small table covered with newspapers. Three large paintings, which are regularly changed, hang on the walls.

A second footman knocks on the door, enters, and asks the guest to follow him. Together you walk down long corridors, past a number of open doors which reveal lovely large rooms in which various people are working quietly. These are the offices used by the Queen's most senior aides and, by tradition, the doors always remain open. The silent corridors are flanked by portraits of former senior advisers.

You are then brought to the aide's room, an unpretentious office. The chairs are upright and the desks leather-topped and wooden. There are also computers, copying machines, and filing cabinets. There is, nonetheless, an air of serenity about the place.

The best way to see and appreciate Buckingham Palace, as a number of American Presidents can testify, is to attend a State Banquet, when all the State Apartments are in use; the servants are in their scarlet-and-gold livery and the guests are dressed in either their national or full-dress uniforms with medals and sashes; the ladies are in full-length ball gowns and tiaras.

As was the case centuries ago, the most rigid hierarchal divisions permeate the Royal Household. At the top are members of the Household, the private secretaries and the assistant private secretaries, and the people who come into daily contact with Elizabeth in her official business. They handle and manage the daily diaries, attend royal functions, organize royal visits, advise the Queen personally.

Their lives are spent in some luxury. They live in rent-free houses and apartments, called Grace and Favour residences. Elizabeth personally decides which home to offer each royal servant, but size and comfort depend on title and position. The highest paid earn $100,000 a year, and the majority of the top advisers receive less than $75,000. They tend to remain in the monarch's employ for decades, and the perquisites are extensive. They can call on assistants and secretaries; they have servants to pack, unpack, and press their clothes, wait on table, run errands, or pour a drink. Whenever they travel on the Queen's business they will go first-class, stay in the very best hotels, and have chauffeur-driven cars.

All this pomp reflects the glory of the monarchy. It also enhances the reputation of those senior advisers who are "close" to Her Majesty. Most of the people immediately surrounding Elizabeth are men. Their wives adore the prestige and glamour attached to the fact their husbands work "at the palace."

Many who hold senior posts are former officers of the armed forces. They claim that they "know the form," palace parlance for how to behave in the presence of Her Majesty. Just as important, Elizabeth, and more so Prince Philip, are sticklers for planning, protocol, and timing. Army officers believe they are uniquely trained for such duties, which they maintain are all essential for the efficient running of the monarchy. Others, more critical, see the system as "jobs for the boys."

Usually, retired former officers already receive a service pension. The Queen gives them a small salary, rent-free accommodations in the heart of London, and a position with unique privileges.

After the members of the Household come the officials, responsible for the efficient day-to-day running of the palace itself. They include qualified accountants who authorize payments, pay royal bills, decide staff levels and pay. These employees, with decades of loyal service, organize the royal functions and the feasts, the kitchens and the food, the gardens and the automobiles. Yet these men and women could never climb to the next rung on the ladder, never become members, who are the officer corps of royal service. The officials know their place. In most circumstances they earn more pay than the members but don't receive as many privileges. Those I have spoken to show some jealousy toward their "superiors" who, without their years of training, have many of the perks and privileges without the burden of everyday responsibility.

Finally, the Royal Household Staff make up the lowest grade. These are the two hundred or more workers—the maids, domestic servants, junior clerks, laborers, and other workers who live all their lives "below stairs." Here also, the pecking order is strictly adhered to, just as it was decades ago. None of these people would ever address the Queen or Prince Philip without first being spoken to. Indeed, they would hardly ever see the royal couple, and most would go out of their way rather than come face-to-face with Elizabeth or Philip, discreetly disappearing around a corner if they saw them approaching down a corridor.

At all levels, there is unquestionably a determination on everyone's part to dedicate one's working life to the service of the sovereign, and most believe they are part of a very large team, working together to ensure that the monarchy runs like a well-oiled machine.

Just as in the armed services, how the palace staff address one another provides the clue as to the relative standing of each. Members address each other by their first names, no matter how junior or senior their position; officials are always addressed by their surname, preceded by Mr., Mrs., or Miss, but never Ms. "Ms." is a term never permitted in royal circles. The officials call the members by their titles, Sir So-and-so or Colonel So-and-so. The staff—the workers—call everyone above them strictly Sir or Madam.

The Queen's Household is made up of six separate departments: the Private Secretary's Office, the Keeper of the Privy Purse, the Lord Chamberlain's Office, the Crown Equerry, the Master of the Household, and the Royal Collection.

After the Queen, the most important person in Buckingham Palace is the Private Secretary to the Sovereign, a far more important person in real terms than the titular head of the Queen's advisers, the Lord Chamberlain, and more important than Prince Philip. This man (thus far the position has always been held by a man) shares all the sovereign's secrets, reads all the secret state and government papers, and has access to every piece of information given to the Queen. Provided with all that knowledge, it is his duty to advise her on all matters, including government affairs and the monarchy.

The Right Honourable Sir Robert Fellowes, who is married to Diana's sister Jane, has held that post since 1990. He has many of the right credentials for the post, but many doubt whether he has the intellect to carry out the job properly or the authority with the Queen to push through the radical reforms the Palace so obviously needs to haul it into the next century. He has two major problems: Sir Robert is fifteen years younger than the Queen, and his knowledge of the workings of the monarchy is very limited compared to hers; second, his father, Sir William Fellowes, worked for the Royal Family for much of his life as their land agent at Sandringham, a position which some critics believe did not equip his son with sufficient credentials, social status, education, or professional experience.

Sir Robert's background, however, is impeccable: educated at Eton, service in the Scots Guards followed by nine years in the City as a director of a discount brokerage. He was invited to join the Palace staff in 1977 as an assistant private secretary. Sir Robert married Jane in 1978 and has a son and two daughters. He possesses all the interests of a typical English aristocrat—hunting, shooting, fishing—although he does not look like a sportsman, being tall, thin, and bespectacled. He belongs to the right clubs (Pratt's and White's), loves watching cricket, and occasionally plays a round of golf. Those who have seen him in the presence of Elizabeth observe that he seems to be in awe of her, ready at a moment's notice to do her bidding, but not bright enough or prepared enough to challenge his boss on any matter.

Sir Robert made a poor impression in the 1991 BBC film *Elizabeth R*, a look at a year in the working life of the Queen. As the Queen's principal adviser, he was unable to answer Elizabeth's simple, straightforward questions with any authority. He was obviously poorly briefed, unsure of his facts, and rather uninspiring. All he seemed to have in his favor was impeccable breeding, impeccable manners, an upper-class accent, and well-tailored clothes. He rather resembled the famous P. G. Wodehouse character Bertie Wooster.

Some of his colleagues credit him with a quick brain and a sense of humor and say he gets on well with the other courtiers and those he meets at his various clubs. Others at the palace confirm Sir Robert possesses great integrity, high principles, and a ready wit. But he is a man who is about as streetwise in the ways of the world as an Australian aborigine would be in New York City. Except for what he reads in the tabloid press, he has no idea what the ordinary people in the factories, the offices, or the shops think about.

And this, of course, must be an indictment of Elizabeth herself. Her previous Private Secretaries were the tried, tested, and trusted courtiers of a bygone era, but they displayed some intellectual capability. Sir Alan Lascelles, Sir Michael Adeane, Sir Martin Charteris, and Sir Philip Moore were all older than Elizabeth, and she listened to their advice and learned from them. Sir Robert's immediate predecessor, Sir William Heseltine, whom most at the palace called Bill, was an affable, rather aggressive Australian who would challenge the Queen when he thought it necessary. He had been much closer to ordinary people before starting his career at the palace.

Today Elizabeth prefers to surround herself with people like Sir Robert Fellowes who make the monarchy run like clockwork with everything in its correct place. Now nearing seventy years of age, Elizabeth does not welcome change. Not many older people do. This inflexible attitude exists at a time when the monarchy is under attack, when change is swirling around the Palace and many other British institutions. Elizabeth seems to hope that by surrounding herself with those gray men, the monarchy can ride out the storm.

The Private Secretary is in absolute command. He holds power over the Queen's diary, the functions she attends, the visits she makes, the people she sees, as well as serving as her guide in advising ministers of the Crown, foreign statesmen, and heads of state. He also sees every piece of correspondence addressed to Her Majesty and has responsibility for drafting all her speeches and official letters.

Perhaps the most important part of the Private Secretary's job is that he is the principal link between the sovereign and the Prime Minister and all other branches of government. He is informed about everything that occurs in government, knows everything that is going on in politics, and yet he must remain completely objective in his political views, for the government may change from Tory to Labour and back again. Like the monarch, he must be seen as absolutely impartial.

Many presume that the Queen, the whole Royal Family, and their senior advisers are biased toward the Conservatives; after all, the Conservatives are known as the hunting, fishing, and shooting party. Most official biographers suggest that the Royal Family and their senior advisers favor neither side.

The Private Secretary is the Keeper of The Queen's Archives. He has overall responsibility for cataloging and filing all Elizabeth's correspondence, which is stored in the Round Tower at Windsor Castle. These documents are watched over by the Queen's Librarian, a post now filled by Oliver Everett, who was not only a good friend to Prince Charles for many years and a polo playing pal, but also his assistant private secretary.

The Private Secretary is also responsible for liaison between the Queen and the armed forces. Throughout this century there has always been a close relationship between the House of Windsor and the military: A many members of the family have served, and still serve, in the army, navy, and air force. As a result, the Palace has its own Defense Services Secretary, the link man between the Palace and all three services.

Finally and most important, the Private Secretary has total responsibility for the Buckingham Palace Press Office, the link between Elizabeth, the press, and the nation. The press secretary's job has become increasingly difficult since the tabloid press shows no inhibitions in its coverage of the Royal Family, particularly the younger members. He must also contend with the paparazzi, those freelance photographers with their all-intrusive long lenses whose main mission is to invade the Royal Family's privacy. While the British press claim they do not employ paparazzi and never permit their own staff photographers to intrude on the Royal Family, the tabloids will happily pay tens of thousands of dollars to any photographer who turns up at their office with sensational, exclusive pictures.

A spectacular example involved the photographs showing Sarah Ferguson, the Princess of York, sunbathing topless in St. Tropez, kissing and frolicking in the pool with her "financial adviser," John Bryan. The *Daily Mirror* bought these pictures, taken by a paparazzo in the summer of 1992, just after the breakup of her marriage to Prince Andrew. The *Mirror* paid over $100,000 for them and sold nearly one million extra copies of that day's paper. The public reveled in the scandal of the half-naked Fergie all but making love in broad daylight. At a stroke, Fergie lost any remaining public sympathy because she had been captured on film making a sexy spectacle of herself in front of her young daughters, Bea, then four, and Eugenie, two. Elizabeth was furious that she could have been so mistaken about Fergie, whom she felt had let her down.

In November 1993 another set of royal photographs caused an uproar when the Mirror Group published pictures showing Princess Diana, in a leotard and Lycra shorts, working out on a leg-press machine at a London fitness club. The photographs were taken secretly by a New Zealander, Bryce Taylor, thirty-nine, owner of the LA Fitness gymnasium in West London, which Diana joined in 1990. A former squash coach, Taylor revealed how he had bought a Leica for $4,000 and installed it in the ceiling above the leg press, taking photographs of the Princess on three separate occasions during the spring of 1993. Taylor sold the photographs to the Mirror Group for $150,000, and his agent maintained he would make about $1,000,000 from worldwide syndication.

Diana expressed her "distress and outrage" at the "gross intrusion" into her privacy and ordered lawyers to sue Mirror Group Newspapers and Mr. Taylor over publication of the Peeping Tom photographs. She also won an immediate injunction banning publication of further pictures in Britain.

Mirror Group were condemned throughout the newspaper industry and, inevitably and understandably, Members of Parliament renewed calls for laws to shackle Britain's newspapers by bringing in restrictive privacy legislation.

The palace press office also fields a thousand questions a week from journalists covering every aspect of the Royal Family. Many are on sensitive matters. Generally speaking the press office does not comment on stories that appear almost daily in the British national press because Buckingham Palace believes the best way to deal with these stories is to ignore rumors, allegations, fantasies, and hypothetical questions which provide so much material for the tabloids.

Of course, this means on occasion Buckingham Palace, and therefore the Royal Family, can be less than candid. I reported in my book *Diana: A Princess and Her Troubled Marriage* that by the autumn of 1988, Charles and Diana were living apart most of the time and a year later Charles had moved to his country home, Highgrove, while Diana stayed at Kensington Palace. Yet, even when my book was published, in the spring of 1992, Buckingham Palace still refused to comment on the Waleses' living arrangements. Not until November 1992, just before the official separation was announced, did the Palace hint that there might indeed be problems within the marriage.

No information is ever released to the media, either in a formal statement or in any off-the-record comment by the palace press office, without the knowledge of the Private Secretary. Since 1990 Sir Robert

Fellowes has had absolute authority over the press officers and responsibility for every statement made. But this official job description doesn't take account of one vital aspect of life at Buckingham Palace.

On the surface all appears friendly between everyone working at the palace. The senior advisers are expected to be cordial toward one another, seeing themselves as brother officers in the same regiment. In reality, much of the time, ruthless power politics are the order of the day.

One example involved the separation of Andrew and Fergie in March 1992. Within hours of the official announcement, Charles Anson, the pleasant, affable, and competent press secretary, talking to the BBC's royal correspondent, attacked Fergie with almost personal abuse. He told the BBC that Fergie had ordered media leaks about her marriage, employed a high-powered public relations firm, and, worse still, had revealed by her behavior that she was unworthy of being a member of the Royal Family. No one in the media had ever heard such a personal attack on a Duchess of the House of Windsor on any other occasion going back half a century.

The day after Anson made the critical remarks, which were reported in TV news bulletins and in the newspapers, Elizabeth ordered Anson to make an unprecedented, humiliating public apology to the Duchess of York and herself for the criticisms themselves as well as for suggesting that the criticisms had been endorsed by the Queen. Anson said, "I have apologised to the Queen, and both Her Majesty and Her Royal Highness have been kind enough to accept these apologies."

In fact, Anson had been briefed by Sir Robert Fellowes, who told him how to suggest, off the record, the Palace's view of the Duchess of York to a few selected journalists. Sir Robert had never been fond of Fergie.

His attitude had been colored by his repugnance for her father, Major Ronald Ferguson, who consorted with prostitutes and massage-parlor girls. He also had the reputation of trying to seduce the wives and girlfriends of friends he met in the polo world. According to Sir Robert, after his daughter married Prince Andrew, Major Ferguson had been told to forbear lewdness for fear he would damage his daughter and the Royal Family if his activities ever became public.

Not surprisingly, Major Ferguson's seamy adventures were reported in the newspapers and, as a result Ronald Ferguson lost his job with the Guards Polo Club, his role as Polo Manager to Prince Charles, and he later lost another $50,000 job with the Royal Berkshire Polo Club. His behavior brought disrepute on the entire Royal Family, but proved especially embarrassing to his daughter Fergie.

Sir Robert had formed the opinion that Sarah Ferguson, with her "past"— various sexual adventures, including living with a wid-ower—made her unsuitable as a member of the House of Windsor. He was dismayed when it became obvious that Prince Andrew was about to ask Fergie to marry him, and he advised Elizabeth of this circumstance. He had hoped that Andrew's mercurial sexual adven-ture with Fergie would end as his affair with Koo Stark did: Andrew had enjoyed sowing his wild oats with the porn film star, and then the affair was over.

From the beginning of their marriage, Sir Robert pressured Fergie to behave appropriately, but he was not prepared for her gutsy response. She was far less amenable to his powers of persuasion than her sister-in-law Diana. In short, Fergie refused to be ordered about by Sir Robert and told him so in no uncertain terms.

A row occurred in 1989 when Fergie wanted to travel overseas on a holiday. There was no reason why she should not go; there was no suggestion of any impropriety, but Sir Robert believed the Royal Family's image would suffer if Fergie took too many overseas holidays. He asked to see her in his palace offices. The meeting ended with Sir Robert shouting at the top of his voice: "You will do as you are told, and you will take advice from me. That is my job and I expect the advice I give you to be obeyed."

Sir Robert went on, "I have the authority and I will use that authority if I think fit to make you understand that now you are a member of the Royal Family you will behave as all members should. Do you understand that, young lady?"

"Go to hell," Fergie said, and stormed out.

From that moment, Sir Robert lost hope of any successful relationship with Fergie, and she had made an enemy of the most powerful person in the Palace. He would make life difficult for her.

Sir Robert demanded that Fergie carry out duties, functions, and visits which he arranged and which were all but impossible for her to cancel. He began to criticize her, pointing out that her speeches weren't good enough; her dress sense was often inappropriate; her demeanor wasn't sufficiently royal. As a result Fergie lost confidence in herself and began to rebel more openly against the system until she felt she simply could not carry on. Some courtiers believe Sir Robert was determined to hound her from the palace.

Sir Robert saw his chance when Fergie came to tell Elizabeth she could no longer remain a member of the Royal Family, that the pressures had become too great, and that reluctantly she had to ask Andrew for a separation. He briefed the luckless Anson, his press secretary, what he should say to the media.

Anson was called to see Her Majesty, and Sir Robert Fellowes stood in the room while the Queen told Anson of her severe displeasure for the way he had criticized the Duchess of York and thereby involved herself and the Royal Family. In those circumstances, Elizabeth can produce a cold, hard, some would say withering look when she wishes, and the recipient is left in no doubt that he or she has transgressed. Sir Robert stood there and said nothing while Anson took the blame.

The job of royal press secretary was instituted in 1918 during the reign of King George V, but thirteen years later he dispensed with it. In 1944 King George VI saw that a press secretary could be useful in feeding information to the media, and the post has continued to the present day. So far, there have been only ten office holders. The press secretary is in direct contact with Elizabeth and is equipped with a mobile telephone so that he can be contacted at any time. Elizabeth believes such modern contraptions are not necessary for those working at Buckingham Palace, but accepts that the press secretary should carry one. Despite the direct access to Elizabeth, however, most contacts come through the Office of the Private Secretary.

The link between the Royal Family and the media has become so important that other members of the House of Windsor now have their own press officers, all of whom take their orders from Sir Robert Fellowes. In addition to directing the press office, Charles Anson has been given special responsibility for the Queen. His number two is responsible for Prince Philip and The Princess Royal, Princess Anne.

Another assistant press secretary is responsible for Andrew and Edward as well as Princess Margaret. Still another works practically full-time for both Charles and Diana, but since their separation they now have their own press officers. The Queen Mother had her own man at Clarence House, while press matters involving the Duke and Duchess of Kent, the Duke and Duchess of Gloucester, Prince and Princess Michael of Kent, and Princess Alexandra are dealt with by their respective private secretaries, but only after consultation with the Buckingham Palace Press Office or Sir Robert Fellowes.

The Private Secretary is also responsible for the Information and Correspondence section. Besides all the official correspondence, the Queen also receives another 250 letters a day, close to 100,000 a year, from members of the public, all of which receive a reply. Sacks of mail follow a visit by the Queen to a part of Britain or an overseas tour. There are daily requests for information on every aspect of the Queen's life, including her horses, her corgis, her wealth, her homes, her clothes, and even her diet. A team of seven sift, read, and then reply to the ceaseless torrent of mail.

Officially, the head of the Royal Household and the man with overall responsibility for all its departments is the Lord Chamberlain. Since Elizabeth came to the throne in 1952, there have been five, all chosen for the job by Elizabeth herself. The present holder is the Earl of Airlie, a former chairman of merchant bankers Schroder Wagg. Recently, Lord Airlie has been most helpful with all the discussions and publicity concerning the Queen's finances. Like the Private Secretary, the Lord Chamberlain has nothing to do with the day-to-day running of Buck House. Lord Airlie's duties range from ceremonial occasions to royal weddings and funerals and the care of the five thousand or so pictures in The Royal Collection.

The Lord Chamberlain is also responsible for many other senior royal appointees, such as the Marshal of the Diplomatic Corps, whose prime duty is to keep happy all members of foreign embassies, consulates, and delegations in their dealings with the Palace; the Constable of Windsor Castle, who has overall responsibility for the efficient running of the castle; the Clerk of the Closet and three Priests in Ordinary, all involved with the religious aspect of the monarchy; and he has responsibility for the Medical Household, pharmacists who attend when necessary.

The Lord Chamberlain also has the delicate task of instructing incoming diplomats on the ritualistic customs of Buck House when they come to present their credentials to Her Majesty. All nations are treated as equals, and some ambassadors of the smaller nations have a rather grandiose view of their own importance, which can cause problems. It is all done most correctly, starting with a ride in an open horse-drawn landau from the embassy to Buck House, with much bowing and scraping as they enter the Bow Room on the ground floor, accompanied by various royal officials. Then the ambassador and the Queen are left alone to chat for five minutes before the ambassador's entourage is formally presented. Finally, the ambassador's wife is invited to join the group and must curtsy on meeting the Queen.

In the late 1960s Elizabeth did away with one embarrassing point of protocol. Until then ambassadors, their entourage, and their wives had to leave the room backward. Today, once they reach the doorway, they all must turn and bow. Everyone turns and bows.

The Lord Chamberlain is responsible for making sure that no "undesirables" are allowed access to the court or permitted to meet the sovereign for fear the Crown might be tainted by scandal. What constitutes scandal changes through the centuries, but it was Queen Victoria, followed by the high-handed Queen Mary, who banished all divorced men and women from the palace or any royal gathering. Some time after Elizabeth came to the throne, she relaxed this rule. Those divorced politicians who needed access to Her Majesty were accepted only in their "official capacity," a typical yet neat British way of circumventing the problem. Put another way, they never met her on a personal basis. At first the Queen allowed only "innocent parties" in divorce cases to come to court and be presented to her, but the divorce explosion in Britain meant the strict rules had to be relaxed. It was dropped quietly in 1970. Even today, however, no one is presented at court who has a serious criminal record or has ever been involved in a major scandal.

Three times a year the forty beautiful acres of gardens that surround Buckingham Palace are thrown open to invited guests for the legendary garden parties where Elizabeth, Philip, and often other members of the family mingle and chat with the privileged and their partners, while taking afternoon tea. It is a special day for the ladies, some of whom spend fortunes buying expensive haute couture creations, and always with a hat, to parade before Her Majesty, the cameras, and each other. Though debutante dances were canceled as passé in the 1950s, garden parties somehow managed to survive the rigors of time and the changes in Britain's social structure.

The three parties are held in the summer months, and around twenty thousand people in all attend. (One garden party is also held each year at the Palace of Holyrood House in Scotland). Each party costs about $80,000, the guests consuming 30,000 sandwiches, 18,000 cookies, and 2,000 gallons of ice cream. An outside caterer provides everything. While everyone else scoffs up the food and drinks the tea, however, Elizabeth remains aloof. Her special tea and her favorite cucumber sandwiches are brought to her on a silver salver, during the party.

Every name on every invitation must be vetted, but not for security reasons. Rather, Palace officials go to great lengths to be sure Elizabeth will not be tainted by meeting anyone undesirable. Until recently, anyone found guilty in court of riding a bicycle without lights thirty years ago would be barred from attending a garden party, for life. And there was no appeal.

The garden parties are considered so important that a special Garden Party Office employs nine middle-aged ladies for six months of the year to sift information while checking invitations and people's reputations. The office holds cabinets filled with "top secret" garden party files, which include thousands of names of people blacklisted through the years by the Lord Chamberlain's Office. One strict rule still applied is that no one is allowed to seek an invitation to a garden party, either directly or through a third person. Anyone caught lobbying is barred for life, and so is the person for whom he or she is trying to secure an invitation. Anyone who falsely claims to be related to So-and-so, or uses a title or a decoration to which they are not entitled, will never be invited.

A special file, known as the black box, contains anonymous letters sent to the palace every year by disagreeable, jealous people, including maladjusted misfits outraged that someone else should have received a garden party invitation. These letters invariably contain unsavory allegations about individuals. The Garden Party Office must check out each one by judicious questioning of the appropriate authorities. If the allegations are well founded, the accused person will not receive an invitation or will have the invitation rescinded, since it is the Lord Chamberlain's job to ensure the sovereign does not meet "the wrong

332 • QUEEN ELIZABETH II

sorts." Care is also taken to ensure that innocent people are not victimized.

One odd responsibility for the Lord Chamberlain is the Crown Jewels, which officially come under his jurisdiction. Others are the Royal Bargemaster and the Queen's Watermen, responsible for the sovereign's safety when on board a craft on the River Thames. Perhaps the most extraordinary group of men are the so-called Queen's Swan Uppers—still active today—who catch and inspect all the young cygnets on the River Thames. Swans that belong to the Queen are not marked, but every swan must be identified. These men are called Uppers because when they sight a cygnet, they shout "Up, up, up" as they move in to catch and inspect the new arrival.

The Lord Chamberlain is also in charge of the Lords-in-Waiting, who represent the Queen at funerals or memorial services, meet and say farewell to important visitors; the Gentlemen Ushers, who conduct guests around at official royal functions, making sure everyone is in the right place; Sergeant at Arms, the oldest armed royal guard in England but now purely a symbolic post, awarded for long service; the Central Chancery of the Orders of Knighthood, which provides employment to a dozen older men whose full-time task is to record and maintain the lists of millions of people awarded a medal, a decoration, or any honor. The name of every single man and woman, living or dead, who has ever received an honor is stored there.

The Master of the Household is in charge of the three hundred men and women who are now considered necessary to take care of Elizabeth's domestic needs and all those who live and work at the palace. His job can be described as that of headwaiter, majordomo, restaurateur, head porter, head butler, employer, housekeeper, and bookkeeper all rolled into one. For all this work he receives,$60,000 a year.

He divides his kingdom into three categories: food, general, and housekeeping. About fifty men and women work in the royal kitchens as chefs, underchefs, pastry cooks, vegetable cooks, kitchen porters, and the very lowest rung in the ladder, dishwashers.

Another eighty are footmen, stewards, pages, upholsterers, seamstresses, and cellar men. Their main concern is the palace's furniture and fittings. Another fifty are maids and cleaners.

Getting a job at Buckingham Palace is quite easy. There are frequent vacancies, even in times of recession and severe unemployment. Many people are simply frightened of the prospect of life below stairs in Buck House. And the pay is poor. Maids, cleaners, and dishwashers earn $120 a week, about the same as for working at a third-rate London hotel. They are provided with training, a uniform, and free meals, but there are no tips. Unmarried people can live in, occupying spartan single rooms on the top floor with bathrooms located at the end of each corridor. Until the 1960s young men and women slept in separate dormitories accommodating up to twenty people. Fun, but not very private. The boys and girls were strictly monitored, and the dormitories more than a hundred yards apart.

Work conditions in the palace have improved greatly since the end of the nineteenth century. Then it was fourteen-hour days, six days a week, with strict discipline. Today, alarm clocks ring at 7:15 A.M. Breakfast for all the staff is served from 7:30 to 8:30 A.M., all with strict adherence to seniority, the members in one dining room, the officials in another, and the staff in a third. A full English breakfast of orange juice, porridge or cereal, bacon and eggs, and tea or coffee is provided in all three dining rooms. And all are self-serving, including, surprisingly, Elizabeth and Prince Philip, who hate fuss at breakfast time. Even when the entire Royal Family breakfast together, for example at Windsor or Balmoral, the morning meal is a self-service affair, with the food being provided in covered warm-plates for everyone to help themselves.

After breakfast each goes about his or her work as in any other large establishment, with breaks for coffee, lunch, and tea. But life in Buckingham Palace *is* different. The atmosphere is quiet, somber, monastic; some would say funereal, others would say serene. And there is, of course, never-ending obsequious behavior at all levels, some long-serving and senior servants demanding such treatment from those they see as their inferiors. Elizabeth seems to treat all her servants, for that is what they are, as equal to each other, demanding the same respect from her most senior courtiers to her most junior footmen.

Whenever a royal servant meets the Queen in the palace, he or she will either bow or drop a "bob" curtsy but will never say hello or good morning. Every servant calls the Queen Ma'am (rhymes with *jam*) and

Prince Philip Sir. And, if by chance a servant should meet Philip or any other member of the family while walking along a corridor, the servant must wait until the royal has passed by. Only then may he or she proceed. Under no circumstances must any servant talk to any member of the Royal Family unless spoken to. And yet, it must be said, when this author has been in Buckingham Palace the attitude of all the staff, from the highest to the most junior, has been relaxed, none appearing nervous or agitated by their permanent proximity to the sovereign.

After dinner, at about eight, the footmen, pages, and anyone else still working is finally free to come and go as they please. Friends are allowed to visit the palace but must be out by ten. Overnight visitors are strictly forbidden and, if a man or woman lets anyone, of either sex, stay overnight, they are promptly fired.

Senior courtiers do enjoy certain privileges not given to the most junior dishwasher. One is the palace indoor swimming pool. Senior members of the Household can use the pool in the early morning, but never when a member of the Royal Family is there. Indeed, if courtiers are in the pool when a member of the family wishes to swim, they must immediately leave the pool. (Diana swam there frequently.)

The Keeper of the Privy Purse looks after the Queen's private financial affairs. He is also called her Treasurer, and in that capacity he keeps an eye, with her full permission of course, on her various bank accounts. His other responsibilities include the finances of the royal estates, the royal horse stud, and the not inconsequential expenses of the Queen's favorite hobby, horse racing.

The current Keeper of the Privy Purse is Major Sir Shane Blewitt. He is next to Sir Robert Fellowes in order of precedence. Now that the Queen has agreed to pay income tax like every other British citizen, Sir Shane will have to deal with the tax inspectors. The finances of the Royal Family, and particularly those of Elizabeth, are complex and have, until now, remained secret.

Sir Shane is the one man who knows how much the Queen is really worth. For years it has been accepted that the Queen is one of the world's wealthiest women, a billionaire many times over, but that is a misleading fact because the great majority of her fortune is not hers at all but owned by the state.

A Committee for the Crown Lands published a special report in

1955 detailing the monarch's estate. No official, authorized list of the Queen's English properties was meant to exist, yet the report contained one. It revealed that Elizabeth, as sovereign, owned two thousand buildings in London, including part of Regent Street, office blocks, a number of embassies, hotels, and stores, including the famous Liberty's. Outside London she owned four hundred thousand acres of land, the bed of the sea three miles offshore, and almost all foreshores. She also owned Buckingham Palace and Windsor Castle. Today, however, all these are classed as Crown Estates, that is, state-owned for most purposes, and none of the income goes to the Queen.

One myth about the Queen's fortune is easily dismissed. She owns no real estate in the United States, despite rumors she owned skyscrapers on New York's Park Avenue.

The Queen inherited the world's largest collection of jewels in private hands, the Crown Jewels alone being incalculable in value. She also inherited the greatest array of paintings in private hands, including Canalettos, Holbeins, Leonardo da Vincis, Michelangelos, Raphaels, and Van Dycks; a magnificent stamp collection, wonderful tapestries, and a vast array of French antique furniture. But all these are the inalienable property of the monarchy which she can never sell.

Some newspapers have suggested she is worth $6 billion, others $10 billion. But that would include such items as the Crown Jewels, Buckingham Palace, the Royal Collection, and other inherited wealth belonging to the nation, entrusted to the monarch only for his or her lifetime. They, too, cannot be included in her fortune.

Elizabeth's *personal* wealth includes only her stock portfolio, Balmoral and Sandringham (together worth about $150 million), and her string of racehorses. The only parameters ever volunteered came in 1972 when Lord Cobbold, then Lord Chamberlain, in evidence to a House of Commons Committee examining royal finances, said, "Estimates of Her Majesty's private wealth as being between $75 million and $150 million are highly exaggerated."

At that time her stock portfolio was probably worth about $50 million. Sensibly invested in U.K. shares it should have grown to about $750 million by 1993, if all dividends had been reinvested and the Queen had spent none of the capital. But she has spent most of the dividends and dug deep into her capital, mainly to help other members of the Royal Family and for the upkeep of her personal homes, Balmoral and Sandringham. Today her stock portfolio is worth approximately $100 million, earning perhaps $7 million a year.

The Queen's other private income comes from the Duchy of Lancaster, which consists of large tracts of land, farms, and property in six different counties as well as the piece of ground on which stands the famous Savoy Hotel in London.

The Duchy of Lancaster has been passed down from monarch to monarch since 1399, when Henry IV was on the throne. The monarch automatically inherits all the duchy and all its wealth and property, and it is still tax-free. This income, about $2.5 million a year after all expenditures, is paid directly into Elizabeth's private bank account.

In all, Elizabeth has at her disposal the income of about $7 million from stock investments, plus perhaps another $1 million from the Duchy of Lancaster, an annual income of $8 million.

From this $8 million she pays toward staff pensions, various amounts to minor royals for carrying out their duties, numerous charitable donations, her racing stables and string of horses, and her extensive wardrobe, an absolute necessity for her role as Queen.

The Keeper of the Privy Purse must check all the Civil List finances, those moneys voted to the monarch by Parliament to enable her to pay her staff, run her palaces, operate her aircraft and boats, in other words, the money needed to perform her duties as head of state. The Civil List is exactly parallel with funding for the office of the President of the United States, and includes personal costs of the Queen, the Royal Family, and staff salaries, amounting to approximately $12 million a year.

The Civil List does not include a salary for the monarch or any other members of the Royal Family. Every cent must be accounted for, and it is all spent on expenses. Over and above the Civil List, the government meets other royal expenses. In 1992–93, for example, the upkeep of the royal palaces—Buckingham Palace, Windsor Castle, Kensington Palace, St. James's Palace, Hampton Court, and Holyrood House—cost about $42 million; the Queen's Flight about $12 million; the Royal Yacht *Britannia* $15 million; and the royal train another $5 million, a total of $74 million, all paid for by the government.

The Crown Equerry is another man of considerable importance. Officially responsible for the Royal Mews, he is in fact in charge of virtually everything outside the palaces. That includes the five Rolls-

Royce limousines painted royal maroon and the chauffeurs, all the gardens and the grounds, the horses, and the priceless collection of state coaches, landaus, and carriages. In Victoria's day more than two hundred horses were kept in the Royal Mews at Buck House. Even today there are thirty—twenty bays and ten grays—all used for ceremonial purposes. The job may not sound arduous; however, in addition to the normal daily duties, about 150 events take place each year.

Then there are the ubiquitous women whom people always hear mentioned but never seem to see, hear, or meet: the ladies-in-waiting. All female members of the Royal Family have ladies-in-waiting but none are so vital or important as those who wait on the Queen. Whenever Elizabeth sets forth from any of her palaces on any occasion, whether it is a ten-minute meeting or a full-blown month-long foreign visit, she is accompanied by at least one and usually two ladies-in-waiting. They are the invisible but indispensable aides who smooth the way, chat to a dignitary, check the Queen's dress, and, of course, stand ready for any emergency.

Today Elizabeth has fourteen ladies who take turns being on call and who are on duty at all times of the day and night. It is the most extraordinary job which carries no pay whatsoever and no perks other than the highest status in class-conscious British society. Ladies-in-waiting work, live, and have the ear of the most important person in the land, the Queen.

A good lady-in-waiting is discreet and tactful; she displays refinement, taste, a ready smile, and the ability to conduct small talk with anyone. She must also know when to hold her tongue, which is the case most of the time she is on duty. She must also know how to dress so as never to detract from the glamour or the limelight of the center of attraction, Elizabeth.

Ladies-in-waiting must also learn to smile discreetly. On most occasions they ride in the chauffeur-driven limousine sitting beside the Queen, but they cannot smile too much or appear more enthusiastic than the sovereign.

When the Queen is entertaining, a lady-in-waiting is always present to hold bouquets and presents given to the Queen; to take any messages; to provide an arm or a hand if necessary; to relay phone calls; to check what Elizabeth is being given to eat and drink; to be on hand with Elizabeth's favorite Malvern mineral water, headache pills, handkerchief, or on rare occasions, on hand with any money she may require.

Ladies-in-waiting also deal with Elizabeth's personal correspondence, especially writing letters to the young and the old. One or two ladies also do some of Elizabeth's personal shopping.

The Queen's ladies-in-waiting are considered so important that the senior positions are given titles. The most senior is Mistress of the Robes, who by tradition is a duchess; then there are two Ladies of the Bedchamber, who are always peeresses, and two Women of the Bedchamber, daughters of aristocrats. The rest are described as Extra Ladies. Most duties in fact are carried out by the four Women of the Bedchamber, who are younger, more agile, and more capable of sustaining the sometimes arduous travel and long hours involved.

Elizabeth has a favorite lady-in-waiting who has become someone with whom she can confidentially discuss many of her personal thoughts as well as the problems of her children and her daughters-in-law: Lady Susan Hussey, sister of the Conservative politician William Waldegrave. She is married to Marmaduke ("Duke") Hussey, a former director of *Times* newspapers who is now chairman of the BBC.

For the past twenty years Lady Hussey has been among Elizabeth's most important "eyes and ears" to the outside world, informing her of the moods of the nation and of the people's attitude to the monarchy, to herself, and more particularly to the behavior of the younger royals. Unfortunately, Susan Hussey has little idea of what the ordinary man or woman in the supermarket thinks or talks about, and can only tell Elizabeth the mood of those at the highest echelons, the gossip she hears at influential lunch and dinner tables, and gatherings of the rich and famous.

Finally, there are the faceless but important people who care for all the Queen's inherited wealth: the paintings and drawings, the engravings and etchings, the furniture and the exquisite objets d'art which in total number about one million different items and are part of The Royal Collection.

Management consultants, hired in 1986 to reduce the royal retinue, recommended that all the paintings, the library, and the works of art should be put under the direction of one man, Surveyor of the Queen's Pictures. At that time the post was held by Sir Oliver Millar; today the

Surveyor is Sir Geoffrey de Bellaigue. Elizabeth insists that a handsome profit must be made from this great collection, which otherwise has no income except from exhibitions and the Queen's own purse. For example, whenever a photograph of one of the Queen's pictures, paintings, or works of art is used anywhere in the world, in any form, a reproduction fee is paid. In this way, not only are the running costs kept to a minimum, but the salaries of those employed in the department are covered.

Craftsmen are constantly engaged in restoring furniture, preserving the objets d'art, cleaning the paintings, keeping the superb collection in perfect condition. Three people alone look after the three hundred clocks in the Queen's four residences. Elizabeth decreed in the 1970s, again following advice, that every one of the one million pieces in The Royal Collection should be listed and categorized on a computer. That enormous task is still going on, and some three years later a small team of photographers is still engaged in photographing, printing, and developing pictures of every single item so that a precise, detailed record can be obtained.

This is the way Elizabeth likes assignments carried out—unhurried and diligently, with care and attention to detail. Ever since she was a little girl Elizabeth has been like that, careful and surefooted, but always with a quiet determination and a confidence that her wishes will always be met. For the greater part of her reign that systematic way of doing things has worked without fail. But today the world is moving much faster, and the great institutions on which she has built her monarchy are no longer so steady. It is unclear whether her old approach will continue to suffice, or if a new one is necessary to keep the influence and authority of the monarchy from eroding.

VI

ELIZABETH AND HER PRIME MINISTERS

FOURTEEN

THE WOMAN WHO WOULD BE KING

When Margaret Thatcher became Prime Minister at the age of fifty-four, in May 1979, Elizabeth was fifty-three and had been on the throne for nearly thirty years. There had never before been a woman Prime Minister. Also, Margaret Thatcher was unknown to the Queen. For most of her reign Elizabeth had known the politicians who became Prime Minister for some years as they climbed the political ladder. Margaret Thatcher had held a Cabinet position under Edward Heath's premiership in the early 1970s and had been leader of the Opposition since 1975, yet Elizabeth rarely had a long conversation with her and certainly never had an intimate head-to-head chat in private over political or any other matters.

Elizabeth of course followed every campaign for Prime Minister. Now from her private sitting room she watched on television as Mrs. Thatcher entered No. 10 Downing Street for the first time as premier and recited a magnanimous exhortation from St. Francis of Assisi:

> Where there is discord, may we bring harmony.
> Where there is error, may we bring truth.
> Where there is doubt, may we bring faith.
> Where there is despair, may we bring hope.

When Elizabeth met Mrs. Thatcher at the first weekly audience she asked if the quotation from St. Francis was the basis of her political creed. "Absolutely," Mrs. Thatcher replied, "absolutely." Later, as Mrs. Thatcher confronted the trade unions and attacked the fabric of Britain's welfare state, Elizabeth commented to a friend, "It seems a pity that Mrs. Thatcher seems to have forgotten the words of St. Francis."

In retrospect, Margaret Thatcher, still finding her way as premier during those early months, did not know how to treat Elizabeth, a woman she had been brought up by her royalist parents to respect and admire, if not revere. While Mrs. Thatcher never appeared nervous when confronting her political opponents or her Cabinet colleagues, she did find her weekly audiences with Elizabeth difficult.

She would arrive every Tuesday evening between fifteen minutes and half an hour early for her private chat, whereas other premiers would appear perhaps five to ten minutes before the appointed hour. Mrs. Thatcher would read through her notes and chat with one of Elizabeth's senior advisers, waiting for the summons from the Queen. After a few weeks a Palace adviser suggested to Mrs. Thatcher that she might like to save time and leave No. 10 a little later. She replied that she left so early to give herself sufficient leeway in case of heavy traffic, an extraordinary reply because Buckingham Palace is only half a mile from Downing Street and the Prime Minister's car is always flanked by a police escort which would ensure that traffic give way for the Prime Minister.

Her reply suggests her nervousness at having to talk for thirty minutes with the Queen from a subservient position. The daughter of an alderman (local councilor) from middle England, Mrs. Thatcher had achieved a remarkable rise to the pinnacle of power through dogged determination and political good fortune. She also knew that her power could be swept away within hours either by her Conservative party colleagues or by the voters in a general election, whereas the Queen would remain in power till the day she died, or chose to step aside.

Elizabeth could have seen Mrs. Thatcher as soon as she arrived at the palace so that her Prime Minister did not have to wait, patiently, for the appointed time. But that was not Elizabeth's nature. She has always demanded punctuality, which she believes shows respect, not for her, but for the monarchy. And that was the lesson she continued to give Mrs. Thatcher: respect for the monarchy was paramount; Prime Ministers had to wait. Of course, being forced to wait riled the already uncomfortable Mrs. Thatcher.

Those who saw Mrs. Thatcher in company with Elizabeth noted

that her behavior was very contrary to her usual rather bossy nature. Margaret Thatcher would curtsy far more deeply and bow her head far lower than most women when meeting the Queen in public, as though trying to exaggerate her respect. As one South American ambassador noted, "Watching Mrs. Thatcher curtsy was like watching a magnificent crimson sun sink beneath the horizon."

The Prime Minister held a deeply royalist view of the monarchy. In an interview Mrs. Thatcher paid tribute not only to Britain's unwritten Constitution, based on a hereditary monarchy, but also to the work of the monarch. In so doing of course, she paid unsolicited praise to Elizabeth herself.

"A monarchy, a hereditary monarchy," Mrs. Thatcher said, "is wonderfully trained, in duty and in leadership, which understands example, which is always there, which is above politics, for which the whole nation has an affection and which is a symbol of patriotism. . . . It gives a nation stability and assurance. . . . It is not only a symbol of unity, but you respect and admire the monarch as well."

Margaret Thatcher began her relationship in awe of Elizabeth and her position of ultimate power as the Queen, but that was to change as Mrs. Thatcher became more and more confident, more in control of her party, her Cabinet colleagues, the House of Commons, and the country. Friction developed which never disappeared.

Margaret Thatcher's long period in office—from May 1979 to November 1990—was remarkable in postwar Britain, but many people felt she soon became too authoritarian and overconfident, even more royal than the monarchy itself. Elizabeth was one of the first to note her regal ways.

At the close of the Conservative Party Conference in October 1990—when Mrs. Thatcher was still leader—the entire assembly rose and, in customary style, stood respectfully as the national anthem was played. As they stood singing, the BBC television cameras panned slowly along the government ministers standing in line on the platform and closed in on the face of Mrs. Thatcher just as the last line, "Long to reign over us, God save the Queen," was sung. Even the hundreds gathered in the hall experienced the combination of her face and those words on the huge screens on either side of the platform.

Mrs. Thatcher, standing erect as a guardsman and dressed in her royal blue suit, looked suitably regal. She was at the height of her power, treating the electors, some foreign ministers, and all her own Cabinet ministers as mere subjects to heed her words of wisdom and obey her commands. She had become intolerable in Cabinet meetings, treating her ministers, who were part of the government, as mere ciphers who were to subscribe to her views, decisions, and commands.

One apocryphal story illustrates how people felt about her. The headwaiter serving dinner to Mrs. Thatcher and the entire Cabinet asks what she would like to eat. She replies, "Oh, a small steak please." The headwaiter then asks, "And the vegetables, Ma'am?" She replies, "Oh, they'll have the same as me."

It didn't actually happen and was only a House of Commons joke, but the story touched a raw nerve in the country, particularly among government ministers. For that was how the nation perceived Mrs. Thatcher had come to treat even her Cabinet members.

There were no jokes between Elizabeth and Mrs. Thatcher during their eleven years of weekly meetings, which was unusual for Elizabeth. She had got on remarkably well with most of her Prime Ministers, beginning with the father-daughter relationship with Winston Churchill back in the 1950s, and they often shared lighthearted comments.

The two women were expected to reach an early understanding, for they had much in common. Both were mature women with families, holding the most responsible positions, sacrificing their lives for the nation, and devoted to duty. And neither was particularly interested in fashion, music, or the arts.

The product of small-town life in Grantham, Lincolnshire, Mrs. Thatcher grew up above a grocer's store; her father, the grocer, was enmeshed in local politics. Her quick brain and determination helped her go to university and she carved out a major political life for herself. Elizabeth, born into a royal household and destined to be Queen, was a country woman at heart. They had no common interests. The irreverent British TV puppet show *Spitting Image* portrayed Elizabeth and Mrs. Thatcher as sharing nothing except the way they both clung, leechlike, to their handbags.

The first hint of trouble between the two women came in 1982 when the political journalist Anthony Sampson wrote that "the weekly meetings between the Queen and Mrs. Thatcher are dreaded by at least one of them." Mrs. Thatcher may have been nervous to start with, but Elizabeth perceived a woman who seemed to think she should lecture and pontificate rather than hold a discussion and inform her sovereign about what was going on. "Dreaded" may have been an overstatement, but probably neither looked forward to the meetings.

Mrs. Thatcher's regal approach to her own position provided some amusement for Elizabeth. It is not known exactly when Mrs. Thatcher began using the royal *we* when referring to herself, but she used the famous royal expression frequently, even after she was forced from office. Elizabeth, on the other hand, has never used it in public except when outlining the government's program at the start of a new parliamentary session. One of Mrs. Thatcher's more famous examples came en route to Moscow when she said, "We are in the fortunate position in Britain of being, as it were, the senior position in power."

Another instance which caused much hilarity and scoffing throughout the country occurred on a television interview, when she rejoiced that her daughter-in-law had just given birth: "We are a grandmother!" She also spoke often of "my factories" and "my coal mines."

Her regal attitude also had its serious side. Many people, both inside and outside Parliament, believed that Mrs. Thatcher deliberately used the royal *we* to suggest her own near-regal, permanent position in the nation's political life, just like that of the monarch.

Like the Queen, Mrs. Thatcher preferred to have men advise her and work with her. Even today, save for ladies-in-waiting, maids, and dressers, Elizabeth employs virtually no women who work closely with her. All senior advisers, courtiers, and those in charge of various departments throughout the palace are men. During her eleven years as premier, Mrs. Thatcher was dismissive of the possibility of employing women in senior government positions. She did have women in her Cabinet, but not for very long. When a Cabinet vacancy came about it was frequently suggested that perhaps she would want a female replacement. Every time Mrs. Thatcher replied firmly, "No," but gave no explanation.

And it wasn't only women about whom Mrs. Thatcher seemed dismissive. Elizabeth was informed, unofficially, by one of her mandarins that Mrs. Thatcher was having problems with senior civil servants: relations were described as "dreadful." Mrs. Thatcher had made little attempt to conceal her contempt and mistrust for their ineffectual and detached attitude to her priorities. In 1980 Elizabeth was told that the Prime Minister had held a dinner for Permanent Secretaries—very senior civil servants—at which she had berated them all evening. In the end she had insulted them all, saying, "If only I had officials like the man [herself] they had come to see, things would be a lot better."

At one of her subsequent weekly meetings, Elizabeth let Mrs. Thatcher know that she had been informed of the problems she was having with her civil servants. Mrs. Thatcher told her, "There is no problem. You know what servants are. I just wanted to put the fear of God in them."

Problems continually arose between Buckingham Palace and No. 10 Downing Street when tragedy occurred. The 1980s saw a spate of air disasters. In such circumstances, it has always been the tradition that the Queen would select a member of The Firm to travel to the scene of the tragedy to show the nation that the royals cared. Elizabeth, however, had always told the respective authorities that no one would attend immediately for fear of getting in the way or being a nuisance when the emergency services needed all their energies caring for the dead and injured. As a result, members of the Royal Family would usually arrive a few days after a disaster.

Before Mrs. Thatcher became Prime Minister, there had been no problem over such matters between the Palace and No. 10. Discussions would take place and a schedule coordinated, with the Queen always being granted her wish so that the royals would not be upstaged by a politician. Mrs. Thatcher put an end to that cozy relationship. She wanted the nation to see *her* caring side.

Despite Mrs. Thatcher's explanation that her instinct was to rush to the scene of a disaster to offer comfort and help, most people believed she did so primarily for political gain, and she was accused of using tragedies to further her own ends. Since she would rush off to any tragedy without consulting or advising the Palace, her behavior did not help the relationship between the Queen's advisers and Mrs. Thatcher's senior aides. She was roundly criticized for deliberately upstaging the royals, particularly the Queen, who knew only too well that her Prime Minister was happy to use every such occasion for her own advantage.

So angry did Elizabeth become with Mrs. Thatcher's behavior that she ordered her advisers to collate evidence of people's reaction when a member of the Royal Family did not turn up at the scene of a disaster. They reported that people felt neglected if a royal did not quickly appear. "If Mrs. Thatcher can arrive within hours, why can't a royal?" was the usual complaint.

Elizabeth discussed the problem with Mrs. Thatcher and gave her the evidence of the Palace research. The Prime Minister not only ignored it, at one stage she issued orders to her aides that they must never permit the Queen or any royal to arrive before she did at the scene of any disaster. Such behavior explains the occasional icy coolness that existed when the two women met each Tuesday evening.

Hugo Young, in *One of Us*, his fine biography of Mrs. Thatcher, states that when the cross-channel ferry, *The Herald of Free Enterprise*, sank off Zeebrugge, Belgium, in March 1987, with the loss of two hundred British lives, Mrs. Thatcher "firmly instructed her staff to see to it that the Palace presence, in the persons of the Duke and Duchess of York, did not upstage her own." Knowing how sensitive the Queen was on such occasions, the Prime Minister's actions indicate the depths to which their relationship must have sunk to treat Elizabeth with such disrespect.

Although some described the formal relationship between the two women as "frigid" or "cool," more in the Palace and government circles preferred the word "professional."

One senior Palace adviser commented, "Mrs. Thatcher was punctilious in all modes of address and courtesies." He continued, "Mrs. Thatcher of course acknowledged the Queen's right to be kept informed and to be consulted. On the Queen's side, she acknowledged, as she must, a Prime Minister's right finally to take the decisions. Her Majesty is very capable of offering her own opinions about things, when she holds them, and would certainly express them if they were contrary to those of her Prime Minister. However, once she had done that she would feel that she had exercised her constitutional rights and prerogatives, and it was the Prime Minister who had to take the decisions."

In reality, Mrs. Thatcher treated the Queen the same way she treated her husband Dennis. "Of course I consult Dennis," she said once. "Then I make the decision."

Another major area of conflict between the two matriarchs

concerned the Commonwealth, that great conglomerate of emerging nations, mostly from the Third World, many former members of the old British Empire, on which the British government once boasted "the sun never set." Elizabeth had always been passionate about the Commonwealth; her feelings for the organization, its peoples, and its nations, had been heightened in part because she was invited to become its leader. She had been voted into that position by the Commonwealth leaders and she had accepted it as a privilege and a duty.

At the end of World War II, some said Britain lost an empire without finding a role. Elizabeth was determined to do all she could to promote the Commonwealth of Nations into a force for good throughout the world. Elizabeth took the concept from a former Conservative minister, Rab Butler, the same man who had tutored Charles during his three years at Cambridge. Butler's vision was of "a Commonwealth of independent nations, emerging out of an Empire, purged from superiority of race and the false pride of dominion."

When Elizabeth succeeded to the throne in 1952 there was only a handful of Commonwealth nations, and many people felt that with the emergence of a European Common Market, the Commonwealth of Nations would wither and die. Far from it; today there are more than fifty members, and Elizabeth is still Head of the Commonwealth. Throughout her years on the throne Elizabeth has devoted much time to the Commonwealth, visiting each of its countries. She insists on attending every single Commonwealth Conference, held every two years, where she has private meetings with every head of state. On occasion, Elizabeth has acted as a diplomatic go-between, for many heads of Commonwealth countries remain in power for decades and they happily discuss their nation's problems with the Queen. They not only trust her but realize that she has no political axe to grind.

Mrs. Thatcher had little time for the Commonwealth. Sir Shridath Ramphal, former Commonwealth Secretary-General, once commented, "Mrs. Thatcher came to the Commonwealth not knowing, not caring, very much about it. Then she came to like the style of the heads of government meetings, but grew more and more irritable with the critics of her South Africa policy. Mrs. Thatcher argued that imposing sanctions against South Africa only hurt the black majority. She had a schizophrenic attitude where the Commonwealth was concerned, and I must say I never felt that there was a wholly relaxed attitude between herself and the Queen. No warmth on either side."

Throughout the 1980s Elizabeth became less and less impressed with the Prime Minister as well as her attitude and policies regarding the unemployed and the underprivileged. Mrs. Thatcher's great battle was fought against the National Union of Mineworkers, who feared their jobs were at risk under a Thatcher government. As the strike ran into weeks and months, and miners' families found life extremely difficult, Elizabeth repeatedly raised the question of miners' wives and their families with Mrs. Thatcher during their weekly meetings. As a result the atmosphere became more frosty as the Queen asked pointed questions which Mrs. Thatcher found irritating.

The Prime Minister's second general election victory gave her a fresh mandate and further confidence to continue her "Thatcherite" policies. Elizabeth could only note that she had the continued confidence of the electorate and, as a result, their weekly chats became less confrontational and more amenable. The two women seemed to come to an understanding: they had to work together so they developed as congenial a partnership as possible.

The whiff of confrontation between the two women continued to emerge from the Palace and No. 10, and the media sniffed a good story. The problems between the two women exploded into the open in 1986 when an article in *The Sunday Times*, entitled "The African Queen," suggested the Queen was disturbed at what she sensed was a lack of compassion in some of Mrs. Thatcher's policies toward the underprivileged in Britain and her attitude toward sanctions on South Africa. During Mrs. Thatcher's eleven-year premiership, the poorest among the electorate became financially worse off. Elizabeth also believed that trade sanctions against South Africa should not be lifted. At the time, these were two of the most divisive domestic and foreign issues facing Parliament.

The Palace was horrified. Never had any suggestion been made at any time during her reign that the Queen wanted to interfere with government policies, whether Labour or Tory. Senior courtiers were most concerned because, constitutionally, the British monarch is not permitted to become involved or even utter an opinion in public on domestic or foreign politics. If the monarch were to intervene, it is possible the great mass of the people might prefer the policies of the monarch to those of the elected government, and that could lead to political turmoil and all sorts of constitutional problems.

The Sunday Times report was accurate, however. Elizabeth has always held the vision of "One World," working toward the unification of black and white nations. She believed fervently that South Africa should be punished for its apartheid policies, its suppression of free thought, and imprisonment of government critics.

The crisis over South Africa threatened to break up Elizabeth's beloved Commonwealth and, as its head, she was determined to use her influence to prevent that. By doing so she set herself against Mrs. Thatcher. She let the Commonwealth Secretary-General know that if there was anything she could do to save the situation, she would happily use her influence. The row over sanctions ended with sixteen Commonwealth nations boycotting the Commonwealth Games of 1986, but the Commonwealth itself remained intact.

No other matter of policy throughout Mrs. Thatcher's eleven years in office proved so divisive for her relationship with Elizabeth. For a time during 1986, unspoken hostility between the two women made their weekly meetings extremely difficult.

There were other differences. One involved the Church of England, which the monarch heads. Margaret Thatcher, a devout churchgoer, had numerous run-ins with the Palace of Lambeth, the Church's London headquarters. She demanded a greater say in the appointment of bishops but they, understandably, did not want Mrs. Thatcher poking her nose into affairs of which she knew little and had no experience.

As Prime Minister, however, Mrs. Thatcher had the right to "advise" the Queen on her choice of senior bishops. A commission, as customary, produced two names for the Prime Minister, who selected one and sent it to the Queen for approval. Elizabeth had no choice; she was obliged to sign the recommendation.

Toward the end of her premiership, the time came to appoint a new Archbishop of Canterbury, the highest office in the Church. Two names were put forward: Dr. John Habgood, the Archbishop of York and the favored choice, and Dr. George Carey, Bishop of Bath and Wells, a 25-to-1 outsider and the Prime Minister's choice. Again, Elizabeth had to honor Mrs. Thatcher's recommendation, but she was not at all happy.

George Carey was the personification of Thatcher's self-made man; the son of a Cockney hospital porter, he had left school at fifteen and worked his way to the top of an intensely political clerical establishment. Today, three years after his appointment, critics within the Church now openly attack his leadership, under which the Church has lurched from one crisis to another. His promised decade of evangelism has degenerated into a series of crises and a vacuum of leadership, with the very legitimacy of the Anglican communion as the established Church of the land now in question. Thatcher must have known that Elizabeth would have much preferred Dr. Habgood, a highly intelligent man, a leading liberal, and a friend of Elizabeth's.

Cynics muttered that the decision to go for a relatively inexperienced figure was Margaret Thatcher's final revenge on the Church which, under Lord Runcie, had frequently challenged her policies.

Margaret Thatcher was the first woman Prime Minister of Britain and the first Elizabeth had to deal with. It was perhaps natural there should be some settling-in difficulties, but those who suggest that the two women got on quite well for most of the eleven years are incorrect. Their meetings frequently proved difficult. If Elizabeth asked any questions, Mrs. Thatcher frequently took them as a criticism of her and her government, which riled her, particularly as her confidence grew and her authority became greater.

Mrs. Thatcher was never happy with her relationship with Buckingham Palace. In an angry aside, she once commented, after a row with senior Palace aides, "Politics is meant to be a dirty game, but we politicians could never teach those at the palace anything."

Elizabeth knew from past experience that one day Mrs. Thatcher would go the way of all Prime Ministers—removed from office. But no one had any idea that the departure of Margaret Thatcher, in November 1990, would be so dramatic. She was still Prime Minister with a large majority in the House of Commons and, so she believed, in absolute control of her party and her Cabinet. But the Tories knew from their grassroots supporters that Mrs. Thatcher was becoming a liability and that under her the Tories were likely to lose the next general election. Tory leaders gathered and plotted her downfall, and Mrs. Thatcher realized too late that her support inside the party had vanished. She quit six weeks after she had stood, queenlike, at the Conservative Party Conference. And the strong woman premier who had appeared so tough and invulnerable for so long left No. 10 in the back seat of her official Jaguar, with tears streaming down her face.

In her memoirs, *The Downing Street Years*, published in October 1993, Mrs. Thatcher barely mentions the Queen in her nine-hundred-page tome. Only in chapter 1 does Mrs. Thatcher write of her relationship with Elizabeth: "The Audience at which one receives the Queen's authority to form a government comes to most prime ministers only once in a lifetime. The authority is unbroken when a sitting prime minister wins an election, and so it never had to be renewed throughout the years I was in office.

"All audiences with the Queen take place in strict confidence—a confidentiality which is vital to the working of both government and constitution. I was to have such audiences with Her Majesty once a week, usually on a Tuesday, when she was in London and sometimes elsewhere when the royal family were at Windsor or Balmoral."

Mrs. Thatcher gave a brief insight into those meetings. She wrote, "Perhaps it is permissible to make just two points. Anyone who imagines that they are a mere formality or confined to social niceties is quite wrong; they are quietly businesslike and Her Majesty brings to bear a formidable grasp of current issues and breadth of experience. And although the press could not resist the temptation to suggest disputes between the Palace and Downing Street, especially on Commonwealth affairs, I always found the Queen's attitude towards the work of government absolutely correct."

Mrs. Thatcher ended her three paragraphs about her relationship with Elizabeth, commenting, "Of course, under the circumstances, stories of clashes between 'two powerful women' were just too good not to make up. In general, more nonsense was written about the so-called 'feminine factor' during my time in office than about almost anything else. I was always asked how it felt to be a woman prime minister. I would reply: 'I don't know: I've never experienced the alternative.'"

All other references to the Queen in Mrs. Thatcher's memoirs are only mentions of her being in attendance.

Throughout her forty-year reign Elizabeth has found friendship, even affection, with several of her former Prime Ministers, who now number eight men and one woman. Framed photographs up the stairway at No. 10 start with Winston Churchill and continue through Anthony Eden, Harold Macmillan, Alec Douglas-Home, Harold Wilson, Edward Heath, James Callaghan, Margaret Thatcher, and John Major.

James Callaghan (1976–79), with whom Elizabeth got on remarkably well, commented after leaving office about his relationship with her. He said, "What one gets is friendliness but not friendship. Indeed, one gets a great deal of friendliness. And Prime Ministers also get a great deal of understanding of their problems—without the Queen sharing them, since she is outside politics.... Of course she may have hinted at things, but only on the rarest occasions do I remember her saying, 'Why don't you do this, that or the other?'. . . She is pretty detached on all that. But she's very interested in the political side—who's going up the ladder and who's going down."

Lord Charteris, who was Elizabeth's first Private Secretary and saw six Prime Ministers come and go, commented, "The universal response is one of admiration, respect, and a warm regard for the Queen. They all come out of the audience on the balls of their feet, having gone in on their heels. She obviously has the same tonic effect on them as she does on others."

The two Labour leaders, Harold Wilson and James Callaghan, were evidently Elizabeth's favorite premiers; she found them more friendly that some of the Tories, particularly Edward Heath, whom she found "very hard work."

Her relationship with Churchill was difficult because she had relied so much on him when she became Queen in 1952. Churchill was almost certainly the greatest Englishman of the century: statesman, politician, writer, and painter. He had led his country to victory in a war it had come close to losing. In 1953 he was venerated almost like a god. He had not only been Elizabeth's hero but her father's as well, and, most importantly for Elizabeth, the man who had put such faith and power in the hands of Lord Mountbatten. It was difficult for Churchill, too. In their own ways both were nervous of the other but for very different reasons.

Elizabeth used to worry that anything she said to Churchill might sound stupid; he was nervous, as many old men are at the prospect of having to chat with a pretty young woman who understandably made him feel positively ancient. The old man, who was eighty when Elizabeth became Queen, told his secretary Jock Colville at the time,

"How can I adapt to her after serving her father for seven years? I don't know her. She's a mere child. I knew the King so well and had a deep affection for him." And that was the trouble. Churchill, who was then becoming senile, did treat Elizabeth like a child, explaining everything to her in such a way that their audiences became tiresome, and Elizabeth prayed that their Tuesday meetings would end quickly, even though she knew she had so much to learn. It was during these years that she began to cling tenaciously to her Uncle Dickie for advice, a relationship which continued until his murder in 1979.

Fortunately, the nervousness on both sides disappeared, and when Churchill finally left office in April 1955, a special relationship had developed between the old man and the young Queen. Elizabeth has always said there was a special feeling for Winston Churchill that she never had with any other Prime Minister. When someone asked her, "Which of your prime ministers, Ma'am, did you enjoy your audiences with most?" she replied immediately, "Winston of course, because it was always such fun." She has never changed that view.

According to Churchill the "fun" he had with Elizabeth consisted mainly of racing talk. It was true that his Tuesday audiences got longer and longer, sometimes lasting nearly two hours instead of the usual thirty minutes. After most meetings with the Queen, Churchill told his private secretary rather mischievously, "Nothing to report, we talked about racing."

Elizabeth's three years with Churchill helped the young sovereign gain confidence and experience in her new role that stood her in good stead in the years to come. When Elizabeth became more confident she took the advice of Lord Charteris and Dickie Mountbatten and began to show her mettle, deliberately putting the Prime Minister of the day under pressure. She would read her state papers with great care and then ask relevant questions, often concerning obscure matters, which sometimes caught out the Prime Minister, making him feel unprepared, a most serious matter. It was a wonderful way of making Prime Ministers realize that she not only read the state papers, but also understood them. It also ensured that no Prime Minister ever treated her as someone who did not know precisely what was going on and gained their lasting respect. It was a neat trick which Elizabeth has often used since, sometimes to the annoyance and embarrassment of certain premiers.

As Harold Wilson confessed some time after he left office, "Whenever the Queen quoted from a state paper that I hadn't read, I felt rather like an unprepared schoolboy."

Elizabeth had to be on her mettle with all her Prime Ministers. Following in the footsteps of Churchill came Anthony Eden (1955–57), who had been deputy to the grand old man for some years. He was broken by the failure of the ill-judged Suez campaign, when the United States threatened to intervene if Britain and France sent forces to depose the new Egyptian leader, Gamal Abdel Nasser, in 1956. Apparently she found Eden tense, a little twitchy, and awkward to talk to.

Elizabeth got on well with Harold Macmillan (1957–63), an astute man who handled the young Queen with gentleness and consideration. She had faith in his ability and experience, and she regarded him as "one of us," with his background of Eton and the Guards, and his pretense of being an amateur when it came to politics. In fact he was professional to his fingertips, but he never let on.

The Scottish aristocrat, Sir Alec Douglas-Home (1963–64), who renounced his title in order to enter the House of Commons and take over as Prime Minister, seemed "at home" with the Queen and her Scottish family. They shared a love of Scotland and the wild country north of the border. But he was not around long enough to build a real relationship with Elizabeth.

Harold Wilson (1964–70 and 1974–76) began his relationship with Elizabeth rather warily but ended up adoring her. As Richard Crossman, who served in Wilson's cabinet, related in his diaries, "The nearer the Queen they get the more the working-class members of the Cabinet love her and she loves them."

As Prime Minister John Major arrived at Buckingham Palace in November 1990 to accept the office of Prime Minister, a senior member of the Royal Household recalled, "Her Majesty seemed very happy to welcome him. She was smiling broadly."

VII

THE THREE WITCHES
OF WINDSOR

A chauffeur-driven limousine, an armed detective at the wheel, arrives at the front door of a London house in a wealthy residential area of the city. A young lady, immaculately and expensively dressed, sits discreetly in the backseat, head slightly bowed, trying to look invisible. The chauffeur jumps smartly out of the car, opens the rear door, and the young lady slides decoratively out and hurries across the sidewalk to the house. As she climbs the steps, the door opens and she disappears inside. Outside, the chauffeur returns to his car to wait patiently.

After an hour or two the young woman, still immaculately dressed, reappears. She does not look back as she hurries to the car and slides into the back seat. Within seconds the car speeds away without the woman glancing or waving toward the house.

For most of the past hour the young woman, a married lady of the Royal House of Windsor, was making love to a man who was not her husband.

This has been the secret life of three members of Britain's Royal Family in the 1980s and 1990s. The three young women leading adulterous lives were commoners who had married into Britain's Royal Family.

The first young woman, one of the most famous faces in the world, was Diana, Princess of Wales, married to Prince Charles, heir to the throne; the second, Sarah, Duchess of York, married to Prince Andrew, third in line of succession; and the third, Princess Michael, wedded to Prince Michael of Kent, the Queen's first cousin. All three took several lovers during those years and indulged their passions in what they mistakenly believed were safe houses around London.

The houses of course were not safe. The identities, backgrounds, jobs, personal lives—even the sexual preferences—of each and every man they took to bed was known not only to Britain's security services, but also to Sir Robert Fellowes, the Queen's Principal Private Secretary, and to the Royal Protection Squad. More important, Elizabeth was fully informed about the adultery of all three women. She knew the names and backgrounds of their lovers.

Among senior officials at Buckingham Palace, the three women became known as the Three Witches of Windsor.

FIFTEEN

PRINCESS MICHAEL OF KENT

Princess Michael was the first to stray. Born Baroness Marie-Christine von Reibnitz in Czechoslovakia, in January 1945, she was the daughter of Baron von Reibnitz, an SS officer during World War II. Marie-Christine's mother and father separated after the war; Marie-Christine, her mother, and her brother emigrated to Australia in 1949, and her father went to live in Africa.

In Australia her mother remarried, this time to a Czechoslovakian count, but there was no money in the family. They all lived in a charmless little house on the outskirts of Sydney. By the age of eighteen Marie-Christine decided she wanted to be rich. She was tall, with a good strong figure, dark hair, a strikingly beautiful face, and a charming, bubbly personality. She soon became part of the elite set of rich young men and women.

She needed money for clothes, jewelry, and expensive accessories, and she found herself a job as a secretary at J. Walter Thompson, the advertising agency. She was popular with her fellow workers, particularly the young men, but they weren't wealthy enough or socially important enough for her.

She decided that with her background and title she could make more money as a dressmaker to the rich and famous, so she quit J. Walter Thompson to set up her own business. At age twenty, she met Ted Albert, the son of a wealthy Australian family of high social standing which had made its fortune by selling sheet music. Ted Albert's father, Alexis, had known Prince Philip during the war, and he was also an honorary aide-de-camp to Sir John Northcott, then governor of the State of New South Wales. Ted Albert was exactly the kind of young man Marie-Christine wanted for a husband.

Despite Marie-Christine's titles, however, and Ted Albert's passion for her, his mother dismissed Marie-Christine as a wartime immigrant, a new-Australian, unworthy of her son. Mrs. Albert threatened to cut off her son's inheritance if he continued the relationship. Angry and humiliated, and recognizing that she would never marry young Ted, Marie-Christine quit Sydney and took a boat to London.

In Australia Marie-Christine had discovered a useful gimmick to make sure she was always noticed. Before going to the races or attending a charity bash, she would telephone society editors of the Sydney newspapers and inform them that Baroness Marie-Christine von Reibnitz would be present, wearing whatever and partnered by So-and-so. As a result she appeared regularly in the social columns. In Britain she was determined to make a good marriage and decided to use the same technique to promote her ambitions, but it didn't work as well as in Australia. Like many other young starlets with obscure European titles in London at that time, she discovered she was only one among many.

To make herself more socially acceptable, Marie-Christine took drastic action. She dropped her Australian twang and adopted a more sophisticated mid-European accent; changed from brunette to blonde; and studied design at the Victoria and Albert Museum. But she needed to work to survive, and so she joined Charles Baker, another upmarket advertising agency. She was twenty-two and caught the eye of a number of wealthy, attractive men. She began to date in earnest, living life in the fast lane.

While flying to Austria for a wild boar hunt, Marie-Christine met her first husband, Tom Trowbridge, a handsome banker. They both spoke German and Marie-Christine actually fell instantly in love. They were married just one year later. It was at her wedding that Marie-Christine met her first member of the Royal Family, the bachelor Prince William of Gloucester, then twenty-nine, and an old friend of Tom Trowbridge. Captivated by his friend's wife he became a regular visitor to their London Chelsea home.

One day, Prince William invited them for a weekend house party at his family home, Barnwell Manor, in Northamptonshire. Another guest was Prince Michael of Kent, then twenty-eight and also a bachelor. A woman guest later recalled, "By the end of that weekend, Marie-Christine had both Princes eating out of her hand; she flirted outrageously with them and they did with her. She adored it."

Back in London, the Trowbridges and the two Princes became a regular foursome, with Marie-Christine the only female. They attended parties together, went to dinners, social events, and weekend house parties. Marie-Christine was in her element, and those also present noted that she spent most of the time flirting with Prince William. A year later tragedy struck: Prince William died in an air crash while piloting a light aircraft in the Goodyear Air Race.

Tom Trowbridge took a job in Bahrain and Marie-Christine joined him there for a while, but Bahrain society wasn't big enough for her; she wanted to be back in London, enjoying high society life, getting to know the Royal Family, and, more important, being near the handsome Prince Michael.

Prince Michael was a charming bachelor who had spent most of his adult years away from the royal limelight in one of Britain's senior regiments, the Royal Scots Greys (named after the color of their horses). There he enjoyed such a quiet life that no one realized he was the Queen's first cousin (he is also Princess Alexandra's younger brother). Not being the firstborn son, he wasn't required to carry out any official royal duties and he didn't want to either. He much preferred the seclusion of the officers mess, where he was extremely popular. Bob-sleigh racing, for which he showed great talent and considerable courage, became his great hobby. He was somewhat shy around women, and although he was often seen with different attractive young ladies on his arm, he rarely became romantically involved with them. Marie-Christine would change all that.

For the next three years Tom Trowbridge worked in Bahrain, while in London Marie-Christine spent as much time as possible mixing in circles where she would constantly meet Prince Michael. And whenever she met him she would take the initiative, inviting him to various events, organizing parties for them to attend together, and making it clear she wanted him.

According to Marie-Christine, their relationship began quietly, introspectively: "For a long time Michael and I cried on each other's shoulders. For a year I saw him simply as a friend. Then, by 1975 I knew I was in love with him. Now I'm glad we had that time, because friendship is something you never lose—and when you are in a rocking chair, friendship is what counts."

It became known that Michael and Marie-Christine were lovers. Whenever they were out together, at parties and dinners, Marie-Christine would spend the whole time on his arm, holding his hand, nuzzling his neck. Occasionally he would seem rather embarrassed by her attentions, but he liked the fact that Marie-Christine was a striking, sexy young woman.

Marie-Christine and Tom Trowbridge were divorced in 1977, and Tom Trowbridge's family and friends gave a great party for him to celebrate his freedom from her.

I came to know Marie-Christine around that time, for she stabled her Arab horse at the same stables at Ham, near Richmond Park, where I kept my polo ponies. She rode out most days and was to say later, "As luck and Cupid would have it, my beautiful dancing Arab steed fell madly in love with this rather churlish animal, ridden by Prince Michael, and from miles away would whinny and gallop up to him. Then it was 'Oh, hello, what a surprise. How nice to see you.'" Marie-Christine made it all sound like some ten-cent novelette.

Prince Michael seemed as keen as Marie-Christine to marry. He loved showing off Marie-Christine, proud that such a good-looking young woman should find him such an attractive man. Prince Michael asked Marie-Christine to marry him and she was overjoyed with his offer.

There were two problems: Marie-Christine was Catholic, and she was divorced. Under the Royal Marriages Act of 1772, Prince Michael needed the Queen's permission, which, since he was over twenty-five, should have provided no obstacle. Elizabeth disliked the idea that Prince Michael wanted to marry Marie-Christine, primarily because she was a divorcée. She asked Sir Philip Moore, then her Private Secretary, to organize a detailed briefing on her life, which included her rather dubious ancestry and details of her earlier years in Australia, and she was not impressed with what she read in the briefing some weeks later. The Palace was also inadvertently helped by the press, which had investigated Marie-Christine when it became public knowledge that she and Prince Michael seemed about to become engaged.

Elizabeth still believed that divorce was not only a taboo at court, but she was deeply disturbed that a member of the Royal Family, particularly someone as close as her first cousin (although only sixteenth in line to succession) could even countenance marrying a divorced person. She believed the Royal Family had to set an example, and marriage to Marie-Christine would set a very poor example indeed.

In early 1978 senior courtiers advised Prince Michael that he might find a more suitable bride, primarily because of the Queen's attitude to divorce and the effect it might have on the Royal Family. After all, it was only forty years earlier that Britain's King had been stripped of his crown and exiled for the remainder of his days because he wanted to marry a divorcée. Worse still from the Queen's view, as Head of the Church of England and Defender of the Faith, this divorcée was a Roman Catholic as well.

To circumvent the growing opposition to the marriage, Marie-Christine came up with a new strategy: she would have her marriage to Tom Trowbridge annulled.

She immediately approached the Catholic Church and argued that Tom Trowbridge had never wanted children, which she claimed was sufficient reason for annulment. In all cases of annulment, the Catholic Church requires the spouse to give supporting evidence. Tom Trowbridge was extremely surprised by his ex-wife's allegation, and even more surprised when he was not invited to give evidence to the Vatican. Astonishingly enough, in 1978 the Vatican granted an annulment to the marriage, and Marie-Christine, then thirty-three, immediately reverted to her maiden name, Baroness von Reibnitz. She was now free to marry whomever she wanted.

Elizabeth discussed the whole matter with Princess Margaret, then forty-eight, one reason being that twenty-five years earlier Margaret had been forbidden to marry the divorced Group Captain Peter Townsend. Margaret was appalled by the idea that Marie-Christine should marry Prince Michael, primarily because she believed, from all the gossip, that Marie-Christine was an opportunist whose only reason for marrying Michael was to reach the ultimate social rung, becoming a member of the House of Windsor. She questioned Marie-Christine's love for Michael; hadn't she first fallen for Prince William and only changed tack on his untimely death?

Princess Margaret argued against Elizabeth's giving her permission for yet another reason. Marie-Christine had happily married Tom Trowbridge in a Church of England ceremony, yet had claimed a burst of Catholic religious fervor when she needed an annulment. The Princess scented fundamental hypocrisy. She described Marie-Christine as "an upstart."

Margaret told a close friend at the time, "I know what that woman is playing at, and she is twisting poor Michael round her little finger. I have seen her with him and it is all but obscene the way she behaves towards him."

Princess Margaret wrote to Marie-Christine before her marriage to Prince Michael, informing her that if she did not "do the decent thing" and convert to Anglicanism—the Church of England is the established church of the House of Windsor and of which the Queen is head—she would never speak to her again. Marie-Christine did not convert, and the enmity between the two women has continued to this day.

In desperation, Prince Michael turned to Uncle Dickie Mountbatten—Mountbatten was also *his* uncle—and appealed for help. Michael said he was in love with Marie-Christine and wanted to marry her, but he did not want to upset or anger the Queen, nor did he want to do anything that might bring the Royal Family into disrepute.

Mountbatten asked him outright, "What do you think would do more harm to the Royal Family, for you two to live in sin together or get married?" Michael shrugged his shoulders and replied with little conviction, "Live in sin."

"Right," Mountbatten replied. "Then if you are determined to live with this young woman we had better find a way for you to marry her. After all, she is not a shop girl. She comes from a good family. She's a natural." Mountbatten himself came from a high-ranking German noble family.

He invited Prince Michael and Marie-Christine to dinner and was rather taken by the flamboyant, attractive young woman. He did, however, see another side to her. During the meal, he slipped a note to John Barratt that read, "If that woman doesn't stop talking, I shall scream."

Once more Mountbatten was in his element. Pitched into the center of a family fracas, he found himself with the opportunity to manipulate royal events yet again. After much lobbying from Mountbatten and direct pleas from Prince Michael, Elizabeth finally gave permission for the marriage to go ahead, but only if Michael renounced his claim to the throne while married to a Catholic. If Marie-Christine died or they divorced, Michael would be entitled to ask to have his claim re-established, but it would not necessarily be granted. He was only too happy to do so.

Marie-Christine was now determined to have a full-blown white wedding in Westminster Cathedral, the principal Roman Catholic church in England, as though she had never been married before. In this she was to be thwarted. As a member of the Royal Family, Michael was not permitted to be married in a Catholic church or a register office, so the marriage would have to take place abroad.

As the daughter of an Austrian nobleman, and having reverted to her Austrian maiden name, Marie-Christine decided to get married in Vienna. She booked the world-famous Vienna Boys Choir, arranged for the ceremony to take place in the Schottenkirche, a church in the aristocratic quarter of Vienna, and spent days agonizing over the guest list.

Then the Vatican stepped in and forbade a church wedding because Marie-Christine had agreed to raise any children of the marriage in the Church of England. She flew into a fury, storming up and down her drawing room and swearing vehemently.

In the end a chastened Marie-Christine married her royal Prince in the Vienna Town Hall.

On her wedding day, a beaming Marie-Christine, resplendent in the Kent jewels, walked toward the Town Hall where, waiting to greet her, were Mountbatten, Princess Anne, Prince Charles, and some other members of the family. In a bitchy swipe at the arrogant Marie-Christine, Anne queried with a smile, "'Do we curtsy to the new Queen of Czechoslovakia, or is it a Republic now?'"

Marie-Christine would, however, win in the end. After five years of constant badgering by Princess Michael, Pope John Paul II announced his recognition of the marriage in July 1983, which permitted Michael and Marie-Christine to renew their vows in church. The Vatican had changed its mind because Prince Michael had permitted the children of the marriage to be brought up as Catholics.

Once she had actually married into royalty, stories about Marie-Christine's arrogance became legion. On one occasion, two girls were standing atop ladders fixing curtains, but she ordered them to descend after she entered the room so they could curtsy to her. She insisted that all her staff bow and curtsy to her whenever she passed them in the house or walked into a room; she insisted that everyone, even many old friends, call her Your Royal Highness whenever they met.

One day, Queen Elizabeth commented, "Marie-Christine sounds far too grand for us."

Marie-Christine pushed Michael to become more "royal" as well. Before his marriage, Prince Michael was a delightfully quiet, amiable sort of fellow who went about his everyday business in the Scots Greys and kept very much to himself. Now the irrepressible Marie-Christine first persuaded Michael to quit the army immediately, which he did; then she persuaded him to grow a beard in order to look more dashing and authoritative; then she set about organizing parties to which she would invite high-profile, well-connected names from London's financial district, people who might be interested, for a considerable sum of money, in having Prince Michael of Kent as one of their company directors, his name on their letterhead. This ploy worked to a small degree, mainly because Michael was thought of as a "most decent type."

Marie-Christine's ambitions knew no bounds. She wanted a country mansion, fit for a princess, and went in search of one. Because Princess Anne lived in Gloucestershire, she decided to reside there, too. She first checked out Highgrove, the Gloucestershire home Charles eventually bought before marrying Diana, but that wasn't large or grand enough. Finally, in 1979, she decided on Nether Lypiatt Manor, also in Gloucestershire, which unfortunately needed $150,000 to bring it up to her exacting standards.

The antagonism Charles felt toward Marie-Christine, which continues today, bubbled over when she announced her decision to buy Nether Lypiatt, just fifteen miles from Highgrove, which Charles had by then decided to purchase for himself. He first tried to prevent the sale of Nether Lypiatt, and then told his secretary, "Let that woman know that she will never be invited to Highgrove at any time or for any reason. Also let her know that I don't ever want to be invited to her place either. Nor do I want to speak to her." To this day Princess Michael has never been invited to Highgrove, nor has Charles ever visited Nether Lypiatt.

The only way Prince Michael could afford to grant his wife her wish was to sell all his private investments. By the early 1980s they had their wonderful country home, interior design by Princess Michael, but very little money.

To earn some money, Marie-Christine turned her talents to writing books, something she had never tried before. She decided that royal subjects could make bestsellers. Her first book, about European royal princesses, sold quite well, despite the fact that two writers accused her of plagiarism.

In another money-raising idea, Princess Michael decided she and Prince Michael should hire out themselves for functions, since they were not included on the Civil List. She argued that other royals indirectly earned money for attending royal occasions, so she didn't see why they shouldn't be paid directly; it amounted to the same thing. She believed that the Queen's first cousin, Prince Michael of Kent, and therefore his wife as well, should be on the Civil List because, she felt, they were popular with the general public and would be an asset compared to "some of the stuffier" royals. She argued that Princess Alexandra, her husband's elder sister, was on the Civil List, and therefore Prince Michael certainly should be, too.

For royals to hire themselves out like entertainers is anathema to the monarchy, but undeterred, Marie-Christine went ahead. She and Prince Michael charge from $1,000 and $10,000 per attendance at social events.

Still, their income proved insufficient to match their expenditures, for Princess Michael was determined to lead the life of a high-profile royal. At Nether Lypiatt she employed a staff of five for the manor, as well as four gardeners, a groom for her three horses, and a chauffeur for her Rolls-Royce. They also had to pay toward the upkeep of their London apartment in Kensington Palace.

Elizabeth, who learned about the couple's lifestyle and financial contrivances from her Private Secretary, made it plain she did not wish ror require Prince Michael to take on any royal duties, despite frequent appeals to do so from both Michael and Marie-Christine. This was the most insulting way to dismiss Princess Michael's appeal, for Elizabeth did not even bother to address herself to Marie-Christine, who was furious at being ignored.

Marie-Christine managed to annoy Elizabeth even in petty matters. Having been advised on one occasion to wear black to a funeral, Marie-Christine turned up in black but carried a black handbag with gold clasps. The following day Elizabeth sent a note: "I say black I mean black. Not a black handbag with gold clasps." Marie-Christine let fly a stream of abuse.

She became more recalcitrant. During a television interview she committed what many would describe as the "ultimate sin" in the eyes of the Royal Family, suggesting that the Queen's corgis "should be shot."

As Prince Michael's wife she had been invited to the Royal Family's traditional Christmas dinner at Windsor in 1986. She felt the rest of the family was ignoring her, so she stayed away from the dinner table, a serious insult to the Queen after accepting her invitation.

Hours later Marie-Christine received a typewritten memo from one of the Queen's senior staff. It read, "It is understood that in the future you will join the rest of the family for dinner." Infuriated by the note, Marie-Christine ordered her bags packed and left immediately for London.

Marie-Christine had gone too far. Elizabeth refused to speak to her for some years, either by phone or personally. If she needed to give the Princess any information she would write a note.

Determined to force the Queen's hand, Marie-Christine tried another tack. She would make herself so popular that, by public demand, the Queen would have to rethink whether she could afford not to involve the Kents in royal duties. Marie-Christine knew that if she and her husband carried out royal duties they would automatically be entitled to receive money from the Civil List, which covers all travel, a substantial clothes allowance, and contributes toward administrative costs for royals who carry out official duties.

Marie-Christine desperately wanted to be on the Civil List because to her that was the mark of being a truly royal, full-fledged member of the House of Windsor and that had always been her goal. Despite her considerable intelligence, she had grossly underestimated the Palace and Elizabeth.

She continued offering her services, and those of Prince Michael, to anyone who would accept them as royals, opening garden fetes, clubs, shows. If asked, they would travel anywhere. At first they carried out all these functions for no money, but their bank account soon dwindled to nothing, which led Princess Michael to comment rashly, "I would go anywhere for a free meal."

Her secretary was John Barratt, who had been a good servant and close confidant to Earl Mountbatten for twenty years, until Mountbatten's assassination in August 1979, after which he had been taken on by Prince Michael. Barratt organized their schedules, their charity work, and their growing number of public engagements.

He recalled some of Princess Michael's antics: "I remember on one occasion she opened a store for a well-known electrical firm and a few days later a van arrived at the house with ten TV sets which she had asked as a gift from the firm. They were for the servants' rooms. She was shameless."

She received gifts, including horses, cars, holidays, airline tickets, jewelry, perfume and cash, checks, and any items offered by whatever firm or person she met. But that wasn't enough for Marie-Christine. She was prepared to go to any lengths to obtain the money she needed to pursue the life she wanted. She began to date some of the world's wealthiest men, disappearing with them for nights, weekends, trips, and holidays, in return for which they would give her clothes, jewelry, and money.

As one loyal friend of the Royal Family put it, "I am afraid you cannot escape from the fact that Princess Michael was behaving more or less like a harlot."

She took numerous lovers, including a wealthy Arab prince who was heavily involved in arranging deals on behalf of the Saudi Royal family, Senator John Warner (of Liz Taylor fame), and Ward Hunt, cousin of the Texas billionaire Bunker Hunt. She had met Hunt in Texas in 1983 at a fund-raising dinner for the United States Friends of the English National Opera, and they became lovers a year later.

Ward Hunt, a wealthy, forty-four-year-old millionaire, had been divorced by his wife Laura in 1984. He lived in a luxurious Dallas apartment where Marie-Christine used to visit. On occasion he traveled to London. Once he visited with his mother and they stayed at Kensington Palace.

Marie-Christine would take extraordinary risks to be with Ward Hunt, who lavished gifts and money on her. On one occasion she and Prince Michael were visiting Dallas, staying at the Turtle Creek Hotel, when Marie-Christine told her secretary to arrange for Prince Michael to be flown to New York ahead of her because she wanted to see Ward Hunt. The two men in fact almost met in the lobby; Prince

Michael was escorted to his car while Ward Hunt sat in the lobby waiting for him to leave. That night Marie-Christine and Ward Hunt stayed in Dallas, and she joined her husband the following day.

Marie-Christine enjoyed her lover's company, and his presents even more so. She recklessly invited Ward Hunt to London for a week's holiday, but those closest to her decided her behavior was becoming too scandalous. Royal servants, at every level, know that the private and intimate lives of those they serve is none of their business and that on most occasions their duty is to look the other way. But Marie-Christine's behavior went beyond the bounds of recognized adultery. It wasn't that she had taken a lover; she was, more or less, prostituting herself and therefore risking scandal for her husband Prince Michael and the Crown.

Details of her numerous affairs had already been passed to Elizabeth, through the usual channels of private secretary to private secretary. Appalled, Elizabeth decided the time had come to put an end to Marie-Christine's activities.

Stuart Kuttner, an assistant editor with the Sunday scandal paper the *News of the World*, with excellent contacts in royal circles, takes up the story. "One day I was invited to lunch and as we walked by the Thames that afternoon I was asked whether we had noticed how often Princess Michael of Kent visited America. It was suggested to me that my paper should investigate the record of her trips.

"By the end of the conversation I had the name 'Ward Hunt' and the rest was left to us to investigate. I thought it would take time."

Within a matter of weeks the same royal contact phoned to say that Ward Hunt was arriving in London on June 24, 1985, and would stay at the Carlton Tower, a luxury hotel in Cadogan Square, near Harrods. Before Hunt arrived Kuttner received another call from his source, informing him that Hunt would now be staying at a private luxury apartment which belonged to the brother of Princess Esra of Hyderabad, a mutual friend of Hunt and Marie-Christine who lived in California.

Kuttner continued, "We were informed that Ward Hunt and Princess Michael would spend a couple of days at the apartment and then move to the country, to Rosie Northampton's country home in Gloucestershire. On the appointed day Princess Michael arrived at the apartment with groceries and an ill-fitting red wig. Later Ward Hunt

Prince Charles's mistress, Camilla Parker Bowles, with her husband, Andrew, attending a polo match at Windsor Great Park in 1992.

Prince Andrew, the Duke of York, with Sarah, Duchess of York and their younger daughter, Eugenie, in 1990, after her baptism.

Three photographs reprinted in the Italian magazine *Oggi* in 1992 show Sarah Ferguson after her separation from Prince Andrew. She is pictured with her lover Johnny Bryan on holiday in the south of France.

Elizabeth on horseback riding down the Mall for Trooping the Colour in 1985. A year later she would be shot at as she rode past the same spot.

Elizabeth with Prince Andrew and his wife, "Fergie," pictured with one of Elizabeth's favorite courtiers, Sir John Miller, at Windsor in 1987.

Princess Diana and Sarah, Duchess of York, sharing a joke at Royal Ascot in 1987, while Prince Charles stands by.

Elizabeth with Philip at the Royal Windsor Horse Show in 1988.

A rare picture showing Elizabeth together with Prime Minister Margaret Thatcher at Windsor in 1988.

Queen Elizabeth "pressing the flesh" royal style at the official opening of the Royal Mint in 1989.

Queen Elizabeth and Princess Diana at London's Victoria Station, in 1989, waiting for the arrival of a head of state.

Queen Elizabeth and Prince Philip at the Royal Gallery in 1989.

Queen Elizabeth and Prince Philip arriving at Royal Ascot in traditional style, riding in an open carriage, June 1989.

Queen Elizabeth with Prince Philip attending the state opening of Parliament in 1990.

Elizabeth attending the christening of her granddaughter Eugenie, younger daughter of Prince Andrew, Duke of York, and Sarah, Duchess of York, in 1990.

Queen Elizabeth and Prince Philip waiting at Windsor in 1990 for the arrival of a head of state.

Prince Charles with Princess Diana celebrating Queen Elizabeth's fortieth year on the throne in October 1992. One month later they would separate.

Elizabeth sharing a joke with the England polo team at Windsor in July 1993.

Happy family. Charles and Diana bicycling with their sons William and Harry in the Scilly Isles in 1989.

Charles and Diana at the Festival Hall, London, in 1983.

Prince and Princess Michael of Kent enjoying the tennis at Wimbledon in 1988.

The Prince and Princess of Wales on an official royal visit to Hungary in 1990.

Princess Margaret and her former husband, Lord Snowdon, at Ascot in 1966.

Princess Margaret with her lover Roddy Llewellyn on holiday in Mustique in 1989.

Princess Alexandra and her husband, Sir Angus Ogilvy, at a wedding in 1988.

arrived, and there they stayed together. All the time they were watched by *News of the World* reporters, and whenever they left the apartment, photographers hiding nearby caught them on film."

Having quit London to spend a few days together in the country, Princess Michael received a mystery phone call informing her that the *News of the World* had photographs and details of her liaison with Ward Hunt, and that the story would hit the headlines the next day. Distraught at being caught in flagrante delicto, Princess Michael arranged for a helicopter to fly Ward Hunt from the country house where they were staying to Manchester, 150 miles north, so that he could catch a plane to New York. Once he had left, Princess Michael announced she was suffering from exhaustion and went straight into hospital, where she remained until the fuss had died down.

A few days later, she was photographed with her husband Prince Michael at the Wimbledon tennis championships, holding his hand, leaning on his arm, and acting like an attentive, charming, smiling wife. Elizabeth, however, was not fooled, even if Prince Michael did accept whatever excuse was proffered by his money-grabbing wife.

When Elizabeth saw the photographs of Prince Michael and his wife together at Wimbledon, she was amazed at Marie-Christine's effrontery, for she had expected that the scandalous newspaper headlines would finish their marriage and that Marie-Christine would be sent packing, certainly out of the Royal House of Windsor, and perhaps out of the country. Phone tapping had revealed that Ward Hunt was in love with Marie-Christine and wanted to marry her. He believed she was fully prepared to leave Prince Michael, obtain a divorce, and make a new life for herself with him in Dallas.

Elizabeth's handling of this incident illustrates the lengths to which she, supported by her senior advisers, will go to uphold the dignity of the Crown and to remove someone likely to bring disgrace to the monarchy. Elizabeth never forgets that her principal task in life is to uphold and, if possible, strengthen the Crown. One way of upholding that dignity is to keep scandal at arm's length. Only a few years later, Elizabeth again showed her ruthlessness when she had to deal with the sexual adventures of the Duchess of York.

Princess Michael did not end her marriage and return to Dallas with the likable, wealthy Ward Hunt for three principal reasons: the first concerned her two royal children; the second was that she loved being a royal princess; and the third was that she had discovered his divorce settlement had been costly and Ward Hunt was not as wealthy as she had first thought.

Marie-Christine's first child, Lord Frederick Windsor, was born in April 1979, just nine months and five days after she was married to Michael, and her second, Lady Gabriella, arrived exactly two years later in April 1981. After her daughter was born, Princess Michael said, "April is the ideal time to have a baby. You can have the pram outside and the fresh air on that child for the whole spring, the whole summer and the whole autumn. That was why my second child was also born in April. I organised it like that so that both my children could have this benefit."

Princess Michael is known to believe in discipline for both her children, and they are both indisputably well behaved; it is also obvious from those who see her with her children that she cares for them. But it was not always so.

Frederick was a beautiful baby and child. Some described him as having "chocolate-box looks." Gabriella, however, did not meet her mother's exacting standards. She confessed to John Barratt, "I am really beginning to hate this child, she is so plump and unattractive. Why can't she be like Frederick, who is so beautiful?"

Princess Michael knew she would not be permitted to take her son and daughter to America if she left Prince Michael and set up home with Ward Hunt. Elizabeth would have issued instructions to Prince Michael that his children must be brought up and educated in Britain and not allowed to live with their mother.

With the evidence of Princess Michael's sexual adventures in hand, Elizabeth had planned to instruct Prince Michael to make them wards of court, if necessary, and so obtain care and custody of the children legally. All this was explained to Princess Michael through the private secretaries, and she was left in no doubt that if she divorced Michael and quit Britain, she would lose her children.

Elizabeth made sure never to see her or speak to her on any occasion. Princess Michael was cast into outer darkness to repent and atone for her sin of bringing the monarchy into disrepute by being discovered cheating on her husband.

Elizabeth banned Marie-Christine from attendance at any public functions where she would be present and vowed never to permit her to become part of the Civil List. Through Palace officials Elizabeth let it be known that she was most displeased with Princess Michael of Kent and that invitations sent to Princess Michael should not associate her in any way with the Royal Family.

Princess Michael vented her fury on her hapless husband, accusing him of being weak and pathetic, of not standing up to the Queen, and of not defending her own good name. Ever since their marriage Marie-Christine has talked to Michael as if he were a servant rather than her husband.

When she felt Prince Michael was not supporting her in her continuing battles with Buckingham Palace, she would sometimes shout at him, "Call yourself a man. You're no better than your father and he was a transvestite, homosexual drug-taker." His father, who had died in 1942, was George, Duke of Kent, the brother of King George VI, Elizabeth's father.

Princess Michael has been known to harangue her husband even in public, ordering him about, criticizing and making fun of him in front of guests, treating him without the slightest respect or affection. She frequently refers to Prince Michael as "an arsehole." So very, very different from those days before they married when she referred to him as "my beloved Michael."

To top it all, Marie-Christine has the most fearsome temper and will change in a second from a pleasant, smiling woman to what has been described as a "true virago": foul-mouthed, swearing at everyone until the moment of fury has passed and she calms down again. Prince Michael has been on the receiving end of much of her venom.

Despite her sexual adventures, which continue even today, it is Marie-Christine, now forty-nine, who threatens Prince Michael whenever they have an argument. Repeatedly she has told him that if he dares seek a separation or a divorce, she will make sure he never sees his children again. There is no need for this, however, because Prince Michael worships her and above all else, he dearly loves his children. His temperament and personality are such that he is not only prepared to put up with his wife's shenanigans, but is happy to do so.

Prince Michael is well aware of his wife's continuing illicit trysts. She has an ironclad rule which Prince Michael and both children obey. Every evening between six and seven, Marie-Christine retires to her bedroom and insists on not being disturbed, not even by her husband.

During what she calls her "hour of privacy," she makes and receives telephone calls on a private phone specially installed in her room. There she chats and makes her plans for lunches, dinners, parties, and weekends.

Since those torrid days and nights with Ward Hunt, Princess Michael has been somewhat less forward than in the first few years of her marriage, but she still flirts madly with various men and somehow makes ends meet financially. To this day, neither Princes or Princess Michael of Kent has ever received money from the Civil List, and they still charge handsome fees to attend functions and events and open exhibitions. Payments for their appearances are their only source of income, and Princess Michael still works hard at making herself as popular as possible, hoping to widen her net and attract more people, organizations, and companies willing to buy their presence.

After eight years in the wilderness, the Queen now permits Prince Michael to attend royal functions, occasionally. The effervescent Marie-Christine, however, is usually, but not always, excluded from royal gatherings, much to her chagrin.

SIXTEEN

DIANA, PRINCESS OF WALES

The second witch of Windsor perhaps least resembles a classical witch: the lovely, beautiful, megastar Lady Diana Spencer, who became the Princess of Wales in a splendid fairy-tale wedding which captured the hearts of nations when she married Prince Charles in July 1981.

The innocent, shy, sweet, gauche young woman of twenty would change dramatically within a few years into someone barely recognizable to those who knew her well and worked with her during her early twenties.

Diana had a rotten childhood. Born in July 1961, on an estate next to the Royal Family's country home at Sandringham in Norfolk—when Prince Charles was nearly thirteen years old—Diana was only six when her mother bolted the family home. It is ironic that Diana's love life and married life should so closely mirror that of her mother Frances.

Frances was sixteen when she met her husband-to-be, Johnny, then an officer in the Brigade of Guards, an equerry to the Queen, and a man-about-town. She fell hopelessly in love with him, obsessed with this good-looking, wealthy aristocrat in the same way that Diana, thirty years later, would fall in love and become obsessed with Prince Charles.

The similarity of their lives continued. Married at eighteen, Frances recalled an idyllic first few years, like Diana, before the rot set in. She became bored with her handsome husband, who had taken to the country life of a gentleman farmer and enjoyed his quiet existence in the backwoods of Norfolk. Surrounded by his children and happy with his beautiful, still young wife Frances, he seemed to love his life.

Frances had had five children: Sarah, born in 1955, with whom Prince Charles was to have a love affair lasting several months; Jane, their second daughter, born in 1957; the third, John, born in 1960, who lived only ten hours; then their third daughter, Diana, born in 1961; and finally a son and heir, Charles, born three years after Diana, in 1964.

After the birth of Charles, Frances began visiting London more frequently, visiting friends, attending parties, dinners, the theater. Then in 1966 she took an apartment in fashionable Cadogan Square.

Before many months Frances fell in love. Peter Shand Kydd was a married man, a wallpaper millionaire, a graduate of Edinburgh University, and a former Royal Naval officer, when he began an affair with the attractive Frances. He had taken his wife, a talented artist, and three young children to Australia, and bought a five-hundred-acre sheep farm. When that venture failed, he returned with his family to England, and met Frances.

In a sensationally frank statement to the press in 1967, Frances announced, "I am living apart from my husband now. It is very unfortunate. I don't know if there will be a reconciliation."

To her husband Johnny, at their farm in Norfolk, the statement came as a thunderbolt. He later said, "How many of those fourteen years were happy? I thought all of them, until the moment we parted. I was wrong. We hadn't fallen apart. We'd drifted apart."

Diana was just six, her brother Charles only three at the time. After her parents divorced the young Diana told one of her nannies, "When I marry it will be forever. I will never, never get divorced." Twenty-five years later, when Diana forced Queen Elizabeth and the British Prime Minister to agree to a formal separation from Prince Charles, her sons were a little older: William was ten, Harry just six.

Her parents' divorce had a devastating effect on Diana. She changed from a happy, smiling, sociable little girl full of confidence to a rather unhappy, often miserable child who lost much of her confidence and became obstinate and shy.

Diana now attributes much of that to the trauma her mother's abandoning the family home and the bitter divorce action in which Frances lost custody of her four children. Diana and her siblings spent the greater part of their young lives with their father in Norfolk, away from her mother, except for occasional visits to the home Frances set up when she married Peter Shand Kydd in 1969.

Diana's childhood experience of loneliness and misery is the principal reason she will never relinquish care and custody of Wills and Harry. Everyone who has seen Diana with her two sons agree that a strong bond exists between her and the two boys, and thus far she has proved a loving mother to the two Princes.

Like her mother Diana yearned for the bright lights and the good times. Like her mother she was fed up with her married life and her dull, boring husband. Johnny Spencer enjoyed the peace and quiet of the country and loved farming; Charles loves life in the country, tending his private walled garden and taking long walks. Both Frances and Diana preferred a much more social life, partying, meeting people, dancing, and gossiping over long lunches. In the same way that Frances could not bear an isolated life in Norfolk, nor the restrictions, discipline, and commitment of marriage to Johnny Spencer, so Diana could not stand living in Kensington Palace, nor the restrictions, discipline, and commitment of marriage to Prince Charles.

In her divorce action Frances accused Johnny Spencer of mental cruelty and more, and Princess Diana similarly has complained to friends of the mental cruelty she has endured while married to Charles. Diana has also accused Charles of turning his back on her, spurning her love, and leaving the marital home to live with his lover Camilla Parker Bowles at his country home, Highgrove in Gloucestershire.

A further extraordinary coincidence is that both Frances and Diana separated dramatically from their husbands at exactly the same age, when they had just turned thirty.

In her desire to escape from her boring, restrictive life, Diana's view of her husband changed completely, from obsession with her "wonderful prince" who could do no wrong to regarding him as a rather strange, commonplace man with opinions, hobbies, and interests completely different from hers.

Education became one of the major problems that divided Charles and Diana. Prince Charles had attended a good preparatory school and a stringent but good public school, Gordonstoun, where he left with six "O" (Ordinary) levels and two "A" (Advanced) level exams. He spent three years at Cambridge and graduated with a B.A. honors degree in Class II, division II (called a 2.2 in university parlance), a rather ordinary degree. His tutors, however, were convinced that if he had not been subjected to royal disruptions (for example taking a three-month break to learn Welsh at Aberystwyth University), he would have earned a much higher degree, possibly first-class honors.

By contrast, Diana's education was abysmal, her achievements nil. She took six "O" level exams and flunked them all, retook four "O" level subjects and failed those too. Indeed, she has the remarkable but unenviable achievement of having attended good schools from the ages of six to seventeen and gaining not a single exam pass in any subject. That fact embarrassed her greatly. She not only tried to hide her failure, but frequently lied, telling friends and others that she did have a few "O" level passes. Since the world discovered the truth some years ago, Diana has sensibly changed tack, frequently joking about her lack of brainpower.

But the jokes were a cover for embarrassment. In their early days together Charles would tease Diana about her education and the fact she had never passed an exam and, jokingly, tell her she had little intelligence. Diana laughed at his comments and Charles would comfort her by telling her it didn't matter that she had no exam passes because he loved her anyway.

When problems began to emerge in the marriage Diana took exception to the frequent teasing, not only from Charles but also other members of the Royal Family—Prince Philip, Andrew, and Edward. It made her more shy and embarrassed and she would sometimes end up in tears.

She was teased mercilessly when she began making public speeches. Shy and embarrassed ever to speak in public, it took her four years to summon up the courage to make her first speech. Her delivery was poor, her voice strained, and it seemed as if she had received no instruction whatsoever. She blushed as she spoke, had difficulty completing sentences, and fluffed her lines even though she read the two-minute speech from a piece of paper she was holding. Charles and Andrew wouldn't stop mimicking her strained, rather squeaky voice and hesitant delivery. She would look at them and laugh, but deep down she was hurt and humiliated.

As she told Sarah Ferguson, then her close buddy, "It just makes me want to curl up and die. I hate making speeches because I know what they will all say afterwards. Even the Queen looks at me oddly after I've made a speech and she unnerves me."

Diana was an anomaly, not only for the Royal Family, but for the British public. On the one hand she appeared to be semiregal and had more English blood than Prince Charles himself; strictly speaking, most of Charles's blood is either German or Danish. Despite the fact she worked as a nursery teacher, she was called by press and public Lady Di from the very beginning, never simply Diana. (Incidentally, she hated being called Lady Di, and no one addressed her that way within the walls of Buckingham Palace.)

When she appeared on the royal scene in 1979, she was very different from most of the girls the world had seen with Charles. She seemed like an ordinary young woman with no pretensions, shy and reserved. She had none of the brash sophistication of the typical Sloane Ranger, those upper-crust young women who live around Sloane Square, in Chelsea, London. They have no particular ambition but swan around looking beautiful, waiting to snare some young man from a wealthy background and with his own handsome income. She wore little makeup, spoke without the strangulated accents of her class, and dressed in a manner more akin to her mother's generation.

Her poor educational standards endeared her to many ordinary Brits, as well as the fact she had worked as a mother's helper—for some months even as a cleaning lady—to earn some money for herself. And she lived happily with several young women in a London apartment, surviving on spaghetti and other inexpensive meals, just like the great majority of other young people. Even Barbara Cartland, whose daughter Raine would marry Diana's father, Lord Spencer, described Diana as "a perfect Barbara Cartland heroine," which of course she was. A true-life Cinderella, Diana was noble yet humble, living an ordinary life, yet known to royalty from birth, waiting like the quintessential virgin for a prince to find her and love her, so that they would live together happily ever after.

From the moment of her engagement to Prince Charles in February 1981, the media made Diana into a worldwide cover girl even before her magnificent wedding in July of that year. The world wanted to know every detail about this young, virginal beauty; from Arizona to Arabia, from Kentucky to Kyoto, her face literally sold a million magazines.

Even the austere Archbishop of Canterbury began his nuptial address in St. Paul's Cathedral with the words, "Here is the stuff of which fairy tales are made." And due to the arrival of satellite TV, the whole world was able to attend the ceremony and the spectacular royal occasion. Even today, thirteen years after the event, there are people who can remember the tears that welled in their eyes as they witnessed Diana's wedding.

This single event propelled the British monarchy into a false state of security. Elizabeth read the reports that flowed into Buckingham Palace during the ensuing weeks from every corner of the globe, reinforcing the belief that a constitutional monarchy makes a modern nation strong. Diana's wedding also helped dispel the idea of republicanism in Britain, though, ironically, the ending of her marriage to Charles eleven years later stirred the entire nation to debate whether the British monarchy might wither and die at the end of Elizabeth's reign.

The wedding created a star, and although Charles and Diana kept out of the limelight as much as possible, the tabloid press were determined to keep their readers titillated with every morsel of gossip and innuendo. The fact that much of what they wrote was untrue did not trouble the media one bit.

The American tabloids and magazines followed the British press coverage, but the European media wanted more sensational stories. The Italians, allegedly from interviews with unnamed housemaids at Buckingham Palace, described Diana as a "sexual volcano" who studied Japanese erotic manuals. Apparently, she was determined to exhaust "Prince Charles day and night so that Il Principe Dongiovanni" would have no surplus energy for other women. The Germans quoted Diana as saying her main aim in life was to be a "good housewife," while the French concentrated on "the fortunes" she spent on clothes.

Magazines around the world began providing readers with enough detail on Diana's habits—her clothes, shoes, makeup, hair, diet, and her lifestyle—so that readers could copy whatever they wanted of the fairy princess's life. In Britain in particular, whenever Diana altered her hairstyle, thousands of young women would copy it within days. Whatever little fashion accessory she decided upon, for example when she wore a small bow on the heel of her stockings, manufacturers produced copies within days. The demand was insatiable.

The world expected Diana to play their version of a dream role, and the less she did the more she captivated everyone's attention. In those first few years Diana rarely appeared in public, preferring to retain her privacy inside Kensington Palace. She continued to look shy, to smile engagingly, and to chat with little children. So the media pounced on what they could—her appearance, her clothes, and rumors. During this time she transformed herself from a round-faced, overweight, rather awkward kindergarten teacher into a sophisticated, elegant, beautiful model the world wanted to emulate and the fashion designers to dress.

No one seemed to care much what effect all this adoration might have on the young, impressionable Diana. Never before had there been an instant creation of a global megastar whose girlish looks and shy simplicity were dramatically catapulted into every corner of the world, all enhanced by the dreamlike overtones of royalty. Queen Elizabeth, and her senior advisers, should probably have investigated how this notoriety affected the new member of the Royal Family who had arrived like a shooting star to outshine them all.

But no one thought to help the inexperienced Diana put her new life into perspective—not Elizabeth, nor Charles, nor Philip. Nor did any advisers try to help her when all this worship proved too much for her to handle. Within a couple of years Diana was on her way to becoming an enchantress who began to believe in her own powers. Every day she would order all the newspapers and magazines, and then sit and read everything written about her; she examined the pictures of herself and talked to her ladies-in-waiting about the outfits she should order to keep up appearances for the avaricious press. She spent more time selecting her clothes and examining herself in front of the mirror before leaving Kensington Palace to attend royal engagements.

Diana needed help settling into a life so different from anything she had experienced before. Until her engagement to Charles, Diana had been a free spirit, moving around London unnoticed, unattached, and happily going about her life in complete freedom. Overnight, all that changed and she could not cope. She felt trapped in the palace by all the unceasing public attention. In addition, her two pregnancies, coming so early in the marriage, intensified her feelings of being confined. Diana herself did not wish to be seen in public or photographed looking big and, in her eyes, hugely unattractive, so she hardly ever appeared in public when heavily pregnant and stayed inside the palace for weeks at a time.

As she struggled to come to terms with herself and her new cloistered life, Diana took out much of her frustrations on Prince Charles. Diana sought from Charles the love she had not received as a young child; she wanted and needed reassurance and comfort; to have her confidence boosted continually. Diana believed Charles to be the one person who could do these things for her. She had worshipped him. She would look at him making speeches with pride and love in her eyes and, some thought, adoration. No man could have provided Diana with all she needed, and unfortunately Charles least of all.

Shortly after their wedding, the image began to crack and Diana realized her Prince was mortal, not unlike her father who also had been unable to give her the love, the confidence, and the reassurance to tackle the world.

Often in Kensington Palace the staff would hear Diana plead with Charles, "Please don't leave me. Please, please, darling, don't leave me. I can't cope without you." And then the pleading would often end with Diana screaming at Charles, often swearing at the top of her voice, "Don't you realize I fucking well need you here? Don't you ever bloody well consider me and my needs?"

Usually the rows would end with Charles leaving, looking shaken and sheepish, and Diana in tears in her room.

Diana was jealous of the officials who spent hours with Charles throughout the day. She seemed unable to understand that Charles, as Prince of Wales, had a varied and busy life; that he had a vast estate, the Duchy of Cornwall, to preside over; that he had hundreds of official duties and functions, visits, and speeches every year, many of which had to be written and checked.

Frances had told Diana she should be sure to appoint her own advisers when she moved into Kensington Palace so that she would not have to rely on Charles's old cronies, many of whom had been with him for years and who owed their allegiance solely to her husband.

Diana believed that all would change for the better if she got rid of all Charles's secretaries and officials who had always had access to him. That was one of the prime reasons his old cronies began leaving his staff in those early years of the marriage. Diana would pick battles with them, be rude, and deliberately make life awkward for them until, in the end, they had no recourse but to resign. The more of Charles's retainers quit, the happier Diana became.

Perhaps the best example of Diana's wayward nature was her treatment of Oliver Everett, a longtime friend and former aide to Charles who abandoned his career with the Foreign Office to return to royal duty as Diana's private secretary shortly before the royal marriage. Everett knew the ropes, and Charles asked him to educate Diana, train her, look after her, and guide through the labyrinth of life inside the Royal Family. Everett is handsome, intelligent, and witty, and she thought he was wonderful.

After William was born, Diana became particularly petulant and demanding, perhaps suffering from postnatal depression. She accused Everett of keeping an eye on her for Charles, reporting everything back to his former polo friend and boss. Everett was patient, perhaps treating her too much like a schoolgirl, and she became irritated with him. In the end, whenever Everett was around, she would shout at Charles, "Get that man away from me." One morning she put a large piece of paper on Charles's desk with the words written in capitals: OLIVER MUST GO.

Everett reluctantly appealed to Charles to let him go because he felt his presence harmed Diana and was straining their marriage. The day Everett quit, Diana was in an ecstatic mood, dancing around the palace shouting out, "Hurrah, hurrah, he's gone, the ogre's gone, I'm free, I'm free."

Many who knew Charles, Diana, and Everett believe this was perhaps the most catastrophic resignation out of the forty-odd that occurred in those first few years after Diana's marriage. (Charles was able to secure for his friend the key librarian's job at Windsor Castle, and they still meet. Now that Charles and Diana have separated, some hope there might be a way back for Everett, perhaps as Charles's private secretary, for he would make a first-class senior adviser.)

There were other good men whom Diana managed to fire, or more usually, persuade to resign, including one of the best legal and constitutional brains working in the palace, Edward Adeane, Prince Charles's private secretary and principal adviser. Diana was jealous of the access Charles permitted Adeane, and she repeatedly appealed to Charles to fire him. Charles always refused.

Edward Adeane had been no Palace flunky. His great-grandfather, Lord Stamfordham, had been Private Secretary first to Queen Victoria and later to the Prince of Wales in the early years of the century. Lord Michael Adeane, Edward's father, had been at first equerry and then Principal Private Secretary to Elizabeth. Edward was a brilliant barrister. Nine years older than Charles and with an impeccable background of Eton and Cambridge, he was the perfect royal courtier and had skillfully advised Charles for many years. Confronted by Diana's impossible demands to fire Adeane, Charles went to consult his mother.

Elizabeth gave him no advice at all. She simply said, "You will have to make the decision. It is your problem."

Charles tried unsuccessfully to placate both Diana and Adeane. Finally Adeane, angry, resigned. Diana was triumphant. Within days of leaving Adeane predicted trouble ahead for the marriage, so disturbed was he that Charles had permitted Diana to wield such influence and power.

When news of Adeane's departure was reported to Elizabeth, she commented, "How unfortunate."

Despite her victories within the palace and the forced resignations of over forty royal servants, Diana's anxiety became more frenzied and acute after the births of both Wills and Harry. Most now attribute her state to postnatal depression coupled with her inability to accept the restrictive atmosphere of the palace.

The renowed royal gynecologist Mr. George Pinker, then fifty-seven, brought Diana's two sons into the world. He apparently did not find it necessary to seek the help of a psychiatrist, a psychologist, or a dietician to help Diana overcome her state of depression or check her eating habits. Diana should have been seen by a young psychiatrist, trained in postnatal care, to ensure she came through the ordeal happily. But that wasn't Buckingham Palace practice. The failure to help her would have the most disastrous effect on Diana, her health, and on her relationship with Charles.

A few months after William's birth Elizabeth asked Diana one day, "Are you feeling well? You look a little peaky." Diana gave a half-smile and said she felt rather tired. Elizabeth told her she thought it was probably due to the effects of feeding young William and left it at that. There were no follow-up inquiries, no concern despite the fact that Diana looked far too thin and was obviously in need of some medical help and advice. Elizabeth did nothing.

Elizabeth's apparent total lack of concern for her daughter-in-law reflected her lack of mothering instinct. None of her children received much maternal attention and spent very little time with Elizabeth.

Perhaps the most extraordinary example of Charles's upbringing began when he was four. Whenever he met his mother in public he had to walk up to her and shake her by the hand, even if it was their first moment together after she had been away for months on an overseas royal tour.

Elizabeth herself had not been brought up in such a strict, Victorian manner and some of the blame must be placed on Prince Philip, whose Teutonic attitude to children, coupled with the discipline instilled in the Royal Navy, resulted in his believing the old adage that children should be seen and not heard.

The nation, however, remained unaware of life behind the high walls of the palace. All they saw were pretty pictures of the Royal Family smiling at the camera in idyllic surroundings, well-dressed and spotlessly clean children with their loving parents, fixed smiles on all their faces. Virtually every photograph Buckingham Palace released to the media in those first years portrayed the perfect family, the image Elizabeth wanted to project to the nation.

After official royal photographs had been taken by the appointed photographer and the film processed, every frame was sent to the palace, where Elizabeth insisted on seeing each one, not just a selection. In consultation with several senior advisers, Elizabeth decided which photographs should be given to the media, to ensure that the correct image was being seen by the people.

Following the birth of Harry, in 1984, Diana again suffered from postnatal depression. She turned to Charles for help and comfort, but as Diana became more demanding, the couple began to drift apart emotionally. Charles found he was unable to give the support and comfort Diana needed.

Diana feared losing Charles's love, and the more demands she made on her husband, the more pressure Charles felt. For four years Charles had done everything to please his young wife, giving in to all her demands. He found her moods becoming more intense, more unyielding, and they would change dramatically without reason. Diana would cry over minor matters, seemingly unable to stop the flow of tears. She demanded all Charles's time and his constant attention.

Charles encouraged her to see a doctor but Diana refused, saying repeatedly, "There is nothing wrong with me at all. I am perfectly well. It is you who have changed." He had no idea at that time, in 1985, that she was suffering from anorexia nervosa.

Unable to cope, not knowing what more he could do to help his tearful wife, Charles would shrug and leave Diana miserable and in tears while he went about his royal duties. He acted toward his wife in typical Windsor fashion—as he had always seen his father and mother behave toward him—exhibiting little or no warmth, very little kindness, and no genuine concern for her problems.

As Diana became more unpredictable and irrational, Charles began to feel he had done all he could to help her settle into royal life and had nothing more to offer. He simply left her alone in Kensington Palace, with Wills and Harry for company.

Diana's mother Frances Shand Kydd could have stepped in and taken charge of her daughter. They talked frequently on the phone, but she didn't see enough of her daughter to know that she needed medical attention. Furthermore, their relationship was still strained since she had abandoned the family, and Frances thought she shouldn't interfere. Ironically, as a result of Diana's marital troubles, Frances and her daughter have become closer and see each other more often.

Diana's depression brought on anorexia nervosa and then bulimia. The one led to the other and she suffered the effects for three years. Following the births of her sons, Diana had difficulty controlling her eating habits as depression gripped her. But the claim by some writers that she suffered from bulimia for nine years is simply not true. Anyone who sees photographs of the athletic, radiant Diana from 1986 onward can tell that the stories of her condition during those years were grossly exaggerated. Medical experts who regularly deal with cases of bulimia know it would have been impossible for Diana to look so good if she had suffered from serious bulimia for years.

Six months after Harry's birth, Diana did occasionally take a handful of laxatives for days on end to make sure she carried no excess weight; she did make herself sick from time to time by drinking salt water, and she occasionally made herself vomit by sticking her fingers down her throat.

Yet Diana never sought medical advice for her condition. She didn't want to reveal to royal doctors she was suffering from a serious eating disorder, and she simply didn't know what to do or whom to turn to. She felt Charles cared neither about her nor her health.

She talked to former girlfriends about her condition but never detailed how badly she suffered. By the beginning of 1986, she believed her relationship with Charles had all but broken down. Diana found she couldn't control her tantrums and bad moods. She screamed and shouted at Charles, picking arguments each and every day, and even refusing to attend royal functions or some of the engagements at which she had agreed to appear. To Charles, brought up to put duty first at all times—duty to the nation, to the monarchy, and most important of all, to his mother the Queen—Diana's attitude amounted to monstrous dereliction of her responsibilities. Charles could not forgive this selfishness, and nothing angered him more than Diana's refusal to carry out royal functions.

In desperation, Diana turned to others for help. In early 1986 she sought the advice of Penny Thornton, an astrologer who was well known in aristocratic circles. Penny Thornton believed that no emotional problem was insoluble if you placed your faith in the stars. She had told Sarah Ferguson, the Duchess of York, that she had used astrology to help save a number of marriages.

Penny gave Diana hope for the future, which raised her spirits. "Penny was a revelation to me," she said. "She made me totally rethink my life. She taught me things about myself I never knew. She has been a godsend."

Unable to cope with his wayward, demanding wife and no longer willing to listen to nonstop arguments, Charles would escape from Kensington Palace as much as possible. He would go to Scotland to fish or shoot or stalk deer; he would escape to Highgrove to tend his beloved garden and relax in peace; and he would invite the one woman who had always understood him to come visit Highgrove from her home, which was just fifteen minutes away. That woman was Camilla

Parker Bowles, whom Charles had first fallen for when he was a young man of twenty-three and she an unmarried debutante.

Charles sought her advice, talked to her about Diana and the problems of his marriage. But once again, love blossomed between the two as it had done twice before. The first time was in 1973 when Charles first met Camilla, née Shand, the daughter of one of Britain's wealthiest property owners. At that time Camilla was also dating the dashing cavalry officer Andrew Parker Bowles, ten years older than both Charles and Camilla. In fact, Camilla was two-timing Andrew because she and Charles were sleeping together at Broadlands, Mountbatten's country home. But Charles was about to go to sea for five years with the Royal Navy, and marriage was far from his mind. Within six months of Charles's departure Camilla had married Andrew.

Their second love affair began in September 1979, following the IRA's assassination of Earl Mountbatten while he was fishing in Ireland. Charles was angry, frustrated, depressed, and traumatized by the murder of his Uncle Dickie, the man who had been more of a father to him than Prince Philip. Camilla had saved his sanity then. They spent six months together, seeing each other most days, while she nursed Charles back to the man he had been before the tragedy struck.

During those months they spent days and nights together, indulging in the most passionate sexual relationship Charles had ever experienced. Fortunately for both Charles and Camilla, Andrew Parker Bowles was serving with Lord Soames in Rhodesia for six months while that former British colony introduced black majority rule and the country became Zimbabwe. Elizabeth had been consulted prior to Parker Bowles's posting, and she agreed to the plan, as long as Parker Bowles raised no objection.

But Charles, who barely knew Diana at this stage, understood that he could never marry Camilla and remain heir to the throne. Elizabeth, the Queen Mother, the establishment, the Church, and the government would forbid that. Together Charles and Camilla discussed what might have been. Both knew the trauma of Edward VIII's abdication for the sake of the divorcée Wallis Simpson and their lifelong exile. Camilla, too, recognized that if they were to marry, Charles would have to abdicate. While Charles wanted to marry

Camilla and turn his back on the throne, his upbringing forced him to put duty first, his own wishes a distant second.

Indeed, it was the sensible, down-to-earth Camilla who finally persuaded Charles to take the advice his great-uncle Dickie had given him some years earlier: "A young man in your position should go out, sow his wild oats, and then find a young virgin; marry her, and train her to be the next Queen of England." Within a matter of weeks he met the lovely Lady Diana Spencer, only nineteen, a virgin, and a girl who had been in love with him from afar for years. Charles was captivated by the nubile, lovely young woman who was so desperately in love with him that she could not bear to be separated from him for more than a day.

Diana certainly knew that Charles had many girlfriends before she began dating him. She had known the intimate details of the on-off love affair between Charles and her own sister Sarah, which had lasted nearly a year. By simply reading the newspapers Diana had become aware of the girls Charles had known. Most, though not all had been catalogued, noted, checked, and probed by the insatiable tabloid press. And quite early in her relationship with Charles, she had learned of Camilla Parker Bowles.

At first Diana believed that Camilla and Charles were "just friends" who had known each other since they were teenagers. She believed that out of friendship, Camilla had given Charles a shoulder to cry on following the murder of Mountbatten. She had not known of the deep love they had for each other, nor of their heavy sexual and emotional relationship. And she had no idea that Charles had seriously considered giving up the throne to marry Camilla.

It had been in the cabbage patch at Camilla's country home, not far from Highgrove, that Charles had first asked Diana to marry him. He had told Diana that his old friend Camilla was thrilled by his decision to marry her. He had often referred to Camilla, quoted her, spoken admiringly of her. He also hinted that Diana could learn a great deal from Camilla, praising her as an example of a wonderful wife and mother.

Diana, suspicious, would ask Charles about his relationship with Camilla, but Charles would hedge, never revealing the depth of their involvement. He would tell Diana that Camilla had been his Girl Friday, someone who happily did odd jobs for him. She sensed there was more to this relationship and was jealous of Camilla when Charles would invite her and Andrew to Highgrove for lunch, tea, dinner, and other social events.

Sometimes, however, her instincts about Camilla drew Diana to the wrong conclusion. Days before her wedding, Diana found a small package in her office in Buckingham Palace and assumed it was yet another wedding present. In a small leather case she discovered a solid gold bracelet engraved with the initials *GF*. She immediately knew the bracelet was a gift from Charles to Camilla, *GF* standing for Girl Friday. Distraught, she ran from the room in tears.

On this occasion Diana was wrong. The bracelet was indeed intended as a gift for Camilla from Charles, but only as one of six thank-you gifts he was giving to people who had been good friends during his bachelor days. Three gifts were for women, three to men. It had never occurred to him to tell Diana about these personal items.

In late 1986, when Charles began to spend so much time at Highgrove, Diana knew instinctively that Charles was seeing Camilla. She directly accused him of sleeping with Camilla, but Charles denied this for several months.

The more time Charles was away from Diana and Kensington Palace, the happier he became. He spent days in Scotland fishing, stalking, or shooting; he hunted; he played polo for three months every summer. He undertook his official royal duties. He spent time with Camilla.

In 1987 Charles concluded that his marriage to Diana had changed dramatically. The love and passion had evaporated, just as it had in so many marriages of his friends and relatives. He didn't try to win Diana back or even help her with her problems. He simply accepted the breakdown of their marriage as a part of life and ignored his wife.

Unaware of Diana's medical problems, Charles thought she had spurned his love and affection. He saw how much she enjoyed herself in the company of her young male friends and concluded that she was bored with him. He also naively thought she would simply accept the situation of marital breakdown and make the most of her life as the Princess of Wales. She adored their two children; she had friends and servants, an expense account, her royal privileges; and she looked forward to the prospect of being crowned Queen of England.

Charles still believed he had made the right decision to marry her, especially after the birth of Prince William in 1982. With her he had fulfilled one of the most important duties of his life, producing an heir to the throne for the House of Windsor.

Charles had never understood Diana, and he had no idea his walking away from her was emotionally devastating. Her distress became more apparent, and she became convinced that Charles was reserving all his time and attention for someone else, Camilla.

One day, in January 1987, Diana decided to put her theory to the test and drove down to Highgrove, unannounced. Later, she told a girlfriend what happened. "As I drove up to Highgrove early one morning, around eight-thirty, with my detective in the car, I saw a car driving away through another exit. It was Camilla. I went straight in and Charles was having breakfast. I asked him if Camilla had been there, and he looked away and asked me why I wanted to know.

"That made me see red and I raced upstairs to the bedroom, my bedroom, and the bed was unmade. It was obvious that two people had slept the night there. I went down again and asked him again whether Camilla had been there. He didn't answer.

"I then knew for sure that he was having an affair. I kept challenging him, but he wouldn't answer me and I lost my temper. I just had a go at him, telling him what a shit he had been, having an affair with an old girlfriend, treating me like shit, leaving me in London with the children while he bonked away at Highgrove.

"In the end I just broke down in tears. I didn't know what to do. All my worst fears had been proved. I knew he didn't love me any more. I knew he loved someone else. It was awful, awful."

From that moment on, Diana changed her view and feelings about Charles, her own marriage, and, more important for Elizabeth, her duties as Princess of Wales. Seemingly overnight she became a spurned woman. The Princess of Wales, mother of two children, the next Queen of England, was twenty-five years old and she had her whole life ahead of her, a life with a husband who didn't love her anymore and for whom she had lost all respect.

Later she told two of her girlfriends over lunch, "It was the worst moment of my life. I felt my life was over and, worst of all, I didn't know what to do or whom to turn to."

After spending weeks turning everything over in her mind, seeking advice from Penny Thornton, her sister Sarah, and some old

394 • QUEEN ELIZABETH II

girlfriends, she turned to her mother. Frances Shand Kydd advised her daughter to find a life of her own, letting Charles continue the life he chose while she enjoyed her friends and, of course, her two sons.

It was sometime in 1987 that the new Diana emerged. And what a change had come over the Shy Di everyone loved.

The new Diana went out of her way to attend every social event, when and with whom she wanted. She put out the word that she wanted to party to old friends such as heiress Kate Menzies, Anne Beckwith-Smith, and handsome young men such as her old flames Major David Waterhouse of the Brigade of Guards and City banker Philip Dunne. Later, Diana would add Major James Hewitt to her list of men to whom she became physically attracted.

Sir John Riddell, her private secretary at that time, could barely cope with her succession of instant parties, dinners, cocktails, nights-on-the-town, theater and cinema outings. He asked Prince Charles if he could kindly speak to Diana about her spur-of-the-moment activities. Diana's schedule, planned six months in advance—as all royal diaries must be—would be changed at a whim as she accepted casual appointments, making Sir John's life most difficult.

Charles did speak to Diana, to no avail. She told him bluntly, "It's my life and, like you, I'm going to do what I want to do." Sir John was left with few options. He resigned.

Diana had a ball. She flirted outrageously. She dined and danced and partied with whomever she wished. She had affairs with various men, including Dunne, Waterhouse, and Hewitt, and she didn't care if Charles knew. But Diana did try to be discreet around the press, because she didn't want her mother-in-law to know what she was doing. Diana was frightened of the Queen and had always been like jelly in her presence.

One example suggests Diana's relationship with Elizabeth. Like many other members of the Royal Family, Diana has become rather a good mimic. Indeed, one of their traditional games is to make innocent fun of others by mimicking them outrageously. In The Firm it is bound to earn a good laugh and not a little ribald fun, and Diana found that she was quite good at it. On one occasion she proved too good.

At Balmoral one evening while waiting for the Queen to come down to dinner, the family were all standing around, as they always do, for the arrival of the monarch. While they waited Diana began to mimic the Queen, adopting the same high, rather shrill, pathetic voice which the TV show *Spitting Image* always uses for the Queen.

It has forever been a golden rule within The Firm that no one ridicules the Queen. Indeed, even in the privacy of the royal kitchens at Buckingham Palace, no servant would dare mimic the Queen because such an act would probably end in instant dismissal. On this occasion, however, Diana, who had been practicing the Queen's *Spitting Image* voice, was doing her impression when Elizabeth walked in.

Diana didn't see her mother-in-law until silence descended like a blanket. And then Diana saw Elizabeth, her eyes blazing as she pierced her with a withering look. Diana fell instantly silent in mid-sentence and blushed a bright red. "I was only joking," she stammered nervously as Elizabeth continued to glare at her. Elizabeth did not reply and never spoke a single word to Diana that entire evening.

That was typical Diana, not thinking before launching into something she thought amusingly naughty. It was also typical of Elizabeth, who never forgets that she is the monarch and as such insists that every single one of her subjects give her the respect due to the Crown.

Diana knew that the power of The Firm lay with the Queen, and if you crossed her your life would become a misery. Her mother-in-law had the whip hand and would use it whenever she thought the reputation of the monarchy was being threatened.

Diana's popular support had waned as the media gave the impression that she was a spoiled brat, causing trouble within the palace, firing Charles's staff, and spending tens of thousands of dollars of taxpayers' money on clothes for herself.

Until Harry was about twelve months old, Diana was patron of only a few charities and organizations, always taking advice from the Palace and from Charles. As a result she was hardly ever seen in public except when attending royal functions, usually accompanying Charles, where she would be photographed in a sensational full-length ball gown, usually topped with a tiara, and looking stunning. But that wasn't the real Diana.

Diana has always shown considerable warmth when dealing with people, particularly one on one. Whenever she tours hospitals, old people's homes, or child care centers, the effect is remarkable: everyone she meets comments on her warmth and sincerity. It is a quality neither Elizabeth, Prince Philip, Charles, nor any of Elizabeth's children possess. Indeed some describe Elizabeth, and members of her immediate family, as "cold fish."

Diana decided to involve herself with more deserving charities. A week never goes by without at least two or three letters arriving at Kensington Palace asking her to be patron of their particular charity or organization. She began to select which to support.

As a result, from 1986 onward she came into contact with far greater numbers of ordinary British men and women, and particularly children. She had an immediate rapport with them. People turned out in hundreds to catch a glimpse of her, waiting patiently in all weather to see her, wanting to meet her, cheer her, and, if possible, talk to her. The press suddenly changed tack, giving her their support as she took on more charities and showed she had what every other member of the Royal Family, including Elizabeth, lacks—the common touch. Suddenly, people believed that Diana cared, really cared, not just for herself but for everyone, especially those in need, in poor health, or suffering.

Diana volunteered to become patron of those charities that other members of the Royal Family fought shy of. Heart-searching discussions occurred within Buckingham Palace when Diana announced she wished to become patron of an AIDS-related charity. Some courtiers advised Elizabeth that the monarchy would be tainted if Diana were associated with charities for gay men who had contracted the disease.

Elizabeth had a word with Diana and asked whether she thought it was a good idea. Diana played her part brilliantly, showing unusual courage before her mother-in-law. Diana realized that Elizabeth's apparently innocent question was her way of expressing disapproval. Diana told her that she thought it vital that someone from the Royal Family be seen openly supporting AIDS patients and she would be happy to do so. Her decision to become the patron won much praise and public acclaim.

Diana would be photographed touching lepers and hugging AIDS patients, talking enthusiastically to drug abusers, the terminally ill, the handicapped, and the homeless. She became their friend, talking and touching the undeserving or the embarrassing in the same way she bobbed down on her heels to talk to small children. Some cynics called her a publicity-seeking disaster junkie, a "Mother Teresa in a tiara." But charity workers knew better.

By the end of the 1980s Diana had become patron to more than 110 charities and organizations. And she worked hard. Those who ran the charities talked of her "wonderful commitment" and testified that her involvement did not cease when the spotlights were turned off.

Diana's self-confidence rose during the late 1980s as she began to make a life for herself away from Charles who, she believed, had lost all interest in her. She overcame her shyness and her eating disorders, she swam every day, played tennis two or three times a week, attended a gymnasium, and, as a result, felt like a new person. And her new confidence spilled over into her personal life. She became a bewitching woman, using all her seductive powers, from fluttering her eyelashes to running her hand through the hair of the man she fancied. She danced with whom she wished at parties; she loved being the center of attention and would raise the eyebrows of other women in the party as she brazenly flirted on the dance floor. She was seen dancing so closely with Philip Dunne and David Waterhouse during smoochy numbers that she appeared to be all but making love as they moved slowly around the dance floor.

Even when Charles accompanied his wife to parties, Diana would continue her new flirtatious role. She seemed to revel in being outrageous with a number of the men whenever Charles was present. Some believed she wanted to interest her husband, others that she wanted to make him jealous, but most believed she was trying to discredit Charles, seeking revenge for his going off with Camilla and leaving her miserable and alone.

Despite the occasional newspaper story, the general public had no idea of what Diana was up to, knew nothing of her outrageous behavior, showing off among her friends, acting like a bachelor girl rather than the wife of the Prince of Wales and the next Queen of England. And the public did not want to believe those few stories that did emerge, for they believed Diana could do no wrong.

In the autumn of 1990 Charles phoned his mother and asked to visit her. It was most unusual for Charles to want to drop by "for a chat."

Mostly they talked on the phone about formal matters and hardly ever indulged in idle gossip. Elizabeth feared the worst.

Charles and his mother had always had an exceptionally polite relationship. Charles had been brought up to show remarkable deference to his Mama, the name he always called her as a child.

Twenty-four hours later Charles walked into the lovely, airy drawing room overlooking the gardens at Buckingham Palace. It was time for afternoon tea. During the hours waiting to see her son, Elizabeth had been nervous, hardly able to eat or sleep, instinctively fearing Charles wanted to see her about Diana.

Elizabeth had prayed that Charles's marriage would not go so disastrously wrong that it would be impossible to salvage. Every Sunday for the past few years Elizabeth had knelt in church and prayed for their marriage; she had prayed at bedtime that all would be well. Elizabeth had told the Queen Mother of her fears and she, in turn, had told her daughter to relax and pray everything would work out.

For some years, Elizabeth had known that Charles and Diana were living separate lives. Diana spent most of her life at Kensington Palace with the children while Charles stayed a hundred miles away at Highgrove, in Gloucestershire, where he had moved his office in 1989. Stubbornly, she hoped that one day they would understand that an accommodation had to be reached for the sake of the children and, above all else, for the monarchy. They had an arrangement until Diana demanded formal separation.

The separations and divorces of Elizabeth's sister Margaret and her only daughter Anne could not compare to the trauma that the rocky marriage of Charles and Diana caused her. Elizabeth knew that if Charles and Diana separated, or worse, divorced, it could damage, if not destroy, the Crown, because Charles was destined to be King.

Elizabeth knew she could rely on Charles; she always had done so and he had never let her down. Charles would never suggest a separation. He knew he had to remain married even if he could not bear to see or talk to his wife.

The Queen had never interfered in Charles's love life, even when he produced a string of girlfriends, many of whom were unsuitable as candidates to become the next Queen of England. She had not advised Charles about his intended marriage to Diana. Indeed they hardly spoke about it. Elizabeth saw Diana as a lovely young girl, shy, retiring, and virginal, perfectly suited to be his bride and the future Queen. Philip hardly said a word to his son but commented to a former polo pal, "I am very happy that the girl he has found to marry is a long-legged, good-looking blonde. I feared he might decide on someone awful."

Charles would have continued his bachelor life but for Mountbatten's murder, which made him realize how thin was the dividing line between life and death. He realized it was his duty to produce an heir to the throne, a view his father repeatedly pointed out to him.

Since his marriage in 1981 Charles had became lonely. Those he had relied on for advice and friendship had been forced to quit; his father had never been a friend to him, and his relationship with his mother was one of respect, not friendship.

Elizabeth found it difficult to talk to Diana about anything except superficialities. She commented on one occasion, "It seems that the only topics of conversation one can have with Diana are about clothes or the weather."

On another occasion Elizabeth said, "It's not as though she hasn't a brain in her beautiful head, but she certainly acts as though she doesn't. I try everything to talk to her, to bring her out of her shell, but I simply cannot get her to relax and chat to me in the same way as I can Anne or Sarah [Ferguson]."

It did not take Elizabeth long to see selfishness and determination behind Diana's apparent bashfulness and nervous disposition. She watched Diana change from a nervous teenager into a young woman who would seemingly stop at nothing to get her own way. Elizabeth had been unhappy at the way Diana talked to Charles, causing trouble until he acceded to her demands. Yet Elizabeth felt she should not intervene as she witnessed Diana manipulate and control her eldest son.

Only once had she talked to both of them, some time after Harry was born in 1984 when she sensed things were going badly wrong. Elizabeth considered Diana strong-willed, even willful. She knew Diana had caused the ferment and argument, and she believed the only way the marriage could succeed would be for Charles to be more forceful. To Charles's surprise and Diana's delight, Elizabeth had spent most of the time castigating Charles for not taking control of his marriage. She had told him quietly but forcefully that his marriage was his business, but that if it was going to be successful he had to be more authoritative. She reminded him that one day he would be King, and that would mean taking command of everything, including the entire Royal Family.

Elizabeth had hoped the arrival of William and Harry would not only help bring Charles and Diana closer but would channel Diana's energies toward her children and away from constant confrontation with Charles. She also hoped it might help break down the barrier between Diana and herself, a barrier which Elizabeth knew often disappeared when young wives become mothers themselves.

Elizabeth was sitting on the sofa in the drawing room when Charles walked in for his chat. She had three of her pet corgis around her, talking to them as though they were children. They were hoping for a tidbit from the royal hand, but Elizabeth's mind was elsewhere.

Charles rang for the maid to bring tea and sat down at the other end of the sofa. Dressed in a double-breasted gray suit, blue shirt, and tie, Charles coughed and, between sips of tea and a biscuit, delivered the bombshell his mother had feared. Diana wanted a separation.

"Are you sure?" Elizabeth asked her son, repeating her question as Charles sat holding his hands, playing with the gold signet ring on the little finger of his left hand. The ring was decorated with a fleur-de-lys, the emblem of the Prince of Wales.

"Well, yes, that's what she says she wants," he replied. "She seems very determined, very determined indeed."

Elizabeth looked worried, wanting to know the precise details. She asked what Diana meant by "a separation." They were already living apart. Had Diana mentioned divorce or, by asking for a separation, was Diana in reality intending this as only the first step toward a full, legal divorce?

In her clipped tone of voice, which Elizabeth often employed on business occasions, she asked brusquely, "Does Diana realize that she and you cannot divorce?"

Charles replied that she knew that full well, that it had all been explained to her before they became engaged. Charles had told her so a hundred times during the last few years during arguments and rows.

Charles explained that Diana demanded they separate so that she could have the same freedom he enjoyed. Elizabeth asked what she meant, but Charles told his mother he wasn't exactly sure. It was a white lie; Charles knew exactly what Diana meant.

Charles had no intention of telling his mother that Diana was in fact demanding the same sexual freedom that he enjoyed. Many were the occasions that Diana would rage at Charles about his relationship with "that woman," Camilla Parker Bowles.

Charles told his mother that Diana had become distressed by the innuendos about her and her so-called lovers in the tabloid press. He explained that Diana persistently described most of the press accusations as "fabrications." Actually, Diana's exact words were "absolute balls."

Elizabeth didn't know how to respond. Charles knew that his mother's marriage had not been a success, that she had endured years of drama and much unhappiness. Elizabeth knew from her own experience how the wronged person felt and understood what Diana had been going through, alone at Kensington Palace, while her husband spent his days in Gloucestershire and his nights in the arms of another woman.

Elizabeth knew that Charles had found in Camilla the woman he wanted to share his life with. As a woman and a mother, however, Elizabeth felt sad for Diana, although she believed Diana had acted without thinking in her demands on Charles.

Elizabeth did not know what to do so, she decided to follow the advice given her as a young woman being trained to succeed her father: seek advice. Uppermost in her mind that afternoon, however, was the conviction that Diana must be dissuaded from the idea that she could simply separate from Charles, like any other unhappy young woman who wanted out of a marriage.

Before Charles left, his mother explained how "very, very serious" the whole matter had become and said she needed to think about everything before discussing the matter further.

Elizabeth would need to discuss all the implications with her advisers, constitutional lawyers, Church leaders, the Prime Minister, the Attorney-General, and other political figures. She would need to brief her own lawyers in case separation papers needed to be drawn up. First and foremost she needed to talk to Diana.

She asked Diana to come and see her at Buckingham Palace. After meeting with his mother Charles phoned Diana to tell her. For months Diana had asked, pleaded, and demanded that Charles raise the matter of separation with Elizabeth. Excited by the news, Diana prepared herself for the confrontation with her mother-in-law.

Diana had persuaded Charles to speak to his mother about a

separation only after threatening him that she would tackle Elizabeth herself. Charles had tried to persuade Diana that it would be no use, that they had to make the best of their marriage because divorce for them was impossible. He hoped to persuade her to accept that marital breakdown did not mean they had to separate formally; they could carry on leading separate lives.

Frequently, Diana had shouted at Charles, "If you're so bloody important and your position is so vital, why do you spend your life screwing another woman and leaving me vegetating? Tell me, answer that."

Charles would usually not reply directly but would try to persuade his wife that they had to accept the situation and get on with their lives as best they could.

Despite the fun that family, people, and some newspapers made of Diana's apparent lack of intelligence, Charles had known for some years that beneath Diana's apparent airhead attitude, her impulsive, irrational behavior, was a woman perfectly capable of looking after her own best interests. Charles never underestimated the determination of his wife, particularly when it concerned her own wishes and her future.

A few days after Charles had talked to his mother, Diana arrived at Buckingham Palace for what she knew would be the most important conversation of her life. Diana was clear about what she intended to say. She had talked the matter through, time and again, with her old friend James Gilbey, a bachelor in his thirties whom she had known since her teenage years.

Gilbey was six feet, three inches tall, a member of the wealthy Gilbey gin family, and a well-educated man-about-town. He had always cherished his unique relationship with Diana. They had met in the late 1970s shortly after leaving school and had kept in contact. The more Diana became estranged from Prince Charles in the 1980s, the more she found solace and comfort with James Gilbey. In the early 1980s, Gilbey had lived a champagne lifestyle, but the severe British recession took its toll on his secondhand-car business, which went into liquidation in 1991, leaving debts of $1 million. Gilbey, with deep personal debts as a result, then joined Lotus, the British specialist car manufacturer, as marketing director.

Feeling miserable and lonely during the years after Harry's birth, Diana found Gilbey a man in whom she could confide. He was gentle by nature and, for some reason, attracted to emotionally vulnerable women. She needed a man who would listen to her wounded heart, flatter and comfort her. She also needed someone to take her side in a hostile world.

Since 1986 Diana had felt trapped, left to rot by her uncaring, unloving husband, and with only her children on whom to lavish her affection. The children were the only ones who loved her, and only with them did she feel happy, tender, and warmhearted. Gone forever were those wonderful heady days when she worshipped the ground Charles walked on. Now she couldn't even bear to share his bed.

The breakdown in her marriage had taken a severe toll on Diana, and she knew it. She hated feeling desperately unhappy most of the time; she hated the problems of bulimia. Diana would complain to a number of her girlfriends: "No one seems to care about my feelings now. They don't seem to care whether I'm miserable or happy. They think I'm dispensable now. I've finished my life's work: I've produced two male heirs."

Gilbey reveled in his newfound role, for he had worshipped Diana for more than ten years, but she had never wanted to be involved with him. In 1992, when their relationship resembled an affair, she told one of her girlfriends, "Oh no, never. James asked me out when I was a teenager and I didn't want to know then. He has been very, very kind to me, but there was never anything between us, never; though he was rather keen."

Diana's relationship with Gilbey was close—they called each other darling and behaved lovingly—but from everything Diana has said, it is doubtful they became lovers. Diana liked Gilbey's being "in love" with her. It boosted her confidence, made her feel good. They would hold hands, kiss frequently but never passionately. Sometimes Gilbey would smother her hand with kisses and profess his love for her. Their phone conversations were smoochy.

Elizabeth was first informed of the existence of James Gilbey in 1989, when a senior member of the Royal Protection Squad had informed her officially—through Sir Robert Fellowes—that Diana had spent three hours one night—from 8 P.M. to 11 P.M.—at Gilbey's

Knightsbridge apartment. Elizabeth ordered that a watch be kept on the relationship but that no action should be taken.

Diana had no idea she was being observed, for she believed her own personal police bodyguard was answerable only to her and treated everything she did or said with total confidence. It was part of her naïveté not to understand the extent to which those in command at Buckingham Palace have the most extraordinary powers, their tentacles capable of reaching into every nook and cranny of British society, whether political, legal, ecclesiastical, the civil service, the armed services, or the City.

Protecting Diana and keeping her confidences formed only part of her bodyguard's job. As Princess of Wales, Diana could be vulnerable not only to physical attack or kidnap by some deranged maniac, but also to a more subtle approach. Chancers, society smooth-talkers, or more perverse people might try to blackmail her or simply try to use her position for their own unscrupulous advantage. Every eventuality had to be guarded against by those whose duty it was to protect her. And a most important part of her bodyguard's responsibility included reporting back to his superiors any visits or friends Diana made that could be questionable or a possible embarrassment to her, to Charles, or to any member of the family.

Eyebrows were raised and senior courtiers became anxious when Diana's friendship with James Gilbey seemed to be turning more serious. Gilbey had always been on Diana's Approved List, those privileged few whose phone calls would be put through immediately to her apartment. All members of the Royal Family have such a list, and most are restricted to remarkably few people. The royals like to do the phoning and not be hassled by people they don't want to talk to.

After Diana's visit to Gilbey's apartment in 1989, a tap was placed on the phone calls he made to her. Not constantly, but from time to time a tape would be made of his calls so that senior Palace advisers could ascertain the state of their relationship. Ostensibly it was done for "security reasons."

The greater Diana's need for emotional security, the more she poured out her heart to Gilbey. He came to know the secrets of her marriage. He listened with concern and sympathy as she recounted her problems and her unhappiness. He heard the bitterness in her voice. She told him of her anorexia, of her eating binges, of her bulimia, just as she had told two or three of her girlfriends. But to Gilbey she dramatized everything out of proportion. The more she poured out her heart, the more concerned he became. She had his full attention, and Gilbey enjoyed the privilege of being privy to the innermost secrets of the royal marriage.

Diana also told him that she had sometimes even considered suicide.

During her meeting with Elizabeth that day, Diana was quiet and composed. She did not complain about Charles, Camilla Parker Bowles, or the state of her marriage. She simply told her mother-in-law that the marriage had broken down and she wanted a separation.

Elizabeth asked her daughter-in-law whether she realized that she and Charles could never divorce and whether she had known this when they married. Diana replied that she did know, that Charles had explained the situation before they became engaged.

The Queen asked her why she now wanted a separation. Diana replied that the situation had changed so dramatically that to all intents and purposes she was no longer Charles's wife and she felt it would be better if they separated.

Elizabeth told Diana that there was no possibility that she and Charles could divorce and that she would have to seek advice as to whether a separation could be permitted. She explained it was all a matter of the Constitution and she would have to consult lawyers. Elizabeth urged Diana to think long and hard about the course she wanted to take, emphasizing the effect a separation could have on William and Harry. She also talked of her responsibilities as the wife of the Prince of Wales and of her duty to consider the succession to the throne, the future of the monarchy, and the role she would play in the future as Queen of England. To all Elizabeth's words of wisdom Diana nodded.

Significantly, Elizabeth did not ask if there was anyone else in her life. Diana knew that Elizabeth would have read in the press of her alleged affairs with the banker Philip Dunne and the Guards officers Major David Waterhouse and Major James Hewitt. But the matter was not even mentioned.

In her heart Diana believed the Queen would never allow her to separate. She was angry that no one, including Elizabeth and Prince

Philip, seemed to care that Charles lived in sin with his mistress while she was expected to lead a virtuous life in London looking after the two heirs to the throne.

Diana demanded a separation for many reasons. She wanted to show the world that life with Prince Charles had become so unbearable that she had to escape from the marriage; she wanted her own independent life totally separate from the husband she had come to detest and despise; and she wanted the opportunity to live her own life as a free woman, unshackled from the strictures of married life. She felt spurned by Charles and believed that one way to right the wrongs she felt he had done her would be to demand a separation causing him as much public embarrassment as possible. She also hoped that the separation would cause such friction within the Royal Family that he would be forced to give up his adulterous affair with Camilla.

As one of her oldest friends put it: "Diana had reached the stage when she was spitting blood. She was so angry."

Whenever Diana went out alone—to lunch, to the cinema, to a party, to friends—she felt guilty, although the occasions were more often than not innocent. The tabloid press knew when and where she would be out alone or with a man, and the paparazzi would be there to capture the moment on film. Diana felt a conspiracy against her.

Yet she also felt quietly confident. Since 1987 she had become the darling of the British people, adored by everyone, and becoming increasingly popular. She knew that no other royal, including Charles or the Queen, attracted the same interest and enthusiasm as she did. None compared to her popularity.

A 1991 Gallup Poll named Diana the favorite royal, with 22 percent of the votes, almost twice as many as in a 1988 survey. Prince Charles, first in the earlier poll, had been pushed into a second-place tie with his sister, Princess Anne, both with 15 percent. The Queen Mother, then ninety, was next with 14 percent, and Elizabeth had only 12 percent. The remaining 22 percent was divided among the rest of the Royal Family, each with just a few points.

Elizabeth was disturbed that Diana, an outsider who was causing problems by her risqué behavior, had become the most popular royal. She knew that Charles could no longer stand Diana; that any love he might have had for her had gone forever; that he was happily and discreetly ensconced in the country with the admirable Camilla. What particularly worried Elizabeth was the growing number of reports of Diana's indiscretions as she seemed to be flaunting her sexuality and her lovers to an ever-growing circle of people. Elizabeth knew it would not be long before the media discovered Diana with a lover, and that would be disastrous for the family and perhaps the monarchy itself.

Throughout her life Elizabeth has gone along with the simple principle which has guided the Royal Family for a century or more: it doesn't matter what members of the family do, the only sin is being found out. That is the overriding principle which governs the response to any problem.

Elizabeth was more concerned with the institution of monarchy and its effect on society as a whole than about the difficulties of any one individual, such as Diana. Neither she nor the public had any idea how miserable Diana had become or how determined she was to break with Charles.

One day while talking with Gilbey, the idea came about that Diana should let her side of the marriage be told in a book, a truthful book which would reveal details about her marriage, her loneliness, and the treatment she had suffered. Her good friend Gilbey would be only too happy to help.

Diana believed such a book would so shock the nation that her millions of loyal supporters would understand her demand for a separation. She believed the British people would support her decision to let the truth to be told. It all seemed so easy. She never gave a second thought to how her revelations might affect the monarchy.

Diana did recognize that she must distance herself from the book, otherwise it would be seen as a self-serving plot, and that wouldn't win her any support. Diana's friends, however, could speak out on her behalf, giving evidence that the marriage had seriously affected her health.

Some time in 1990, after discussions with his London publisher Michael O'Mara, Andrew Morton decided to write a book about Diana's marriage. Similarly, after much discussion with O'Mara, Diana's late father Earl Spencer, who died in 1992, agreed to allow unpublished childhood photographs of Diana to be included in a royal book O'Mara was planning. In return, O'Mara apparently agreed to pay $150,000 to Diana's favorite charities.

The faithful Gilbey told Diana that he would make certain the book would tell her side of the marriage honestly and completely, so the world would see how appalling her life had become. Those of Diana's friends who were contacted by Gilbey and Morton checked with Diana and were told it was all right to speak to them. Generally, they spoke about Diana's unhappiness and her eating disorders.

Gilbey was true to his word. He did all in his power to ensure that Diana's life with Charles was portrayed in accordance to what he believed were the facts. Painful, unhappy, lonely, miserable—so awful that Diana had allegedly tried suicide five times. In the published book, however, only Gilbey talked of the suicide attempts. None of her other friends had ever heard Diana mention wanting to kill herself.

From the time the book idea was first mooted until publication in the summer of 1992, two years elapsed. Diana became impatient for a separation and would frequently ask Charles when a decision would be made or why such a simple matter was taking so long. Sometimes she raised the subject on weekends when she would travel down to Highgrove with Wills and Harry so the boys could spend some time with their father.

The weekends at Highgrove were hardly ever happy family affairs. Charles would spend much of the day in his walled garden, from which Diana and the children were forbidden. Diana didn't even have a key to the walled garden, and this infuriated her. Charles did sometimes take the boys into his garden to show them around and explain things to them, but they preferred to go swimming or riding or playing around the grounds with their mother. They weren't keen on gardening at this young age.

Most weekends Diana knew an argument—more often than not, a violent shouting match—would occur, and she would end up driving back to London angry, frustrated, and fed up.

As one of the kitchen staff revealed, "Diana would get so angry with him. She would shout and scream at him, telling him she had no intention of letting their marriage continue; and warning that unless some action occurred soon then she would go her own way and get a divorce."

Fergie and Andrew had recently separated. This gave Diana every confidence that Elizabeth could not deny her permission to separate, having just permitted Prince Andrew, fourth in line, to do so. Diana

believed that when the nation realized what a dreadful life she had
lead, and how disgracefully she had been treated by Charles, a wave of
concern and sympathy would mean the Queen would have to consent
to an immediate separation.

By the summer of 1992, Diana had been trying to secure an answer
from Elizabeth about her separation for almost two years. Elizabeth
had taken advice from all the responsible quarters—from government
ministers and senior civil servants, the Church, her palace advisers,
constitutional lawyers, and her mother. All had greeted the suggestion
of a separation with horror, certain that nothing but harm would
ensue. They were all concerned that such a separation would markedly
weaken the authority and the prestige of the monarchy. Elizabeth
thought precisely the same, although she didn't let on when taking her
soundings. Each and every person Elizabeth turned to for advice had
given her the same reply: everything must be done to ensure that
neither a separation nor a divorce will take place, under any
circumstances.

Elizabeth had taken most of these soundings before the Yorks'
separation was announced. She well understood that the public
breakdown of Andrew's marriage had made a split between Charles
and Diana even more disastrous for the image of her family and the
House of Windsor.

Ever since Diana first told her she wanted to separate, Elizabeth had
been at her wit's end, unable to find a way to prevent the split. She had
been able to cope with the other separations and disappointments in
her family's marriages, but this one challenged the very fabric of the
Constitution.

During the summer of 1992, Elizabeth told a lady-in-waiting, "I
have had nightmares and so many sleepless nights worrying about
Charles and Diana, knowing that a breakup in their marriage could
cause so much harm. I kept remembering the effect the abdication
had on the family, and especially on my father who had to step into the
breach. People don't realise the strain everyone was under at that time.
We can't let it happen again."

Secretly, Elizabeth hoped Diana would agree to let the marriage
continue as it had for the last few years, in the interests of the family
and the Crown. Elizabeth knew it was Diana's duty to do so, but she

was not confident Diana would agree to pretend the marriage was safe when everyone knew it wasn't. She knew she had to find a solution suitable to Diana.

Elizabeth, under no illusion concerning Diana's determined nature, believed that Diana could well go ahead of her own volition, instructing lawyers and applying to the Family Court for a separation. That would be disastrous for Elizabeth's image because it would reveal to the world the Queen had refused a separation and Diana had been forced to take the drastic step on her own.

I had already decided to write a biography of Princess Diana when, in 1988, I discovered the couple were living virtually apart. The British publishers that I approached, however, were loath to publish a controversial book which detailed the loveless marriage of Charles and Diana and revealed not only Charles's love for Camilla, but the fact that the Prince and Princess of Wales were, to all intents and purposes, living separate lives. *Diana: A Princess and Her Troubled Marriage* was finally published in May 1992.

Andrew Morton's book, *Diana: Her True Story*, had appeared days earlier. Diana was livid. She complained that the book depicted her as naive and foolish, grossly exaggerating her life with Charles, and she knew the alleged suicide bids were rubbish. Further, she had been exposed as the person behind the book, the precise opposite of her intentions. Instantly she had earned the enmity of senior Palace advisers, who could never excuse anyone, not even Princess Diana, for jeopardizing the reputation of the House of Windsor.

Publication of that book ended Gilbey's relationship with Diana at a stroke. She severed all contact with Gilbey, who had provided much of the information. Diana ordered his name be immediately struck off her Approved List at Kensington Palace.

Elizabeth was furious. The Morton book made it seem that Diana's life had been such absolute hell that she had repeatedly attempted suicide, and Elizabeth knew that to be nonsense. She wondered how much was authentic and feared that so many readers would believe Morton's version that she would be forced to grant Diana an immediate separation. Some of her courtiers were convinced that, one way or another, Diana had consented to the book's being written and had perhaps been instrumental in collating the facts.

· The morning that the *Sunday Times* published extracts of the book,

Diana went to Windsor Castle to apologize to Elizabeth. She told the Queen she had given permission for her friends to cooperate by giving information of her life with Charles. She talked about her regrets and her stupidity at letting friends talk about her life. Diana did *not* tell Elizabeth her principal reason for encouraging her friends to speak out: she wanted to humiliate Charles and expose Camilla Parker Bowles as an adulteress.

Elizabeth did know that Diana had once claimed to have taken an overdose of pills but had immediately made herself sick. The Queen felt the overdose was merely a ruse to get Charles's attention, or perhaps to warn him of what she might do if he continued his relationship with Camilla. Elizabeth called in the three royal doctors who cover any medical problems at Buckingham or Kensington Palace. They assured her they knew of no attempts by Diana to commit suicide, but they did know she had tried to wound herself on occasion when angry and depressed.

Elizabeth knew Diana had suffered from anorexia and touches of bulimia, but due to her conversations with the royal doctors, she believed the picture drawn in the book had been exaggerated.

Three months after both books were published, Camilla Parker Bowles was invited, with her husband Brigadier Andrew Parker Bowles, by the upmarket Dunhill Company to their sponsored day at the Guards polo grounds at Windsor Great Park. As usual, Dunhill sent through to Buckingham Palace a list of the guests they intended to invite to see whom the Queen would like to invite into the Royal Enclosure.

Those privileged to attend the match, as well as the media, were amazed to find that sitting in the Royal Enclosure that day was Camilla Parker Bowles, the woman the nation knew to be Prince Charles's mistress and who had been identified in every newspaper as Princess Diana's sworn enemy. Sitting beside her was Brigadier Andrew, the cuckolded husband.

As newspaper photographers clicked away at this unexpected scene, Elizabeth went even further. In full view of everyone, including the photographers, she politely waved to Camilla. And during the tea interval, Elizabeth sought out Camilla for a chat while everyone stood by, fully understanding the remarkable statement Elizabeth was making. The Queen was deliberately giving tacit but public approval to Charles's relationship with Camilla. But there was even more to this gesture. Elizabeth knew accepting Camilla that day would be taken as a deliberate snub to Diana, and a warning of possible future treatment if she didn't toe the line.

From that day in August 1992, Camilla Parker Bowles, the country woman whom some believed responsible for the breakup of the Prince of Wales's marriage, had been accepted, awarded the highest respect by the sovereign herself, and officially welcomed at Elizabeth's court. By her action Elizabeth showed everyone, including Diana, that Camilla, far from being shunned, would now be treated as a close friend of the Royal Family and given the respect that entailed.

Hardly a week had passed since the sensational photographs of a near-naked Fergie at St. Tropez been flashed around the world than rumors of risqué tapes involving Diana and a mystery lover began to circulate through the media. Back in January 1990, Murdoch's *Sun* tabloid had been given a tape which they decided not to reveal but kept in their safe at Wapping, Murdoch's London headquarters. When the *National Enquirer* published a transcript of that same tape, however, in August 1992, *The Sun* decided to release their "Dianagate" tape.

In the tape, a woman's voice, later verified as Diana's, spoke of her life "being a torture . . . of [her] uncaring, selfish husband." There was also much romantic talk, the couple calling each other "darling" and talking of "love." The man kept calling Diana "Squidgy." *The Sun*'s twelve million readers were invited to telephone a special number to listen to the twenty-three-minute tape and hear the full conversation themselves. The recording was most revealing and highly personal. Later, it was confirmed that the man on the tape was James Gilbey.

Cyril Reenan was a highly respectable retired bank manager who loved listening to other people's car-phone conversations on his ham radio. He told how he had picked up the "royal" phone call on New Year's Eve, 1989, and had handed the tape to *The Sun*. The tape was examined by Sony experts, one of whom, Martin Colloms, concluded the tape had been made from "a direct wire tap onto a telephone line" and that this "had been processed afterwards so that superficially it sounded like a cellnet broadcast." Experts concluded this meant Diana's phone had been tapped by person or persons unknown, and that somehow this conversation had ended up being broadcast when monitored by people such as Reenan.

Some British newspapers delved deeper, asking, "How could the Princess's telephone at Sandringham have been bugged? Who had the technical expertise to do this? Why would those responsible waste time by broadcasting the tape? How could they be sure anyone would pick it up and sell it to a newspaper?"

As a result some of the most responsible and distinguished members of society, such as Lord Rees-Mogg, chairman of the Broadcasting Standards Council and a former editor of *The Times* newspaper, maintained the whole Dianagate scandal was a conspiracy perpetrated by the security services and that this tape had been deliberately leaked. But once again the questions were asked: "Why? And by whom?"

Later, further extracts of the Dianagate tape were revealed in which Diana talked of the fear of becoming pregnant and referred to an episode in an English TV soap *Eastenders* (one of her favorite TV shows) in which a character had had a baby by a man who was not her husband. Many people believe this particular tape confirmed that Diana was having an affair with Gilbey, but that is not the case. Diana did not have an affair with him. In fact, the reference to pregnancy was Diana tactfully trying to put off Gilbey, implying she didn't want a sexual relationship with him for fear of becoming pregnant. Further, others suggested, if their relationship was so physical and sexual, it was strange that there was no reference to any past or planned sexual intercourse between them.

The tapes were highly embarrassing to Elizabeth. She ordered one of her private staff, who knew Diana well, to phone *The Sun* hotline, listen to the tape, and let her know whether he believed the voice was that of Diana. Thirty minutes later the confidant returned to say that he was "virtually certain" it was Diana.

The revelation that Diana had been having some sort of love affair with a mystery man helped to balance the allegation that Charles had been having an affair with Camilla. The public were left in no doubt that all the blame could not be laid entirely at Charles's door, and that perhaps Diana had not been the innocent, blameless wife after all.

Throughout the autumn of 1992, Elizabeth stepped up her interviews with all those who needed to discuss the matter of the marriage of the heir apparent and how to proceed if Diana persisted in demanding a legal separation. During her weekly meetings with Prime Minister John Major, Elizabeth spoke at length of the probability that Diana would insist on a separation. She spoke to the Archbishop of Canterbury about the possibility of a divorced man becoming Head of the Church of England.

Elizabeth told both Charles and Diana that the monarchy and the House of Windsor came before all else. If the intended separation would cause any major problem to Britain's unwritten Constitution or meant that Charles could not accede to the throne or succeed as Head of the Church of England, then both would have to accept that a separation would not be permitted. The Constitution might be unwritten, but its disciplines had been honed throughout the past three centuries and continue to be debated by constitutional lawyers and academics.

She reminded them that they had both given assurances that no matter what happened, they would remain married "until death us do part." And married they would have to remain. Charles readily agreed to what his mother said, while Diana said she would wait and see what the constitutional lawyers ruled.

Elizabeth talked to Bobo, then eighty-eight, to her mother, ninety-two, to her senior ladies-in-waiting, as well as to lawyers and her advisers inside the palace and a few close friends she trusted. All were sworn to secrecy and all kept their word. She took Charles into her confidence, so that at all stages, Charles would be fully aware of the constitutional position.

Elizabeth tried one last time to bring the two together in an effort to avoid the split. Charles told his mother he would be fully prepared to continue the marriage, continue the life fashioned over the last four years for the sake of everyone, but especially for the House of Windsor. When Diana came to see Elizabeth, she answered by shaking her head and telling her that in all conscience she could not continue with the marriage, and she begged her to permit a separation.

The die was cast. Elizabeth had failed to persuade Diana. The Queen prepared to face the darkest days of her forty-year reign.

On December 9, 1992, to a hushed House of Commons, Prime Minister John Major read out the statement that the Prince and

Princess of Wales were to separate after eleven years of marriage. The only surprise, which brought gasps of disbelief from the crowded Commons, was when Major announced that there would be no constitutional implications and that Diana could still be crowned Queen. The statement made clear that the couple's decision to lead separate lives had been reached amicably, that both would continue to carry out public duties, and that both would participate fully in the upbringing of their two children.

Buckingham Palace announced that the Queen and the Duke of Edinburgh, although saddened, understood and sympathized with the decision and hoped that intrusions into the couple's privacy would cease. Elizabeth watched the Commons announcement live on television, alone in her sitting room. Then she rang the bell and asked that tea be brought immediately.

Elizabeth and her Palace advisers knew Diana had to shoulder most of the responsibility in this crisis for the monarchy. The Queen firmly believed that whatever had happened, Diana should have abided by the agreement she made not only in her marriage vows in front of the world, but also in private before she even became engaged. Elizabeth believed it was Diana's duty to stay married. She also knew she would never, and could never, forgive her daughter-in-law for what she viewed as gross dereliction of duty and the height of irresponsibility.

Now that the Waleses' marriage had been revealed as a sham to the world, Elizabeth believed that nothing more could possibly go wrong.

Within weeks, however, Elizabeth and Charles were faced with yet further embarrassment. In Australia, *New Idea*, a magazine owned by Rupert Murdoch, published intimate details of an alleged conversation of a remarkable, frank, and sexual nature between Charles and Camilla Parker Bowles. The magazine claimed the conversation, which inevitably they dubbed "Camillagate," had been taped on December 18, 1989, about the same time that Diana's conversation with James Gilbey was taped. There is no doubt that the voices on the tape are those of Charles and Camilla.

New Idea commented, "For the first time, amazingly intimate details of a bedtime phone call between Prince Charles and Camilla Parker Bowles have shown why Princess Diana pulled the plug on her sham of a marriage.

"In the touching late-night conversation, the depth of the star-crossed couple's love for each other, and their desire to be together, comes across with shocking frankness.

"And it finally confirms Camilla's long-standing, passionately familiar relationship with the man who would be King.

"The sexy secrets of the conversation will shock those convinced Charles is a 'cold fish' because he hasn't had a physical relationship with Di for years. He shows that with the woman he loves, he can be warm and unashamedly physical."

The conversation loses some impact in print. I have myself listened to the tape, and the warm intimacy of a couple familiar with each other for some years is unmistakable. When listening instead of reading, one hears the deep underlying longing for each other, the anguished sexual desperation. It is touching and moving.

In the tape Charles tells Camilla, "Your great achievement is to love me. I adore you—I'm so proud of you."

Part of the tape is openly sexual and intimate.

CHARLES: I want to feel my way along you, all over you and up and down you and in and out.
CAMILLA (in a breathless gasp): Oh, oh.
CHARLES: Particularly in and out.
CAMILLA: Oh, that's just what I need at the moment . . . I can't bear a Sunday night without you.
CHARLES: What about me? The trouble is I need you several times a week.
CAMILLA: Mmm. So do I. I need you all the week. All the time.
CHARLES: Oh, God. I'll just live inside your trousers or something. It would be much easier.
CAMILLA (laughing): What are you going to turn into, a pair of knickers? (Both laugh) Oh, you're going to come back as a pair of knickers.
CHARLES: Or, God forbid, a Tampax. Just my luck. (He laughs)

They end the phone call with Charles saying sleepily, "I love you," and Camilla replying in a hushed voice, "Good night, my darling. Love you."

The source of the Camillagate tape stirred controversy in Britain, as with the earlier Dianagate conversation. That phone calls from both Charles and Diana should have been accidentally taped by amateur radio hams was highly implausible.

Further fuel was added to the flames when a third tape suddenly appeared, this one a recorded telephone call between Prince Andrew and Fergie, again recorded in 1989, and again with one of the callers speaking on a mobile phone. Like the other two taped calls, this one included sexy conversation.

The quality of the Camillagate tape was superb, and most media commentators concluded that the bugging had to be the work of professionals. In all three cases one party had been on a mobile phone and the other on a fixed line. Those arguing that the recordings were purely accidental claimed that calls on mobile telephones were easily picked up by radio hams with inexpensive scanners. Experts, however, pointed out that recording both sides of overheard telephone calls is extremely difficult and requires highly sophisticated equipment. Furthermore, to record both sides with the clear audibility of the royal tapes would mean scanning across hundreds of channels to find the other half of the conversation, a virtual impossibility.

The quality of all three conversations, their detail and content pointed to their being recorded at the fixed-link end. That meant the installation of a device, sending out a signal to a recorder. As the arguments raged, nearly every expert consulted came to the same conclusion: the phone calls must have been bugged by professionals.

As speculation intensified over who had the resources and the motive to make these tapes, MI5 officials tried to shrug off accusations that their agents were responsible. Security sources simply indicated that the allegations were too insubstantial to warrant a response. In the United States, given the same circumstances, members of Congress or investigative journalists would have insisted that security authorities investigate such claims.

But in Britain in the 1990s, it is still accepted that security organizations like MI5 can simply refuse to answer questions, as though they are unaccountable to higher political authority, and the public simply accept that no answer will be given.

Those close to government power and many political journalists believe MI5 simply lie when they believe it is "in the national interest" to do so. That "national interest" often includes the reputations of those in the government of the day, Cabinet ministers as well as senior civil servants. Such matters point to the extraordinary secrecy which still prevails in much of Britain's public life and to how little the government does to ensure greater accountability.

As monarch, Elizabeth has both the power and the right to be informed of such matters, but even she is not always told the truth. In the 1970s, the British security services wire-tapped their own boss, Prime Minister Harold Wilson, who theoretically should have been informed of all issues affecting national security. Security service chiefs alleged they had information indicating pro-Communist contacts may have been trying to influence the Prime Minister. But in reality, the security services did what they believed was right at that time, without political supervision and without authority.

Some believed MI5 taped the three conversations to ascertain that no security risk existed involving the behavior of the younger royals. Others suggested the tapes had been smuggled onto the open market by a renegade or greedy agent, or by someone wanting to push the republican cause in Britain. But few, including all members of the Royal Family, believed for one minute that the phone calls were "picked up" accidentally.

Elizabeth demanded of Prime Minister John Major, the ultimate boss of the security services, any information he had about the source of the tapes. It is not known what action the Prime Minister demanded, or indeed whether he had been informed by the head of MI5, Mrs. Stella Rimington, if any agents had been involved, with or without direction or supervision. Nor is it known what Major told Elizabeth.

Elizabeth was seriously worried. She feared the monarchy was under attack on many different fronts and that the younger royals, those commoners her royal advisers called the witches, were primarily responsible. She hoped that the horrors of 1992—the most dreadful year of her reign—would fade, but throughout 1993 she became increasingly anxious that the forces opposed to the monarchy were gaining ground and that the defenses she could call on were weakening.

SEVENTEEN

SARAH, DUCHESS OF YORK

Diana and Princess Michael had, in Elizabeth's eyes, behaved deplorably, reneging on their duty to their husbands and the House of Windsor, and that was considered a major sin. The third witch, whom Elizabeth warmed to and whom she liked far more than either Diana or Princess Michael, was to behave like a loose cannon, leading a truly amoral life and apparently not caring who knew.

Sarah Ferguson, daughter of Major Ronald Ferguson, known all her life as Fergie, was a surprise choice for Prince Andrew to marry. With her titian hair and well-built figure, she was not the usual type of girl Andrew liked to bed.

Andrew was regarded as arrogant, proud, high-handed, and a swank show-off. He seemed to have inherited those genes from his father, which did not make him very popular either at school or in the Royal Navy. And, perhaps more important as far as Fergie was concerned, he believed, as his father did, that he was irresistible to women.

Andrew had known virtually nothing of sex until he was in the Caribbean, serving as a junior officer on a few days' leave from his Royal Navy ship when he met Vicki Houdge, a beautiful, mature fashion model. He was just twenty-one. They spent the best part of a week together, and in that time Vicki taught Prince Andrew a good deal about sex. A colleague of Prince Andrew said later, "When Andrew left that island he was dead on his feet; he had been well and truly decanted."

A strong sexual chemistry existed between Andrew and Fergie. For their first few months together Andrew and Fergie could not keep their hands off each other and would spend as much time as possible in bed. Great sex, and a sense of fun, kept them together. They enjoyed each other's company. Neither Andrew nor Fergie is very bright, but they both enjoyed active sports and liked the same television shows, films, and music. Both loved kidding around, throwing bread rolls in a restaurant or indulging in cream bun fights, enjoying the attention and the limelight.

Elizabeth and Philip had welcomed Fergie's arrival. They felt she would be a far better member of the House of Windsor than Andrew's previous girlfriend, the attractive American actress Koo Stark who, it was revealed by the investigative tabloid press, had had various live-in lovers as well as starring parts in soft-porn movies. In fact, Koo Stark was typical of the women that Prince Philip had found so attractive throughout his life and could not resist bedding. In this Andrew was maintaining tradition. Many royals through the ages have had affairs with actresses, not the least of them Edward VII who, at the turn of the century, had a long-lasting affair with the British sex symbol and leading actress of that era, the lovely Lily Langtry.

Both Elizabeth and Philip had known Fergie, whom they both called by her given name of Sarah, off and on all her life. She had an impeccable upper-class English background which included Charles II as an ancestor. Her father, Major Ron Ferguson, had once commanded the Sovereign's Escort of the Household Cavalry Regiment. He had not only played polo with Prince Philip for some years after World War II, but had also been appointed Polo Manager to Prince Charles. Elizabeth and Philip had first seen Sarah when she was brought to polo matches at Windsor as an infant.

Fergie had virtually grown up with Andrew. She was well acquainted with the rules of royal protocol and etiquette, and she knew how the Royal Family worked. Elizabeth rather liked Fergie's freshness and vitality. She and Philip both wanted their boisterous second son to settle down, get married, and start a family, hoping this would make him more responsible. When Andrew announced he wanted to marry Fergie, his parents were genuinely pleased and relieved. They believed Sarah Ferguson would keep their son in line.

Elizabeth and Fergie got on famously together. Fergie's bubbly personality brought out the friendly, relaxed side of Elizabeth's nature. And the Queen enjoyed the younger woman's company, especially at weekend parties. They had much in common. Both enjoyed country life, riding, stalking, polo, and walking the dogs. Elizabeth also liked Fergie's dress sense, more practical than fashionable.

Elizabeth agreed to give them whatever wedding present they wanted, and they decided on a brand-new ranch-style home near Windsor. Elizabeth paid for everything, including the carpets, the furniture, and the instant garden. Despite the cost of $750,000, architectural snobs thought their new home was in poor taste, some describing it as "cheap and nasty," more like a "burger restaurant" or "supermarket" than a home.

Elizabeth had no idea what a little vixen Fergie really was, nor that Fergie had a remarkable sexual appetite and was genuinely unconcerned with morals. Her character was to be her undoing. As an insecure teenager, Fergie had had a number of lovers, none of whom lasted very long. She seemed to need to have a boyfriend on hand at all times for her self-confidence, and it was during those years that she realized her sexual needs were prodigious.

During the early 1980s Fergie had been in love with Paddy McNally, a man twenty-two years her senior, a wealthy motor racing manager who lived in Verbier, Switzerland, with his two teenage sons. His wife had died of cancer some years before. For three years Fergie and Paddy had all but lived together during the winter ski months. Fergie was a good skier and a good hostess for Paddy, but in this relationship she was always the underdog, pushing for McNally's affection and love.

Paddy did little for Fergie's confidence. He often invited other good-looking young women to his home. McNally liked to keep an open house where people, particularly attractive young women, could always find a bed. Finally, in October 1985, six months after her first date with Prince Andrew, McNally told Fergie he did not want to marry her, and indeed didn't think he would ever remarry.

The ending of that relationship hit Fergie hard. It wasn't the first time she had been rebuffed by a man she loved, and she had set her heart on staying with McNally. Another of Fergie's earlier loves, Kim Smith-Bingham, a handsome British ski bum, had also lived in Verbier, known affectionately to Brits as "Chelsea-on-Ski." Their affair went well until Fergie went to Argentina to visit her mother, Susie

Barrantes. On her return to Smith-Bingham's Verbier apartment, she discovered that another girl, Sarah Worsley, a niece of the Duchess of Kent, had taken her place. Fergie was distraught.

Ever since her mother had fled the family home to live with the wealthy Argentine polo player, Hector Barrantes, Sarah had lacked confidence. She was thirteen at the time, a vulnerable age. Her father, Major Ron Ferguson, had treated Sarah more like a teenage son than a daughter. As a result Fergie became a first-class horsewoman and a good skier, but she was unsure of herself with young men and would fall in love instantly if any man showed interest. Despite good advice from many girlfriends, no one could help Fergie as she stumbled from one disastrous love affair to another.

Paddy McNally was the last straw. She had given her all to him, indulging his sexual adventures and other girlfriends while running his house for him as well as sharing his bed. One of Fergie's girlfriends who spent the next summer on the Mediterranean island of Ibiza with her, recalled, "During those weeks together Fergie poured out her heart. Her life had been shattered, her relationship with McNally had eroded her confidence. And Fergie believed her fling with Andrew was just that, a fling. She was not a happy lady."

Fergie believed she would never find anyone to love her when she met Prince Andrew at a dinner party in London. They had known each other since childhood, and now Fergie was bowled over. One of the reasons she loved her relationship with Andrew in those early months was the fact that he wanted her, wanted to spoil her and be with her all the time, so very different from Paddy McNally.

Naturally Fergie loved it all, and Andrew's attention gave her the confidence she needed. They enjoyed each other's company immensely, both in and out of bed. To Fergie and Andrew, a good sex life was of paramount importance in a relationship. After a six-month courtship Andrew, age twenty-six, proposed, and a deliriously happy Fergie, twenty-seven, accepted. A magnificent royal wedding at Westminster Abbey followed in July 1986.

Despite having grown up around royals, Fergie seemed not to have the faintest idea how to behave when she married Andrew and became the Duchess of York. Marrying into the Royal Family seemed to go to her head; she acted as though she could now do anything and everything she wanted and yet accept no responsibility. She spent

Andrew's 1987 allowance of $140,000 from the Civil List as if it were hers to do with as she wished; she accepted every freebie on offer—every flight, every holiday, every weekend away.

She refused to accept advice given her by Palace officials, by her ladies-in-waiting, or by friends she had known for years. The newspaper attacks on the life she was leading hurt her feelings, but she made no effort to change. She believed she was entitled to rampant hedonism simply because she had joined the Royal Family. Andrew might have reined in her excesses, but he was away at sea most of the time and in any case lacked the strength of character to control his wayward wife.

During those first few years Fergie came in for the most appalling roasting from the tabloid press, which, with inverted snobbery, had decided from the very beginning that Fergie wasn't royal enough for the House of Windsor. It was ironic that in the last decades of the twentieth century, the republican-biased British press devoted so many pages to attacking Fergie for being too ordinary and not sufficiently royal for their tastes. At every opportunity they criticized her figure, her makeup, her hairstyle, her clothes, her holidays, her sense of fun, and her lack of commitment. According to the popular press Fergie could do nothing right.

Fergie didn't do much to ameliorate the situation. Throughout 1990 she carried out only 108 royal engagements, just ten more than the Queen Mother, who was ninety that year. She also played into her critics' hands by indulging in a never-ending round of dinners, balls, society events, and parties. She seemed to take overseas holidays every other month at fashionable beach and ski resorts. She was dubbed "Freebie Fergie" and later "Doolittle Duchess" for two reasons: she wasn't doing much for the Yorks' $400,000-a-year paycheck from the 1991 Civil List, and she behaved like the uneducated Cockney, Eliza Doolittle.

Much of the criticism was unfair, but she believed the underlying fact was the ever-present comparison with the perfect princess, Diana. Seduced by the beautiful Diana, the people of Britain believed in the 1980s that to be a "real princess" one had to be a Diana look-alike: super-slim, super-cool, super-sophisticated. Fergie was none of these.

The incessant onslaught from Fleet Street finally got to Fergie, and she decided to change everything about herself: her image, her looks, her wardrobe. First, Fergie needed to slim down. From her teenage years she had always been a bit heavy but had lived with the problem and had accepted the teasing and the jokes. Now she went on a crash diet and lost nearly thirty pounds. She bought a new wardrobe to suit her new svelte body, changed her hairstyle, and had experts revamp her makeup. Nevertheless, the press critics continued their attacks.

Fergie then turned to an astrologer, a medium, and a palmist in an effort to become a "new woman." Perhaps the most famous was Madame Vasso, a Greek mystic healer who practiced New Age philosophies such as the healing power of the pyramid. Fergie would go to Madame Vasso's very ordinary basement apartment in an unfashionable part of London and sit on a stool under a blue glass pyramid while the astrologer tried to drain away all her tensions. The technique seemed ineffectual.

Like Diana, Fergie also sought the help of the astrologer Penny Thornton. Indeed, she was prepared to try anything and anyone to help her. She experimented with facial massages, hypnotherapy, aromatherapy, and acupuncture, all in an effort to become a new, slim-line, more beautiful woman. Just as she seemed to be winning the battle of the bulge, Beatrice arrived in 1988, and then Eugenie in 1990.

Both Andrew and Fergie were perceived as the living epitome of bad taste. When they allowed themselves to be photographed in their new home, which they had helped design, the press christened the place "Southyork" because it resembled a ranch house from the TV series *Dallas*.

Elizabeth saw the mistakes the couple were making and tried to advise Fergie. She knew how wounding journalists could be, particularly to someone like Fergie, whose figure wasn't that of a catwalk model and whose natural personality was bubbly and excitable. Elizabeth wanted to help Fergie because she believed she would be good for Andrew and, therefore, beneficial to the House of Windsor.

Shortly after her marriage, Fergie discovered that being a member of the Royal Family distinctly encouraged men to come forward, to show interest, to flirt. She had never experienced such attention before and she reveled in it. Even when pregnant Fergie sought the attentions of young men.

In November 1989, five months pregnant with Eugenie, Fergie went on an official royal visit to Houston, Texas, representing the

Queen at the British Festival at the Houston Grand Opera. There she met Steve Wyatt and fell in love. To start, Fergie fell for his good looks. Wyatt, thirty-five, was a serious, athletic man with a mahogany suntan. Fergie was the guest of Wyatt's mother, Lynn Sakowitz Wyatt, heiress to the Houston department store and the wife of oil billionaire Oscar Wyatt, who had adopted Steve and his brother Douglas, when he married their mother. It was Lynn who introduced her son to the Duchess at their Houston mansion. He did not smoke, drink, or take any form of drugs. Fergie became smitten by his talk of karma, astrology, divinity, and other New Age subjects, interests dear to her heart and a million miles from the conversations she had with Andrew. She spent much of that evening dancing with Steve. It was a real-life fatal attraction.

The die was cast. Fergie invited him over to London, invited him to Buckingham Palace, arranged invitations for him to lunch at the palace and take dinner at Windsor Castle, and she introduced her "new friend" to Prince Andrew. Apparently, they all got on famously and would have supper and barbecues together. In 1990 when Fergie took Bea and Eugenie on holiday to Morocco, Wyatt went along too. Unknown to Andrew, Fergie was in love with Wyatt and they were having a passionate fling. Back in London, Wyatt took an apartment close to the palace, and the two spent afternoons and evenings making love there. Fergie seemed unable to say no to Wyatt, risking her marriage, her future, and the lives of her two daughters whom she professed to adore.

Andrew, the cuckolded husband, was blind to what was going on, but the Royal Protection Squad was not. Every date, every clandestine meeting would be reported back to the squad's senior officers who, duty-bound, gave the information to their seniors in the palace. Eventually, the reports ended up on the desk of Sir Robert Fellowes. It is not known at what stage Sir Robert passed the information on to the Queen, but at some point she was informed of the affair.

Alarm bells rang in 1991 when Wyatt escorted Fergie to a private London dinner party to which he had not been invited. He sat down next to her with the immortal words, "Mah woman and I"—"Ah" rhyming with "Mah"—"sit together"—words that were reverberating around Buckingham Palace and the corridors of MI5 within twenty-four hours. The guests and the hosts were flabbergasted at Wyatt's effrontery and the fact that the Duchess of York did exactly as he commanded.

During the summer and autumn of 1991 Fergie continued to stray. Sir Robert Fellowes asked to see her. At their meetings Fellowes tried to make Fergie understand that rumors suggested she was seeing Wyatt and that people might jump to the wrong conclusion. Worse still, if the press discovered Wyatt's existence, they would have a field day.

The police continued their surveillance, and Fergie was called in to see Sir Robert again. This time she was left in no doubt that the Palace knew what had been going on. She was told the Queen had been informed, and she was advised most strongly to stop fooling around.

Fergie still continued to see Wyatt. Fellowes realized he had to stop the affair because not only was Fergie risking her marriage, but if the affair became public knowledge she would involve the House of Windsor and the monarchy in a scandal they could ill afford. He was angry that Fergie ignored his warnings and seemed equally oblivious to potential scandal.

Throughout her marriage Fergie had frequently been called to see Sir Robert about a variety of incidents and stories that appeared in the press. At first he had tried to be friendly, to educate her on how to behave, what to wear, and the hundred and one idiosyncrasies of royal life and traditions. He also warned her to end her casual affairs and behave herself. He told her she must not demand payment for newspaper and magazine articles or accept freebie trips and holidays or any invitations that didn't come through the Palace.

Fergie felt the Palace wanted to control every aspect of her life, and she rebelled. In one memorable shouting match with Sir Robert, she said, "If I can't lead my own life without you telling me what to do, then I'll go my own way. I'm fed up being told what I can and cannot do—by you."

Fergie pleaded with Andrew to demand that Sir Robert leave her alone, because she was at the end of her tether. She told Andrew, "I can't take any more of him preaching and shouting at me. You must make him stop." Andrew replied that he could not become involved, that it was a matter for her and Sir Robert, whose duty it was to advise the younger royals.

Fergie began losing her temper at her meetings with Fellowes, and he, unable to make her come to her senses, began to shout at her. Their meetings became more heated. Fergie resented his tone, his criticisms, and his attitude: sometimes she would leave his room in tears, at other times in a rage. She began to refer to him as "Bellowes," to rhyme with "Fellowes."

Then, for no apparent reason, Wyatt suddenly announced to Fergie in the fall of 1991 that he had decided to return to America. He said his father wanted him back to help run the family business. He had never even hinted he was planning to go home, and Fergie knew in her heart that the establishment had been at work. Someone had spoken to Wyatt. In that most discreet British way, Wyatt had been quietly advised to leave London. Not seeking trouble, Wyatt agreed. Fergie was left behind, angry and upset, and once again feeling rejected by the man she loved.

Alone, Fergie grew nervous. She believed she was being followed everywhere she went, that her phones were tapped, her mail checked, her life subject to scrutiny, all orchestrated from the Palace. By the fall of 1991 Fergie went to pieces.

In a remarkably candid interview in the summer of 1991, Fergie described how she felt "owned and controlled" by the Royal Family. She agreed to be interviewed by the *Tatler* magazine in the Yorks' office in Buckingham Palace, a chaotic room, part nursery, part gymnasium, part workplace. Fergie wore no makeup and her hair was still damp from a recent workout on her exercise bike. Little Princess Beatrice, then three, ran in and out throughout the interview, half-naked, and at one point, Prince Andrew walked in, did a double-take, and tiptoed out, a pantomime expression of comic horror on his face. This was no normal royal interview where the agenda is agreed beforehand, where a Palace press officer is present, and where the royal is seen perfectly dressed, perfectly made up, and in command. Fergie was none of these.

Fergie was reacting against being "on-show" twenty-four hours a day, unable to escape the intense heat of the limelight. She said, "Real life isn't like this, living in a palace. I don't even feel happy at Sunninghill, what the tabloids call Fergie's Dallas Palace. I love to get away, to have my own privacy. I don't even feel any privacy at Sunninghill. Some nights I ask every member of staff to leave so that we can be a family, on our own, like a normal family."

She went on, "I just have to get away from The System and people saying to me all the time 'no you can't, no you can't.' That's what The System is like. I can't stick to all the guidelines, to all the rules because they're not real. It's not a real life living in a palace. And so I feel inhibited."

Fergie explained that she liked to relax by escaping to the mountains to ski. She said, "If I lived in Europe no one would be the wiser if I went to the mountains. I could go skiing for the weekend and no one would bat an eyelid. But here, everyone thinks skiing is an elitist sport. The mountains are my security. I love them. The mountains talk to me and they give me strength. And I'm not allowed to go because of being seen, because of what people might say or write, and all because I'm owned. Therefore I don't go and I feel trapped. And it's The System that is trapping me."

She confided that she was hurt by the constant criticism, much of which, she claimed, was totally incorrect. For example, after Eugenie was born Fergie's hair began to fall out and, on advice from her hairdresser, she had much of it chopped off. One newspaper proclaimed that she did it purely to spite Prince Andrew because he liked her hair long.

After saying that she tried to keep herself as independent as possible, she concluded, "At the end of the day you die alone. As long as you're kind, and you get up in the morning and you're happy to look at yourself, and you're straightforward and thank God for everything you do because He knows, they can write what they want to write. . . ." She did not finish the sentence because tears were forming in her eyes.

Andrew, fed up with press stories about Fergie's love affair with Steve Wyatt, a man he had invited into his home and trusted, began to shun his wife and spend much more time on the golf course. Fergie couldn't cope. With Wyatt gone, Fergie had no one to turn to. She tried to talk things through with her father, but he urged her to make it up with Andrew.

Fergie found solace and companionship with Johnny Bryan, a friend of Wyatt's from their school days together at St. John's High School in Houston. Bryan, another American, was a tall, balding, well-built bachelor in his late thirties who described himself as a financial adviser. He listened to Fergie's problems and offered to help. As troubles brewed between Andrew and Fergie, she asked Bryan to act as peacemaker. He went along to Sunninghill and talked to both of them, ostensibly in an effort to help sort out their marriage problems. However, the more times Fergie spent with Bryan, the more she became attracted to him. Andrew witnessed that attraction. He didn't want to know about patching up the marriage, and Fergie realized that she was being edged out of the family.

As a financial adviser, Bryan was able to help Fergie professionally. During the first years of married life, Fergie had not been idle in feathering her nest. She had seen how her father had struggled through most of his life, always being short of real money and often living hand-to-mouth, sometimes needing to borrow from friends and family. She wanted to ensure that never happened to her. She had given interviews to newspapers for money, one to the *Daily Express* for $150,000, and another to *Hello Magazine*, which paid her $300,000 for a set of photographs showing Andrew, herself, and the children inside Sunninghill. She had also written highly successful children's books about Budgie the Helicopter which had earned her $500,000.

But within a short time, Johnny Bryan had taken over where his friend Wyatt had left off—he became Fergie's new lover. Within days of their sleeping together in 1992, Buckingham Palace was made fully aware that Fergie had gone off the rails again.

Sir Robert Fellowes, Elizabeth's most senior adviser, ordered a report to be drawn up on Sarah. It revealed many of Fergie's past sexual trysts as well as extramarital affairs that had taken place during the months Prince Andrew served at sea. The report described Fergie's sexual appetite as "almost insatiable."

Fergie and the Palace had also had to contend with the scandalous behavior of her father, Major Ronald Ferguson. While Fergie was expecting her first baby in 1988, Ronald Ferguson returned to his old antics, frequenting brothels. He had become a member of the Wigmore Club, a high-class brothel with attractive young prostitutes who specialized in massages. Ferguson not only enrolled at the club under his own name, but openly bragged to the girls who worked there that he was the Duchess of York's father and a close friend of Charles and Diana.

In May 1988, *The People* newspaper ran a front-page story about

Ferguson. The headline read FERGIE'S DAD AND THE VICE GIRLS. The story said, "To the outside world Major Ron is a friend to the Queen, polo manager to Prince Charles, confidant to Princess Diana, and one of the royal circle's most colorful characters.

"But attractive young prostitutes working at a high-class London brothel, called the Wigmore Club, know another Major Ferguson. He is one of their most valued, regular customers. The galloping major pays blondes, brunettes and redheads for sexual services—and even rewards his favorite girls with gifts of perfume."

Elizabeth and senior aides at Buckingham Palace were outraged. Fergie was desperately ashamed. Six months earlier Major Ferguson had been sternly warned by a senior Palace official that his involvement with vice girls could lead to deep embarrassment to the Queen.

Ferguson took no notice of the warning, believing that since his daughter was now a royal, he was free to behave however he wished.

Days after Sarah's engagement in 1985, Major Ron had thrown a celebratory dinner party, inviting a number of people to an expensive restaurant in fashionable Pont Street. One guest commented, "I remember it well because Ron never threw dinner parties. This was an exception."

Someone at the next table heard Major Ron boast, "Until this moment I have been a nobody all my life, but now I am a personality everyone knows and I am beginning to like it."

He was wrong in thinking that his daughter's position would allow him to do as he pleased. The Palace had no intention of permitting Major Ron to continue his scandalous life.

Yet another matter concerning Fergie's father was distressing the Palace. He was using his daughter's position and title—the Duchess of York—to make money for himself in secret.

Unbeknownst to Fergie, her father would arrange dinner parties, polo events, cocktail parties, and other occasions and would promise people that—for a suitable sum of money, payable in cash—his daughter, and sometimes Prince Andrew, would attend. The people he invited never imagined they would be privileged enough to rub shoulders with royalty, let alone meet, chat, and dine with them. They jumped at his offer; their wives were overjoyed.

The Major had a copy of his daughter's diary and would schedule his "private" events so as not to conflict with others in her life. Most people were happy to pay $2,000 to $10,000 for the privilege of meeting the Duchess. And, because Fergie believed she was helping her father's polo sponsorships, she happily agreed to attend the odd dinner, polo match, or other social occasion.

Diana and Fergie had been close pals, indeed best friends (BFs in Sloane Ranger slang) for some time during the 1980s, and both knew full well that neither of them was happy. Fergie had helped Diana come to terms with her role as princess during that time. She encouraged her to develop a more positive attitude by leading a more active, independent life, branching out on her own, and involving herself in charity work. Fergie felt Diana was cloistering herself too much in Kensington Palace.

In late 1991, when she knew that Diana wanted to separate from Charles, Fergie had confided to Diana that she couldn't cope with life married to Prince Andrew. Diana knew precisely how Fergie felt. She had often broken into tears when telling Fergie about her own life and the collapse of her marriage. They both knew that Diana would have a far greater problem in "ditching" Charles, heir to the throne, than Fergie would in leaving Andrew, who, after the births of William and Harry, had dropped to fourth in line of succession.

Five years and two children after their wedding in 1986, Fergie had come to the conclusion that she and Andrew had never really known each other before they rushed into marriage. She now saw that their relationship was based on sex as much as anything else, and, worse, she had married Andrew on the rebound.

The fact that Diana had broached the subject of separation with Elizabeth gave Fergie confidence to do the same. Fergie was fed up with the restrictions of royal life, fed up that she never saw Andrew because he was always at sea with the Royal Navy. The spark had gone out of their marriage, and their sex life had lost the urgency Fergie craved. Buckling from the constant stream of criticism from Palace advisers and the tabloid press, Fergie knew she could no longer take the pressure.

Fergie decided she wanted out, and in February 1992, went to tell the one person she believed would help, her mother-in-law Elizabeth.

As she sat down Fergie said, "I've got something awful to tell you. I cannot take it any more. Everyone at the Palace is against me, and it has ruined our marriage."

Elizabeth reassured Sarah that it was quite wrong for her to think there were people in the palace who wanted her out of the Royal Family. She said that everyone took their orders and instructions from her and the last thing she wanted was a broken marriage in the family.

Frustrated and angry that Andrew and Fergie, who in many ways appeared ideally suited, seemed unable to make a go of their marriage, Elizabeth tried to persuade Fergie to change her mind. She called Andrew home from the Royal Navy and discussed the situation with him. In the previous year Andrew had spent only forty-three days at home, the rest either away at sea or at his naval base. She thought a home-based posting might heal the rift between them, and she arranged for the Admiralty to organize a management course at the college near their Windsor home, so that Andrew could live with his wife and young family.

Andrew had told his mother that Fergie was in control of the home and the children and behaved exactly as she pleased, independently and selfishly, no matter what he said. Andrew said that during the last few months when he had been at home, they had fought constantly. He also told his mother that Fergie believed senior Palace officials wanted to be rid of her.

In fact, Fergie was correct. A number of senior Palace advisers did want to be rid of her, convinced her behavior would only bring discredit to the family.

It was Prince Andrew who finally convinced his mother that his marriage to Fergie could not survive. He had known of her adultery with Steve Wyatt, and he had witnessed at first hand Fergie's attraction to Johnny Bryan as she flirted in front of him at their Windsor home. Andrew believed that the love that once existed between them had all but disappeared and that Fergie had no further interest in him. Andrew told his mother he believed the marriage to be a lost cause.

Eventually, Elizabeth reluctantly agreed that discreet actions could be taken so that Fergie would obtain a legal separation from Andrew, but only on terms that were advantageous to the House of Windsor. More than anyone, Elizabeth knew how precarious Charles's marriage had become, and she had been doing all in her power to ensure Charles remained married to Diana. To be faced with another marriage failure was too much.

Later Elizabeth told one of her ladies-in-waiting, "One day I had just had enough. I went to my bed and lay down and wept. I didn't even know whom the tears were for, myself, my children, or the awful, frightful situation. Those months were the worst of my life. Sometimes as I thought how dreadfully everything had turned out for my children, tears would fill my eyes and I would have to retire. It was awful."

Nonetheless, Elizabeth was now persuaded that Fergie, and her father, were putting the Royal Family at such risk that it was better to oust Fergie and face the consequences of what the press and public would see as another royal marriage disaster, than to let things continue as they were.

Days later, in February 1992, photographs were discovered in Wyatt's old London apartment showing Wyatt on holiday in Morocco with Fergie, Bea, and Eugenie. The pictures, which had never been seen before, were splashed all over the tabloid press.

During the previous few months Andrew had frequently confronted Fergie about her relationship with Wyatt. But Andrew, not a strong character, was no match for Fergie's fire. She would round on Andrew for daring to suggest for one minute that she would be unfaithful.

Now the pictures did three things. First, Prince Andrew saw that his wife had obviously been having an affair with Wyatt for some time. One picture in particular infuriated him, for it showed Wyatt holding Bea in a most paternal pose. Second, the pictures outraged the press and the public, convincing the nation that Fergie was beyond the pale, indulging in open and blatant adultery. No one could or would condemn Prince Andrew if the Yorks separated and eventually divorced. Third, the pictures meant that Fergie had no chance of remaining as a member of the Royal Family.

The pictures had allegedly been found accidentally on top of a wardrobe by a cleaner working there some months after Wyatt had quit the apartment, but the hand of Britain's security services was suspected. Conspiracy theories had mushroomed in Britain ever since the 1970s, after a former MI5 agent, Peter Wright, angry and appalled at the license taken by the most senior officers of MI5 to interfere in the politics of the nation, retired to Australia and wrote *Spycatcher*, a book detailing the activities of his former bosses. Wright had revealed that officers of MI5 had spent the 1970s burgling and robbing their way across London in the most brazen fashion, with utter disregard of the law. The British government had tried to prevent the book's publication, but after a series of famous court cases in the 1980s, the book finally appeared, causing considerable political damage and enormous embarrassment to MI5.

John Barratt, private secretary to Dickie Mountbatten until his murder, and then to Prince and Princess Michael of Kent, knew most members of the Royal Family extremely well and many of the family secrets. He also knew everything that was going on behind the scenes. He commented, "There was no doubt that the Duchess of York was pushed. She didn't just walk. The establishment realized that the Duchess would become a danger to the family, and they persuaded the Queen that it was necessary for her to be ousted so she could bring no further discredit on the family. So out she went."

Fergie now sees that she behaved stupidly, thinking that as a fully-fledged member of the Royal Family she could do whatever she wanted without being reprimanded. She had failed to realize that before she could behave as she pleased, she first had to earn the respect of the nation, the media, members of the Household, and the rest of the Royal Family. She had won over none of those vital constituencies, and she paid the price.

If Fergie had taken a leaf from Diana's book, however, all would have been fine, for Diana made sure that she was firmly established in the hearts and minds of the nation and the media before she decided to cut loose and make her own dash for freedom.

Yet it would be unfair to point the finger of blame solely at Fergie. Prince Andrew was always thought of as the good-looking Windsor, the macho one with the flashing smile and daredevil image whom some girls considered the British equivalent of a Hollywood hunk. They didn't know what the real Andrew was like.

Andrew's arrogance was overwhelming. Even at his predominantly male private school, Gordonstoun, Andrew was called "The Great I Am" because of his self-regard. To young women in particular he was disrespectful to the point of being boorish. As a Prince of the Realm,

Andrew believed that all young women would happily fall into his arms no matter how he treated them.

Andrew would pat the backside of a girl he had only just met; put his hand on girls' thighs under the dinner table, pinch their buttocks when they were walking past, and fondle their breasts, assuming they would understand this as a joke! As one girl who spent some time in the Andrew group explained, "Andrew became truly embarrassing in a party. He thought he had the right to every girl in the group, to grope them, flirt with them and, if he fancied them, kiss them. And if he thought he could get away with it, he would openly suggest bedding any girl that took his fancy. At first it was very difficult for girls to know how to react, but after a while they learned how to say 'no' to him without bruising the royal ego too much. But he was pretty awful."

Andrew didn't earn his sobriquet "Randy Andy" for nothing. Others quipped, "Like father, like son."

Most of the girls Andrew met were too shy to deal with the bumptious Prince as they should have. But Fergie wasn't. At one dinner party, when Andrew tried to force Fergie to eat three chocolate profiteroles, knowing she was on a diet, she turned and slapped him hard across the face in front of everyone. A moment's stunned silence, then everyone cheered. Andrew blushed, not only from the hearty slap, but because he realized in that instant what all his friends thought of him. Some contend that at that moment Andrew fell in love. He had met a girl who would put him in his place, and that was really what he wanted.

From the outset of their five-year marriage, Fergie took command. Macho Andrew, the young Royal Navy helicopter pilot who had won his spurs in the heat of battle during the Falklands war of 1982, was no match for Fergie's forceful personality. Overnight, the arrogant Prince was reduced to following the lead provided by his wife.

Fergie called all the shots. She chose the setting for their dream home, Sunninghill, on the edge of Windsor Park; she approved the architectural design; she selected the interior color schemes of their home as well as the furniture, the curtains and carpets, the dinner services, the cutlery. She decided on their autos, their holidays, their dinner and weekend guests, the food they ate, the staff they employed, even the television shows they watched.

Fergie's mother, Susan Barrantes, saw the danger in such a one-sided marriage. After the separation she said, "Prince Andrew's weakness was the reason the marriage failed. I am afraid he is spineless and lacking in character. Andrew is a good-looking boy who has a heart of gold to the point he would be without money himself to help someone. But he has not got any character, absolutely none. If he had, maybe this marriage would not have broken up."

Susan Barrantes was not trying to excuse her strong-willed daughter but simply described what she saw in the relationship: the forceful Fergie dominating the rather weak Andrew.

Queen Elizabeth and Susan Barrantes, then living in Argentina, spoke on the telephone about the breakup. They had not spoken since chatting at the wedding in London in 1986.

"Is there anything that we can do," Elizabeth asked, "anything at all?"

Susan replied, "It seems to me it's all too late. They have decided the marriage is over and they both want out. What could we possibly do?"

"Yes, I know," Elizabeth replied.

After a moment's silence Susan commented, "Do we know what arrangements are to be made for the children... that seems very worrying... life could be rather difficult for them in the circumstances."

Elizabeth said, "Please be reassured. Everything will be done for them. There is no question at all that any action would be taken without the full cooperation and approval of Sarah."

Elizabeth continued, "I had high hopes for both Andrew and Sarah... I thought they were so well suited... Sarah seemed so very good for him... I thought she was making a man of him... it is so very, very sad for everyone, and of course for the children... we must do everything for them."

Buckingham Palace officially announced the formal separation of the Duke and Duchess of York on March 20, 1992. The announcement was worded to indicate that the Duchess had instituted the proceedings, not Prince Andrew, to put the blame for the separation on Fergie's shoulders, so that the public would see Andrew as the innocent party.

While briefing the BBC's court correspondent, however, the Queen's respected and experienced Press Secretary, Charles Anson, attacked Fergie with almost personal abuse. Never before had royal reporters heard such venom from a Palace spokesman about a member of the House of Windsor. Anson told the BBC that the Duchess had deliberately ordered media leaks, that she had personally employed a high-powered public relations firm, and that her behavior showed she was not fit to be a member of the Royal Family.

Anson specifically criticized Fergie's behavior on a commercial flight returning to London from the United States with her father earlier that year. On that flight she put a paper bag over her head, stuck her tongue through a hole in the bag, and then pelted her father with bread rolls and sugar lumps. All this in full view of a number of British journalists, who had never witnessed royals behaving so crassly.

As noted earlier, Anson publicly apologized the next day, with perhaps the most humiliating statement to have ever been read out by a senior official at Buckingham Palace. But Elizabeth knew where the true blame lay, for she knew better than anyone how the Palace hierarchy worked and who had briefed the wretched Anson on all matters, great and small. She knew Sir Robert Fellowes was responsible.

Some sections of the press reveled in the royal embarrassment and pontificated on the reasons for the marital failure. Elizabeth was not spared.

BLAME THE WAY YOU BROUGHT 'EM UP, MA'AM, proclaimed *The Sun* in big headlines. "Kids starved of affection," suggested the tabloid under the headline DEATH OF THE ROYAL MARRIAGE. The Comment column read, "The Queen must take some of the blame for the breakdown of the royal marriages.... Her distant relationship with her children starved them of affection and left them unable to form loving partnerships.... Such youngsters often end up divorcing...."

The Sun maintained through interviews that the young royals never knew the kisses and cuddles most children take for granted from their parents... had to learn to suppress their emotions... were packed off to tough boarding schools... and were always taught that duty to the nation came first.

Further evidence of the Palace attitude toward Fergie and their treatment of her was revealed by a woman with no axe to grind and whose views could be taken as thoroughly objective. Lesley Abdela, who stood for Parliament and founded the all-party 300 Group for women in public life, remembers the problems facing the Duchess of York when she came to speak at the Woman of the Year lunch at the Savoy in October 1991. She also remembers the extraordinary behavior of Palace officials.

Fergie had been given a prepared speech which read so badly she had to discard it and speak off the cuff. As a result Ms. Abdela wrote to the Palace mildly, criticizing officials for not preparing the Duchess sufficiently.

She recalled, "Afterwards I got a phone call from a guy at the Palace who said they take these things extremely seriously and asked me to help them by saying what had gone wrong at the lunch. He told me he had shown the letter to the Duchess. I was devastated. I really felt for her. I didn't want to hurt her. I wanted to have a go at the professionals so they could do a better job. Suddenly he said words to the effect that if you haven't got a good product to work with in the first place, you can't do much about it. I was amazed. There was definite contempt for her and it was obvious that it was not just him who felt this. He kept saying 'we,' so I knew it was more than one. I got the impression there was this rather old-fashioned male group at the Palace who didn't approve of her."

A week later Ms. Abdela received a phone call from the Palace. Fergie was on the line and told her, "I was deeply hurt by your letter. You have no idea how it hurt me. I really like to get things right and that's why I'm phoning you."

Fergie continued, "There are people at the Palace who are really quite happy to see me fall on my face . . . some are quite happy to see me fail . . . I even believe some are deliberately trying to drop me in it and enjoy it happening."

Ms. Abdela went on, "Fergie indicated that she was actually beleaguered and being frozen out or even sometimes virtually set up. That 'they' at the Palace were working against her, not with her. She was calm, factual, and sad, not in the least hysterical or neurotic, but she seemed obviously fed up and impatient."

Fergie herself said later, "I frequently feel trapped in a Grimm brothers nightmare, alone at one end of a lonely castle; the corridors are long and echoing; and at the other end a light burns; around the light a group of Cyclopses are plotting my downfall."

Elizabeth decided to use the breakup of Fergie's marriage as a sign to Diana of what fate would befall her if she pursued her intention of seeking a separation. It seemed that Elizabeth was sacrificing a pawn to retain a queen.

The Queen's personal lawyer, Sir Matthew Farrer of Farrer & Co., arranged the financial side of the settlement, in which a trust was set up for Bea and Eugenie which would cover their every need, including clothing, private education, and a substantial dowry when they married. A house would be purchased for Sarah and the children near Windsor. Fergie would be given a generous annual allowance, out of which she would have to pay staff, bring up the children, as well as feed and clothe herself.

Throughout her short marriage, Fergie had been most judicious with her own money, not spending a cent of it while happily running up a substantial overdraft of more than $150,000 on Andrew's account, despite receiving an allowance of $400,000 a year. Much of Fergie's expenditure had been on dresses, ball gowns, and overseas travel.

After Elizabeth had briefed him, Sir Matthew Farrer personally informed Fergie of the separation terms. She would be permitted to keep her title, Duchess of York, on separation, but would have to quit the family home immediately. The Queen had decreed she would never be included in any future Royal Family gatherings and would be excluded from representing the Royal Family at any event or function. Fergie was also told that the Queen had not yet decided for which charities she would be permitted to continue as patron but would be informed later after Palace officials had talked to the charities involved.

Stripping Fergie of her charity patronages would, in effect, end all Fergie's royal status. By giving her breathing room, Elizabeth put Fergie on parole, hoping she would realize that she now had to behave and take great care of her two daughters. Elizabeth's concern was twofold: to tame Fergie's wild behavior, and to make sure Bea and Eugenie were brought up properly.

Weeks later, the nation observed the consequences of the separation during Ascot Week, the height of the racing season, when the Queen, other members of the Royal Family, and members of the aristocracy spend four days at Royal Ascot. In 1991 Fergie rode in an open carriage down the center of the course in the celebrated royal parade. In 1992, television viewers saw Fergie and her two daughters watching from a distance, three lone figures standing half hidden by trees, as the Queen and her retinue swept past. In one of the carriages rode Diana, who smiled and waved at Fergie and her children. That sight must have brought home to Diana what fate awaited her if she, too, decided to fly the royal nest.

Within months of her separation, Sarah Ferguson found herself at the center of yet another sex scandal. A set of photographs showed Fergie lying topless by the side of a swimming pool at a St. Tropez villa, kissing and cuddling with a man she had told the nation was her friend and financial adviser, Johnny Bryan. The pictures provoked outrage because playing around the sun lounger, while Fergie and Bryan engaged in openly sexual activity, were Fergie's children, Princess Bea, then four, and Princess Eugenie, two.

All four were pictured frolicking in the sun by the side of the pool. The photographs showed the bald Bryan leaning over Fergie and kissing her full on the mouth. Bryan was also pictured lasciviously sucking Fergie's big toe. This display from a man who had denied, repeatedly, any romantic involvement with Fergie.

The photographs were taken by paparazzi Daniel Angeli who, photo-journalists judged, made more than $1.5 million off them. The pictures appeared to have been taken from inside the villa grounds, and one or two showed the children's bodyguard sunbathing in swim trunks when allegedly on duty. Newspapers pointed out that if a photographer could take snaps twenty to thirty yards from the children, a gunman could just as easily have lain in wait on the grounds. Royal Protection officers said it was "beyond credibility" that a photographer would have been able to infiltrate a private villa, remain on the grounds for some time, and emerge undetected without someone knowing he was there.

Angeli refused to say how he knew where and when Fergie, Bryan, and the children would be at the private villa, which could not be seen from any public road or path. He did not claim he had accidentally stumbled across them on holiday. He simply said he had been informed.

Once again, the question raised speculation: Who had revealed Fergie's whereabouts? And why?

Many believed that, once again, MI5 had tipped off the photographer in order to expose the Duchess of York as unfit to remain a member of the House of Windsor because of her sexual proclivities. They informed Angeli when Fergie and Bryan would be in residence at the holiday villa. Others were adamant that ultimate permission for the pictures had to come from inside Buckingham Palace. It would not have been the first time senior courtiers at the palace had arranged for a newsman to be on hand to deliberately embarrass a member of the Royal Family.

Neither Elizabeth or senior Palace aides approved of Johnny Bryan. Following the announcement of her separation, Bryan had appointed himself her public relations man, to disseminate her side of the story. He talked to journalists off the record, blaming Fergie's problems "on those bastards at the palace" and describing the Royal Household as "a sick bunch." Bryan once shouted at the editor of a glossy magazine that the Duchess was not some "dead common fucking trashy little model."

No one could understand why Fergie allowed such an uncouth loudmouth like Bryan, with no knowledge of the Palace or the establishment, to take command of her life and, in the process, orchestrate the destruction of what little remained of her reputation. Fergie needed sound financial advice, but Johnny Bryan began escorting her around the world, visiting such exotic locations as Phuket in Thailand, Buenos Aires, New York, and Paris. In London Fergie would spend evenings at fashionable Annabel's nightclub in Mayfair, drinking bottles of champagne, and always in the company of her financial adviser.

The press began asking questions about Bryan's real relationship with Fergie. Repeatedly, he denied any romance between them, claiming their relationship to be that of client and financial adviser. "My job is to negotiate a fair and equitable settlement for the Duchess of York," he would reply with a confident smile. "There is absolutely no question of any romance between the Duchess of York and myself, nor will there ever be."

August 1992 brought the St. Tropez photographs which were to reveal Bryan as Fergie's lover. As the French papers put it with Gallic amusement, "Fergie's breasts shake the royal palace."

There was little amusement that day at Balmoral, where Elizabeth had just started her summer holidays. From Elizabeth's standpoint, Fergie's decision to take Johnny Bryan as her lover, or even as her financial adviser, ranked as one of her more crass ideas. Anthony John Adrian Bryan was born in Wilmington, Delaware, in June 1955, the son of Tony Bryan, an Englishman who grew up in England but flew Spitfires for the Royal Canadian Air Force in World War II and won the DFC for gallantry. His mother, Lida Redmond, was from St. Louis, Missouri. Bryan's father graduated from Harvard Business School and was a shrewd businessman, eventually appointed to the boards of both Chrysler and Federal Express. He, too, was something of a ladies' man. In 1964 he divorced Lida and married a wealthy Houston heiress, Josephine Abercrombie. That marriage ended in scandal when he began an affair with the wife of Houston department store magnate Robert Sakowitz. After a much publicized divorce action, Bryan married Pamela Sakowitz in 1978.

Johnny Bryan decided to follow in his father's footsteps. He studied for a master's degree at Katz Graduate School of Business at the University of Pittsburgh. He became renowned as an all-round sportsman, playing tennis, golf, ice hockey, squash; he also skied and flew aircraft. And he had a reputation with the girls. He loved to be thought of as a macho American male with rippling stomach muscles and a good body.

Little is known of his early business career, but in 1985 he put together a consortium of investors which raised $1 million to take over Encom Telecommunications and Technology in Atlanta, Georgia. Bryan became vice president of business development, negotiating rental deals for spare satellite channels. The venture was a disaster: the company crashed in four years and the investors lost their money.

Among the investors was Taki Theodoracopulos, the Greek millionaire and columnist, who had put in $50,000. He said, "I was obviously disappointed when the deal went sour but not angry. Bryan is not a bad fellow. He is a sweet guy really, a typical, loud American full of shit, but basically decent."

Father and son came to London in 1987 and took over Oceanics, an ailing marine electronics company. Within two years they had recouped their investment and made a healthy profit. But Oceanics then ran into trouble and losses mounted. The Bryans did the decent thing and resigned, but Johnny Bryan kept his stake in the German offshoot, Oceanics Deutschland, which has an office in Frankfurt. In 1993, the German company was believed to be worth around $25 million.

Johnny Bryan fell for the social side of life in London and became something of a Don Juan. Prematurely bald, Bryan acquired the nickname "Osram," because his head looked like a light bulb. Osram is a well-known maker of light bulbs. Nevertheless, he squired the most fashionable and sophisticated society girls, most of them heiresses with fathers worth fortunes. But his reputation began to sink fast.

Girls talked openly about the sort of man Bryan had become. A Houston photographer, Pam Francis, who dated Bryan at university, branded him "a little rat"; another former girlfriend described him as "the greatest château-bottled shit of the 1990s." An English girl from a wealthy family, Catherine Loewe, seduced by Bryan's charisma and persistence, later described him as "sneaky, devious, and a King Rat." However, Catherine also said, "Johnny was very much into fitness. He was Action Man between the sheets, a very aggressive, very active lover who could keep going for a long time. I felt at one point he could go on for ever and ever. That's probably one of the reasons Sarah became so attached to him. She's a very sexy lady."

One of his father's ex-wives, Pamela, commented, "It is perhaps no coincidence that his father seemed to single out wealthy, influential, and sometimes married women for conquests, me included. I think John has the same approach."

Once Bryan's true role became known, he decided to launch the Duchess of York on the open market, offering her to newspapers and magazines for photographs and interviews, at a price. He did this through ASB Publishing, which he set up in 1990, two years before the Duchess decided to leave Andrew. When Bryan hawked his own story, "Fergie and Me," around Fleet Street, one tabloid agreed to pay $400,000 but the deal fell through.

Bryan even offered to sell a story to *The People* newspaper which named a girl with whom he claimed Prince Andrew was having an affair. He said he wanted $35,000, telling the executive, "I want it on goddamn publication, baby. I want immediate payment." When *The*

People discovered the story was bogus, Bryan claimed the whole thing had been a joke. When *The People* reported the incident, however, they pointed out there was no joking whatsoever in the discussions before they discovered the story was without foundation.

Another story is told by Lesley Player, the beautiful thirty-four-year-old divorcée and successful businesswoman who fell in love with the game of polo. She found herself at the center of a sensational scandal that revealed her affairs with both Major Ron Ferguson and Fergie's lover, Steve Wyatt, a scandal that would embarrass both Elizabeth and Fergie.

When Lesley Player first met Bryan, he claimed to be in the film business, part-owner of a New York nightclub, and in the process of building a hospital in Germany. Later that evening, after she had seen him snort cocaine through a rolled £10 note, he invited her and another girl to join him in a "three-in-a-bed" sex romp.

Later Miss Player wrote a book, *My Story: The Duchess of York, Her Father and Me,* detailing her affair with Major Ronald Ferguson. She was not flattering to him. She wrote, "I couldn't help noticing how thin his legs were. I expected iron-man thighs from someone who rode as often and brilliantly as he did."

She claimed Fergie connived at the affair, providing a bedroom at her new home, Sunninghill, so that Player and Fergie's father could sleep together. At the time Fergie's two daughters Bea and Eugenie were at the house as well.

To Fergie's greater embarrassment and humiliation, she recounted how the Duchess had enabled Player and Ron Ferguson to continue their affair for free around the world by appointing Player "acting" lady-in-waiting. Thus when Fergie traveled abroad, the whole party traveled free, all expenses picked up by their hosts.

Of her affair with Steve Wyatt, whom she met in the spring of 1991, Lesley commented, "With his permanent tan and easy charm he reminded me of the actor George Segal and radiated a similar boyish charm. Within three days the handsome Texan had romanced me into bed."

Lesley claimed she had no idea Steve Wyatt was having an affair with Fergie at the time. She claimed to be amazed when Major Ron told her Wyatt was two-timing both her and his daughter.

There were more embarrassing claims. Lesley said Major Ron

explained that his daughter was so involved with Wyatt that she no longer wanted to stay married to Prince Andrew. She also described a dinner Wyatt had with Major Ron at Claridge's in which he all but asked for Fergie's hand in marriage, even though she was still ostensibly married to Andrew.

Lesley Player claimed she offered Fergie the loan of her basement apartment in London as a safe house where she could meet Wyatt in secret, but Fergie declined, believing it too dangerous. Lesley Player's relationship with Fergie and her father came to an abrupt end, however, when Wyatt confessed to Fergie he had been having an affair with Lesley. She wrote, "We were all in Florida together when she took a phone call from Wyatt. Within seconds her attitude to me changed. She turned her back on me, refused to answer my letters, or take my phone calls. She began to chill me out the way she in turn would be chilled out by the Royal Family a few months later."

To Elizabeth's advisers and those connected with the Royal Family, Bryan is regarded as a sleazy opportunist, a deeply insidious influence on the Duchess of York, who has brought nothing but shame and dishonor to her and further embarrassment to the beleaguered House of Windsor. Bryan's activities on behalf of Fergie also demonstrated to Elizabeth the risks involved in exiling someone from the Royal Family. No one had considered the possible damage to the monarchy if Fergie should fall in with a person or a set of people ruthless enough to manipulate her and her two daughters for gain and profit.

As a result of the Bryan factor, however, Elizabeth, with advice from Philip and others, became determined not to make the same mistake if and when Diana should go through with her threat to separate from Charles. Diana, as Princess of Wales, is constitutionally far more important than Fergie and consequently at far greater risk to possible manipulation by adventurers and opportunists. Diana had already demonstrated her naïveté about the real world by permitting James Gilbey to tell her "true story" in a book that caused untold embarrassment for her, Prince Charles, her children, and the entire family. Elizabeth realized that she would need to treat Diana's separation with great diplomacy and not permit her to quit the family or become a loose cannon capable of causing even greater damage.

As Bryan's affair with Fergie continued through 1992 and 1993, he became the favorite uncle to Bea and Eugenie, growing in confidence as he took greater control of Fergie's business affairs. They were seen everywhere together.

One of Bryan's former lovers, Catherine Loewe, who knew him for two months, warned, "Johnny Bryan is into all the things that men like him want in life: power, money and status. And he acted like an American on the make, telling me all the time he was determined to crash the royal inner circle, and it was blatantly obvious that both he and Steve Wyatt set out deliberately to do just that."

She added a rider: "But I honestly cannot believe for one minute that Johnny Bryan is in love with Sarah."

And then came the appalling St. Tropez photographs, splashed across the front pages of newspapers and magazines throughout the world. Once again Fergie had been found guilty of the greatest crime in the Windsor mind: being discovered and exposed. The British public agreed with the Windsors, and Fergie's reputation and popularity plumbed new depths.

"This is disgraceful, absolutely disgraceful," Elizabeth said as she looked at the photographs, shaking her head in disbelief. She immediately instructed her Press Office to issue a statement in her name and Prince Andrew's, which said, "We strongly disapprove of the publication of photographs taken in such circumstances." Once again Elizabeth and Philip tried to lay the blame on the press, but they knew all the blame was Fergie's.

Reaction from politicians was divided. Some MPs felt the controversy demonstrated, once again, a need for privacy legislation to guard members of the Royal Family. Others argued that public figures, including the royals, had to recognize that their behavior was of public interest and should act accordingly.

Elizabeth knew full well that the problem for both Diana and Fergie was that they weren't born royal. On marrying, both had accepted the condition that no separation or divorce would be permitted, but now they chose to ignore what they had openly and plainly agreed to. Both young women had taken all the privileges, the glamour, the money, and the titles but had refused to accept the sacrifices and the responsibility that came with royal marriage. She knew that neither duty or self-sacrifice came easily to nonroyals who enter the unreality of the Royal Family, and she understood the strains of marriage between prince and commoner. Yet throughout her entire life, she had accepted that duty came above all else, and she was angry that both her daughters-in-law acted as if they could walk out on their obligations without thinking of the effects their decisions might have on others.

That summer Elizabeth spent a good deal of time thinking about the consequences of marital and social breakdown and their effect on the nation. As monarch, she felt at her most vulnerable since she had ascended the throne in 1952. Increasing numbers in the media, the establishment, and both Houses of Parliament, the Commons and the Lords, feared any more such revelations might undermine the monarchy itself.

VIII

"WHERE PEACE AND REST CAN NEVER DWELL"

—MILTON

EIGHTEEN

ANNUS HORRIBILIS

On a gray, overcast Tuesday in November 1992, Elizabeth, accompanied by Prince Philip, drove in one of her stretched Rolls-Royce limousines from Buckingham Palace to London's Guildhall, virtually unnoticed by the office workers and shoppers as they hurried about their business.

This lunch was the City of London's principal celebration marking the Queen's glorious jubilee. Guests included dignitaries of the City of London, leading politicians, members of the establishment, lords and ladies of society, the legal profession as well as the pillars of the nation's financial empire, the City. There were aldermen and councilors of the City of London in their exotic robes and finery, the same as worn by their forebears two and three hundred years before. The lunch, given by the City of London, had been planned for more than two years to celebrate the fortieth anniversary of the Queen's accession to the throne.

It was far from being a magnificent celebration: Elizabeth made one of the most remarkable personal speeches of her life, which amounted in effect to an extraordinary public confession.

Never before had the nation seen the Queen so downcast, so open, and so apparently vulnerable. Her speech was broadcast on television and radio for the nation to see how their Queen had survived the most traumatic year of her reign.

That November day she suffered from a cold which made her voice croaky. She barely spoke above a frail whisper, which added to the poignancy.

There were those at Buckingham Palace who advised Elizabeth against such an open speech to her people. She had asked that two speeches be prepared for the jubilee lunch: one more upbeat, challenging, looking into the future, ignoring the travails, embarrassments, and traumas of 1992 which had wreaked such havoc and disappointment for her and her entire family. But Elizabeth also demanded that another speech, the one she finally delivered, be written as well. She wanted to open her heart to her people and win their moral support.

As she rose to polite applause at the middle of the top table in the huge Guildhall to address the five hundred people present, Elizabeth seemed a slight, inconspicuous figure in her dark-green, short-sleeved dress and matching hat.

The Queen's accession to the throne at the age of twenty-five, coming so soon after the end of a war that had sapped the lifeblood of the nation, provided cause for hope that her reign would be as glorious for Britain as that of her namesake, Queen Elizabeth I, who reigned for forty years in the sixteenth century.

On Coronation Day in 1953 Winston Churchill had said, "The gleaming figure whom providence has brought to us—and brought to us in times where the present is hard and the future veiled."

Forty years later Elizabeth's speech broke with tradition, tearing away the mystery of the divine right of kings in which Elizabeth had for so many years believed.

She told the privileged assembled listeners, "There can be no doubt, of course, that criticism is good for people and institutions that are part of public life. No institution, City, Monarchy, whatever, should expect to be free from the scrutiny of those who give it their loyalty and support, not to mention those that don't. But we are all part of the same fabric of our national society and that scrutiny, by one part or another, can be just as effective if it is made with a touch of gentleness, good humor, and understanding."

Elizabeth was hoping not only to rein in the more violent attacks on her and her family, which had reached crisis proportions during the previous two years, but also to win the moral high ground, appealing over the heads of the critics and the press directly to the people. She believed the bulk of the nation was behind her and her family, and she was prepared to take the risks of appealing to them directly.

She pushed home the point still further. "I sometimes wonder how future generations will judge the events of this tumultuous year. I daresay that history will take a slightly more moderate view than that of some contemporary commentators. Distance is well known to lend enchantment even to the less attractive views.

"After all, it has the inestimable advantage of hindsight. But it can also lend an extra dimension to judgment, giving it a leavening of moderation and compassion—even of wisdom—that is sometimes lacking in the reactions of those whose task it is in life to offer instant opinions on all things great and small."

And she went on. "No section of the community has all the virtues, neither does any have all the vices. I am quite sure that most people try to do their jobs as best they can, even if the result is not always entirely successful."

She had begun her speech ruefully, commenting, "This is not a year I shall look back on with undiluted pleasure. In the words of one of my more sympathetic correspondents, it has turned out to be an 'Annus Horribilis.'*

"I suspect I am not alone in thinking it so. Indeed, I suspect that there are very few people or institutions unaffected by these last months of worldwide turmoil and uncertainty." This was a reference to the three years of severe recession, with three million unemployed in Britain, a record number of people whose homes had been re-possessed, a record number of personal bankruptcies, and thousands of firms and companies going bust. Elizabeth knew she would win support from many in linking her misfortunes with those of her subjects.

She ended her speech by reminding her critics of the wide range of support she still attracted, saying, "Your hospitality today is an outward symbol of one other unchanging factor which I value above all—the loyalty given to me and my family by so many people in this country, and the Commonwealth, throughout my reign."

Elizabeth's speech had broken the golden rule of monarchy articulated by the most famous of British constitutional advisers,

---

*The Queen's reference to 1992 as an Annus Horribilis (Horrible Year) was an allusion to John Dryden's poem "Annus Mirabilis" (Year of Wonders). Dryden's poem describes the events of 1666, the year of the Great Fire of London as well as the plague. Dryden (1631–1700) was perhaps the most famous Restoration poet and playwright. London's theaters had been closed down during Oliver Cromwell's interregnum and also by plague and fire. Dryden wrote "Annus Mirabilis" while staying in Wiltshire in 1666, after London's theaters were reopened. The poem is a tribute to King Charles II for leading his nation in the war against the Dutch and against the disasters striking London.

Walter Bagehot. He wrote that for the Crown to retain its dignity, honor, and glory, "Magic should not be exposed to the light of day." On this occasion she had revealed a great deal about herself, her fears, and her regrets.

Little did the public or press know when she made that historic Guildhall speech that forty-eight hours later, Prime Minister John Major would announce to an astonished House of Commons that the Queen had decided the time had come for her to pay taxes on her private income. Furthermore, she had agreed to meet the working expenses of most members of the Royal Family.

John Major told the Commons, "The Queen had approached me in July 1992 to ask for a change in the current arrangements to be considered. She asked me then to consider the basis on which she might voluntarily pay tax and further suggested that she might take responsibility for certain payments under the current Civil List arrangements."

The Queen's decision to pay tax and meet the working expenses of her extended family removed at a stroke the two principal sources of irritation with the monarchy which a growing number of her subjects had come to question during the past decade. Whenever one of the junior royals, or lesser far-flung members of the Royal Family, did anything outrageous, ridiculous, or scandalous, or appeared to be trading on their privileged position, the tabloid press always posed the same question: "Why should the nation pay people, who lead such privileged lives, vast sums of money when they behave so badly and without apparent due reverence?"

It was a question which the Press Office at Buckingham Palace, and those courtiers and advisers close to the Queen, had been finding more and more difficult to answer, as revelations about the intimate lives of Princess Diana, Sarah Ferguson, and Charles, the heir to the throne, flooded into the public domain.

Twenty years earlier, Earl Mountbatten had strongly advised Elizabeth to clarify the royal finances for the British people. Even then he was concerned about the escalating cost of the monarchy, particularly because the nation, fed inaccurate stories by the press, believed Elizabeth to be enormously wealthy. In fact, however, 85 percent of her fortune was in paintings, ornaments, furniture, and the state-owned palaces which brought in no income and which cannot be sold. Mountbatten, always a close reader of public opinion, had written to Elizabeth, "The image of the monarchy will be gravely damaged unless the nation realises the truth of that fortune."

Mountbatten ended his note saying, "Will you please ensure all this gets into the public domain, perhaps in an authoritative article in *The Times*, and both please believe a loving old uncle and *not* your constitutional advisers, and do it." It took Elizabeth nearly twenty years, and a never-ending spate of scandal, to heed Mountbatten's advice.

The growing public enthusiasm to see the Queen pay tax represented less a taxpayers' revolt than a growl from an increasing number of loyal subjects who sensed that the royal image had become tarnished and thought lesser royals were having too easy a life. In this they were encouraged by a press which seemed gleefully mean-spirited and irresponsible toward the Royal Family throughout the late 1980s and early 1990s.

Elizabeth's decision to pay tax had been the subject of intense debate inside the Palace during most of 1992. No legal requirement exists for the Queen to pay income tax: all revenues collected in her name are by right exempt. Some Palace advisers believed that acquiescing to such demands was caving in to the Queen's critics, especially the republican sections of the press, the same argument the advisers used against Mountbatten's proposal nearly twenty years before. In the current Palace debate, some of the more ardent monarchists argued that becoming more like an ordinary citizen and accepting the social necessities of every other member of society created the possibility that the monarchy was moving toward extinction.

But Elizabeth was worried. She believed that the Royal Family had sustained so much damage throughout 1992 that she, as head of state, must do something to appease the critics. For some months during that year, Elizabeth had difficulty sleeping through the night as she agonized over how she could stem what seemed to be a rising tide of resentment toward the Royal Family.

Outwardly, and at all the official functions she attended, Elizabeth displayed not the slightest sign of anxiety. Back at Buckingham Palace, however, she ordered her staff to keep her informed of any changes they perceived in the mood of the nation and people's attitude toward the throne. She approached many friends and advisers as well as politicians, including Prime Minister John Major, The Lord Chamberlain, Lord Airlie, seeking advice as to what would be best for the monarchy. Above all else, however, she wanted to know the mood of the people.

Throughout 1992 she paid close attention to opinion polls that were frequently published about the Royal Family, analyzing them for any signs that the public mood was changing toward her and her family—and the job they were doing.

As late as November 1992, Elizabeth still hadn't made up her mind about whether or not to begin paying taxes. Apparently oblivious to any forthcoming change, Chancellor of the Exchequer Norman Lamont told the House of Commons that month, "There are no plans for the Queen to pay income tax." The Labour benches were angry, and some MPs called for a review of the royal finances. Elizabeth could see the criticism getting stronger.

The last straw came when Diana had insisted on a formal separation from Charles. The Queen had already suffered appalling personal embarrassment when the love tapes between Diana and her confidant James Gilbey and between Charles and his mistress Camilla Parker Bowles were published. It seemed the image of royal behavior could sink no lower. Then came Diana's demands. Elizabeth did her utmost to persuade her not to seek a formal separation, but Diana was adamant. She had had enough.

Elizabeth recognized that something had to be done to appease the public's attitude of resentment and derision toward the royals in general. She knew that with the nation's favorite royal, Princess Diana, wanting out of the Royal Family the dam had burst. Elizabeth felt physically sick with the turmoil that was devastating her family. Never a week seemed to pass without some further embarrassment with which she felt unprepared to cope. Now the family's problems had reached to her son, the heir to the throne, to the man who would be responsible for upholding the name of the House of Windsor and family values and who, on the day of his coronation, would become the most important person in Britain. Now, due to Diana's intransigence, he would be seen as an irresponsible adulterer, virtually living with a woman who was married to someone else. It was too much.

To Elizabeth, Philip seemed more of a hindrance than a help in her hour of need, occasionally exploding in anger that the turmoil in the family was symptomatic of the lack of discipline throughout British society and the fact that the young people seemed to have lost all sense of responsibility and duty.

Her advisers urged her that something should be done to try to divert attention away from the personal life of Charles and Diana. The question of tax was one possible diversion. She was fully aware paying tax was a major retreat for the monarchy but worried that her decision to pay tax would be seen as the result of press criticism. And Elizabeth did not want to be seen to be bowing to pressure from the press. Particularly as she, other royals, and her senior advisers despised most of the tabloid newspapers. Agreeing to pay tax would be one single, but important step to show that Elizabeth was in touch with the life and concerns of the ordinary citizen as well as a gesture of penance acknowledging that many members of the extended Royal Family had not been earning their keep.

One day in November, Elizabeth called Charles to her rooms and, over tea, told him of her decision. Charles, who had always believed the Royal Family should not be regarded as a burden on the taxpayer, had encouraged his mother to pay tax voluntarily, rather than being seen as being forced to pay tax because of the nation's mood. Elizabeth, however, was worried that the nation, and particularly some newspapers, would seize on the fact that her decision to pay tax had come only after mounting press criticism. Prime Minister John Major came to her rescue, explaining to the House of Commons that the Queen had discussed the possibility of the sovereign paying tax a year before the decision was taken. Major's statement certainly helped to ease Elizabeth's embarrassment.

Charles told his mother that he would enthusiastically follow her lead and agree to pay income tax on all his personal income as well. Indeed, Charles went further, as he informed a close adviser after the tax changes were announced.

He had told his mother, "I have been wondering when you would take this step; I absolutely and totally agree with it because I believe it will bring us and the people closer together. With all that is going on now, the troubles in our family, the problems facing unemployed millions and families in debt being thrown out of their homes, it is, I believe, the right decision, and the sooner the better."

Elizabeth and Charles's decision to pay tax on their private incomes had nothing to do, however, with the Civil List, the money Parliament agrees to pay the monarch to carry out royal duties on behalf of the nation. Its origins date from 1760, when George III agreed to surrender certain hereditary revenues in return for a set sum agreed to by Parliament. At that time the List was set at £800,000 ($4,500,000), a vast amount in 1760.

Through the last two centuries the principle has never changed, though there have been frequent wrangles between monarchs and Parliament. But income tax was a different matter. Only in this century has the sovereign been relieved of paying income tax. Queen Victoria (who died in 1901) and her son Edward VII (who died in 1910) both paid income tax. In 1910, however, when George V came to the throne, Parliament agreed to abolish tax for the sovereign when the Welsh politician, and later Prime Minister, David Lloyd George convinced Parliament that it was pointless to hand over money to the sovereign with one hand and take it away with the other. George V paid some form of income tax, but Elizabeth's father George VI, who reigned from 1937 to 1952, paid none.

The shape of the current Civil List was set in 1952, when the sovereign agreed to surrender the Crown Estates—250,000 acres of prime agricultural land and substantial property in London—to the government in exchange for a fixed income. In 1972, annual increases in the Civil List were introduced when it became apparent that the Queen's private income was being used to supplement official expenses. Roughly 70 percent of the Civil List pays staff salaries, and 30 percent is spent on official travel, entertaining, and administrative costs.

In 1990, Prime Minister Margaret Thatcher announced a fixed ten-year settlement of the Civil List, hoping to end the annual public wrangle over the Queen's finances and the perennial tabloid headlines, BIG PAY RISE FOR THE QUEEN, which ignored the fact that inflation made the increase necessary. The 1990 agreement would allow the Royal Household to plan ahead on the basis of a known income. It was proposed that from 1991 till the year 2000, about £10 million ($15 million) would be shared out each year among eleven members of the Royal Family.

Neither Prince Charles nor Diana received anything from the Civil List. As Prince of Wales, Charles had inherited the Duchy of Cornwall, which owns substantial agricultural land as well as property in London. By agreement with Parliament, Charles takes 75 percent of the revenue from the Duchy tax-free and the remaining 25 percent goes to the Exchequer. This income has been the Waleses' primary support since their wedding in 1981. In 1991 the Duchy earned approximately £3 million ($4.5 million) profit; the net income to Charles amounted to less than £2 million ($3 million).

Now, however, like his mother, Charles has readily agreed to pay income tax at the full rate of 40 percent. On the other hand, like every other citizen, Charles will be able to deduct legitimate expenses against tax such as staff wages and administrative costs. As a result he will probably gain financially from the new system, but the arrangement will be understood to be fairer. Like everyone else in the land, Charles's income and what he pays in tax will be a private matter between himself and the tax man.

While married to Charles, Princess Diana received no income in her own name, but all her expenses were met by her husband. Her store cards, credit cards (including American Express) were paid for by the Prince of Wales. She has always had her own checkbook and her own bank account, which Charles's bankers replenish with £5,000 ($7,500) every month for pocket money.

Despite their separation, there has been no change in this arrangement. Charles still picks up all Diana's credit-card bills and has continued his monthly standing order.

No one knows the precise annual income of the Queen nor the amount of money she will pay in tax. She is entitled to keep those secrets like every other taxpayer in Britain. In April 1994 the Queen paid income tax on her private income for the first time. Arguments as to the Queen's worth have raged for decades but, as previously stated, her private income is approximately $8 million a year based on her stock portfolio of about $100 million and income from the Duchy of Lancaster.

Sources close to the Palace suggest the Queen paid around $2 million for the tax year ending April 1994, after all expenses and allowances had been deducted. The exact amount will of course never be revealed, which will be a blessing for the Royal Family. Until she decided to pay most of the Civil List herself, all payments were made public, to the embarrassment of some of the lesser royals.

From April 1993 the Queen will still receive money given by Parliament under the Civil List, a total of $12 million a year. The only other Royals still receiving money from the Civil List will be Prince Philip, on $540,000 a year, and the Queen Mother, who receives $1 million.

Elizabeth has assumed the expenses of all the other lesser royals who used to be paid through the Civil List. She pays for Prince Andrew ($375,000), Prince Edward ($150,000), Princess Anne The Princess Royal ($350,000), and Princess Margaret ($330,000). For two years the Queen had been paying another $1 million to the Dukes of Gloucester and Kent as well as Princess Alexandra for the duties they carry out on her behalf. In all, she now pays a total of $2.2 million for costs formerly covered by the Civil List.

The state, however, will continue to pay $74 million a year toward the upkeep of the royal palaces, including Buckingham Palace, Windsor Castle, and Kensington Palace, where a number of royals, including Diana, live. Much of that money will pay for staff salaries as well as for maintenance and repairs. Some will go toward the upkeep of the Royal Yacht *Britannia* and the Queen's Flight of three small aircraft and the royal train.

The new arrangements meant that the principle of the state's funding the Royal Family's public duties remained intact, even though the Queen now receives money from the government which she in turn repays in tax on her private income. Elizabeth and her advisers were adamant that her gesture be considered voluntary and that her decision to pay income tax on her personal income was not a precedent that Prince Charles or any other monarch should have to follow upon accession to the throne.

In fact, Elizabeth had felt coerced into this decision by plummeting public opinion. She was unhappy about eroding the mystique of the monarchy by becoming an ordinary taxpayer like everyone else. In one discussion in the autumn of 1992, Elizabeth said to one of her political advisers, "I believe that if the monarch agreed to pay tax, then there would be no difference between the monarch and the people. And that cannot be good for the Crown. There has to be a difference and the people should see there is a difference."

Elizabeth believed her decision would result in loss of the respect and esteem with which the great majority of her subjects had regarded her for forty years, but that this loss would be less severe than the consequences of doing nothing. Intensely annoyed by the decision she felt forced to make, she blamed her plight on the weakness of Charles and the selfishness of his wayward, headstrong wife, Diana.

As a result, the gulf between Diana and Elizabeth widened. They had never been close. Diana had told Charles and other friends that she felt "very awkward" whenever she was in the presence of her mother-in-law and had never been able to relax when they were together. As Diana explained to close friends, "Whenever we are together, at tea or lunch or whatever, everything is so formal. I cannot relax for a minute and I feel so embarrassed all the time not knowing what to talk to her about. We all know that most young women don't get on very well with their mothers-in-law. Well, think what it's like having the Queen as your mother-in-law."

Elizabeth was well aware that her daughter-in-law had difficulty talking to her and tried over the years to find a way through to Diana so that they could chat happily together. But as Diana explained, "The only thing we seem to have in common are children. She asks me questions about Wills and Harry, but I just get the feeling that she's only asking the questions because she feels she should, not because she really wants to."

Diana was aware of what her mother-in-law thought of her because she had read it often enough in the press. "Life is more difficult now that we've got this tiresome girl," Elizabeth is alleged to have said of Diana. Elizabeth read the same report and told Diana to pay no attention to newspaper accounts, the stories were just made up. Diana wasn't so sure.

Diana saw another side to Elizabeth. "Charles has always told me his mother expects respect from her children," she said, "and they all show her enormous respect. But I never saw her show much motherly love toward any of her children. Now, it seems she wants the same respect from her grandchildren as well. Whenever she meets Wills and Harry, which is very rarely, she tries to be sweet to them, but it all seems rather forced."

As Elizabeth struggled to come to terms with the breakdown of Charles's marriage throughout 1992, however, hardly a month went by without a fresh scandal pushing the House of Windsor hither and thither. It would have been difficult for anyone, much less the Queen, to face so many disasters within one year.

The final tragedy was the fire that erupted at Windsor Castle on November 20. It began when a strong halogen lamp ignited inflammable liquid being used to restore paintings in the private chapel in the castle's Chester Tower. The resulting fireball set light to tapestries and drapes that had been coated with protective fluid, and within seconds the wood-paneled walls were ablaze.

Minutes later the fire had spread along the ceiling to neighboring St. George's Hall, the magnificent scene of State Banquets, where many American Presidents have been entertained in true royal style during the past decades. The alarm was raised immediately and restorers and workers frantically began removing paintings, pictures, and any other works of art and furniture they could carry.

Prince Andrew, on leave from the Royal Navy, was in the castle when the fire alarm rang out. He took charge, galvanizing as many staff as possible to help in the dramatic rescue work as the flames moved with terrifying speed through the castle. His military training to cope under pressure helped that day, and much that would otherwise have been destroyed was rescued, particularly priceless paintings hanging in St. George's Hall.

Inflammable materials are essential to the restorer, for example, as solvents to remove old varnish. Halogen lamps generate extreme heat, so they are never allowed near the surface of a picture, but the brightness of a halogen lamp is needed to enable restorers to clean and patch the surfaces of paintings.

That night, television viewers in Britain and around the world saw the flames leaping hundreds of feet into the air as fire crews fought to bring the blaze under control in an effort to preserve one of Europe's most magnificent castles. But the shock to the nation came after the fire had been extinguished and TV cameras revealed the full horror of the destruction.

Many were moved as they saw Elizabeth, a small figure beside the well-built, uniformed firemen, walking through the gutted state apartments. Their hearts went out to her as they watched her, dressed in a long, waterproof, hooded coat looking sad, and some thought rather pathetic, as she surveyed the damage. She appeared worried and stern, some thought angry, as she squelched in her green Wellington boots through the debris-strewn quagmire of water and burned embers. Of all her residences, Windsor was the one she always thought of as home. (Buckingham Palace she considers her office; Sandringham and Balmoral are her holiday residences.) The fire was personally devastating for her.

The horrible stench of burning hung over the castle and the town of Windsor; one tattered, discolored British flag flew sadly from the ramparts. Aircraft flew overhead en route to Heathrow, giving passengers an overall view of the gutted, roofless ruins. The rain never let up.

For centuries the castle had seemed impregnable, especially to the townspeople of Windsor, but suddenly they realized it was as vulnerable as anyone else's home. More important, the fire seemed like a sign from heaven, graphically illustrating to the nation as well as to Elizabeth that she was a human being as vulnerable to life's travails as any other citizen.

After spending an hour surveying the damage, Elizabeth emerged into the pouring rain and approached her youngest son Edward. At one point she laid her head on his chest, as though in despair and resignation, and he, in turn, put a comforting arm around his mother's shoulders.

St. George's Hall lost its famous, centuries-old roof; its immense carvings were gone completely. Along the length of the great room a visitor saw only a huge pile of black rubble. The adjacent Waterloo Chamber, said to be the most beautiful room in the world, was just an empty, stinking shell.

Historian Sir Roy Strong, former director of London's Victoria and Albert Museum, had often spent days inspecting and surveying the pictures and other works of art at Windsor Castle. "Windsor Castle is home to the Queen's private collection of art works—perhaps the greatest and most important in the world," he said. "In reality, the treasures there are priceless. Windsor is a lump of England, a huge chunk of our heritage and history. The castle is like an A to Z of the history of Great Britain, from the portraits of all our Kings and Queens, to the maps and books."

The collection at Windsor includes paintings by Michelangelo, Raphael, Gainsborough, Rembrandt, Van Dyck, Rubens, and Canaletto; the Garter Throne Room is lined with portraits of the nation's sovereigns from George I to the present Queen; the finest examples of furniture from the reigns of French kings, including Louis XIV, XV, and XVI; statues of Kings, Queens, and noblemen, magnificent carvings, and centuries-old pieces of armor. Throughout the castle are priceless carpets, tapestries, and drapes as well as drawings and sketches by Leonardo da Vinci and Holbein. A magnificent royal library houses books and maps dating back hundreds of years.

The nation was fortunate that the staff and restorers were able to save many of the works of art and that the fire crews could contain the blaze. But the mood of the nation, fanned by the sensationalist press, was so resentful toward the Royal Family that gratitude for the preservation of a treasure trove of historical artworks was overcome by spite and meanness.

Believing he was speaking with the support and sympathy of the great majority of the British public, Heritage Secretary Peter Brooke, in his upper-crust, rather plummy, aristocratic voice, stood before the ruins and proclaimed that the government—that is, the taxpayer— would pay the full cost of the repairs to the castle, which would come to at least $75 million, since Windsor was not insured. (In Britain, government and public buildings are never insured.) This had been accepted practice for decades: the British taxpayer was responsible for keeping and sustaining their monarch in luxury and splendor. Little did The Right Honorable Peter Brooke realize that day how the mood of the nation had changed.

Hours later, ITV's *This Morning* program asked callers to phone in their answers to the question: Who should pay for the repairs to Windsor Castle? An astonishing 95 percent, out of a total of 30,282 callers, said the taxpayer should not have to foot the entire bill and urged the Queen to contribute.

The tabloid press took up the cry. "Give and take," screamed a Murdoch tabloid, *Today*. "We're giving, the royals are taking." The right-wing *Daily Mail* asked the question: "Why should a populace, many of whom have had to make huge sacrifices during the most bitter recession, have to pay the total bill for Windsor Castle, when the Queen, who pays no taxes, contributes next to nothing?"

The left-leaning *Daily Mirror* accused the House of Windsor of "sowing the seeds of its own destruction—meanness, greed, and blinkered disregard for the feelings of the people are the mark of a dying, not a lasting dynasty."

Murdoch's tabloid *The Sun* also organized a phone-in and revealed that 48,876 readers said the Queen should pick up the tab to repair her own castle; only 2,877 reckoned the taxpayer should pay.

The Times, another Murdoch paper, commented that the announcement that the taxpayer was to pay for the repairs "had struck a jarring note. The fire had brought to a head questions that can no longer be fudged...the crunch comes with the decision over who is to pay."

The intellectual, politically independent *Guardian* newspaper put the accusation most succinctly: "All the warm words of sadness for the Queen in the House of Commons can't hide the growing wash of public cynicism; not yet republicanism, but carping disaffection." There were calls from Labour members of Parliament that the taxpayer should not be called on to pay for the entire cost of repairs, but the MPs' criticism was more muted than the press.

The Windsor fire became the single most important event in Elizabeth's forty-year reign, for it clearly revealed that the British people's attitude to the monarchy and the Royal Family had undergone a sea change. With the fire still smoldering, Elizabeth, the establishment, and Parliament were forced to face the unpleasant fact that the myth that the British people were totally supportive of the monarch and the Royal Family—at any cost—had, almost overnight, been swept away.

During the days that followed Elizabeth read with growing sadness and dejection all the papers—the responsible broadsheets as well as the tabloids—and she could hardly find a crumb of comfort. She became listless and took to her bed for a few days; she found it difficult to shake off the cold she had been suffering. A close woman friend commented, "Her Majesty had realized of course that the mood of the nation was becoming less sympathetic to the royals, but she had not realized there appeared to be such a serious deterioration in their respect and loyalty. That realization seemed to lay her low.

"It is, after all, a devastating realization for someone who has spent all her adult life loyally and honorably serving her people, to the best of her ability, to discover at the age of sixty-six that the nation has become disenchanted with her and her family."

Distinguished royal author Robert Lacey wrote in November 1992, "This has been the year in which the fairy tale ended. If the late 1970s and 1980s were anni mirabiles for the House of Windsor, it is hardly surprising that the current and painful unravelling of all those promises of happiness should be producing an annus horribilis—with the Queen's first tax demand as the price of her children's marital incompetence. They screw up and she pays the price."

As the criticism thundered over Elizabeth's head, there were some loyal monarchists, not only MPs or members of the House of Lords, but ordinary citizens who tried to set the debate on a more even keel in letters to newspapers. The right-wing *Sunday Telegraph* was typical, "Before the Queen-bashing reaches any new harsh pitch of sanctimonious wrath, perhaps we might all bear in mind that this unique and truly noble lady has fulfilled her personal pledge which, so solemnly, she expressed as a young girl.... to dedicate her life to her country and its people."

Another letter writer commented, "The Queen must be particularly dismayed by the stupid, spiteful and small-minded attitudes displayed by so many of those to whom she has pledged her devoted service—the abominable and fickle British public: abominable, because they are prepared to believe any suggestion of royal impropriety, however absurd; fickle, because they feed like voracious vultures on the salacious, regurgitated offerings of the loathsome tabloids. In this respect it seems a pity that we no longer employ an axeman: the thought of serried rows of tabloid editors' heads stuck atop Traitors' Gate is an alluring one, and has much to commend it."

The mood throughout the country, however, seemed inexorably against the Royal Family, despite some strong defenders. The telephone switchboards of radio stations lit up in unprecedented numbers as ordinary people vented their disenchantment with the royals. Many spoke, or wrote to newspapers, along the lines, "Years ago I was an ardent royalist, but over the past few years, my opinion has changed and I now say the Royal Family is a luxury that will have to go."

The influential *Sunday Times*, a Murdoch newspaper, devoted a three-page special focus on the monarchy under the banner headline THE PEASANTS' REVOLT. It detailed the "Seven Days That Shook the Crown," and one article by Godfrey Smith was headlined TIME TO LAY DOWN THE CROWN. Tongue in cheek, he wrote a spoof speech for the

Queen, suggesting that it should be her Christmas message to her people:

"I propose to retire on January 1. Forty years is a good innings and I am already past the age when most of my subjects retire. I do not say abdicate because that would mean I was giving up the throne for a new occupant."

Godfrey Smith then outlined what should happen. Charles would remain Prince of Wales because Britain, now a member of the European Community, was more a principality than a kingdom. He suggested Charles should hold the post until he was sixty, then hand it over to his elder son William. The speech also proposed the Queen should renounce her role as Head of the Church of England, and that the royal palaces and her other residences should be bequeathed to the people.

During that last weekend of November 1992, Elizabeth turned to one of her most senior courtiers and spoke her mind. He revealed later, "Her Majesty spoke quietly and slowly, thinking very carefully the words she was using. She said, 'I wonder sometimes whether I have failed the nation, or the monarchy, or the family. It seems that whatever way we turn there are nothing but disasters surrounding us all. It is all most unfortunate and most disturbing.'"

Elizabeth was more worried than she had ever been since becoming Queen. She knew from all she was reading that the people, her subjects, were turning their backs on everything she stood for. All her life she had endeavored to uphold the traditions and the authority of the Crown, and, by example, to show the nation how a family should behave. Following the example of Queen Victoria and her own father, Elizabeth had tried to emulate them. She had evidently failed.

On every possible occasion throughout her reign, Elizabeth had made it an imperative that the family should show they were a family unit. Whenever state or private occasions, such as royal birthdays, came about, she ordered the family to appear on the balcony at Buckingham Palace. Her family attended church every Sunday, as a family, and especially at Christmas.

Elizabeth had watched helplessly as the nation turned its back on the Church ever since the end of World War II. In vain she had hoped that by example, as the head of the most important family in the land, she could persuade others to follow her lead and attend religious services. As a young girl and as a teenager Elizabeth had seen whole families crowding into church every Sunday, praying together. In the early 1990s a mere 2 percent of the population attended regularly. She found this dispiriting and sad.

"If only, if only I had acted sooner," Elizabeth said to one of her advisers, speaking sternly about herself. "If I had spoken out earlier when I first decided that paying taxes was on my mind, I do believe this awful fire would have helped to heal the rift between us, between me and the nation. If only we had acted sooner." Then she fell silent and walked away, deep in thought.

In February 1993, Prime Minister John Major gave details in the House of Commons about the tax that the Queen and Prince Charles had agreed to pay; he also revealed the tax they would still escape.

Later that day Lord Airlie, Lord Chamberlain, head of the Queen's Household and one of her principal advisers, called the media to St. James's Palace, two hundred yards from Buckingham Palace, and talked for the first time ever about the Queen's finances. Officially, the Lord Chamberlain is in command of the monarch's responsibilities, but his other duties include being in charge of state visits, the royal standard and other flags, the Queen's swans, and even the Queen's barges. Until 1968 he also had to censor every play on behalf of the monarch before it could be performed.* Those days when the government could control literary expression seemed a century ago.

In a remarkably revealing statement, Lord Airlie tacitly acknowledged that it had been increasingly apparent over the last few years that a growing emphasis on royal wealth, tax, and the Civil List was tending to obscure and distort the contribution made by the Queen to the national life. It was a confession that would have been unimaginable only a few years earlier.

He told the assembled journalists, "Paying tax and meeting the costs of other members of the Royal Family will place a considerable burden on the Queen's finances. Her Majesty has taken this decision to ensure the monarchy develops with the times, particularly during a recession. The recent emphasis on royal wealth had tended to obscure the Queen's contribution to national life, and this—not the embar-

---

*From 1570 to 1670, theater censorship existed to protect the monarchy from abuse on the stage; in the eighteenth century, England's first Prime Minister, Robert Walpole, made the scope of censorship political. Under Queen Victoria censorship was extended to "protect" the nation's morals.

rassing publicity surrounding her children—had prompted the change."

Lord Airlie then provided a small clue as to the real wealth of the Queen. He said, "Estimates of the Queen's private funds range from £100 million (US$150 million) to many billions of dollars. But Her Majesty has authorized me to say that even the lowest of these estimates is grossly overstated.

"The wilder estimates frequently include the Crown Jewels, Buckingham Palace and Windsor Castle, and the royal collection of art treasures which belonged to the Crown, and were not the Queen's personal property." He explained that all those items would be exempt from tax, as they are considered part of the national heritage.

Tax experts believe the Queen's main liability for paying tax will be on dividends from the $100 million stock portfolio she is believed to own. As with every other citizen, tax will be levied initially at 25 percent, although most will be at the higher rate of 40 percent. She will also pay capital gains tax on any stock sales.

The Queen owns stud farms with stables at Sandringham, West Ilsley, and Sunninghill Park. They are taxable but most likely will produce a substantial loss each year. So, just like other citizens, she will have an occasional credit. Indeed, Elizabeth may some year come out ahead with the new arrangement.

Elizabeth also agreed to pay tax on private income from what is called the Privy Purse, principally income from the Duchy of Lancaster, which is mainly agricultural land and property, ownership of which dates back to the thirteenth century. These holdings comprise 11,800 acres in Staffordshire, Cheshire, and Shropshire; 10,700 acres in the Fylde and Forest of Bowland in Lancashire; 8,000 acres in Yorkshire, and 3,000 acres in Northamptonshire and Lincolnshire. In 1992 the land and property yielded a net surplus of $5 million. Most of that money, however, goes to meeting official expenditures not covered by the Civil List.

For Prince Charles, who announced that he, too, would pay income tax and would continue to do so when he became King, there is one important difference from the liability of the ordinary taxpayer. Charles will not have to pay the 40 percent inheritance tax which everyone else in Britain does. John Major announced that the Queen would be able to pass on to her successor, tax-free, all her assets, such as her private homes, Balmoral and Sandringham, as well as her private property and her substantial stock portfolio. But bequests and gifts to those who are not immediate family will be subject to inheritance tax.

Mr. Major explained to the Commons why the decision had been taken. "Special arrangements have been made for the Queen's inheritance tax because it is necessary to protect the independence of the monarchy. Any other arrangements would have posed the danger of assets of the monarchy being salami-sliced away by capital taxation through generations, thus changing the nature of the institution in a way few people in this country would welcome."

Neither John Major nor Lord Airlie gave any hint of the extraordinary behind-the-scenes arguments that had gone on before the decision to pay taxes was reached.

Elizabeth did not want to pay income tax at all but felt she had no choice, given the nation's current attitude toward the Royal Family. She refused absolutely, however, to pay inheritance tax as well. Some in Buckingham Palace believed she should have agreed to pay some inheritance tax, perhaps at a lower rate, but she would have none of it, refusing even to hear of such a suggestion. On one occasion she angrily told one of the secretaries, "Do you really think for one minute that I would ever agree to the death of the monarchy by a thousand cuts? I am here to uphold the monarchy. Don't people realize that my duty in life is to preserve the monarchy? I have not the slightest intention of entertaining any thoughts of abandoning that duty, for anyone."

So a way had to be found which would be politically and diplomatically acceptable to the closest scrutiny. Royal trustees, a body set up to watch over the monarch's finances, drew up a report claiming that "the monarchy as an institution needs sufficient private resources to enable it to continue to perform its traditional role in national life, and to have a degree of financial independence from the government of the day." They argued there had to be a distinct separation between Elizabeth's private and official lives.

Two areas proved tricky: the Queen's personal art collection and the Crown Jewels. The art collection, one of the most important private art collections in the world, contains 7,000 oil paintings, 30,000 drawings and watercolors, and 1,000 miniatures. Most of the great names among the Old Masters are present in the collection, which was begun by Charles I in 1625 when he purchased the Gonzaga pictures from Mantua. King George III (1760–1820) purchased the extraordinary Consul Joseph Smith collection from Venice in 1762. King George IV (1820–1830) and Queen Victoria (1837–1901) also bought wonderful Dutch and Italian collections. Though never officially given, its value is estimated to run into billions of dollars. The Crown Jewels are priceless.

The trustees finally came up with the idea of combining the jewels and all the works of art into a special trust set up to conserve the pieces. As a trust no tax will have to be paid, ever. The trust also includes books, furniture, and sculptures. Elizabeth readily agreed, approving of the plan and of the trust's title, The Royal Collection.

Although part of the art collection is always on view at the Queen's Gallery at Buckingham Palace, it is likely that under the terms of the new trust, more of the pictures will be on display or will be lent out to exhibitions around the world. The income from admittance charges, which in 1992 generated $4 million, will help fund the trust and improve the collection.

Most Members of Parliament appeared relieved and satisfied that Elizabeth had finally agreed to pay income tax, but a number, especially those on the Labour benches, felt she should also have agreed to pay some inheritance tax.

The tabloid press smelled blood. The following day the Labour *Daily Mirror* splashed the front page with H.M. THE TAX DODGER, with a cartoon showing Elizabeth, smirking as she worked out her tax return with the aid of a calculator. Inside, under the headline SAVE AS YOU REIGN, the paper argued that Elizabeth's offer was nothing more than a tax dodge, an insult to the ordinary citizen.

But the general view was that Elizabeth had made the right decision. The Conservative *Daily Telegraph* wrote, "Among those who applaud the Queen's consent to pay tax, there are two factions. The first, and by far the larger, merely wishes to see the Royal Family contribute some proportion of its private income to the public weal, as do the Queen's subjects. A much smaller faction regards this as a first step towards dismantling of royal wealth, and reduction of the Royal Family to the economic status of ordinary mortals.

"Those who espouse the latter view should be honest about its logical destination, and admit their republican ambitions. The balance that most of us would wish to see struck is that the Queen should not be so distanced from the circumstances of her subjects that her isolation puts their sympathy at risk. As never before, perhaps, she needs that sympathy. To be a citizen is to be a taxpayer, and one of the roles of a contemporary monarch is to be seen to be chief citizen...a focus of the aspirations and ideals of Everyman, rather than a unique, non-citizen quite unlike everybody else."

The Murdoch-owned *Sunday Times* commented, "By joining the ranks of sovereigns who pay income tax, the Queen has seized the opportunity to sweep away some of the cobwebs that have surrounded the royal finances for centuries. In doing so, she took a historic step towards putting the monarchy on a new, more modern footing, which is to be welcomed."

That her agreement to pay any tax at all was grudging was confirmed by one of her ladies-in-waiting two weeks after the official announcement by the Prime Minister. During a visit to East London the lady-in-waiting was asked by an old woman, "Does the Queen mind having to pay tax now?" The answer was emphatic: "She is not at all happy about it."

But the big question remained. Had she done enough to end the growing criticism of the Royal Family and the monarchy? The days of fawning deference had finally been laid to rest, but there were those who wondered whether the monarchy still commanded the respect that mattered, or whether the events of annus horribilis 1992 had so eroded that respect that the royals had become at best a charade, at worst an affront people could no longer tolerate.

Moreover, the nation had shown it was not prepared to dig into its collective pocket to find the $100 million needed to repair those burned out parts of Windsor Castle. This estimate had risen from $75 million since Peter Brooke's statement immediately following the fire. Six months after the appeal for contributions to Windsor Castle repairs had been opened, only $40,000 had been donated by the public. Another way had to be found.

One of Elizabeth's advisers came up with the idea of opening Buckingham Palace to paying visitors. At first Elizabeth disliked the idea, despite the fact that she had never intended to live in the palace, but simply use it as her office. It was Winston Churchill who persuaded her that she should, as sovereign, spend the weekdays at the palace, as it had become a symbol of monarchy. After all, he told her, her father had stayed there throughout the war, even after the palace had been bombed.

She hated the idea of millions of strangers tramping through "her" home, gawking at everything, prying into her private residence, examining the royal furniture, royal carpets, royal ornaments, royal family portraits. As she commented, "It sends a shudder down my back just thinking about it."

Unless Elizabeth wanted to pay the $100 million herself, however, there was no other way. After much debate it was agreed that the people could see part of the palace, but Elizabeth was determined to keep the hordes away from the private areas as well as the working offices of the palace. She would show them only what she happily showed personal visitors, invited statesmen, and heads of state when they visited Buckingham Palace. Nothing more.

Elizabeth personally walked through those areas which her advisers had suggested be opened, and she made the final decision as to which rooms would be available to the public gaze. As a result, the British people and tourists from around the world now have a magnificent opportunity for two months each year, until 1998, to savor the splendor and enjoy one of the most remarkable royal palaces in the world. No matter how many stately homes and palaces a tourist has viewed, there is nothing to compare with the magnificence a visitor can now see at Buckingham Palace, the working residence of a reigning monarch.

From the soaring grandeur of its Blue, Green, and White Drawing Rooms to the vast gilt-laden formality of the State Dining Room, where American Presidents are royally entertained whenever they visit Britain, the tour is guaranteed to be one of the world's top tourist attractions for years to come. Four hundred thousand visitors a year, paying twelve dollars a head, with reductions for children and the elderly, are expected to visit each year.

During the first year, 1993, a total of 377,000 visitors paid to tour the palace. After deducting administration expenses, the net income amounted to $2 million from attendances and a further $1.2 million from souvenir sales. As a Buckingham Palace spokesperson commented, "We had anticipated 400,000 visitors, but the souvenir sales exceeded our best expectations."

On Elizabeth's insistence, the palace will be opened only during August and September, the eight weeks when she is always at Balmoral, her summer holiday home in Scotland. Elizabeth made it plain that under no circumstances would she ever be at the palace while tourists were flocking through her home.

She also gave instructions that when the last tourist had left the palace at the end of the season, the tour areas be restored to their original state so that not the slightest sign would be visible that any visitors had ever toured her home.

EPILOGUE

Throughout 1993 and 1994 the British people witnessed their Royal Family fading into the background as Elizabeth ordered gatherings of the clan to be severely cut back for royal occasions. Elizabeth hoped that removing from public view those royals who had caused problems for the House of Windsor might help start the long process of winning back the nation's affection and respect.

It had been customary for royal pageants, such as the Trooping the Colour, celebrating Elizabeth's official birthday, to end with all members of her extended family standing on the balcony at Buckingham Palace waving to the cheering crowds below and watching the Royal Air Force fly past overhead.

In previous years Elizabeth ordered all members of her family to attend such events, demonstrating family unity and illustrating the importance of family gatherings in society. No excuses were permitted. Every royal turned out, the men in full military attire, the women in their best finery and always wearing hats. Palace balcony scenes were often used as the first opportunity for royal children to make their public debut, to introduce them to royal life and let the people see how the little royals were coming along.

Only the older royals were on parade in 1993. None of Elizabeth's grandchildren were at her side, and many of the younger generation were missing, including Prince Andrew, Prince Edward, Princess Diana, Princess Anne, and her husband, Commander Timothy Lawrence. Elizabeth was flanked only by Prince Philip, Charles, the Queen Mother, Princess Margaret, and the Duke and Duchess of Kent.

Elizabeth's official birthday celebration on Saturday, June 12, 1993, one week after the fortieth anniversary of her Coronation, should have been one of the most glorious occasions of her reign. Television, newspapers, and magazines had been reminiscing about Coronation Day 1953, with pages of old photographs showing jubilant scenes.

To many, the 1993 official birthday represented a watershed for the

Royal Family. It revealed that Elizabeth herself knew the British people no longer regard their Royal Family as they had only ten or twenty years before. The Mall wasn't teeming with enthusiastic, cheering crowds. Indeed, far fewer people than usual turned out. Rain clouds hung over the palace, but in the good years this would not have kept crowds away.

Only a month earlier Elizabeth had read the latest poll on her family. The poll by ICM (Independent Communications & Marketing), conducted specifically for the anniversary of Elizabeth's Coronation, made for gloomy reading. The nation wanted a dramatic change from the type of distant, aloof, old-fashioned monarchy she had epitomized throughout her reign. They wanted a slim-line, Scandinavian-style monarchy with fewer royals involved. They also wanted all the lesser royals to get proper, worthwhile jobs, rather than just opening the occasional hospital wing or fete, presiding over a charity meeting, or representing the Queen on official occasions.

Elizabeth had known of the nation's changed attitude to the lesser royals, but she was shocked to learn that the majority wanted to do away with Britain's traditional monarchy and install a Scandinavian-style one in its place. She called a meeting of advisers and asked them to put forward suggestions for reversing, or at least halting, what seemed a growing discontent toward her style of monarchy.

The poll had showed 50 percent wanted a cut in the cost of the royals and their upkeep, and 14 percent thought the royals "should not receive any public money at all." People aged 18–34 were especially keen to see a slim-line monarchy, 66 percent of them wanting to cut or eliminate the $74 million taxpayers spent each year on the monarchy.

The public's general understanding of the extent to which privileges were dispensed to Elizabeth's extended family would prove remarkably accurate. However, the public had no precise idea of the favors handed out through the years.

In January 1994, the Heritage Department released details of the royal favors to the House of Commons Public Accounts Committee, which scrutinizes government spending. It revealed that 268 members of the Royal Family, relatives, and staff were living at the taxpayer's expense. This figure was far greater than MPs or the general public had ever suspected.

It showed that aunts, uncles, and cousins of every member of

Elizabeth's "royal" family live, rent free, in grace and favor apartments in royal palaces and all are attended by lavish staff, even though they are not included in the Civil List.

At Kensington Palace, the home of Princess Diana and her two sons, also live Prince and Princess Michael of Kent, who have four bedrooms and six reception rooms; the Duke and Duchess of Gloucester, who also have four bedrooms and seven reception rooms; and Princess Margaret, who has three bedrooms and four reception rooms.

At St. James's Palace, 150 yards from Buckingham Palace, Princess Alexandra and her husband Angus Ogilvy have five bedrooms and four reception rooms, and the Duke and Duchess of Kent four bedrooms and six reception rooms. They also have another home on the Sandringham estate in Norfolk. All, save for Diana and Margaret, hardly ever live in their palace apartments, for they stay at their large, fully staffed mansion homes in various parts of the country.

To service the royals, free homes are provided for 13 chauffeurs, 55 private secretaries, 47 domestic servants, 41 stable and farm staff, and 6 gardeners, along with 42 additional craftsmen, porters, and other staff. Living free at Windsor Castle are 13 military knights, all pensioners, and 27 other pensioners who had previously worked for members of the family.

As Labour MP Alan Williams, who serves on the Public Accounts Committee, commented: "It is outrageous. In no other Western democracy is the wider Royal Family and ancillary people supported by the taxpayer. I do not think it should be allowed to go on."

For Elizabeth personally the poll wasn't very encouraging either, showing the mood of the people had become less favorable toward her. The great majority, 81 percent, believed she had done a "good job" as Queen. But now, there was a feeling of sympathy, even pity for her. Elizabeth wanted the nation's respect and admiration, not their pity. Sixty-five percent believed "she has been a good mother to her children, but they have let her down," but only 61 percent of women thought she had been a good mother.

Despite her conscious effort to smile more and look happier in public, 64 percent said she still looked too glum and urged her to be more cheerful in public. Those who know her well understood, and she knows herself, that she is simply not an innately joyful, happy, smiling person.

For Charles and Diana, Andrew and Fergie, as well as Anne and the younger royals, the poll provided cheerful reading. Most people were unwilling to impose stricter moral standards on the young royals; 57 percent believed they should be allowed to divorce like anyone else. However, 57 percent also thought the younger royals should set an example by not having sexual relations outside marriage.

The public strongly disapproved of the press's publishing of the Dianagate and Camillagate phone tapes, 63 percent believing the media should be banned from publishing people's private telephone conversations.

One important aspect of the poll came as a great relief to Elizabeth and, to a lesser extent, Charles. Even if Charles were to divorce, 76 percent approved of his succeeding to the throne.

For months after Diana and Charles's separation, constitutional lawyers argued over the problems facing the monarchy and Prince Charles in particular. Finally, the lawyers decided that no constitutional implications attached to either separation or divorce prevented the heir from succeeding to the throne. The reason being that the rules governing royal marriages, which go back two hundred years, merely require that the monarch not marry a Roman Catholic. Those acts of Parliament said nothing whatsoever about separation or divorce.

Within the unwritten British Constitution precedence is all-important. And a precedent was found. When George I succeeded to the throne in 1714, he had not only divorced his wife, Sophia Dorothea, but kept her imprisoned for life in a dark, damp, and gloomy castle. Edward VIII's abdication in 1936 was a crisis over convention, not the Constitution. Edward was challenging the rules of morality pertaining at that time and the Church, politicians, the media, and public opinion were not prepared to accept a twice-divorced American as Queen Consort.

Argument suggested it would be unlikely that the Britain of the year 2010, for example, when Elizabeth would be eighty-four, would not accept a divorced King. Diana's position as a divorcée, however, would be far more complicated. At present, Diana owes her position and status entirely to the fact of her marriage to the Prince of Wales.

If Charles and Diana were to remain separated, as opposed to divorced, that status would be unchanged. With Prince Charles's consent, she could be crowned Queen. If, on the other hand, Charles decided to block such a move, it would be totally within his power, and within his rights, to do so. All this has been explained in detail to Diana by Elizabeth and by constitutional lawyers, so that she can be in no doubt what her possible future might be. It is ironic that despite demanding, and being granted, a separation, Diana still finds her future status rests in the hands of her husband.

Despite her attempts to escape from the straitjacket of royal life, Diana recognizes, and is annoyed by, the hold that both Elizabeth and Charles still exert over her. Diana is determined that one day she will sit on the throne as Queen Consort, even if it is beside Charles, the man she grew to despise. And Diana has not yet been able to forget *that bitch*—the words she uses to describe Camilla Parker Bowles. Whatever happens, Diana is determined that Camilla will never sit on the throne next to Charles or usurp her position as the mother of the heirs to the throne, Wills and Harry.

Should Charles and Diana divorce, and if she does not remarry, Diana would continue to hold the rank conferred by the royal marriage, but she could *not* become Queen; on divorce she would become Diana, Princess of Wales. She could also be stripped of the title Her Royal Highness. That decision would be made solely by Elizabeth, although she would take advice first.

Stripping Diana of the title would mean a considerable downgrading in her position; all other family members with the title Royal Highness would take precedence before her. It would also be seen as a direct and very personal insult to Diana by the Queen, for Diana would still be the mother to Prince William, the heir to the throne.

Diana's position would become more difficult if Charles should remarry. There would then be two Princesses of Wales. Diana's position will be dictated by the nature of her divorce settlement, so she will, presumably, make sure her settlement guarantees her position within the family. She holds three strong cards: she is the mother to the heir to the throne, she is the most popular royal, and she is capable of causing severe embarrassment and untold damage to the Royal Family if she ever decided to "kiss and tell."

If Diana remarries, however, her status would change dramatically. She would take her new status from her new husband. It is perfectly possible that the mother of the future King of England could marry a plain Mr. Smith, but Diana would revert to her title at birth and be called "Lady Diana Smith."

Despite the drama of the early 1990s and the collapse of royal marriages, there is no reason to believe in 1994 that a majority of the British people want to be rid of either the House of Windsor or the monarchy. No poll has suggested it, despite the numbers of books, magazine, and newspaper articles on the subject that have led to an open public debate.

The royals remain popular and their efforts for charity are recognized. They also work very hard. In 1992, for example, the royals carried out 2,946 engagements at home, and eleven members of the family kept another 1,112 engagements on official tours abroad. Indeed, the Windsors' productivity, in terms of official visits, has doubled since Charles married Diana in 1981. And requests from organizations for royals to attend their functions still arrive at Buckingham Palace by the sackful.

In Australia, however, growing disenchantment with the monarchy has become a serious political debate. Prime Minister Paul Keating wants to replace the monarchy with a republic, discarding Elizabeth as head of state.

At the end of World War I it was decided that the Commonwealth of Nations was a better title than the British Empire and, after World War II, the name was shortened to the Commonwealth. It is now a free assocation of sovereign independent states, together with a few dependent territories.

But the Commonwealth only really became an entity after Elizabeth arrived on the throne in 1952 and the association of sovereign states decided to hold conferences every second year. She was invited to become head of the association and readily agreed.

Australia today is a parliamentary monarchy with Queen Elizabeth as head of state, just as she is Britain's head of state. In Australia she is represented by a governor-general. If Australia does vote to become a republic it will, more than likely, still decide to remain a member of the Commonwealth in the same way India decided to stay within the Commonwealth when that state adopted a republican status in 1950.

Until recently, Australia has been one of the most loyal Commonwealth countries, with polls showing Australians to be more passionate about the British Crown than British people themselves. The motto of Canberra, Australia's capital city, is "For the Queen, the Law and the People." And Canberra is full of memorials to emotional royal visits. All that warm attachment to Britain and the Crown has changed dramatically, and rapidly.

Monarchists in Britain fear that if Australians should turn republican so quickly, then the day may not be far away when the British people will do the same. The latest MORI (Market and Opinion Research International) poll shows that 85 percent of the population believe the monarchy will still exist in Britain in 2002, but less than half the nation believe it will be around in fifty years' time.

Australia has already taken the first decisive step to becoming a republic by the year 2000, when Sydney will host the millennium Olympic Games. Prime Minister Keating visited Balmoral in September 1993 and explained all to Elizabeth in an hour-long chat. He said afterward, "I explained to Her Majesty that, notwithstanding the deep respect and warm affection felt towards her by the Australian people, there was a growing feeling that Australia should make the necessary constitutional changes to allow the appointment of an Australian head of state."

He told her that it was inconsistent for Australia to have an English monarch as head of state, because Australia had become a multiethnic state, and he believed the time had come to establish clearly Australia's identity as an independent nation.

No matter what she thought, no matter how sad or frustrated she felt that day, Elizabeth could do or say nothing to postpone or halt the process. She is bound by law to follow the advice of the Australian government, in exactly the same way as she is bound to follow the British government's advice.

Paul Keating's visit to Elizabeth sent shivers through royalists who feared the British monarchy might soon be seen as irrelevant. Among the Queen's advisers it is recognized that a British government might demand, one day, to go down the same path. Except for galvanizing public opinion against such a move, the monarch can do nothing but obey the advice of the government of the day.

Australia's apparent keenness to become a republic made Elizabeth realize that other Commonwealth countries might feel the same way. A month after Paul Keating's visit, Elizabeth, who is head of state to sixteen Commonwealth nations, addressed Commonwealth leaders at their biennial conference in Cyprus.

She said, "I have enough experience, not least in racing, to restrain me from laying any money down on how many countries will be in the Commonwealth in forty years' time, or who they will be. I will certainly not be betting on how many of you will have the head of the Commonwealth as your head of state."

The speech revealed that Elizabeth is prepared to move with the times, accepting that nations will want their countries to become republics at some future date. Elizabeth decided she should first broach the subject openly with friendliness and good grace, and her speech was greeted with applause.

Elizabeth fears that becoming irrelevant, more than outright opposition to the Crown, might be the undoing of the British monarchy. Some politicians argued after the announcement of the breakdown of Charles and Diana's marriage that it was preposterous at the end of the twentieth century that Princess Diana's possible coronation should be treated as a matter of national importance and announced in Parliament by the Prime Minister.

Yet most polls barely support a constitutional monarchy. Discussion about replacing the hereditary sovereign with an elected President is rare. There is still so much genuine admiration and affection for Elizabeth, however, that not many would think of rocking the throne while she is still alive.

The consensus seems to be that the British monarchy must change. Elizabeth's decision to pay tax and meet the expenses of lesser royals has been a start. Politicians wonder whether a monarch who has lived her entire life in an ivory tower can be relied upon to make proper decisions. Many politicians believe that her regular advisers are simply not up to the job, being out of touch with "real" life outside the close confines of royal palaces.

For centuries Britain has been governed by those who have lived, worked, and exercised power in three London palaces: the Palace of Lambeth, the epicenter of the nation's established Church for five hundred years; the Palace of Westminster, where the mother of parliaments has held sway for three hundred years; and the Palace of

Buckingham, where the nation's monarchs have lived a privileged existence for one hundred fifty years.

While the next millennium fast approaches, however, all three institutions are in crisis.

Time and again doubts about the survival of the British monarchy have been raised, not just in Westminster and Lambeth, but throughout Europe and beyond. But never has the Royal Family faced the crisis it does today, primarily due to the antics and marital problems of Queen Elizabeth's own children and, more important, her two daughters-in-law, both commoners.

Many senior politicians believe tampering with the present monarchical institutions would start Britain down a slippery slope leading to turmoil. Prime Minister John Major, for instance, believes the monarchy is an essential part of the English landscape and should be left well alone. The entrenched establishment view, behind which the British aristocracy hide with their wealth and privileges, calls for no change.

Other sectors of society, however, call for dragging the monarchy out of the nineteenth century and into the twenty-first. Paddy Ashdown, leader of Britain's third political party, the Liberal Democrats, and a Privy Councillor, calls for "fundamental modernization."

The great majority of Britain's middle class, accounting for 70 percent of the nation, seeks change along the lines of the North European example, which is less aloof and austere, more open and exposed. They want the privileged existence the royals now enjoy to be cut back, if not ended completely for lesser royals.

A survey among one hundred Labour MPs, following the marital breakdowns of both Charles and Andrew, showed republicanism gaining ground. Twenty-four, a remarkably high percentage, said Britain should become a republic; thirty-two said the monarchy should be reformed along Swedish and Dutch models, stripped of pomp and pageantry. Only fourteen wanted no change.

And not only Labour. Strong criticism of the behavior of the royals came to the fore in a survey of more than three thousand grass-roots Conservative party members published in 1994. The unprecedented survey among Britain's traditionally ultra-loyal group by Tory Central Office suggested that while Elizabeth retained the strong affections of

Tory party members, the conduct of others members of her family and the break-up of royal marriages had tarnished their image.

After criticizing the media, particularly the tabloid press, for its portrayal of the Royal Family, many groups expressed the hope the royals would maintain high standards to retain public support.

The nationwide poll revealed the Tory party deeply split over the monarchy's future. While all the 380 local discussion groups surveyed want the monarchy to continue, they are divided over whether the Royal Family should try to preserve its mystique or move toward a Scandinavian-style system closer to the people. Some thought the Royal Family would have to improve its image if it were to survive in its present form.

The same survey revealed strong support for the retention of the House of Lords, although some groups said hereditary peerages should be abolished or phased out. Many felt peers should be barred unless they attended the Lords for a minimum number of times each year.

During Elizabeth's reign there have been some constitutional changes, though minor. Life peerages were introduced in 1958, making the House of Lords more representative; and people wishing to reject hereditary peerages were granted permission to do so in 1963.

But no change has touched the fundamental issue of privilege in Britain where, in the 1990s, 90 percent of the wealth is owned by 5 percent of the people. Those demanding change see Elizabeth as the figurehead of the state of affairs which some describe as "obscene."

Demands for change in the present Constitution are now coming not only from the left, or republicans, or the less privileged, but also from the royals themselves, including both Elizabeth and Prince Charles.

One change which Elizabeth and Charles have discussed is to divorce the Crown from the miter, removing the sovereign as Head of the Church of England. They believe that disentangling Church and monarchy would be in the interests of both institutions.

As Paddy Ashdown commented, "I don't think having the monarch as head of the established Church does the Church any good. I don't think it does the nation any good, nor the system of government, to have a linkage between something which is primarily about ethics of religion and the power of the state."

One suggestion is that the Prime Minister set up a bipartisan commission of Privy Councillors to consider the matter. Elizabeth, the Church's "Supreme Governor," is in favor of reforming the doctrine and severing all links with the state. Both Church and Crown would then be free.

At the same time, Prince Charles believes an urgent repeal of the Royal Marriages Act of 1772 is called for. Under this act Parliament has authority in royal marriages to vet the intended bride or groom. Elizabeth's children were permitted to marry whom they wished. No one, in or outside Parliament, thinks Parliament would now intervene to stop a proposed marriage of Wills or Harry, despite the scandals and disasters.

The most serious threat to the monarchy's future stems not from the few directly hostile to it, but from what I detect is the growing number indifferent to the Royal Family, who believe the monarchy doesn't matter anymore. The malaise is deep. Many of the younger generation no longer feel awe or respect toward the royals; they simply no longer care.

Yet the royals do still command attention from the older generation, who turn out to catch a glimpse of them whenever they visit their hometown. And Princess Diana always attracts crowds, both young and old.

The relevance of the monarchy to Britain in the twenty-first century was debated in London in May 1993, when Rupert Murdoch's London *Times* newspaper and Charter 88, a human-rights group, organized the most comprehensive forum on the subject since the seventeenth century. Indeed, if such a debate had taken place twenty-five years ago, it might have been deemed treasonable, but today's discussion reveals how far public opinion has moved in such a short time.

No consensus emerged from the ninety speakers and five hundred guests, but the conference did capture a mood of national anxiety about the constitutional arrangements that shape the way the British live. More doubt than decision was provoked. Some monarchists were persuaded that the Crown might gain from scrutiny; some republicans were reminded how unpredictable were the upheavals that might follow their success. Elizabeth followed the conference closely, reading the daily reports in all the newspapers.

She noted that the conference viewed the prospect of the European Union as an important momentum for possible change, not just for the monarchy but also the Church, Parliament, and the courts. Many expressed concern that an unwritten Constitution and a hereditary monarchy, like Britain's, would have no place in the new Europe.

Britain's unwritten Constitution, with the sovereign as head of a parliamentary monarchy, could cause problems if Europe does move toward closer political, as well as monetary, unity. All other European Union countries have written constitutions.

The British Constitution is unique in that it does not exist in the form of a single document; it consists rather of an accumulation of customs and precedents, which have arisen in the course of national development, together with a number of laws defining certain of its aspects. And these laws date back to Magna Carta in 1215.

The conference also threw light on Elizabeth's other role as Head of the Church and Defender of the Faith. Few in Britain see Elizabeth in that role, though the letters *DF*, for *Fidei Defensor* (Latin for Defender of the Faith), are on every single British coin.

Senior clergymen in the Church of England are now urging the disestablishment of the Church, an idea that would have been greeted with horror a generation ago. Elizabeth knows the Church is in deep crisis. Since 1945 Anglican church attendance has collapsed, and today only 2.4 percent of the population attend church each week. As a result, the authority of the Church, and its teachings, have diminished accordingly.

The Church's present turmoil has been caused primarily by its decision, taken in 1992, to permit the ordination of women priests. Out of 10,000 Anglican priests, about 3,500 oppose women priests. More than 1,000 traditionalist vicars have said they will leave the church when the first woman is ordained. Many will join the Church of Rome, which already has more weekly churchgoers than the established Church of the land.*

---

*In January 1994, the first royal split with the Church of England occurred when the Duchess of Kent, aged sixty, announced that she was quitting Anglicanism to join the Roman Catholics, the first member of the Royal Family to do so since James II in the seventeenth century. (Although the Act of Settlement of 1700 bars royalty from marrying Catholics, the Duke of Kent's eighteenth place in the succession would not be affected because the Duchess was not Catholic when they married in 1961.) Before taking this dramatic step, the Duchess had asked permission from her cousin Elizabeth.

Elizabeth consulted with senior Church of England bishops. She knew she would have

Elizabeth's dual role as head of state and Head of the Church has also been thrown into doubt by the divorces in her own family and, in particular, the separation of Charles and Diana. The Anglican church is implacably opposed to divorce, yet it seems likely that one day Charles and Diana will divorce, which will mean the Church would have as its head a divorced monarch.

In December 1993, Elizabeth and Charles were openly challenged over the twin questions of divorce and adultery when a senior Church of England figure, the Archdeacon of York, the Venerable George Austin, said that if reports of an affair between Camilla Parker Bowles and Prince Charles were true, it was questionable whether Charles had the right to be the next King.

The Archdeacon said, "Charles made solemn vows before God in church about his marriage, and it seems—if the rumors are true about Camilla—that he began to break them almost immediately.

"He has broken the trust on one thing, and broken vows to God on one thing. How can he then go to into Westminster Abbey and take the Coronation vows? Are we to believe that he will keep those? I think it brings into question the whole attitude of Charles to vows, trust and so on."

Such an extraordinary attack from an authoritative clergyman at such a vulnerable moment in Elizabeth's reign brought back memories of King Edward VIII's abdication. Demands for Edward's abdication first became public knowledge following a senior churchman's remarks.

Both Elizabeth and Charles were furious that such an attack should

---

to accede to her cousin's demand, but she also recognized that if a senior member of the Royal Family left the church, her own position as Supreme Governor would become more untenable.

The Duchess's conversion could not have come at a more delicate time, just months before the first women priests were to be ordained. The Anglican bishops knew the Duchess had spoken out against the ordination of women. Her decision boosted the morale of Anglicans leaving the Church of England, and Lambeth Palace feared other lay Anglo-Catholics would follow her example to Rome.

The Duchess has always been deeply religious. She believes her strong faith saved her in 1977, when she suffered a miscarriage of her fourth pregnancy, at the age of forty-four. She succumbed to prolonged depression, withdrew from public life and all her royal duties, and spent some months in hospital.

Her son, George, the Earl of St. Andrews, married a Roman Catholic in January 1988 and renounced his place in line of succession. His marriage took place in a register office in Scotland, so very different from his mother's magnificent wedding ceremony in York Minster.

be made just days after Diana had announced her decision to retire from public life. They knew the attack would be seen as another destabilizing influence on the British throne, and they needed to end, firmly and quickly, such an argument against Charles's fitness to be King.

Elizabeth has never flinched from her belief that Charles would succeed her. And Charles has always known it was his right and his duty to succeed his mother. Not for one moment has Charles ever considered passing over the throne to his son William, despite rumors and suggestions that he doesn't relish the thought of being King. As one of Charles's former secretaries said, "Charles may not be terribly keen to be King. But he has not the slightest intention of not succeeding when his mother dies. It is his destiny, his duty."

Nicholas Soames, one of Charles's former equerries, the best man at his wedding, and a lifelong friend, spoke to Charles and got permission to step into the fray for the first time since the breakup of Charles's marriage. Minister of Food in John Major's government, Soames went as far as to telephone political editors of a number of newspapers and describe the Archdeacon's attack as "disgraceful, wounding, ignorant, and hurtful."

Soames left the editors in no doubt that he was speaking with the full authority of the Palace and Prince Charles. For this had become one of the most serious attacks ever mounted on the House of Windsor at any time. In effect, the Archdeacon had suggested that the heir to the throne could be picked and discarded at whim.

Soames said, "Being heir to the throne is not an ambition, but a duty and one which will befall Charles on a sad moment later in his life. He will inherit the throne and that is the end of the matter."

At the same time as the storm erupted over Charles's fitness for King, a poll by MORI reported in December 1993 that 65 percent of respondents felt Prince Charles should not become King if he continued his alleged relationship with Camilla, even if he and Diana divorced.

In many respects the MORI poll was more worrying to Elizabeth and Charles than the clergyman's attack, for it revealed the British people were becoming more antagonistic toward Charles because of Camilla. Never before had polls suggested Charles should not succeed his mother. The nation's stance against adultery seemed odd, though, for polls in 1993 also showed that 70 percent of married men and 60 percent of married women in Britain admitted to committing adultery at some point during their lives.

The crises facing Buckingham and Lambeth Palaces were interconnected with Westminster, which also faced radical change and a challenge to its authority. No divorce of church from state could go through without changes to the House of Lords, Parliament's upper chamber. And in such an upheaval, it would be unlikely that the bishops who sit in the House of Lords by right would keep their seats.

Such a move would bring about wholesale reform of the Lords, which many consider little more than a cozy club. Indeed, the Lords is often referred to as "the best club in London."

During the past decade 60 percent of peers didn't bother to attend, and a remarkable 85 percent of hereditary peers never spoke. Many view the unelected Lords, packed with hereditary peers, as a shameless anachronism whereby people have the right to a seat, and vote, solely by accident of birth.

In 1993, Labour leader John Smith spoke for growing numbers demanding change when he said, "The hereditary element of the House of Lords has really got to go. I've never begun to understand how it was remotely possible to defend it." And so thinks most of the British electorate.

The House of Lords in fact has a most important function, serving as a corrective, delaying, and advisory body which is subordinate to the House of Commons and often straightens out poorly written legislation.

Britain, like the rest of Europe, is slowly integrating. In the Treaty of Rome, the legal bedrock of the European Union, direct elections to the European Parliament were introduced. Now, 410 members from across Europe sit in the European Parliament. As Europe becomes more closely integrated, more power will be passed to the European Parliament, undermining the power of parliaments in every European nation, including Britain.

That would affect the power of the British monarchy, rendering it virtually obsolete in its present form. The monarch could remain on the throne, wear a crown, live in Buckingham Palace, and occasionally ride down the Mall in a glass coach. But the sovereign would have less of a role to play in the constitutional life of the nation. A purely decorative monarchy is the recurring fear of Britain's monarchists.

Perhaps more worryingly for Elizabeth, a 1992 MORI poll revealed a remarkable 75 percent of the nation considered the Royal Family too wealthy, while 50 percent regarded them as an "expensive luxury the country cannot afford."

These are the reasons that I believe survival well into the next century depends on further, radical changes being introduced. Those changes Elizabeth has initiated are a start but need to be taken much further so that a modern monarchy emerges, rid of superstition, rid of the divine right of kings and those awful divisions in society that perpetuate the tradition of monarchy. Everything that the Crown stands for—inherited wealth, inherent virtues, inequality—are aspects of the monarchy the people simply will not tolerate anymore, slowly but surely increasing its unpopularity.

Elizabeth's wealth is increasingly regarded as inappropriate for the head of a state, like Britain's, which is now a second-class European power, where poverty increases and public services deteriorate. The image of a Queen with three palaces and other royal residences, in a country which has a substantial housing shortage, is seen as divisive and grossly unfair. The resentment has less to do with envy than with an innate sense of justice.

As the British slowly edge toward a more equable society, there is a belief that the nation's ancient class division—upheld by the traditions of monarchy—has caused so much discord and unfairness that it must come to an end, and soon. The institution of monarchy in its present form encourages deference, glorifies the past, entrenches class divisions, and manifests a divisive feeling of "them and us."

Yet other divisions in society must surely be eradicated if the Crown is to survive, let alone prosper, whether as a traditional or even a Scandinavian-style setup. No division of British society is more damaging than the separation of the races. And in Britain race and religion often go hand in hand. Today, given the diversity of its population, it seems extraordinary that Britain has a head of state that is head of only one brand of religion.

In fact, Elizabeth is also the sovereign of Catholics, Nonconformists, Jews, Hindus, Moslems, Sikhs, and Buddhists. Many maintain the situation is grossly unfair that the monarch is head of an established Church when there are six or seven other faiths for her to defend.

The behavior and nefarious activities of the younger royals which captured the attention of the world have just brought the whole matter to a head and made people examine the need for a constitutional monarchy. Undeniably, it is the younger royals who are responsible for the damage being wreaked on the monarchy. Most opinion polls show that three-quarters of the nation blame their marital breakdowns as responsible for the change in attitude to the Crown. There is still adulation for the lovely Princess Diana and respect for Elizabeth, but scorn and derision for a number of the lesser royals.

A new professional monarchy, which I believe Britain now needs, should be characterized by a conscious attempt to emphasize the similarities between the sovereign and subjects, rather than perpetuate the differences. Much of its bogus mysticism should be stripped away, and clearly defined duties should be carefully stipulated for the sovereign. I believe the rest of the family, save of course for the sovereign's consort and heir apparent, should all lose their special status and become ordinary citizens. Only then can the respect that has been lost of late perhaps be won back.

But it will be an uphill struggle.

All this Elizabeth must tackle, and urgently. She has always professed that her principal task in life has been to uphold the monarchy and the House of Windsor. If she persists in the belief that she was ordained by providence to be sovereign, then she will stand by and watch the British monarchy, and everything she stands for, lose the esteem, respect, and admiration of the nation. I cannot believe that Elizabeth wants that to occur.

It is now that she must seize the day. If she wants the Crown and her family to prosper she must take the crucial decisions, irrespective of the advice offered by some whose heads seem to be buried in the sands of time.

Now sixty-eight, Elizabeth has no one close to whom she can turn for advice. Long ago she recognized the advice offered by Philip as suspect and often subjective. She lost her faith and trust in him because of his demand to lead a life independent of the monarchy and of herself. Elizabeth knows that the support Philip has given her for nearly fifty years has been little more than superficial.

Her beloved Bobo, the nursemaid in whom she put such faith and trust throughout her life, died in August 1993. They had been together since Elizabeth was ten, and no one ever knew Elizabeth better or shared so many private moments. Margaret MacDonald, daughter of a gardener who became a railway worker, would become the only royal servant ever permitted to call the Queen Lilibet.

Elizabeth must decide how much her court and her family should change their ways, live their lives, educate their children, share their wealth. Only now, after a lifetime of dedication to her people has earned their respect, does she have the esteem to push through those changes. She now faces the most fundamental decisions of her entire reign, decisions which will affect the sovereign, her heirs, her subjects, and the nation. Only time will tell whether she has the foresight and the courage to decide wisely.

APPENDIX

INSIDE BUCKINGHAM PALACE: THE ROYAL TOUR

After waiting in line outside the nineteenth-century Ambassador's Entrance, you begin the tour by emerging into the Quadrangle, which gives the first impression of the sheer scale of the place. This huge space is dominated by The Grand Portico, designed by John Nash, the architect who transformed Buckingham House into Buckingham Palace in the 1820s.

You enter the palace proper through The Grand Entrance, the oldest part of the palace and part of the original house built in 1705. You then climb the Grand Staircase into a burst of light and color. The staircase splits in three directions, the whole area dominated by a glass dome. To feel a work of art, run your hand along the sweeping curved arms of the carved gilt balustrade, which in 1830 cost $6,000 (equivalent to $600,000 at today's rate).

You then enter the Guard Room, ingeniously lit from above and hung with magnificent eighteenth-century Gobelin tapestries. Originally intended for palace guards, it was never used for such a purpose.

Next, you come to the dazzling Green Drawing Room, a vision of green, white, and gold hung with shimmering silk and decked out with works of art. All around are dynastic portraits, together with some of the most beautiful, exquisite, and valuable French furniture in existence. There are magnificent cabinets, one by Adam Weisweiler in 1785, the other by Martin Carlin in 1772. On top of the Carlin cabinet is a vase in the shape of a ship, once the property of the famous

Madame de Pompadour. It is the first of countless pieces of Sevres porcelain on view.

Leaving the splendor of the Green Room you enter the Throne Room, though there is no throne to be seen. The Queen never sits there. Instead she stands before a small step, and the place for the throne is marked by a pair of chairs—His and Hers—from the Queen's Coronation in 1953. The ceiling is covered by coats of arms representing England, Scotland, Ireland, and Hanover. Note the early-nineteenth-century French "Oath of the Horatii" clock, just one of the many timepieces on display.

Next comes the Picture Gallery. Within this massive, 155-foot-long room hangs a small portion of The Royal Collection, which has three times as many paintings as London's National Gallery. There are Van Dycks, Rembrandts, and Claudes, among many others. And don't neglect the furniture, or the black Sevres porcelain.

Next, the Silk Tapestry Room, which contains superb French eighteenth-century furniture. Passing through the East Gallery, the Cross Gallery, and the West Gallery, which house more of the Queen's extensive antique collection, you arrive at the State Dining Room. The room is a riot of red and gold, where seated dinner guests can view portraits of the Hanoverian Kings, the forefathers of the House of Windsor.

You will then enter the Blue Drawing Room, lined by no fewer than thirty magnificent Corinthian columns in imitation onyx. There you will see the single greatest piece of furniture on view: The Table of the Grand Commanders, made for Napoleon, in 1806, of Sevres porcelain. It took six years to create and was given to King George IV two years after the Battle of Waterloo in 1815. The table shows Alexander the Great and twelve other commanders all painted in imitation cameos.

The bow-windowed Music Room, lined with huge blue columns, is where royal christenings traditionally take place. The ceiling is a brilliant design of domes and semidomes glittering with gold that seems somehow to float in space.

And into the final room on this floor, the White Drawing Room, another grandiose, high-ceilinged room resplendent with more exquisite French furniture. Much of the French furniture, as well as other fine pieces at Buckingham Palace, were acquired by George IV after the French Revolution, when prized pieces were smuggled out of France.

And this drawing room offers a surprise which has so often brought a touch of humor when assembled dignitaries come to the palace on official visits. At state occasions, the guests are assembled, waiting patiently for the Queen, and sometimes other members of the family, to proceed through the State Rooms to the Dining Room. Suddenly, as if by magic the Queen appears in the White Drawing Room. One of the pair of huge, twelve-feet-tall mirrors is actually on hinges. It swings back to reveal the Queen, hidden in the Royal Closet.

Downstairs to the Marble Hall, and the grand tour is nearly at an end. You will pass through the Bow Room to the terrace overlooking Buckingham Palace's magnificent gardens.

Don't expect to see any of Elizabeth's private apartments or those of any other member of her family. Elizabeth was adamant that nothing of a private or personal nature be seen by the tourists. Nor will visitors see a glimpse of the working parts of the palace—the offices, the kitchens, or any areas where the 300 people who work in the great building actually carry out their everyday jobs.

BIBLIOGRAPHY

All published in London unless otherwise stated.

Alexandra of Yugloslavia. *Prince Philip: A Family Portrait,* 1949.

Bagehot, Walter. *The English Constitution,* 1898.

Barratt, John. *With the Greatest Respect,* 1991.

Barry, Stephen. *Royal Secrets,* 1985.

Birkenhead, Lord. *Walter Monckton,* 1969.

Boothroyd, Basil. *Philip: An Informal Biography,* 1971.

Cathcart, Helen. *Her Majesty,* 1962.

Colville, John. *Footprints in Time,* 1976.

Davies, Nicholas. *Diana: A Princess and Her Troubled Marriage,* New York, 1992.

Dempster, Nigel. *H.R.H. The Princess Margaret: A Life Unfulfilled,* 1981.

Grigg, John. Title TK *National and English Review,* 1957.

Hall, Unity. *The Private Lives of Britain's Royal Women,* Chicago, 1991.

Hall, Unity. *Philip: The Man Behind the Monarchy,* 1987.

Heald, Tim. *The Duke: A Portrait of Prince Philip,* 1991.

Higham, Charles, and Roy Moseley. *Elizabeth and Philip: The Untold Story,* 1991.

Hoey, Brian. *HRH The Princess Anne,* 1984.

Hoey, Brian. *All the Queen's Men,* 1992.

Holden, Anthony. *Charles, Prince of Wales,* 1979.

Junor, Penny. *Diana, Princess of Wales,* 1982.

Lacey, Robert. *Majesty: Elizabeth II and the House of Windsor,* 1977.

Longford, Elizabeth. *Elizabeth R,* 1983.

Morrow, Ann. *The Queen,* 1983.

Morton, Andrew. *Diana: Her True Story,* 1992.

Nicolson, Harold, *Monarchy,* 1962.

Oaksey, John. "The Queen's Horses," *The Queen,* 1977.

Pearson, John. *The Ultimate Family,* 1986.

Philip, HRH Prince. *Selected Speeches,* 1957.

Player, Lesley. *My Story: The Duchess of York, Her Father and Me,* 1993.

Sampson, Anthony. *The Changing Anatomy of Britain,* 1982.

Thatcher, Margaret. *The Downing Street Years,* 1993.

Townsend, Peter. *Time and Chance: An Autobiography,* 1978.

Wapshott, Nicholas, and George Brock. *Thatcher,* 1983.

Wheeler-Bennett, Sir John. *King George VI: His Life and Reign,* 1968.

Windsor, HRH The Duke of. *A King's Story: The Memoirs of HRH The Duke of Windsor,* 1951.

Young, Hugo. *One of Us,* 1989.

Zeigler, Philip. *Mountbatten,* 1985.

INDEX

499